Rio de Janeiro in the Global Meat Market, c. 1850 to c. 1930

This book examines the meat provision system of Rio de Janeiro from the 1850s to the 1930s. Until the 1920s, Rio was Brazil's economic hub, main industrial city, and prime consumer market. Meat consumption was an indicator of living standards and a matter of public concern. The work unveils that in the second half of the nineteenth century, the city was well supplied with red meat. Initially, dwellers relied mostly on salted meat; then, in the latter decades of the 1800s, two sets of changes upgraded fresh meat deliveries. First, ranching expansion and transportation innovation in southeast and central-west Brazil guaranteed a continuous flow of cattle to Rio. Second, the municipal centralization of meat processing and distribution made its provision regular and predictable. By the early twentieth century, fresh meat replaced salted meat in the urban marketplace. This study examines these developments in light of national and global developments in the livestock and meat industries.

Maria-Aparecida Lopes is professor of Latin American history at California State University, Fresno.

Routledge Studies in the History of the Americas

1 **Education in Revolutionary Struggles**
Iván Illich, Paulo Freire, Ernesto Guevara and Latin American Thought
Andrés Donoso Romo

2 **Cartographic Expeditions and Visual Culture in the Nineteenth-Century Americas**
Edited by Ernesto Capello and Julia B. Rosenbaum

3 **The Johnson Administration's Cuba Policy**
From "Dirty War" to Passive Containment
Håkan Karlsson and Tomás Diez Acosta

4 **The Unheard Voice of Law in Bartolomé De La Casas' 'Brevísima Relación De La Destruición De Las Indias'**
David T. Orique

5 **The Nixon Administration and Cuba**
Continuity and Rupture
Håkan Karlsson and Tomás Diez Acosta

6 **Translating Cuba**
Literature, Music, Film, Politics
Robert S. Lesman

7 **Rio de Janeiro in the Global Meat Market, c. 1850 to c. 1930**
How Fresh and Salted Meat Arrived at the Carioca Table
Maria-Aparecida Lopes

For more information about this series, please visit: https://www.routledge.com/Routledge-Studies-in-the-History-of-the-Americas/book-series/RSHAM

Rio de Janeiro in the Global Meat Market, c. 1850 to c. 1930

How Fresh and Salted Meat Arrived at the Carioca Table

Maria-Aparecida Lopes

Routledge
Taylor & Francis Group
NEW YORK AND LONDON

First published 2022
by Routledge
605 Third Avenue, New York, NY 10158

and by Routledge
2 Park Square, Milton Park, Abingdon, Oxon, OX14 4RN

Routledge *is an imprint of the Taylor & Francis Group, an informa business*

Library of Congress Cataloging-in-Publication Data
A catalog record for this title has been requested

ISBN: 978-0-367-52853-9 (hbk)
ISBN: 978-0-367-52854-6 (pbk)
ISBN: 978-1-003-05868-7 (ebk)

Typeset in Sabon
by SPi Global, India

For my parents

Contents

Figures

Tables

Acknowledgments

This book—long in the making—would not have been possible without the support from several colleagues, friends, family members and institutions in the United States and Brazil. The project started years ago while I was concluding my visiting scholarship at the Center for Latin American Studies at Stanford University and beginning my professorship at California State University, Fresno. I had the fortune to consult primary and secondary material at the Cecil H. Green Library at Stanford, whose *Braziliana* collection is one of the best in the United States. In addition, Erik Steiner, Creative Director of the Spatial History Project at Stanford, generously shared data for in Rio's maps; I am deeply thankful for his gesture. At Fresno State, the Provost's office and the College of Social Sciences awarded me release time and financial support to conduct archival research in Brazil and participate in national and international conferences. I am indebted to my colleagues from the Chicano and Latin American Studies and History Departments at Fresno State. Annabella España-Nájera, Cristina Herrera, Ramon Sánchez, and William Skuban who read and provided valuable feedback on sections of the manuscript. We had more conversations than I can remember about my work. I am privileged to be in the company of such generous colleagues and friends, including Lori Clune and Maritere López, who encouraged me along the way.

Many thanks to the personnel of the Henry Madden Library at Fresno State, particularly Gretchen Higginbottom, who located essential materials during this long research process. My ex-students Bailee Roche, Jordan Lapadula, Maria Cabrera, Patricia Brito, and Rebecca Hiura assisted me in gathering primary sources and uploading data. I thank them for their meticulous work, which was supported by the Undergraduate Student Research Grant at Fresno State. Xiaoming Yang from the Geospatial Information Center at Fresno State worked closely with me designing the book's maps. I thank him for his professionalism and patience throughout the process. Chi Kin Leung from the Geography Department also provided valuable feedback on the maps. I am grateful to the administrative personnel at Fresno State who assisted me over the years. I am mostly appreciative of my Fresno State students. On several occasions, when I interrupted our lectures to talk about my research, they were always attentive and asked stimulating questions.

In Brazil, Georgia Tavares from the Arquivo Geral da Cidade do Rio de Janeiro and other staff from the Arquivo Nacional in Rio de Janeiro shared their expertise and intimate knowledge of Rio's archives with me. The Arquivo Nacional maintains an essential online resource, the Biblioteca Nacional Digital, which enabled me to access numerous original sources cited in the book. Eduardo Cavalcante and Kairo da Silva Santos compiled primary material in both archives; Kairo also worked diligently in all maps. Special thanks to Paulo Márcio Leal de Menezes, coordinator of the Laboratório de Cartografia at Universidade Federal do Rio de Janeiro, who generously shared the findings of the project "Involução Cartográfica do Estado do Rio de Janeiro" with me. Horacio Gutierrez and Jonis Freire, whom I met while working at Universidade Estadual de São Paulo, Franca were valuable interlocutors along this journey, so were Carlos Eduardo Valencia Villa, Paulo Roberto Cimó Queiroz, Renato Leite Marcondes, Raúl Jacob, and Sandro Dutra e Silva.

I am indebted to Linda Lewin, who commented on drafts of some chapters and made thorough suggestions. She has become a mentor to me. My friend María Cecilia Zuleta was always available to talk about my research dilemmas. She read parts of the manuscript and challenged me with meticulous observations. I exchanged notes with Roger Horowitz and Jeffrey Pilcher when this project was only beginning; I thank them for the advice and generosity.

Special thanks to all the organizers who put together conferences and workshops where I presented sections of this work and received thoughtful feedback: the 2014 Roger Smith Food+Tech Conference; the 2018 World Economic History Congress; the 2019 Pursuit of Global Urban History Conference; the Latin American Historians of Northern California; the Latin America Brown Bag Series at Fresno State; and the Seminario Interdisciplinario de Alimentación, Instituto de Investigaciones Dr. José María Luis Mora, Mexico. Parts of Chapters 3, 4, and 5 appeared in the article "Struggles over an 'Old, Nasty, and Inconvenient Monopoly': Municipal Slaughterhouses and the Meat Industry in Rio de Janeiro, 1880–1920s," published in the *Journal of Latin American Studies* 47, no. 2 (2015): 349–76. Copyright © Cambridge University Press 2014. Reprinted with permission.

In early 2021, as I conclude this project, I am again the beneficiary of two institutions that have supported this work since its inception. Fresno State granted me a sabbatical year to complete the manuscript; it is a privilege to work exclusively on my research. The Center for Latin American Studies (CLAS) at Stanford awarded me the CLAS Stanford Library Access Grant for Minority Serving Institutions.

Thanks to my family in Brazil, with whom I shared many of the meals mentioned in this book. Thanks to my family in the United States. My kids were toddlers when the project began, now they have questions about my work and are active participants in dinner conversations. Special acknowledgment to my partner, Ricardo Claps, whose scientific viewpoint about my findings was instrumental in shaping the work.

Glossary

açougue	Butcher stall, butcher shop
Câmara municipal	Municipal chamber
Carioca	People, objects, or places from the city of Rio de Janeiro
carne verde	Any fresh meat; in this work, the expression is used mostly to refer to fresh beef
Cerrado	Biome that corresponds to roughly 25 percent of Brazil's territory. It encompasses several states, and houses multifaceted ecosystem: semiarid savanna, grasslands, and riverine forests
Corte	In Rio de Janeiro, the seat of the Portuguese and the Brazilian empires
crioulo	Mixed-blood cattle of Iberian-origin brought to the Americas, (*criollo* in Spanish)
charque	Sun-dried meat or beef. This work uses the terms, salted meat, salt beef or meat, charque, and carne seca interchangeably
charqueada	Charque processing factory
farinha de mandioca	Manioc meal
fazenda	Farm, plantation
feijoada	Black bean stew prepared with loin, bacon, charque, and/or sausages
frigorífico	Meat processing plant
matadouro	Slaughterhouse
mil-réis	The Brazilian unit of currency during the period under study in this work. One *mil-réis* was written 1$000. This work uses the format 1.000 to facilitate reading; values smaller than one *mil-réis* are written as 500 *réis*, for example.
Mineiro	People, objects, or places from Minas Gerais state
Paulista	People, objects, or places from São Paulo state
prefeitura	City council

Riograndense	People, objects, or places from Rio Grande do Sul state
saladero	Salted meat processing plants in Spanish
tasajo	Salted meat
zebu	According to current classification, cattle of European (*Bos taurus*) and Indian origin (*Bos indicus*) are two distinct species; they probably have a common ancestor, *Bos primigenius,* but developed in different regions

Note on Orthography

Brazilian Portuguese spelling has changed considerable since the nineteenth century. For words in Portuguese in the text, I used modern spelling. For citations, proper names, and bibliography, I maintained the spelling as in the original text.

Introduction

Popular and academic interest in the topic of meat production and consumption is growing.[1] Since its inception in the latter part of the nineteenth century, industrial meatpacking has seldom left the news cycle. The first packinghouses publicized their technological wonders in full-page newspaper ads featuring images of their plants (a veiled reference to the primacy of private enterprise over municipal slaughterhouses), claims of their product's wholesomeness, and pledges to make meat affordable to all. Shortly after readers laid eyes on these adverts, controversy ensued. As the case of the United States revealed, these meatpacking plants were anything but wholesome; they exposed laborers to unsafe conditions and engaged in monopolistic work exclusively on my research practices. During the twentieth century, the industry evolved into a global network of animals, meat, and grains. It also perfected the ability to hide from the public view the processes by which ranchers and workers transformed cattle into meat and distributed it to retailers. Most recently, and alarmingly, the 2020 Covid-19 pandemic ushered meatpacking back to the front pages of newspapers. Closures of processing plants in Argentina, Brazil, and across the United States have stoked fears of shortages and raised questions about how food travels from farm to table. The current worldwide crisis has laid bare how crucial aspects of the cattle/meat complex remain unchanged, like industry concentration, and how we continue to conceive of meat as an "essential" food.[2]

Set in a thoroughly different historical context, this book examines the origins of such innovations and discussions using Rio de Janeiro (Brazil's capital city until 1960) as a case study.[3] It ventures through different spatial scales, connecting South American, transatlantic, national, and regional actors involved in Rio's fresh meat (*carne verde*) and salted meat (*charque* or *carne seca*) supply network. This study shows that policymakers in early twentieth-century Brazil—like their counterparts in Europe and the United States—strove to expand pasturelands and promote meat consumption. In doing so, they created enduring global linkages that allow consumers in most urban centers of the Americas to find any meat cut, year-round.

Brazil in the Empire (1822–1889) and the First Republic (1889–1930)

Before the advent of private meatpacking, dwellers in most cities of the Atlantic world trusted that municipal slaughterhouses (*matadouros*) would guarantee them regular access to fresh meat. During the nineteenth century, the city of Rio de Janeiro saw the construction of two such facilities: in 1853, the São Cristóvão matadouro opened its doors and, almost three decades later, the Santa Cruz abattoir began to operate at the city's edge. The latter remained Rio's sole provider until meatpacking companies disrupted the municipal provisioning system. This study examines Rio's meat market from the foundation of São Cristóvão to the introduction of packing plants in Brazil in the first decades of the 1900s.

To a contemporary observer of the nineteenth-century Americas, Brazil was somewhat of an anomaly. Although its independence from Portugal in 1822 was an outcome of the Atlantic Revolutionary wave of the late 1700s and early 1800s, Brazil implemented a successful monarchy. During most of the nineteenth century—excepting 1831 to 1840—two emperors, descendants from the Portuguese Bragança dynasty, governed the country. The monarchical choice was, in no small measure, related to the presence of the Portuguese crown in Brazil. In 1808, they moved the empire's capital from Lisbon to Rio, fleeing the Iberian Peninsula's imminent invasion by Napoleon's army. Upon the court's return to Portugal in 1821, Pedro, the heir to the throne, stayed in Rio as Prince Regent of the Brazilian Kingdom. One year later, he declared Brazil's independence and became its first emperor. Soon after, some politicians began to question Pedro's adherence to the constitution, and thus loyalty to the nation. In 1831, he abdicated in favor of his Brazilian-born son, Pedro II, who ruled as a constitutional monarch from 1840 until 1889.[4]

To some segments of the Brazilian elite and political class, only the monarchy was capable of countering what they saw as Spanish America's misfortunes: territorial disintegration and slavery abolition. Whereas Spanish America fragmented into several nations, most provinces in Brazil—despite numerous separatist rebellions—remained loyal to the monarchy. Likewise, in most Spanish America, the slavery system collapsed some decades after its emancipation wars, but in Brazil—and the United States—the institution endured and strengthened over the 1800s. The end of slavery only came in 1888 and the implementation of the republic one year later.

The city of Rio de Janeiro was central to these political transitions. Notable sectors of the Brazilian political, military, and religious leadership called Rio their residence. Over the 1800s, it housed the Portuguese and Brazilian royal families, the parliament, the ministers of the state, and later the president of the republic and the congress. Rio was one of Brazil's dioceses, and in 1892, it was elevated to an archdiocese. The military academy was founded in the city alongside the army's school of engineering, and other intellectual associations, which were crucial in toppling the monarchy in 1889. Rio was also Brazil's principal port and an entrepôt in the Atlantic for exchanges among Africa, Europe, and the Americas. Between 1808 and 1850, its population increased approximately fourfold.[5] These demographic changes pressured the local government to address housing, food provision, sanitation, and other services. They did so following colonial mandates, according to which municipal chambers were the main guarantor of urban dwellers' wellbeing. These mandates remained in place for fresh meat supplies—with some variations—until the early twentieth century.

The socioeconomic changes this book examines accelerated in the second half of the 1800s, in part because of the expansion of a new crop in southeast Brazil, coffee. From 1850 to 1930, annual coffee production in the country fluctuated between 50 and 70 percent of total global output.[6] Coffee's systematic cultivation began in the province of Rio de Janeiro's southern region, in the Paraíba Valley—a strip of land that runs along the Paraíba do Sul River, encompassing portions of Rio de Janeiro, São Paulo, and Minas Gerais. In 1840, when Pedro II ascended to power, the Rio de Janeiro province housed most coffee estates in the country. It alone was responsible for more than half of Brazil's exports of this commodity. Large and small plantations (*fazendas*) depended on African and Brazilian-born slaves' work. They picked and processed coffee berries destined for Europe and the United States. Slaves also conducted trains of mules that carried bags of coffee beans to Brazil's leading ports.[7]

The coffee plantation, like mining and sugar operations, relied on slave labor. From the colonial era—particularly after the 1770s—until the termination of the Atlantic slave trade in 1850, millions of enslaved Africans arrived in Brazil.[8] The end of slave trafficking greatly stimulated captives' internal movement from the northeast and south Brazil to the southeast. In 1854, slaves accounted for approximately 24 percent of the country's inhabitants. They corresponded to nearly half of the Rio de Janeiro province's population and 40 percent of Rio's city. In 1872, around 15 percent of Brazil's inhabitants remained captive; however, in the Rio de Janeiro province, slaves accounted for twice that number. In the same year, they represented almost 18 percent of inhabitants in the city of Rio, revealing the importance of the free black sector in the Corte.[9] The 1872 census registered that nearly 60 percent of the total African-descent population in the city was free.[10]

The weight of the coffee economy in nineteenth-century Brazil cannot be overestimated. Prominent coffee planters were involved in Brazil's early industrialization, notably in agricultural machinery production for coffee processing and shipping, and in the textile segments. They also engaged with the public sector to incentivize infrastructure to facilitate coffee exports (railroads, ports, telegraphs, and steam navigation) and finance these ventures.[11] Later, such investments helped to overhaul urban centers' public services, sewage, water, gas, and electricity. The first railway in Brazil, the Estrada de Ferro D. Pedro II (later Central do Brasil), built in the 1850s, linked Rio de Janeiro to São Paulo and was a major conductor of coffee from the Paraíba Valley plantations to Rio's port. In 1864, 470 kilometers of railway track covered the Brazilian territory; in 1900, more than 15,000.[12] Low-cost transportation via rails had a decisive role in expanding the coffee frontier to western São Paulo, linking these plantations to Santos, the leading province port. In a show of their political muscle, planters—in conjunction with city officials—made sure that the rails ran near their estates, increasing land prices and expediting transport. Packs of mules continued to carry bags of coffee, but they did so to head stations relatively close to fazendas in key municipalities.[13] The railroad network also boosted the internal market for other goods. Between the 1870s and 1915, foodstuffs and raw materials freight on the major "coffee railways" continually rose. In that vein, the cattle traffic in Brazil's center-southeast lines increased fourfold in the first two decades of the twentieth century. The city of Rio de Janeiro received a considerable amount of rice, coffee, beans, manioc meal, and wheat consumed in the urban grid and its surroundings via rail lines.[14]

Other provinces in Brazil had a different experience. The expansion of coffee plantations in southeast Brazil reinforced geographic inequalities, for most improvements occurred in Rio de Janeiro, São Paulo, and Minas Gerais. Over the nineteenth century, as the exports of traditional crops declined—particularly from the northeast region—coffee remittances soared. In 1913, the latter represented 60 percent of total overseas sales, while sugar and cotton accounted for 3 percent.[15] Concurrently, the northeast provinces lost population in favor of the southeast—first, after the 1850s, due to the internal slave traffic and migration; and later, when slavery's end was imminent, coffee planters alongside the public sector sponsored immigration programs to substitute captives with foreign-born laborers. Although early immigration schemes failed, between 1880 and 1930, more than four million Europeans and Asians migrated to Brazil. Most settled in official colonies and small farms in the south, worked in the coffee fields of the southeast, and in cities, like Rio de Janeiro and São Paulo, where they joined the urban labor force.[16]

In 1900, Brazil surpassed Mexico to become the most populous nation in Latin America. At the time, Brazil had abysmal literacy and mortality rates. In 1872, almost 40 percent of newborns died before turning five years of age, life expectancy at birth was 30 years, and nearly 85 percent of the population was illiterate. These metrics improved during the First Republic (1889–1930), although in some domains, Brazil continued to lag behind its neighbors. Between 1899 and 1933, the number of primary schools grew a little more than threefold, while the number of enrolled students increased almost ninefold. In 1920, one third of Brazilians could read and write—in 1925, nearly 75 percent of Argentineans were literate—but enrollment in technical schools was considerably low. Sanitation works and vaccination campaigns improved living conditions in some regions, and reduced mortality rates, most notably in urban centers.[17]

The data above show that Imperial Brazil was unable to address major social needs and other issues. In 1889, a coalition of military officers, middle-class professionals, journalists, and some farmers (*fazendeiros*) backed the coup that deposed Pedro II. They sought to overturn key aspects of the monarchical establishment: political centralism, Catholicism as the official religion, and economic conservatism (historian Warren Dean called it "hostility towards capitalism entrepreneurship").[18] The 1891 constitution adopted federalism, did not sponsor a religion, and extended voting rights to all males 21 and older who could read and write (which excluded many citizens from voting).[19]

During the First Republic, the government sought to accelerate the pace of industrialization. Before the outbreak of World War I, Brazil had greatly expanded its manufacturing capacity, particularly in the textile, transport, and food-processing sectors. Also, the transition from slave to wage-labor force greatly stimulated the consumer market.[20] Yet, Brazil continued to rely on coffee exports. On several occasions, depressed international coffee prices threatened the entire economy. In such circumstances, the government enacted policies in "defense of the coffee industry." When plantations' output exceeded worldwide consumption, the government limited the production of low-quality beans and bought coffee from planters, storing or burning it to counter low prices. Brazil was fundamentally an agricultural country; primary products dominated the export sector, and only a minority of Brazilians lived in urban centers.[21]

For those residing in cities, the economic expansion of the late nineteenth century provoked new predicaments. Dwellers in the federal capital faced housing, sanitation, and food supply challenges. Concurrently, they found new conduits to channel their grievances, threatening social unrest. The privations of World War I and the 1929 economic crisis only complicated this panorama. In 1930, the government that emerged from these multiple crises endorsed—like most in the Western Hemisphere—policies to address the "social question." Food security gained a preeminent role in the agenda of experts and policymakers. In conjunction with the government, nutrition professionals sought to improve the working poor's well-being and educate them on the benefits of "scientific eating." As national industrialization programs began to move Brazil toward a new economic paradigm, meat industrialization, in particular, undermined the municipal abattoir and ushered in a new epoch of food politics.[22]

Rio de Janeiro: Brazil's Prime City

For the entire period under consideration in this study, Rio de Janeiro was the political and intellectual center of Brazil and, up to the early 1900s, its leading economic and financial hub. In 1763, it became the vice-regal capital of the Portuguese dominions in the Americas. Since the late eighteenth century, Rio was an intermediary port for European vessels heading to India, China, and Australia. During this period, Rio also became the chief slave port in Brazil. The Portuguese crown's transference to Rio in 1808 and the subsequent opening of Brazil's ports to "friendly" nations—mostly Great Britain—strengthened Rio's commercial connections. Brazil had been a relegated territory of the Portuguese empire, but after 1808, Rio de Janeiro transformed into the royal court seat. Administrators established a royal press, schools of commerce, medicine, and war, a botanical garden, the *Banco do Brasil*, bookstores, a theater, a school of fine arts, scientific associations, and the Institute of History and Geography (*Instituto Histórico e Geográfico*). These institutions were instrumental in shaping public policies that sought to administer the city and its inhabitants for decades to come.[23]

William Scully, editor of the *Anglo-Brazilian Times* in Rio, called Rio de Janeiro, "the emporium of South America."[24] His assessment reflected the dynamism of Carioca life in the 1860s, when almost half of Brazil's exports passed through its port. Although in subsequent decades Rio's economy lost steam, in 1908, its port ranked higher than Santos (in São Paulo) in cargo tonnage and vessel numbers.[25] The manufacturing sector in Rio benefited from the city's function as a port, commercial activity, and coffee expansion in its hinterland. In the 1860s, the province and city of Rio de Janeiro housed large textile mills—the chief in the country until the early 1900s—shipyards, and small-scale industries. Between 1850 and 1880, the city's directories registered businesses in the areas of food and beverage, furniture, tobacco, leather and metal works, graphic arts, clothing, hats, and shoe ware, construction materials, and chemical products. In 1920, Rio was the largest Brazilian industrial city; it led the country in production, capital, and employed workforce in the manufacturing sector.[26]

Such an economic drive stimulated a demand for workers, professionals, and investors. During the 1800s, in the city and its port-complex, slaves worked in all sectors—agriculture, commerce, transport, manufacturing, public works, and arts—as well as operating as servants.[27] As a prominent business center, Rio attracted a considerable foreign population. British and Portuguese investors headed large commercial houses. A sizeable number of artisans, shoemakers, tailors, and doctors of French and Spanish origin lived in the city. The Portuguese segment—by far the largest—prevailed in commercial-related occupations, such as clerks and merchants.[28] The 1880s onward witnessed a new migration wave of poor Italian, Spaniard, and mainly Portuguese nationals. In 1890, they represented "39 percent of the industrial workforce and 51 percent of those involved in commerce."[29] During the First Republic, workers from other Brazilian states moved to the city, as did ex–slaves who left the coffee fazendas in the Paraíba Valley. Together with other Cariocas, they made up the city's labor force, competing for the same jobs and struggling to find housing and other resources.[30]

As Rio's population increased—approximately four times, by one account, between 1872 and 1920—dwellers advanced from the original port area to its hinterland.[31] Local administrators created new parishes and shifted the boundaries of existing ones to accommodate neighborhoods. The central parishes, where manufacturing facilities and commercial establishments abounded, were prime locations for workers who lived in old administrative buildings turned into tenements (*cortiços* and *estalagens*). Others settled in the west, where the population growth was most significant, and later in the south. In the 1850s, public transport systems began to bridge these parishes. The railway Estrada de Ferro Dom Pedro II stretched from the city center to its north and west bounds. In 1868, Rio inaugurated its first streetcar, drawn by mules. By 1910, an electric tramway system of approximately 300 km traversed the urban grid.[32]

Like other urban settlements in the Atlantic world, Rio was a city of contrasts. It had better literacy and lower mortality rates than the national average, but it also had striking inequalities. The majority of urban residents struggled with water supply, trash collection, and housing services. They also faced relentless epidemics of yellow fever, tuberculosis, influenza, and smallpox. Since the late 1800s, government-sponsored projects, public works, and health interventions attempted to address some of these issues. By 1910, popular dwellings in the city center were destroyed, hills leveled, and avenues widened. Waterworks and port modernization followed. The latter included building a sea wall and warehouses, and opening routes that linked the port to the commercial center and the railway terminus. In this process, workers and their families were expelled to underserved suburbs. At the same time, they were subject to public health campaigns that established mandatory vaccination. Residents openly resisted these projects, yet scholars credited these interventions to a steady decline in the city's mortality levels.[33]

To administer this burgeoning population during the empire and the First Republic, the city established and followed detailed municipal ordinances (*código de posturas*), which structured public life in two parts: "health" and "safety." The first covered a host of issues determining where to establish and how to manage graveyards, sewage, slaughterhouses and meat retail, manufacturing facilities and hospitals, and banned "objects that corrupt the atmosphere and harm public health."[34] The area of safety regulated housing construction, streets and public squares alignment and cleaning, markets, peddling, drunkenness, yelling, entertainment, games, firearms possession, and public peace. As for food matters, the municipality licensed businesses to operate, and supervised and rented out spaces in the public market. In the late nineteenth century, fresh meat was the only product whose entire provision was in the municipal chamber's hands.[35]

In Rio de Janeiro, as in other cities of the Atlantic word, fresh beef was considered a "food of first necessity"[36] (akin to a public good), which local officials had to make available to residents in reasonable conditions and prices.[37] In 1920, Rio surpassed one million inhabitants, making it the largest consumer market in Brazil and the second in Latin America. As with other services, it became apparent that the municipal meat supply scheme was inadequate to meet dwellers' needs.

Rio de Janeiro: A Case Study of Meat in the Marketplace

As Brazil furthered its economic ties with the Atlantic world in the second half of the nineteenth century, Rio became a microcosm for examining how global exchanges (in animal improvement technology, meat production and preservation, transportation, and nutrition knowledge) transformed the city's meat market and how its inhabitants contributed and responded to such changes. Regional, national, and transnational networks allowed animals, commodities, technologies, ideas, and people to travel from and to the port city of Rio de Janeiro to Brazil's hinterlands, to South American nations, across the Atlantic, and beyond. Drawing from a methodological framework that stresses the linkages among urban and global developments, *Rio de Janeiro in the Global Meat Market* situates Brazil's capital in the realm of other transatlantic cities. It surveys known economic ties between Latin America, Europe, and the United States—primary commodities and technology exchange, for example. Most importantly, it brings other spaces (south-to-south livestock and the salt-meat trade) and themes (tropical ranching) into the contours of Rio's meat marketplace.[38]

In the last two decades, a growing body of literature has examined multiple transformations that the meat supply system underwent in the nineteenth-century city. Mostly, concerns over public health and increasing demand drove the transition from the private slaughterhouse to the municipal abattoir and, years later, to industrial meatpacking. Some investigations focus on how animal husbandry improvements and transport and storage innovations (railroads and mechanical refrigeration) transformed ranching and the networks that connected farm to table. Elsewhere, studies anchored in Geographic Information System (GIS) tools have revealed the polity behind meat retailing in municipal systems of provision. This methodology has been particularly useful where traditional data are not available, underscoring how city administrators supplied this essential foodstuff before refrigeration. Scholarly works have delved into the unequal and slow-paced expansion of industrial meat in urban settings, showing how this staple and other animal-derived food improved the diets of some but not all working-class groups. Finally, food studies have emphasized the changes in eating habits brought about by industrial packinghouses, the political economy that harnessed private plants, and the resistance of cattle purveyors, butchers, municipal officers, and customers against refrigerated meat.[39]

This book builds upon and contributes to scholarship that considers urban Rio de Janeiro in light of global processes. Traditionally, the Brazilian historiography has underscored how critical events in the 1800s—the movement for independence, the end of slave trafficking, and the expansion of coffee cultivation—connected to worldwide developments. Surely, the majority of works tend heavily toward Brazil's ties with Europe or the United States. Still, some scholars have drawn attention to links with Latin America (particularly with southernmost Brazil) and, more recently, with Africa.[40] Concerning Brazil's contribution to the Atlantic market of foodstuffs and other agricultural products, debate has interrogated the extent to which external entanglements determined low domestic output and food shortages. Referring to early-1800s Rio, one historian contends, "No fact was as significant for the lack of basic goods as the guiding movement of the economy for the production of export commodities."[41] Studies dealing with the late nineteenth century follow a similar interpretation. The classic literature posits that foodstuff production for internal consumption was of "little interest to the state" and that farmers dedicated vast swaths of land to export crops (which seemed more lucrative), neglecting those destined for domestic needs.[42]

Yet, because of Rio's function as Brazil's capital, local administrators had a keen interest in keeping the city well provisioned. During the empire and the First Republic, the city's domestic food network stretched from Rio's immediate and extended hinterland to north and southernmost Brazil. Shortages and price hikes were common because of Brazil's structural problems: land concentration, absence of agricultural machinery, and inefficient transportation (most interprovincial trade was carried by mules).[43] Several case studies for Rio's hinterland show that subsistence farmers regularly supplied the city with all necessities—from manioc meal to fruits and vegetables. In Rio de Janeiro, Minas Gerais, and São Paulo, slave plantations and farms (of varied size, based on slave labor or not) cultivated manioc, rice, corn, and beans, and raised and fattened livestock for the city's consumption. Bahia and Rio Grande do Sul also contributed manioc meal and salted meat to the urban market. After the 1870s, large-scale agriculture and ranching persisted while farm equipment usage remained spotty at best. Nevertheless, the railroad network's extension—particularly in the southeast—made the shipping of export and non-export goods quicker, cheaper, and safer. The latter was particularly beneficial to the exchange of foodstuffs and animals arriving in Rio.[44]

This book argues that in the second half of the nineteenth century, the city of Rio de Janeiro was well supplied with animal proteins, particularly red meat. Meat consumption was an indicator of living standards and a matter of public concern. During most of this period, dwellers relied typically on imported charque, then, in the latter decades of the 1800s, two sets of changes upgraded fresh meat deliveries. First, ranching expansion and transportation innovation in the southeast and central-west Brazil guaranteed a continuous flow of cattle to Rio's hinterlands. Second, the municipal centralization of meat processing and distribution made its provision regular and predictable. By the early twentieth century, carne verde was more abundant and affordable than charque, replacing the latter in the urban marketplace.

As this book traces, developments beyond Rio's borders subjected salted and fresh meat deliveries to extreme swings. Large factories in the South American pasturelands manufactured charque, and transnational commercial houses delivered it to the city. The interplay between these actors determined the flow and price of salted meat, which had a shelf life of several months and was available in Rio's numerous dry goods stores. In comparison, fresh meat was suitable for consumption for no more than two days after the animal's slaughter, and only municipally sanctioned butcher stalls carried it. Further, Rio's city council had a monopoly over the handling, distribution, inspection, and pricing of carne verde in the urban grid (abattoir system). The abattoir system gave city officials the means to control the entire supply network of an essential, perishable food item. It also allowed them to ban "interlopers" (*forasteiros*, in their language) in the city's meat business.

In the latter decades of the nineteenth century, Rio's municipality strengthened its grip over fresh meat supplies. It increased the number of butcher stalls in the city, enhancing its capacity to make meat available where the population was growing while managing its price and quality. Simultaneously, charque deliveries underwent a steep decline, thanks in part to Brazil's leading international providers (Argentina and Uruguay) abandoning salt-meat production in favor of refrigerated meat. They, like Brazil would do later, revolutionized cattle raising and meat processing to fulfill domestic and European demands. In the first decades of the 1900s, these technologies challenged traditional provision schemes; meatpacking companies processed animals several kilometers away from the city, effectively superseding the abattoir system. For their part, old butchering methods proved incapable of keeping up with the rapid urban population growth, and the local government began (although not easily or quickly) to retreat from its meat supply duties. The transition from the abattoir system to meat industrialization was convoluted, and often deregulation did not result in more meat at Cariocas' tables.

When meatpacking plants attempted to enter Rio's market, they (alongside some federal authorities) accused city officials of corruption. They discredited the municipal monopoly as obsolete paternalistic economics—which they broadly defined as market manipulation for the benefit of a few. As this book illustrates, several other elements were at play behind the municipal abattoir. From the 1850s to the early 1900s, to maintain a constant flow of fresh meat to Rio's multiple butcher stalls, the city council attempted to surveil all processes involved in transforming cattle into meat. First, it managed the herds that arrived in Rio's outskirts, as they had to be fed and tended to before slaughter. Second, it estimated the number of animals for consumption based on local demand and slaughterhouse processing capacity. Third, it distributed the by-product as quickly as possible. Rio had no access to natural ice (mechanical refrigeration was introduced in the early twentieth century); thus, it had limited storage capacity for meat and other perishables. Fourth, it established meat prices to offset cyclical crises (droughts and floods, for instance) and to provide consumers with a degree of predictability. These complex arrangements, which responded to the extant technologies, gave the municipality and its agents broad control over the meat market. In the 1920s, cold chain and other innovations utterly disrupted the processes described in this paragraph, challenging all actors involved in the cattle/meat supply business and their politics of provision. Rio, in that case, was no different from other cities in the Atlantic world.[45]

The book opens with a description of Cariocas' eating habits. Chapter 1 examines how food intake in Rio evolved during the nineteenth century, thanks to the influx of foreign fare into the urban marketplace. Chapter 2 uses GIS tools and builds on spatial location theory to illustrate fresh beef offerings in the late 1800s. The increment in the number of butcher stalls—where the population was growing—indicates that consumers had daily access to a perishable good at walking distance. Fresh meat provisions also became more predictable and later replaced salted meat in the urban marketplace. Before that, however, charque was one of the primary sources of animal protein for Rio's residents. Through close readings of primary materials, such as newspaper articles and adverts, cookery books, and postmortem inventories, Chapter 3 shows that salted meat was at the table of all Cariocas irrespective of social condition or status.

The next three chapters underscore changes in the Carioca meat market in the late nineteenth and early twentieth centuries. Chapter 4 studies how the expansion of pasturelands and the extension of railroads in the southeast and central Brazil contributed to improving cattle production in these regions and meat retailing in Rio de Janeiro. These processes coincided with the municipal abattoir's apogee and the decline in charque imports into the city. Chapter 5 turns attention to the global cattle trade, considering its impact on charque deliveries to Rio.[46] Argentina and Uruguay were the primary charque sellers to Brazil. As both increased refrigerated meat output for European markets, salted meat virtually disappeared from Rio's grocery shelves. Chapter 6 illustrates how the arrival of meatpacking plants in early-1900s Brazil empowered new interest groups to challenge the monopoly held by the municipal abattoir and a limited number of purveyors. The epilogue reflects upon the environmental costs associated with the growing appetite for meat—and other animal-derived food—in Brazil and beyond.

This case study shows how the Carioca carnivorous diet changed over time, considering local and international conditions that accompanied this transformation. After all, discussions about the social benefits of increasing animal protein intake by the urban poor were as ubiquitous in early-1900s Brazil as in Argentina, Mexico, Great Britain, or France. At the intersection of social and economic history, this book shows that, during this period, a seemingly mundane aspect of people's lives—specifically, eating habits—was shaped by events beyond their control. Then, like now, diet selection was less a matter of individual preference or taste than of how domestic public policies linked to global trends and technologies.

Notes

1 Unless otherwise noted, throughout this study, the word meat refers to beef cattle.

2 Maximo Torero Cullen, "COVID–19 and the Risk to Food Supply Chains: How to Respond?," Food and Agriculture Organization of the United Nations, March 29, 2020, accessed October 16, 2020, www.fao.org/3/ca8388en/CA8388EN.pdf; United States, "Executive Order on Delegating Authority Under the DPA with Respect to Food Supply Chain Resources During the National Emergency Caused by the Outbreak of COVID–19," Executive Orders, Land & Agriculture, April 28, 2020, accessed October 16, 2020, www.whitehouse.gov/presidential-actions/executive-order-delegating-authority-dpa-respect-food-supply-chain-resources-national-emergency-caused-outbreak-covid-19/; Jonathan Safran Foer, "Meat Is Not Essential. Why Are We Killing For It?," *The Washington Post*, May 11, 2020. I thank Robert Wilcox for sharing this article.

3 During most of the nineteenth century, the city of Rio de Janeiro was referred to as Neutral Municipality (*Município neutro*) or the Court (*Corte*), and in the First Republic (1889–1930) as Federal District (*Distrito Federal*). The city is commonly called Rio, and the adjective "*Carioca*" refers to people, objects, places from the city. In the 1800s, the territory that surrounds Rio was called the province of Rio de Janeiro, and after 1889, the state of Rio de Janeiro.

4 Between 1831 and 1840, a regency governed Brazil in the name of the emperor Pedro, who was only five years old upon his father's resignation. Leslie Bethell, "The Independence of Brazil," in *The Cambridge History of Latin America* 3, ed. Leslie Bethell (Cambridge: Cambridge University Press, 1985), 157–96; Boris Fausto, *História do Brasil* (São Paulo: EDUSP, 1995), 106–58.

5 Luciana L. Martins and Mauricio A. Abreu, "Paradoxes of Modernity: Imperial Rio de Janeiro," *Geoforum* 32, no. 4 (2001): 537; Thiago Vinícius Mantuano da Fonseca, "A região portuária do Rio de Janeiro no século XIX: aspectos demográficos e sociais," *Almanack*, Guarulhos, n. 21 (2019): 174; Maria Cecília Velasco e Cruz, "O porto do Rio de Janeiro no século XIX: Uma realidade de muitas faces," *Revista Tempo* 8 (1999): 3; Thomas Holloway, "Prefácio: Haddock Lobo e o Recenseamento do Rio de Janeiro de 1849," *Boletim de História Demográfica* Ano 15, no. 50 (2008), accessed October 16, 2020, http://historia_demografica.tripod.com/bhds/bhd50/thrj.pdf.

6 Francisco Vidal Luna and Herbert S. Klein, *The Economic and Social History of Brazil Since 1889* (New York: Cambridge University Press, 2014), 7.

7 Marcelo de Paiva Abreu and Luiz Aranha Correa do Lago, "A economia brasileira no Império, 1822–1889," unpublished manuscript, n. 584, Departamento de Economia, PUC–Rio (2010): 7; Gustavo Pereira da Silva, "A formação familiar do complexo caffeeiro: a rede familiar e os investimentos dos Lacerda Franco na economia paulista, (1847–1893), *SÆculum – Revista de História* 29 (2013): 189–90.

8 Numbers vary; for current estimations see Slave Voyages, accessed October 16, 2020, www.slavevoyages.org/voyage/database#tables; João José Reis, "Slavery in Nineteenth–Century Brazil," in *The Cambridge World History of Slavery* 4, ed. David Eltis, Stanley L. Engerman, Seymour Drescher, and David Richardson (Cambridge: Cambridge University Press, 2017), 130–31.

9 For national data, see Tarcísio R. Botelho, "População e espaço nacional no Brasil do século XIX," *Cadernos de História* 7, no. 8 (2005): 75–80. Estimations for the city of Rio de Janeiro are in Holloway, "Prefácio," and Herbert S. Klein "The Colored Freedmen in Brazilian Slave Society," *Journal of Social History* 3, no. 1 (1969): 36.

10 Brazil had one of the highest manumission rates in the Americas. The 1872 census recorded that over 40 percent of the country's total population was free blacks, while in 1860 in Cuba, they represented 16 percent. Focusing specifically on the population of African descent, in 1872 in Brazil, 70 percent was free. In 1860s Cuba and the United States, they corresponded to approximately 35 and 11 percent, respectively. Klein "Colored Freedmen," 35–37; Sidney Chalhoub, "The Precariousness of Freedom in a Slave Society (Brazil in the Nineteenth Century)," *International Review of Social History* 56, no. 3 (2011): 406–10.

11 Wilson Suzigan, *Indústria brasileira: origem e desenvolvimento* (São Paulo: Hucitec, 2000), 73; Flávio A. M. de Saes, "A controvérsia sobre a industrialização na Primeira República," *Estudos Avançados* 3, no. 4 (1989): 30–34; Warren Dean, "The Brazilian Economy, 1870–1930," in *The Cambridge History of Latin America* 5, ed. Leslie Bethell (Cambridge: Cambridge University Press, 1986), 716.

12 Nathaniel H. Leff, "Economic Development in Brazil, 1822–1913," in *How Latin America Fell Behind: Essays on the Economic Histories of Brazil and Mexico, 1800–1914,* ed. Stephen H. Haber (Stanford, CA: Stanford University Press, 1997), 45.

13 Francisco Vidal Luna, Herbert S. Klein, and William Summerhill, "The Characteristics of Coffee Production and Agriculture in the State of São Paulo in 1905," *Agricultural History* 90, no. 1 (2016): 32; Robert H. Mattoon Jr., "Railroads, Coffee, and the Growth of Big Business in São Paulo, Brazil," *The Hispanic American Historical Review* 57, no. 2 (May 1977): 285–88; William Summerhill, "Transport Improvements and Economic Growth in Brazil and Mexico," in *How Latin America*, 97.

14 Leff, "Economic Development," 42–48; Summerhill, "Transport Improvements," 99–100.
15 Leff, "Economic Development," 35.
16 Fonseca, "A região," 189; Luna and Klein, *The Economic*, 25–31.
17 Luna and Klein, *The Economic,* 5–26; Kenneth L. Sokoloff and Stanley L. Engerman, "History Lessons. Institutions, Factor Endowments, and Paths of Development in the New World," *Journal of Economic Perspectives* 14, no. 3 (2000): 229; Eileen Keremitsis, "The Early Industrial Worker in Rio de Janeiro, 1870–1930" (PhD diss., Columbia University, 1982), 202; Dean, "The Brazilian Economy," 706.
18 Dean, "The Brazilian Economy," 688.
19 Boris Fausto, "Brazil: The Social and Political Structure of the First Republic, 1889–1930," in *The Cambridge History of Latin America* 5, ed. Leslie Bethell (Cambridge: Cambridge University Press, 1986), 787– 83.
20 Dean, "The Brazilian Economy," 688; Humberto Perinelli Neto, "Nos quintais do Brasil: homens, pecuária, complexo cafeeiro e modernidade – Barretos (1854/1931)" (PhD diss., Universidade Estadual Paulista, Franca, 2009), 175–86.
21 Earl Richard Downes, "The Seeds of Influence: 'Brazil's 'Essentially Agricultural' Old Republic and the United States, 1910–1930" (PhD diss., University of Texas at Austin, 1980), 8–20; Dean, "The Brazilian Economy," 702.
22 John J. Crocitti, "Vargas Era Social Policies: An Inquiry into Brazilian Malnutrition During the Estado Novo (1937–1945)," in *Vargas and Brazil: New Perspectives*, ed. Jens R. Hentschke (New York: Palgrave Macmillan, 2006), 152; Francisco de Assis Guedes de Vasconcelos, "Os Arquivos Brasileiros de Nutrição: uma revisão sobre produção científica em nutrição no Brasil (1944 a 1968)," *Cadernos de Saúde Pública* 15, no. 2 (1999): 310–13; José Arimatea Barros Bezerra, "Educação alimentar e a constituição de trabalhadores fortes, robustos e produtivos: análise da produção científica em nutrição no Brasil, 1934–1941," *História, Ciências, Saúde – Manguinhos* 19, no. 1 (2012): 159–65; Juan Carlos Yáñez Andrade, "Los pobres están invitados a la mesa. Debates y proyectos transnacionales de alimentación popular en América del Sur, 1930–1950," *Historia Crítica* 71 (2019): 69–91.
23 Martins and Abreu, "Paradoxes," 537; Herbert S. Klein, "A demografia do Tráfico Atlântico e escravos para o Brasil," *Estudos Econômicos* 17, no. 2 (1987): 134; Kirsten Schultz, "Royal Authority, Empire and the Critique of Colonialism: Political Discourse in Rio de Janeiro (1808–1821)," *Luso-Brazilian Review* 37, no. 2 (2000): 8–9.
24 William Scully, *Brazil; Its Provinces and Chief Cities; the Manners & Customs of the People; Agricultural, Commercial, and Other Statistics, Taken from the Latest Official Documents; with a Variety of Useful and Entertaining Knowledge, Both for the Merchant and the Emigrant* (London: Trübner & Co, 1868), 165.
25 Lyman L. Johnson and Zephyr Frank, "Cities and Wealth in the South Atlantic: Buenos Aires and Rio de Janeiro Before 1860," *Comparative Studies in Society and History* 48, no. 3 (2006): 653; Cruz, "O porto," 2–3.
26 Ângela Maria de Castro Gomes and Marieta de Moraes Ferreira, "Industrialização e classe trabalhadora no Rio de Janeiro: novas perspectivas de análise," unpublished manuscript (Fundação Getúlio Vargas, Centro de Pesquisa e Documentação de História Contemporânea do Brasil: Rio de Janeiro, 1988): 11–18; Cristiane Silva Furtado, "A Gigante Brasil Industrial: herança e modernidade no Vale Paraíba Fluminense; a Fábrica Paracambi na

segunda metade do século XIX," *Espaço e Economia* Ano 6, no. 12 (2018): 2, accessed October 10, 2020, https://doi.org/10.4000/espacoeconomia.3175; Luna and Klein, *The Economic,* 65.

27 Luis Carlos Soares, *O "povo de cam" na capital do Brasil: A escravidão urbana no Rio de Janeiro do século XIX* (Rio de Janeiro: Faperj, 7 Letras), 300–05.

28 Fonseca, "A região," 174; Rosana Barbosa Nunes, "Portuguese Migration to Rio de Janeiro, 1822–1850," *The Americas* 57, no. 1 (2000): 43–45.

29 Fausto, "Brazil," 786.

30 Fausto, "Brazil," 785; Teresa Meade, "'Living Worse and Costing More': Resistance and Riot in Rio de Janeiro, 1890–1917," *Journal of Latin American Studies* 21, no. 2 (1989): 244; Maria Cecília Velasco e Cruz, "Puzzling Out Slave Origins in Rio de Janeiro Port Unionism: The 1906 Strike and the Sociedade de Resistência dos Trabalhadores em Trapiche e Café," *The Hispanic American Historical Review* 86, no. 2 (2006): 225–27.

31 Rio de Janeiro, *Anuário Estatístico do Distrito Federal Ano IX*, 1941, Estado da população. População do Distrito Federal – 1821/1940 (Rio de Janeiro: Publicação do Departamento de Geografia e Estatística, 1942), 84. In 1872, Rio's population was twice as big as Salvador's, the second-largest city in Brazil. In 1900, it had almost four times more inhabitants than the city of São Paulo. In subsequent decades, although Rio lost its economic primacy to São Paulo, it remained the most populous city in the country until the mid–1900s. Brasil, Instituto Brasileiro de Geografia e Estatística, "População nos Censos Demográficos, segundo os municípios das capitais – 1872/2010," accessed October 10, 2020, https://censo2010.ibge.gov.br/sinopse/index.php?dados=6.

32 Keremitsis, "The Early," 106; Meade, "'Living Worse," 253.

33 Sidney Sergio F. Solis and Marcus Venicio T. Ribeiro, "O Rio onde o sol não brilha: acumulação e pobreza na transição para o capitalismo," *Revista Rio de Janeiro* 1 (1985): 50–54; Keremitsis, "The Early," 21–43; Meade, "'Living Worse," 246–50.

34 Rio de Janeiro, *Códigos de Posturas da Ilustrissima Camara Municipal* (Rio de Janeiro: Emp. Typ. Dous de Dezembro, 1854), 24.

35 Ibid., 3–10; Rio de Janeiro, *Consolidação das Leis e Posturas Municipaes do Districto Federal,* Primeira parte, legislação federal (Rio de Janeiro: Oficinas tipográficas de Paulo Souza & Comp., 1905); Juliana Teixeira Souza, "A autoridade municipal na corte municipal: enfrentamentos e negociações na regulação do comércio de gêneros (1849–1889)" (PhD diss., Universidade de Campinas, 2007), 12–60.

36 Rio de Janeiro, "*Consolidação*," 789. With some variations, a system of monopolies on either cattle transport and processing or meat preparation and retailing—together with other regulations—guaranteed a steady supply to urban dwellers. See Gisela Moncada, "El abasto de carne en la ciudad de México, 1810–1835," in *Integración y desintegración del espacio económico mexicano: mercado interno y abastecimiento de las carnes desde la colonia al siglo XX*, ed. Enriqueta Quiroz (México: Instituto de Investigaciones Dr. José María Luis Mora, Consejo Nacional de Ciencia y Tecnología, 2017), 239–54; Andrea Dupuy, "Los precios de la carne vacuna en Buenos Aires colonial. Una interpelación historiográfica e histórica," *Tiempo & Economía* 1, no. 1 (2014): 61–75; Gergely Baics, "Is Access to Food a Public Good? Meat Provisioning in Early New York City, 1790–1820," *Journal of Urban History* 20, no. 10 (2013): 643–68; Enriqueta Quiroz, "Del estanco a la libertad: El sistema de la venta de carne en la ciudad de México (1700–1812)," in

Mercaderes, comercio y consulados de Nueva España en el siglo XVIII, ed. Guillermina del Valle Pavón (México: Instituto de Investigaciones Dr. José María Luis Mora, 2005), 191–223.

37 Larissa Virginia Brown, "Internal Commerce in a Colonial Economy: Rio de Janeiro and its Hinterland, 1790–1822" (PhD diss., University of Virginia, 1986), 148–50; Richard Graham, *Feeding the City. From Street Markets to Liberal Reform in Salvador, Brazil, 1780–1860* (Austin: University of Texas Press, 2010), 107–20, 178–85.

38 Mariana Dantas and Emma Hart, "The Urban and the Global in the Early Modern Period in a Comparative Perspective," *Almanack*, Guarulhos, no. 24 (2020): 1–10; Sebastian Conrad, *What Is Global History?* (Princeton: Princeton University Press, 2016), 62–89; Katarzyna J. Cwiertka, Megan J. Elias and Jeffrey M. Pilcher, "Editorial Introduction: Writing Global Food History," *Global Food History* 1, no. 1 (2015): 5–12; Wilson J. Warren, *Meat Makes People Powerful: A Global History of the Modern Era* (Iowa City: University of Iowa Press, 2018).

39 For San Francisco, see Andrew Robichaud and Erik Steiner, "Trail of Blood. The Movement of San Francisco's Butchertown and the Spatial Transformation of Meat Production, 1849–1901," *The Spatial History Project*, August 2009, accessed August 10, 2020, https://web.stanford.edu/group/spatialhistory/cgi-bin/site/pub.php?id=31; New York City, Gergely Baics, "The Geography of Urban Food Retail: Locational Principles of Public Market Provisioning in New York City, 1790–1860," *Urban History* 43 special issue (2016): 1–19; Mexico City, Jeffrey Pilcher, *The Sausage Rebellion: Public Health, Private Enterprise, and Meat in Mexico City, 1890–1917* (Albuquerque: University of New Mexico Press, 2006); London, Ian MacLachlan, "A Bloody Offal Nuisance: The Persistence of Private Slaughter-houses in Nineteenth-Century London," *Urban History* 34, no. 2 (2006): 227–54; Paris, Kyri Claflin, "La Villette: City of Blood (1867–1914)," in *Meat, Modernity, and the Rise of the Slaughterhouse,* ed. Paula Young Lee (Durham, NH: University of New Hampshire Press, 2008), 27–45; Barcelona, Manel Guàrdia, José Luis Oyón, Sergi Garriga, and Nadia Fava, "Meat Consumption and Nutrition Transition in Barcelona, 1709–1935," *Urban History* 45, no. 2 (2018): 193–213; Berlin, Dorothee Brantz, "Animal Bodies, Human Health, and the Reform of Slaughterhouses in Nineteenth-Century Berlin," in *Meat, Modernity*, 71–85; and Copenhagen, Mikkel Thelle, "The Meat City: Urban Space and Provision in Industrial Copenhagen, 1880–1914, *Urban History* 45, no. 2 (2018): 233–52.

40 Recent works on the topic are, Nielson Rosa Bezerra, "Escravidão, farinha e tráfico Atlântico um novo olhar sobre as relações entre o Rio de Janeiro e Benguela," unpublished manuscript (Rio de Janeiro: Fundação Biblioteca National, Ministério da Cultura, 2010): 1–62; Thales A. Zamberlan Pereira, "Was it Uruguay or Coffee? The Causes of the Beef Jerky Industry's Decline in Southern Brazil (1850–1889)," *Nova Economia* 26, no. 1 (2016): 7–42; Carla Menegat, "Brasileiros e pecuária no norte do Uruguai: produção e mercado em meados do século XIX," *Mundo Agrario* 21, no. 46 (2020): 1–18, accessed August 5, 2020, https://doi.org/10.24215/15155994e131.

41 Alcir Lenharo, *As tropas da moderação: o abastecimento da Corte na formação política do Brasil* (Rio de Janeiro: Prefeitura da cidade do Rio de Janeiro, 1992), 38; Pedro Henrique Pedreira Campos, *Nos caminhos da acumulação. Negócios e poder no abastecimento de carnes verdes para a cidade do Rio de Janeiro (1808–1835)*, (São Paulo: Alameda Casa Editorial, 2010), 20.

42 Maria Yedda Leite Linhares, *História do abastecimento; uma problemática em questão (1530–1918)* (Brasília: Edições Binagri, 1979), 22–25.

43 Stephen Haber summarizes this debate in "Introduction: Economic Growth and Latin American Economic Historiography," in *How Latin America*, 1–33.

44 Hebe M. da C. M. G. de Castro, "Mercado interno, trabalho livre e escravidão: a agricultura de alimentos na Província Fluminense na segunda metade do século XIX," *Revista Rio de Janeiro* 4 (1986): 88; João Luís Fragoso, "O império escravista e a república dos plantadores," in *História geral do Brasil*, ed. Maria Yedda Leite Linhares (Rio de Janeiro: Editora Campus, 1996), 145–96; Camila Moraes Marques, "À margem da economia: cachaça e protocampesinato negro no litoral sul fluminense (1800–1888)" (master's thesis: Universidade Federal Fluminense, 2011), 18–30.

45 See Paula Young Lee, ed., *Meat, Modernity, and the Rise of the Slaughterhouse* (Durham, NH: University of New Hampshire Press, 2008); Roger Horowitz, Jeffrey M. Pilcher, and Sydney Watts, "Meat for the Multitudes: Market Culture in Paris, New York City, and Mexico City over the Long Nineteenth Century," *The American Historical Review* 109, no. 4 (2004): 1055–83; Ingrid Johanna Bolívar, "Discursos estatales y geografía del consumo de carne de res en Colombia," in *El poder de la carne: historias de ganaderías en la primera mitad del siglo XX en Colombia*, ed. Alberto Guillermo Flórez Malagón (Bogotá: Pontificia Universidad Javeriana, 2008), 230–89, and more recently the dossier "Meat and the Nineteenth-Century City," see Gergely Baics and M. Thelle, "Introduction: Meat and the Nineteenth-Century City," *Urban History* 45, no. 2 (2018): 184–92.

46 Sections of Chapters 3, 4, and 5 appeared in the article Maria-Aparecida Lopes, "Struggles over an 'Old, Nasty, and Inconvenient Monopoly': Municipal Slaughterhouses and the Meat Industry in Rio de Janeiro, 1880–1920s," *Journal of Latin American Studies* 47, no. 2 (2015): 349–76.

Bibliography

Government Documents and Publications

Brasil. Instituto Brasileiro de Geografia e Estatística. "População nos Censos Demográficos, segundo os municípios das capitais – 1872/2010." Accessed October 10, 2020. https://censo2010.ibge.gov.br/sinopse/index.php?dados=6.

Rio de Janeiro. *Códigos de Posturas da Ilustrissima Camara Municipal*. Rio de Janeiro: Emp. Typ. Dous de Dezembro, 1854.

Rio de Janeiro. *Consolidação das leis e posturas municipaes do Districto Federal*. Primeira parte, legislação federal. Rio de Janeiro: Oficinas tipográficas de Paulo Souza & Comp., 1905.

Rio de Janeiro. *Anuário Estatístico do Distrito Federal Ano IX*, 1941, Estado da população. População do Distrito Federal – 1821/1940. Rio de Janeiro: Publicação do Departamento de Geografia e Estatística, 1942.

United States. "Executive Order on Delegating Authority Under the DPA with Respect to Food Supply Chain Resources During the National Emergency Caused by the Outbreak of COVID-19." Executive Orders, Land & Agriculture. April 28, 2020. Accessed October 16, 2020. www.whitehouse.gov/presidential-actions/executive-order-delegating-authority-dpa-respect-food-supply-chain-resources-national-emergency-caused-outbreak-covid-19/.

Newspapers and Magazines

Foer, Jonathan Safran. "Meat Is Not essential. Why Are We Killing for It?" *The Washington Post*, May 11, 2020.

Other Primary Sources

Cullen, Maximo Torero. "COVID-19 and the Risk to Food Supply Chains: How to Respond?" *Food and Agriculture Organization of the United Nations*. March 29, 2020. Accessed October 16, 2020. www.fao.org/3/ca8388en/CA8388EN.pdf.

Scully, William. *Brazil; Its Provinces and Chief Cities; the Manners & Customs of the People; Agricultural, Commercial, and Other Statistics, Taken from the Latest Official Documents; with a Variety of Useful and Entertaining Knowledge, Both for the Merchant and the Emigrant*. London: Trübner & Co, 1868.

Slave Voyages. Accessed October 16, 2002. www.slavevoyages.org/voyage/database#tables.

Secondary Sources

Abreu, Marcelo de Paiva, and Luiz Aranha Correa do Lago. "A economia brasileira no Império, 1822–1889." Unpublished manuscript n. 584. Departamento de Economia, PUC-Rio (2010): 1–44.

Baics, Gergely. "Is Access to Food a Public Good? Meat Provisioning in Early New York City, 1790–1820." *Journal of Urban History* 20, no. 10 (2013): 643–668.

Baics, Gergely. "The Geography of Urban Food Retail: Locational Principles of Public Market Provisioning in New York City, 1790–1860." *Urban History* 43 special issue (2016): 1–19.

Baics, Gergely, and M. Thelle. "Introduction: Meat and the Nineteenth-Century City." *Urban History* 45, no. 2 (2018): 184–192.

Bethell, Leslie. "The Independence of Brazil." In *The Cambridge History of Latin America* 3, edited by Leslie Bethell, 157–196. Cambridge: Cambridge University Press, 1985.

Bezerra, José Arimatea Barros. "Educação alimentar e a constituição de trabalhadores fortes, robustos e produtivos: análise da produção científica em nutrição no Brasil, 1934–1941." *História, Ciências, Saúde – Manguinhos* 19, no. 1 (2012): 157–179.

Bezerra, Nielson Rosa. "Escravidão, farinha e tráfico Atlântico um novo olhar sobre as relações entre o Rio de Janeiro e Benguela." Unpublished manuscript. Rio de Janeiro: Fundação Biblioteca Nacional, Ministério da Cultura (2010): 1–62.

Bolívar, Ingrid Johanna. "Discursos estatales y geografía del consumo de carne de res en Colombia." In *El poder de la carne: historias de ganaderías en la primera mitad del siglo XX en Colombia*, edited by Alberto Guillermo Flórez Malagón, 230–289. Bogotá: Pontificia Universidad Javeriana, 2008.

Botelho, Tarcísio R. "População e espaço nacional no Brasil do século XIX." *Cadernos de História* 7, no. 8 (2005): 67–83.

Brantz, Dorothee. "Animal Bodies, Human Health, and the Reform of Slaughterhouses in Nineteenth-Century Berlin." In *Meat, Modernity, and the Rise of the Slaughterhouse*, edited by Paula Young Lee, 71–85. Durham, NH: University of New Hampshire Press, 2008.

Brown, Larissa Virginia. "Internal Commerce in a Colonial Economy: Rio de Janeiro and its Hinterland, 1790–1822. PhD diss., University of Virginia, 1986.

Campos, Pedro Henrique Pedreira. *Nos caminhos da acumulação. Negócios e poder no abastecimento de carnes verdes para a cidade do Rio de Janeiro (1808–1835)*. São Paulo: Alameda Casa Editorial, 2010.

Castro, Hebe M. da C. M. G. de. "Mercado interno, trabalho livre escravidão: a agricultura de alimentos na Província Fluminense na segunda metade do século XIX." *Revista Rio de Janeiro* 4 (1986): 87–95.

Chalhoub, Sidney. "The Precariousness of Freedom in a Slave Society (Brazil in the Nineteenth Century)." *International Review of Social History* 56, no. 3 (2011): 405–439.

Claflin, Kyri. "La Villette: City of Blood (1867–1914)." In *Meat, Modernity, and the Rise of the Slaughterhouse*, edited by Paula Young Lee, 27–45. Durham, NH: University of New Hampshire Press, 2008.

Conrad, Sebastian. *What Is Global History?*. Princeton: Princeton University Press, 2016.

Crocitti, John J. "Vargas Era Social Policies: An Inquiry into Brazilian Malnutrition During the Estado Novo (1937–1945)." In *Vargas and Brazil: New Perspectives*, edited by Jens R. Hentschke, 143–171. New York: Palgrave Macmillan, 2006, ProQuest Ebook Central.

Cruz, Maria Cecília Velasco e. "O porto do Rio de Janeiro no século XIX: Uma realidade de muitas faces." *Revista Tempo* 8 (1999): 1–18.

Cruz, Maria Cecília Velasco e. "Puzzling Out Slave Origins in Rio de Janeiro Port Unionism: The 1906 Strike and the Sociedade de Resistência dos Trabalhadores em Trapiche e Café." *The Hispanic American Historical Review* 86, no. 2 (2006): 205–245.

Cwiertka, Katarzyna J., Megan J. Elias, and Jeffrey M. Pilcher. "Editorial Introduction: Writing Global Food History." *Global Food History* 1, no. 1 (2015): 5–12.

Dantas, Mariana, and Emma Hart. "The Urban and the Global in the Early Modern Period in a Comparative Perspective." *Almanack*, Guarulhos, no. 24 (2020): 1–10.

Dean, Warren. "The Brazilian Economy, 1870–1930." In *The Cambridge History of Latin America* 5, edited by Leslie Bethell, 683–724. Cambridge: Cambridge University Press, 1986.

Downes, Earl Richard. "The Seeds of Influence: 'Brazil's 'Essentially Agricultural' Old Republic and the United States, 1910–1930." PhD diss., University of Texas at Austin, 1980.

Dupuy, Andrea. "Los precios de la carne vacuna en Buenos Aires colonial. Una interpelación historiográfica e histórica." *Tiempo & Economía* 1, no. 1 (2014): 61–75.

Fausto, Boris. "Brazil: The Social and Political Structure of the First Republic, 1889–1930." In *The Cambridge History of Latin America* 5, edited by Leslie Bethell, 779–830. Cambridge: Cambridge University Press, 1986.

Fausto, Boris. *História do Brasil*. São Paulo: EDUSP, 1995.

Fonseca, Thiago Vinícius Mantuano da. "A região portuária do Rio de Janeiro no século XIX: aspectos demográficos e sociais." *Almanack*, Guarulhos, no. 21 (2019): 166–204.
Fragoso, João Luís. "O império escravista e a república dos plantadores." In *História geral do Brasil*, edited by Maria Yedda Leite Linhares, 145–196. Rio de Janeiro: Editora Campus, 1996.
Furtado, Cristiane Silva. "A Gigante Brasil Industrial: herança e modernidade no Vale Paraíba Fluminense; a Fábrica Paracambi na segunda metade do século XIX." *Espaço e Economia*, Ano 6, no. 12 (2018): 1–15. Accessed October 10, 2020, https://doi.org/10.4000/espacoeconomia.3175.
Gomes, Ângela Maria de Castro, and Marieta de Moraes Ferreira. "Industrialização e classe trabalhadora no Rio de Janeiro: novas perspectivas de análise." Unpublished manuscript. *Fundação Getúlio Vargas*, Centro de Pesquisa e Documentação de História Contemporânea do Brasil: Rio de Janeiro (1988): 1–73.
Graham, Richard. *Feeding the City. From Street Markets to Liberal Reform in Salvador, Brazil, 1780–1860*. Austin: University of Texas Press, 2010.
Guàrdia, Manel, José Luis Oyón, Sergi Garriga, and Nadia Fava. "Meat Consumption and Nutrition Transition in Barcelona, 1709–1935." *Urban History* 45, no. 2 (2018): 193–213.
Haber, Stephen. "Introduction: Economic Growth and Latin American Economic Historiography," edited by Stephen H. Haber, 1–33. Stanford, CA: Stanford University Press, 1997.
Holloway, Thomas. "Prefácio: Haddock Lobo e o Recenseamento do Rio de Janeiro de 1849." *Boletim de História Demográfica* Ano 15, no. 50 (2008). Accessed October 16, 2020, http://historia_demografica.tripod.com/bhds/bhd50/thrj.pdf.
Horowitz, Roger, Jeffrey M. Pilcher, and Sydney Watts. "Meat for the Multitudes: Market Culture in Paris, New York City, and Mexico City over the Long Nineteenth Century." *The American Historical Review* 109, no. 4 (2004): 1055–1083.
Johnson, Lyman L., and Zephyr Frank. "Cities and Wealth in the South Atlantic: Buenos Aires and Rio de Janeiro Before 1860." *Comparative Studies in Society and History* 48, no. 3 (2006): 634–668.
Keremitsis, Eileen. "The Early Industrial Worker in Rio de Janeiro, 1870–1930." (PhD diss., Columbia University, 1982.
Klein, Herbert S. "The Colored Freedmen in Brazilian Slave Society." *Journal of Social History* 3, no. 1 (1969): 30–52.
Klein, Herbert S. "A demografia do tráfico Atlântico de escravos para o Brasil." *Estudos Econômicos* 17, no. 2 (1987): 129–149.
Lee, Paula Young, ed., *Meat, Modernity, and the Rise of the Slaughterhouse*. Durham, NH: University of New Hampshire Press, 2008.
Leff, Nathaniel H. "Economic Development in Brazil, 1822–1913." In *How Latin America Fell Behind: Essays on the Economic Histories of Brazil and Mexico, 1800–1914*, edited by Stephen H. Haber, 34–64. Stanford, CA: Stanford University Press, 1997.
Lenharo, Alcir. *As tropas da moderação: o abastecimento da Corte na formação política do Brasil*. Rio de Janeiro: Prefeitura da cidade do Rio de Janeiro, 1992.

Linhares, Maria Yedda Leite. *História do abastecimento; uma problemática em questão (1530–1918)*. Brasília: Edições Binagri, 1979.

Lopes, Maria-Aparecida. "Struggles over an 'Old, Nasty, and Inconvenient Monopoly': Municipal Slaughterhouses and the Meat Industry in Rio de Janeiro, 1880–1920s." *Journal of Latin American Studies* 47, no. 2 (2015): 349–376.

Luna, Francisco Vidal, Herbert S. Klein, and William Summerhill. "The Characteristics of Coffee Production and Agriculture in the State of São Paulo in 1905." *Agricultural History* 90, no. 1 (2016): 22–50.

Luna, Francisco Vidal, and Herbert S. Klein. *The Economic and Social History of Brazil Since 1889*. Cambridge: Cambridge University Press, 2014.

MacLachlan, Ian. "A Bloody Offal Nuisance: The Persistence of Private Slaughterhouses in Nineteenth-Century London." *Urban History* 34, no. 2 (2006): 227–254.

Marques, Camila Moraes. "À margem da economia: cachaça e protocampesinato negro no litoral sul fluminense (1800–1888)." Master's thesis: Universidade Federal Fluminense, 2011.

Martins, Luciana L., and Mauricio A. Abreu. "Paradoxes of Modernity: Imperial Rio de Janeiro." *Geoforum* 32, no. 4 (2001): 533–550.

Mattoon Jr., Robert H. "Railroads, Coffee, and the Growth of Big Business in São Paulo, Brazil." *The Hispanic American Historical Review* 57, no. 2 (May 1977): 273–295.

Meade, Teresa. "'Living Worse and Costing More': Resistance and Riot in Rio de Janeiro, 1890–1917." *Journal of Latin American Studies* 21, no. 1–2 (1989): 241–266.

Menegat, Carla. "Brasileiros e pecuária no norte do Uruguai: produção e mercado em meados do século XIX." *Mundo Agrario* 21, no. 46 (2020): 1–18. Accessed August 5, 2020, https://doi.org/10.24215/15155994e131.

Moncada, Gisela. "El abasto de carne en la ciudad de México, 1810–1835." In *Integración y desintegración del espacio económico mexicano: mercado interno y abastecimiento de las carnes desde la colonia al siglo XX*, edited by Enriqueta Quiroz, 239–266. México: Instituto de Investigaciones Dr. José María Luis Mora, Consejo Nacional de Ciencia y Tecnología, 2017.

Neto, Humberto Perinelli. "Nos quintais do Brasil: homens, pecuária, complexo cafeeiro e modernidade - Barretos (1854/1931)." PhD diss., Universidade Estadual Paulista, Franca, 2009.

Nunes, Rosana Barbosa. "Portuguese Migration to Rio de Janeiro, 1822–1850." *The Americas* 57, no. 1 (2000): 37–61.

Pereira, Thales A. Zamberlan. "Was it Uruguay or Coffee? The Causes of the Beef Jerky Industry's Decline in Southern Brazil (1850–1889)." *Nova Economia* 26, no. 1 (2016): 7–42.

Pilcher, Jeffrey. *The Sausage Rebellion: Public Health, Private Enterprise, and Meat in Mexico City, 1890–1917*. Albuquerque: University of New Mexico Press, 2006.

Quiroz, Enriqueta. "Del estanco a la libertad: El sistema de la venta de carne en la ciudad de México (1700–1812)." In *Mercaderes, comercio y consulados de Nueva España en el siglo XVIII*, edited by Guillermina del Valle Pavón, 191–223. México: Instituto de Investigaciones Dr. José María Luis Mora, 2005.

Reis, João José. "Slavery in Nineteenth-Century Brazil." In *The Cambridge World History of Slavery* 4, edited by David Eltis, Stanley L. Engerman, Seymour Drescher, and David Richardson, 129–154. Cambridge: Cambridge University Press, 2017.

Robichaud, Andrew, and Erik Steiner. "Trail of Blood. The Movement of San Francisco's Butchertown and the Spatial Transformation of Meat Production, 1849–1901." *The Spatial History Project*, August 2009. Accessed August 10, 2020. https://web.stanford.edu/group/spatialhistory/cgi–bin/site/pub.php?id=31.

Saes, Flávio A. M. de. "A controvérsia sobre a industrialização na Primeira República." *Estudos Avançados* 3, no. 4 (1989): 20–39.

Schultz, Kirsten. "Royal Authority, Empire and the Critique of Colonialism: Political Discourse in Rio de Janeiro (1808–1821)." *Luso–Brazilian Review* 37, no. 2 (Winter 2000): 7–31.

Silva, Gustavo Pereira da. "A formação familiar do complexo caffeeiro: a rede familiar e os investimentos dos Lacerda Franco na economia paulista, (1847–1893)." *SÆculum - Revista de História* 29 (2013): 189–207.

Soares, Luis Carlos. *O "povo de cam" na capital do Brasil: A escravidão urbana no Rio de Janeiro do século XIX*. Rio de Janeiro: Faperj, 7 Letras, 2007.

Sokoloff, Kenneth L., and Stanley L. Engerman. "History Lessons. Institutions, Factor Endowments, and Paths of Development in the New World." *Journal of Economic Perspectives* 14, no. 3 (2000): 217–232.

Solis, Sidney Sergio F., and Marcus Venicio T. Ribeiro. "O Rio onde o sol não brilha: acumulação e pobreza na transição para o capitalismo." *Revista Rio de Janeiro* 1 (1985): 45–59.

Souza, Juliana Teixeira. "A autoridade municipal na corte municipal: enfrentamentos e negociações na regulação do comércio de gêneros (1849–1889)." PhD diss., Universidade de Campinas, 2007.

Summerhill, William. "Transport Improvements and Economic Growth in Brazil and Mexico." In *How Latin America Fell Behind: Essays on the Economic Histories of Brazil and Mexico, 1800–1914*, edited by Stephen H. Haber, 93–117. Stanford, CA: Stanford University Press, 1997.

Suzigan, Wilson. *Indústria brasileira: origem e desenvolvimento*. São Paulo: Hucitec, 2000.

Thelle, Mikkel. "The Meat City: Urban Space and Provision in Industrial Copenhagen, 1880–1914." *Urban History* 45, no. 2 (2018): 233–252.

Vasconcelos, Francisco de Assis Guedes de. "Os Arquivos Brasileiros de Nutrição: uma revisão sobre produção científica em nutrição no Brasil (1944 a 1968)." *Cadernos de Saúde Pública* 15, no. 2 (1999): 303–316.

Warren, Wilson J. *Meat Makes People Powerful: A Global History of the Modern Era*. Iowa City: University of Iowa Press, 2018.

Yáñez Andrade, Juan Carlos. "Los pobres están invitados a la mesa. Debates y proyectos transnacionales de alimentación popular en América del Sur, 1930–1950." *Historia Crítica* 71 (2019): 69–91.

1 Foodways and Diet in Nineteenth-Century Rio de Janeiro

Foreign travelers who visited Rio de Janeiro in the early nineteenth century seemed to agree that Brazil's capital was a crowded, dirty, and noisy city. In one account, at 5:00 a.m., cannon shots from Ilha das Cobras awoke the oblivious guest; 30 minutes later, horns of the national guard called its members to initiate duties; shortly thereafter, church bells rang, inviting parishioners to the morning mass; at 6 a.m., prisoners began shouting at people's houses to collect wastewater. As the day went on, heavily loaded oxcarts crossed the "irregular pavement" of Rio's narrow streets—which one observer judged more appropriate to call "alleys"—producing earsplitting noises.[1] Before 7:00 a.m., a boisterous street market began to take shape, with slave peddlers promoting goods with chants and songs. They hauled water, flowers, and coal, and offered their labor as barbers, barber–surgeons, porters, and carpenters. Freed and slave women (*quitandeiras*) balanced food trays on their heads, hawking fruits, pastries, and vegetables. Other sellers—stationed under canopies near corner stores—sold more substantial viands, salted meat (*charque*) with manioc meal and beans, fried fish, and a stew prepared with manioc meal, offal, and lard (*angu*). The street menu was completed with hot coffee, a refreshing sour, sweet drink made with fermented rice (*aluá*), and various tropical fruits beverages.[2]

This tableau figures centrally in this study, revealing, on the one hand, the existence of a vibrant market in Rio and, on the other, how passers-by—of any social status—had access to a variety of foodstuffs in the urban center. By the second half of the nineteenth century, although travelers continued to decry the city's noisy neighborhoods, they noted significant changes in its infrastructure and street market. They described, for instance, an upgraded sewage system, "carefully" paved streets, and petty commerce whereby slaves alongside poor immigrants peddled traditional and exotic food items. Underlying these observations was Brazil's economic engagement in the Atlantic trade. To sate the ever-growing international appetite for coffee, plantations in the Paraíba Valley expanded clearing areas adjacent to Rio. If in the early 1800s most foodstuffs consumed in the city came from its hinterland, by the end of the century, a larger share of those items arrived from far provinces and abroad.[3]

Two correlated developments accompanied the diversification of Rio's food market. Precisely when Brazil was establishing its first medical schools in Bahia and Rio de Janeiro, knowledge about nutrition science—which had emerged in late eighteenth-century-France—was permeating the global medico-scientific community. By the mid-nineteenth century, those principles entered mainstream Brazilian political discourse via medical publications and theses about the interplay between bodily constitution and food intake. This chapter looks into Cariocas' eating habits in light of such context. It does so, first, by examining the diet of city dwellers in the first half of the century. Second, it considers eating shifting patterns after the 1850s. Lastly, this chapter underscores the significance of animal proteins in Rio's urban market.

The Brazilian Food Triad: Beans, Manioc Meal, and Charque

During the nineteenth century, the staple foods for Brazilians were beans, manioc meal, and salted meat.[4] The triad composed a dish rich in carbohydrates, and vegetal and animal proteins. Typically, eaters mixed cooked beans broth with manioc meal, kneading little cakes that they accompanied with fried charque. In Brazil's capital, several accounts describe the appearance of these three items in the daily meals of all segments of the Carioca society—slave and free, rich and poor, immigrants and travelers, hospital patients and prisoners. Indeed, eating practices, as historiography underscores, highlight the complex relationship between foodways and social class. In the spirit of elucidating this animated aspect of Carioca society, this section discusses how additions to these foods and changes in their preparation reveal social and ethnic divisions in Rio's urban setting.[5]

Manioc (*Manihot esculenta*) is a starchy root, indigenous to South America, domesticated by natives, and regularly cultivated in Jesuit missions during the early colonial period. Manioc can be eaten boiled or when prepared in powder as manioc meal (*farinha de mandioca*). In the early nineteenth century, manufacturing of the latter entailed removing the rigid brown skin of the root. Grated and pressed, the bright white inside dripped out as a liquid; the remaining pulp was toasted in copper pans or large ovens. Manioc meal can be stored for some time, particularly the coarse kind, which contains less moisture and lasts longer than fine-textured farinha. One by-product of manioc (*mandioca*) is tapioca, the main ingredient for porridge and a variety of cakes, including a pancake (*beiju*), which eaters still savor today by folding up and sprinkling sugar, cinnamon, and coconut flakes.[6]

In the early 1800s, several slaved-based coffee and sugar plantations (*fazendas*) surrounded Rio de Janeiro. While intimately connected to external markets, these fazendas produced manioc meal for their consumption. Small farms—that also relied on slave labor— manufactured farinha almost exclusively for Rio's capital, which along with locally grown fruits and vegetables arrived in the city via streams flowing into the Guanabara Bay. Rio de Janeiro also acquired manioc meal from south Bahia and Santa Catarina via coastal commerce.[7] Notwithstanding manioc meal's importance to Brazil's internal market, it played a significant role in the transatlantic trade between Rio de Janeiro and Angola. Farinha de mandioca fed Africans who arrived at Rio's shores from Benguela, and sustained ships' crewmembers sailing in both directions. Rio's port also exported manioc meal to areas under Portuguese control in West-Central Africa, where it had been a staple since the eighteenth century.[8]

"No meal is complete without" manioc meal, stated Mary Graham, the British governess who visited Rio in the 1820s. Other contemporaries noticed its presence in the meals of the poor, slave, and rich, used, according to some, like bread. In his classic sociological study about Brazilian foodways, Luís da Câmara Cascudo disputes this assessment, arguing that manioc meal never replaced bread. In any case, Brazilians ate manioc meal in several forms: uncooked as an accompaniment to any sour or sweet dish. Sautéed with oil or butter, it resembles a dish of breadcrumbs (*farofa*); mixed with fish or meat stock, it turns into a heavy porridge (*pirão*).[9]

Beans were the basic vegetable that accompanied farinha de mandioca—in the case of Rio de Janeiro, black beans predominated. It arrived in Rio from its rural parishes and, increasingly, from nearby provinces in the southeast region. Beans were boiled in water, sometimes seasoned with spices and garlic, or stewed with pork, sausages, and charque. The last was the only item of the triad not produced in Rio's hinterland and probably the most important food item in Brazil's coastal commerce. Throughout the nineteenth century, northeast Brazil, first, and later Rio Grande do Sul, Argentina, and Uruguay regularly supplied Rio's depots with large, folded pieces of salted meat, called *mantas*, which Mary Graham compared to "bundles of thick ragged leather."[10] Retailers hung them in dry good stores alongside bacon and dried fish, cutting them in lengthwise strips and selling them by weight.

Prior to cooking, charque has to soak in water for several hours, which helps to wash out the salt (used for preservation) and softens the meat. Charque is fried, broiled, or cooked with beans; when shredded, it becomes a filling for savory pastries.[11] Aside from salted meat, fresh meat was widely available in Rio, although foreigner visitors often described it as "lean and bad." Bacon was a common substitute for charque, and, apparently, Cariocas consumed pork in large quantities.[12] Hogs arrived from Minas Gerais, and as municipal ordinances attest, small livestock rearing (including pigs and chickens) was ubiquitous in the city center. Milk, by one account, was "scarce and mediocre." When available, the vender would pull a cow through Rio's streets, park the animal in key areas, and retail the liquid in front of residents' doors. The most common cheese was the Minas type (*queijo de Minas*), a fresh, semi-soft variety from the province bearing its name.[13]

Rio had a vibrant fish market located near the customhouse. Based on contemporaries' observations, fresh fish eating was the privilege of a few. Scanty records show its presence in rich families' meals and in restaurants. Dried fish, on the other hand, was frequent fare across the Carioca social spectrum. Noteworthy, the British merchant John Luccock describes a shift in fish consumption in Rio de Janeiro in a matter of a decade. In 1808, when Luccock initiated his ten-year stay in Brazil, he found fresh fish "scarce and expensive" and Cariocas "prejudiced against such food, conceiving it to be unwholesome." By 1818, the merchant claims, locals had developed a "taste" for it, so much that "multitudes resorted to fishing" for trading and "to draw, in an idle way, a bare subsistence from water." Less usual in the first half of the nineteenth century, salted codfish became an everyday occurrence after the 1850s.[14]

Vegetables and fruits came to Rio from nearby big and small fazendas, where slaves harvested palm hearts (*palmito*), cauliflowers, cabbages, carrots, parsnips, spinach, onions, lettuce, and assorted pumpkins. Occasionally, captives had access to small plots, where they cultivated vegetables and fruits for their consumption. Masters permitting, they peddled the surplus in the city market. Banana and orange gardens surrounded the villas adjacent to Rio, hence both fruits were abundant in Brazil's capital, as were cashew fruit (*caju*), guava, watermelon, pineapple, passion fruit (*maracujá*), papaya, jaboticaba, mango, and sugar-apple fruit (*fruta do conde*). Cariocas indulged in sweetmeats. Crystalized fruits, compotes, and guava paste were daily fare, alongside other sweets (*doces*), locally produced and regularly purchased from the city of Itu (São Paulo), famous for its doces. In Rio's street market, one could find slices of sugar cane, beijus, little pastries filled with molasses (*sonhos*), hominy with cinnamon (*canjica*), and rice puddings. To wash down this feast, tropical fruit beverages, mate, coffee, and cachaça were also available.[15]

In the early nineteenth century, the eating rhythm of Rio's inhabitants was no different than that of their rural counterparts. The first meal of the day was a 5:00 or 6:00 a.m. fare of coffee, milk, bread, and butter. Three or four hours later, lunch was served, and 2:00 or 3:00 p.m. was time for dinner. The last was, by one account, a heavy meal consisting of several dishes. Albeit describing a dinner in Rio's countryside, the Irish reverend Robert Walsh provides a glimpse of a 3:00 p.m. repast he enjoyed in the household of Mr. Willis, an Englishman settled in Irajá. The table, says Walsh was covered with several dishes, "salt-fish, with onions ..., at one end; at the other, salt fish, hashed with vegetables, and in the middle a large tureen of ... black beans stewed in ... hog's lard, and beside it a broad platter of farinha." Supper, taken anytime between 6:00 and 8:00 p.m., varied between a light meal and a repeat of jantar.[16]

Unquestionably, such an eating schedule as well as the quantity and composition of each meal's dishes, varied according to social status. Shopkeepers "hastily" ate at their shops, whenever they could. Slaves' mealtimes were subordinate to their labor routine. In the best of circumstances, they had three meals daily, all of which might have included farinha de mandioca, or cornbread and beans, and occasionally charque, fresh meat, or bacon. In his 1839 *Farmer's Manual*, the French medical doctor Jean Baptiste Alban Imbert describes a typical meal routine in a Rio de Janeiro fazenda where slaves had bread and cachaça before starting their workday; at 9:00 a.m. a meal of rice, bacon, and coffee; in the afternoon, salted meat (two days per week fresh meat substituted the latter) with vegetables for dinner; and manioc meal, cooked vegetables, and fruits for supper. In case of illness, the author recommends adding chicken broth to slaves' food intake. In urban centers, slave earners had a less rigorous eating schedule, gathering around quitandeiras, whenever possible, to supplement their meals with the produce and dishes being hawked.[17]

As with timing, the variety of foodstuffs available to Cariocas altered according to social standing. There were not foods exclusive to one group; rather, those who could afford more than charque, beans, and manioc meal added sumptuous items to their food intake. According to an 1829 resolution—which did not materialize—the standard daily meal allotment for captives from the Ministry of Finance should have consisted of salted or fresh meat, bacon, beans, and manioc meal, for a total of 5,546 calories per day. Although this is an unrealistic number—scholars estimate that an adequate, minimum-cost diet amounted to approximately 4,000 calories—it denotes a benchmark to consider variations in captives' diet.[18] Evidently, some masters did not provide enough food to maintain their slaves' health. Their high mortality rate in early-nineteenth-century Rio de Janeiro is evidence of that. Records of the Santa Casa of Rio from 1833 to 1849 collected by Mary Karasch show that several diseases afflicting the urban slave population were due to malnourishment, among them scurvy, rickets, and pellagra. What is more, without essential nutrients and vitamins, captives could not fight infectious-parasitic diseases. Their offspring were particularly vulnerable; as children relied on their mothers who were already malnourished, they lacked, in particular, protein, calcium, and iron. This epidemic worsened after the nursing period, for milk was a rarity. Some reports indicate that slave children as young as two or three years old (and even adults) ate dirt, a condition linked to mineral deficiency. To prevent the practice, slave owners made the use of iron masks compulsory.[19]

Moreover, slave food intake differed according to their condition, location, production unit, and, most importantly, to how it was supplemented.[20] The historiography of the slave diet in Brazil is vast; discussing it goes beyond this chapter's scope. Studies on the topic have evolved from providing a compendium on the "African contribution" to the Brazilian cuisine and idyllic views about the relationship between captives and masters to accounts emphasizing the inhuman treatment to which the vast majority were subject. Indeed, at least until 1850s, the slave population grew in Brazil chiefly because of the continuous flow of Africans. Currently, scholars tend to underscore regional diversities and the means by which captives supplemented their diet. Those who could so, potentially had a more nutritious diet—as they sought to acquire fruits and vegetables, including sweet potatoes, cabbage, spinach, kale, okra, peanut oil, and palm hearts—than their counterparts who relied solely on their masters' allotment.[21]

Although the line that separated rural from urban spaces was not rigid, scholars have shown that in the former areas, slaves could access produce from the plantation or cultivate for their sustenance. In 1813, when the Swedish geologist Gustavo Beyer visited Fazenda Santa Cruz, a massive cattle and agro estate owned by the Portuguese crown, he enthusiastically noted that captives had "a little piece of land and two free days to work for themselves."[22] There were also variations within the rural world. The French painter Jean Baptiste Debret reports that on rich plantations, slaves regularly had canjica, black beans, bacon, salted meat, and fruits, whereas in smaller units, their ration was reduced to boiled farinha de mandioca, orange, and bananas. In the latter case, bacon, charque, or fish were consumed only when slaves purchased those items. In cities, wage-earner slaves could buy "fruits, sweet potatoes, fried 'sardines,' *angú*, *massarocas* ('Indian-wheat boiled'), and *feijoada* [a black bean stew] from the market women." Slave earners in other Brazilian urban centers had similar eating prospects, as Henry Koster observed in Recife's marketplace in the northeast region.[23]

While there is an impressive body of research on the slave diet, little is known about the regimen of poor people. Nonetheless, several sources underscore that their diet had much in common with that of slaves, for they also relied on charque, manioc meal, and beans. Debret left the best descriptions of Carioca foodways across social strata. According to his accounts, in the former's dinner, those who could afford more than charque with manioc meal consumed pork loins or fish cooked with onions, tomatoes, and bell peppers; and even had a dessert course of orange and banana. The diet of the rich had certainly more variety than that of the poor and enslaved. A typical dinner of the well-to-do consisted of several dishes: a consommé prepared with beef, sausages, bacon, tomatoes, cabbages, followed by a plate with vegetables cooked with meat or shrimp, all eaten with manioc meal. Afterward, an "extremely spicy" rice platter with poultry was served alongside chicken or other roasts. The final dish was a salad with onions and black olives. For dessert, the higher classes had a rice cake with cinnamon, Minas cheese, and assorted tropical fruits: pineapple, maracujá, watermelon, mangos, and others. Port wine and coffee washed down this feast.[24]

During the second half of the nineteenth century, Brazil experienced years of prosperity due, in part, to the expansion of coffee plantations in the Paraíba Valley. As the country furthered its economic ties with the Atlantic North, foreign fare became common in the urban marketplace. Apart from the addition of sumptuous and other food items, Cariocas' diet seemed to have diversified, including that of slaves. Simultaneously, physicians and public authorities empowered themselves with the latest European treatises on the relationship between nutrition and chronic disease, disseminating recommendations on how to improve the diet for all. The next section delves into such developments.

The Rise of Nutrition Studies in Brazil and a New Diet for Cariocas

To describe cultural changes of any sort, historians seldom have the luxury of singling out clear-cut events, for cultural shifts usually occur over time and are shaped by multicausal circumstances. In early nineteenth-century Brazil, however, one event brought about considerable scrutiny of Cariocas quotidian habits: the transfer of the Portuguese royal court to Rio de Janeiro in late 1807. Escorted by a British fleet, after Napoleon Bonaparte troops' invasion of the Iberian Peninsula, Prince Regent João VI arrived in Rio de Janeiro in March 1808. In his convoy, apart from the royal family (including his mentally incapacitated mother, Maria, his Spanish wife, Carlota Joaquina, and his son Pedro, who would later declare Brazil's independence), nobles, confessors, servants, and public officials accompanied the prince. It was indeed a momentous occurrence. On the one hand, no European sovereign had ever been in the Americas. On the other, the new center of the Portuguese empire, Rio de Janeiro, had no infrastructure to receive such an entourage; it lacked sufficient housing and some important amenities, notably a royal theater and a printing press. In subsequent years, the cityscape transformed itself to accommodate thousands of exiles, as did its residents' customs, from dressing trends to eating habits.[25]

In his 1852 medical thesis "The Alimentary Regime of the Wealthy Classes in Rio de Janeiro" (*Do regimen das classes abastadas no Rio de Janeiro* [...]), José Maria Rodrigues Regadas captures shifts in the food domain. According to interviews conducted with affluent Cariocas, on the eve of the court's arrival, their typical breakfast consisted of coffee (sometimes drank with milk), tea (albeit rare), beijus, queijo de Minas—"instead of butter," stresses Regadas—and eggs. The lunch comprised soup with meat and rice, roasted meat, "pastries strongly garnished with our pepper and palm oil (*azeite de dendê*)," and shrimp. Variations on this menu included salted or fresh fish and seafood, and manioc meal—raw or cooked in a broth. In addition, there was a daily portion of beans, although some claimed they only savored them sparingly in samba festivities (*batucadas*). For this occasion, beans were prepared with loin, pig's head, bacon, charque, and sausages, "constituting the well-known feijoada." For dessert, oranges, pineapple, and melon (the last two only during the summer) were served alongside guava paste or molasses with manioc meal and queijo de Minas. This feast ended with water and the occasional Porto wine. Fish and rice (prepared with fish's head or shrimp) and cooked hominy comprised supper, the final meal of the day.[26]

However, slowly, Regadas remarks, 40 years after the transference of the Portuguese court to Rio, the upper class sought new cuisine, thanks, in part, to the influx of imported goods. Whereas beijus and queijo de Minas were less frequent in the gentry's meals, bread with butter savored with English tea gained preeminence at lunch. Domestic poultry and a diverse range of fruits from abroad became part of the midday meal, as did pasta and wine. Fish and spicy pastries (*quitutes*) practically vanished from the tables of the rich, while "nutritious and light" bread replaced manioc meal. The other major change was in the size of supper, which turned into a modest fare of bread, butter, and tea. Finally, ice (certainly a luxury) became a common item in well-to-do households.[27]

Judging by the findings of Francisco Fernandes Padilha and Antonio Corrêa de Sousa Costa, authors of two medical theses about the alimentary regime of the Carioca poor, the diets of the less affluent also changed. By midcentury, apart from the triad, their meals included a wide array of legumes and vegetables (sweet potato, cassava, sweet pumpkin, cabbage, turnips, collards [*couve*], corn, and potatoes), codfish, sardines, and other fresh fish, and on festive days pork, although poultry remained expensive. A "heavily seasoned" dish prepared with okra, shrimp, and azeite de dendê (*caruru*) was daily fare for the poor. Fruits, in the words of Padilla, "of all seasons are accessible to all families on the sad scale of poverty." In addition, they regularly had coffee and milk, and observed three daily meals. Other food items thought to be exclusive to the diets of the rich reached the tables of the poor, as they incorporated wine—although one of "mediocre quality" emphasizes Costa—and wheaten bread in their diet. Indeed, Padilla labeled the former "the staple food of the poor class,"[28] which would explain the significant increase in the number of bakeries in Rio de Janeiro. While in 1816 there were only six pastry shops in urban Rio, by mid-century the local Almanac registered as many as 50.[29]

Costa also commented on the alimentary regime of the foreigner poor. The Portuguese—who constituted by far the largest immigrant segment in Rio—if residing with their families observed three daily meals similar to those of nationals: beans with vegetables and a "small portion of salted meat." While some preferred to add slices of bread to their bean broth, others used "our farinha de mandioca." Those who lived alone apparently subsisted on bread and coffee—with the occasional fruit in the morning, charque, salt cod, or sardines, which they accompanied with bread or beans. The poor of French, German, and British origin had a more carnivorous diet, adding meat to potatoes, bread, and rice. They were also less attracted to domestic "condiments and spices," but keen on oranges and bananas.[30]

As for the slave diet, recent studies show that after the 1850s, other items rarely present in slaves' food allotment became common, including rice, coffee, charque (as their primary source of animal proteins), and fresh meat or codfish on selected days. The ways by which slaves supplemented their diets, mentioned in the first section of this chapter, both in the urban and rural setting remained. In the latter areas, produce from the plantation combined with foodstuffs that could be stored for several months determined the type of food slaves had. Hence, the preference of masters for charque, which according to Louis Couty—a French biologist who studied salted meat production in 1880s South America—had a shelf life of eight to ten months.[31] Still, there was enormous variation in slaves' diet. In an article published in the *Annaes Brasilienses de Medicina*, João D. P. da Silva, a medical doctor, notices the low incidence of hookworm disease in the Marquesa do Paraná plantation in the province of Rio de Janeiro because slaves ate charque daily and maintained proper hygiene. However, collaborators in the same magazine stress that, while in some regions of Brazil, slaves had charque twice a week, in others, their regular meal only consisted of "beans and bacon."[32] Contemporaneous sources confirm such a disparity between fazendas, and the presence of codfish as a meat substitute.[33]

The end of slave trafficking in 1850 triggered a series of consequential events for the Brazilian labor market. First, it strengthened the internal trade of captives. Scholars have pointed out that the expansion of coffee plantations during the second half the nineteenth century was based upon the constant flow of slaves from economically "stagnated" regions to southeast Brazil. Second, as early attempts to introduce immigrant labor to Brazil did not bear expected results, captives, who up to 1850 were attainable even to the middling sector, became expensive. Such prospects would suggest that masters sought to improve the living conditions of those hard-to-come-by slaves if anything because of their increasing prices. In his classic work, Stanley Stein affirms, "The end of slave trade forced planters to look more carefully to the physical needs of their slaves to prolong their working existence."[34] Finally, slaves permeated every aspect of the Carioca society and all economic sectors; thus, it is not surprising that as Rio's inhabitants diversified their diet, that of slaves followed suit.[35] In broad terms, however, while some 1850s descriptions about captives' eating patterns might have included more items than those made earlier, variety according to their status, work they executed, location, and labor unit seemed to continue to determine the type and quantities of food they ate.[36]

Authors of the aforementioned medical theses drew careful distinctions between the alimentary regime of urban and rural slaves and in-house versus outside slaves. The former, explains Costa, made three daily meals, and had access to a wide array of foodstuffs. Conversely, those who were rented out and worked as carpenters or bricklayers had meager meals of "three or four sardines, ... angu, or a small portion of salted meat or codfish," which they supplemented with street food, "bad stews[,] and various harmful treats." Costa observed slave eating practices in Rio de Janeiro province and condemned their "regular and uniform ... almost exclusively ... vegetarian meals," which rarely included fresh beef or charque. The medical doctor concluded his work by urging those who had any "interested in the cause of civilization and the progress of agriculture" to pay attention to the alimentary regime of slaves.[37]

These theses present new thinking about diet, nutrition, and its connection to disease incidence. For instance, the "new" diet of the rich mirrors not only the optimum alimentary regime according to the medical view of mid-nineteenth century Brazil, but also the superiority of European tastes. As the diet of wealthy Cariocas became more diverse, a preference for foreign foods arose,[38] notably in the emergence of wheaten bread as a replacement for manioc meal, in the apparent phasing out of spicy foods, and in the controversy over the intake of beans, which were considered stodgy. Not coincidently, these foodstuffs distinguished the alimentary regime of the elite from the poor and enslaved, whose diets, deemed monotonous and insufficient, were made worse by their "immoderate" use of coffee and, most of all, of certain spices (mainly, azeite de dendê), which nineteenth-century physicians associated with "indigestion, diarrhea, dysentery, hemorrhoids and all the diseases of the digestive tract."[39]

These observations are a testimony to the "Chemical Revolution" of the late eighteenth century and its impact on nutritional knowledge henceforth. Particularly significant was the discovery of nitrogen (called "azote") and experiments that determined its content in food compounds.[40] It was also asserted that foods high in nitrogen were inherently nutritious.[41] By the mid-1800s, the German chemist Justus von Liebig went further and classified foodstuffs into two groups: plastic (azotized foods, later identified as proteins) and respiratory (non-azotized foods). Whereas the latter (fats, sugars, and starch) oxidized in the blood, the former, present in animal and vegetal substances, were "the only true nutrient, providing both the machinery of the body and the fuel for its work."[42] Liebig also ascribed a superior quality to animal proteins; in his words:

> The juice of flesh contains, beyond a doubt, the conditions necessary for the formation of the whole muscle ... herein consists, obviously, the high value of flesh, taken as whole, as an article of food. Hay and oats, potatoes, turnips, bread etc., produce in the living body blood and flesh; but none of all these substances reproduces flesh with the same rapidity, or restores the muscular substance, wasted by work, with so small an expenditure of organic force as animal food.[43]

To be sure, other scientists questioned Liebig's assertions, yet the German scientist influenced a vast group of researchers, doctors, and chemists in Western Europe and elsewhere.[44] In the late 1800s, his propositions merged with purported connections between protein requirements and prosperity; that is, individuals who partook in protein-rich foodstuffs were healthier and better off than their counterparts who did not. Indeed, governments, nutritionists, and public officials came to promote high-protein foods as wholesome and nutritious.[45] Liebig also sponsored the industrial production of a beef extract, which became a staple in households in the United States and some European countries (discussed in Chapter 3).

In 1832, the first Brazilian medical schools opened their doors in Rio de Janeiro and Salvador (Bahia). Two decades later, the city of Rio de Janeiro established the Junta Central de Higiene (1850) whose scientific nutrition parameters entered the Brazilian medical discourse and the public policy establishment.[46] Profoundly influenced by European scientific thinking, the theses mentioned above, alongside medical newspapers, articulated a vision according to which nourishment, weather, and morality shaped civilized individuals. In their evaluation, Brazil's environment took center stage, for there was a belief that tropical climates impoverished the blood, which along with inadequate eating and housing produced a series of diseases common to Rio. Such assumptions are tributary to miasmatic theories. The latter identifies corrupt air as the cause of most maladies. Tropical environments received particular attention given the prevalence of heat and humidity, thought to "favor the multiplication of harmful microorganisms." Contemporaneously, other doctors—although not abandoning the environmental framework—started to introduce parasitological knowledge to the field. Known as *Tropicalistas*, a small group of physicians, mainly in the province of Bahia, conducted groundbreaking research, identifying, for instance, hookworm disease as a parasitosis. The group, as such, dwindled by the 1880s in part because most of their proposals had entered the mainstream scientific and medical fields in Brazil.[47]

Not coincidentally, some theses from Rio's medical school include a chapter on diet, another on living conditions, and descriptions of

Brazil's—Rio's in particular—climate. Antonio Corrêa de Sousa Costa, author of a thesis abovementioned, provides lengthy accounts of "lower-classes" housing and considerations about their clothing. The poor, in his words, "go through the year in the same clothing [moreover] instead of wearing woolen garments, at least in certain seasons, they cover themselves with cotton fabrics."[48] These writings convey parameters about appropriate taste and hygiene rules, suggesting that those who followed such advice would be less vulnerable to the epidemics. Behind this reasoning was also the belief that Rio's environment played a seminal role in its residents' "temperament, constitution, and habits." Costa further explains that the "almost exclusive vegetable" diet of the poor (and slaves) would be suitable for inhabitants in other climates, but not to those in Rio, where the "hot air … results in less oxygen," which in turn causes blood poverty and overall weakness. The city's sea-level location, high humidity, and surrounding swamps contributed to an insalubrious setting, made worse by dwellings inadequately ventilated. Hence, to better guard the poor and enslaved from the elements, it was essential to increase the amount of animal-derived foods they relied on.[49]

As Cristiana Loureiro de Mendonça Couto evinces, physicians in Brazil quickly adopted the principles mentioned above, citing European studies to attest to the nutritional value of indigenous foodstuffs. In his work, Antonio Corrêa de Sousa Costa quotes experiments that the French chemist Anselme Payen had conducted to justify that yams were less nutritious than wheat, as they comparatively contained a smaller amount of "azotized matter." By doing so, Costa and his contemporaries implicitly recommended substituting native foods with others believed to be more wholesome. The most notable "victim" of the new taste was manioc meal, as some associated it with hookworm disease, a parasitic illness that, in Brazil, was called *hypoemia intertropical* or *opilação*.[50] Beans, for instance, were judged to be of "low digestibility" and unhygienic because of their "flatulent" properties. Along these lines, the weekly Carioca newspaper *O Jornal do Agricultor* (The Farmer's Newspaper) claimed that "vegetables are little nutritious[,] weakly excite the stomach [, and] diminish the energy of all functions." While a diet based on vegetables and fish was associated with the poor, spicy foods were thought to "provoke inflammations in the digestive tract," for which they should be avoided. These appreciations echo medical wisdom as much as the ideal "exquisite but not strong" flavors of the French cuisine. Not coincidently, according to some, the upper classes had phased out those food items from their feasts.[51]

Gilberto Freyre labels this process the "de-Africanizing the Brazilian table," whereby European treats replaced domestic vegetables, "typical desserts" (honey, cane juice, and canjica), and condiments and spices on the Brazilian table—all of which were deemed harmful.[52] When Costa and his peers discussed the alimentary regime of the Carioca poor and enslaved, they were convinced that, to balance out harmful consequences of Rio's climate, it was vital to increase the amount of meat they ate.

Two Commodity Chains: Charque and Fresh Meat in Rio de Janeiro

The mid-nineteenth century saw what scholar Vaclav Smil classifies as a "dietary transition," whereby "agricultural productivity, rapid industrialization, and widespread urbanization" combined not only to improve people's diets, but also to dramatically change our relationship with food. In this process, popular perceptions about the superiority of animal protein in the human diet gained traction. Gradually, as chemistry's significance for nutrition knowledge became prominent, meat reigned as an "element of human health and … as a matter of public policy."[53] In Europe, governments, public officials, and even consumers saw the "absence of meat in the diet of the masses a sign of deprivation."[54] The Brazilian medical community was clearly in tune with these observations. Medical practitioners did believe that a proper diet was a balanced one. In the words of Francisco F. Padilha, "The exclusive animal regime produces violent and unbridled passions … the vegetable regime … makes men sweet and compassionate,"[55] but they regarded fresh meat, as a nutritious food per se.[56] However, when Padilha defended his work at Rio's medical school, it is likely that the vast majority of Cariocas relied on salted rather than fresh meat.

Salted meat was widely available in rural and urban South America. The abundance of livestock and of land (and water) to feed those animals in a scarcely populated subcontinent resulted in the renascence of ancient meat preservation methods, chiefly salting and drying, which delays spoilage and allows storage for several months. The widespread assumption that in colonial South America gauchos slaughtered their animals with the intention of only commercializing their skins leaving carcasses putrefying in the prairies, although partially accurate, does not do justice to the processes by which wild herds were rounded up and domesticated during early colonial times.[57] The advent of salt-meat factories (*saladeros* in Spanish, *charqueadas* in Portuguese) was, then, a response to a pastoral environment marked by abundance. These plants slaughtered cattle (mostly) for the production of charque, but also of a wide range of by-products including hides and skins and talon, highly valued in international markets. Since the late eighteenth century, cattle, charque, and other animals' by-products were exchanged in South America and traded in the Caribbean and Europe.[58]

South American charque sustained the free and the enslaved in Brazil. In Rio de Janeiro, the figures for the second half of the 1800s show that supplies were plentiful. Between 1869 and 1874, more than 30,000 metric tons of charque arrived at Rio's port annually.[59] Although milk and butter were a rarity, the city also consumed significant amounts of fresh meat. By one generous account in the early 1870s, approximately 102,000 cattle, 19,000 sheep, and 18,000 pigs annually were shipped to Rio.[60] These annual aggregates certainly do not provide an accurate picture of what reached Cariocas' tables. Nevertheless, they suggest that there was no shortage of animal-derived foods in Brazil's capital, although supply was subject to pronounced oscillations due in part to technological constraints.

One of the most emblematic images of Rio's fresh meat market in the early 1800s is Debret's panoramic view of the Santa Luzia matadouro. In the background, at the beach of the same name, shirtless slaves carry large pieces of severed animals over their heads; in the front, two captives pull an oxcart loaded with parts of quartered carcasses. The scene evokes a rather rustic view of Rio's meat production and distribution.[61] By the 1850s, fresh meat supplies gained renewed life with the opening of a new slaughterhouse in 1853 (and another one in 1881) and the implementation of railroads for transporting cattle from Brazil's interior to Rio de Janeiro as well as meat delivering within the urban grid. No other foodstuff received more attention from local authorities. Newspapers regularly published the number of cattle slaughtered for the city's consumption, while the municipality made strides to monitor meat retailing and setting up prices.

This study sheds light on the elaborate national and international network of ranchers, merchants, manufacturers, shippers, and providers who transformed animals into meat—salted and fresh. Although both are by-products of the same raw material, not only were the techniques utilized in their preparation different, but also, as the nineteenth century progressed, the animals themselves were of varied quality. Hence, two supply networks operated in South America to provide fresh and salted beef to Rio de Janeiro. Fresh meat that arrived in Rio's butcher stalls came from cattle that had traveled on the hoof from the grazing lands of center and southeast Brazil to the pasturelands of Minas Gerais, São Paulo, and Rio de Janeiro provinces. After several months of fattening, herds arrived at the outskirts of Rio, where they rested for a few days before being "disassembled." Large quarters of freshly butchered beef reached Rio's main depot in the city center, which delivered the product to municipally supervised butcher stalls. Although some foreign cattle might have entered Mato Grosso and made their way into the pasturelands of southeast Brazil, the transformation of cattle into fresh meat was essentially a domestic undertaking. For the most part, charque that landed in Rio's ports started its journey from animal to processed flesh in the fertile pampas, either in Rio Grande do Sul, Uruguay, or Argentina. These animals came to the region's saladeros or charqueadas, where highly skilled workers (slaves in the case of Brazil) transformed their muscles into mantas of salted meat. These mantas traveled in barrels or stacked on the decks of vessels on the south Atlantic coast, landing at Rio's innumerous storehouses. They later made their way to an even higher number of dry good stores, where costumers purchased small strips of the product. When fresh and salted meat arrived in Rio, they intersected with social practices and public policies, which this work examines.[62] The next chapter deals with fresh meat supplies; the subsequent studies charque consumption in Rio.

Notes

1 Ernst Ebel, *O Rio de Janeiro e seus arredores em 1824* (São Paulo: Editora nacional, 1972), 13–14, 40–98; Jean Baptiste Debret, *Voyage pittoresque et historique au Brésil ou séjour d'un artiste français au Brésil depuis 1816 jusqu'en 1831 inclusivement* (Paris: Firmin–Didot, 1834), vol. 2, plate 52, 57, vol. 3, 141; John Luccock, *Notes on Rio De Janeiro, and the Southern Parts of Brazil: Taken During a Residence of Ten Years in That Country, from 1808–1818* (London: Printed for Samuel Leigh, in the Strand, 1820), 38, 190.

2 Luccock, *Notes*, 38; Debret, *Voyage*, vol. 2, 35, 101; Gilberto Freyre, *The Masters and the Slaves = Casa-Grande & Senzala: a Study in the Development of Brazilian Civilization* (New York: Alfred A. Knopf, 1971), 461–67.

3 George Gardner, *Travels in the Interior of Brazil, Principally Through the Northern Provinces and the Gold and Diamond Districts During the Years 1836–41* (London: Reeve Brothers, King William Street Strand, 1846), 537; William Scully, *Brazil Its Provinces and Chief Cities; the Manners & Customs of the People; Agricultural, Commercial, and Other Statistics, Taken from the Latest Official Documents; with a Variety of Useful and Entertaining Knowledge, Both for the Merchant and the Emigrant* (London: Murray & Co, 1866), 150–51; Ina von Binzer, *Os meus romanos: Alegrias e tristezas de uma educadora alemã no Brasil* (São Paulo: Editora Paz e Terra, 2004), 53; François Auguste Biard, *Dois anos no Brasil* (Brasília: Senado Federal, 2004), 27; Thomas Ewbank, *Life in Brazil* (London: Sampson Low, 1856), 70–93; Mary C. Karasch, *Slave Life in Rio de Janeiro, 1808–1850* (Princeton: Princeton University Press, 1987), 144; Stanley Stein, *Vassouras: A Brazilian Coffee County, 1850–1900. The Roles for Planter and Slave in a Plantation Society* (Princeton: Princeton University Press, 1985), 90.

4 Cláudia Moraes Trindade, "Doenças, alimentação e resistência na penitenciária da Bahia, 1861–1865," *História, Ciências, Saúde – Manguinhos* 18, no. 4 (2011): 1081; Lisanti Luis, "Sur la nourriture des 'Paulistes' entre XVIIIe et XIXe siècles," *Annales. Economies, sociétés, civilisations* 18e année, no. 3 (1963): 539; Ramiro Alberto Flores Guzmán, "The Feeding of Slave Population in the United States, the Caribbean, and Brazil: Some Remarks in the State of the Art," *América Latina en la Historia Económica* 20, no. 2 (2013): 24–27.

5 Biard, *Dois anos,* 43; Ebel, *O Rio de Janeiro,* 60, 132–33; Biblioteca Nacional, "Requerimento dos presos sentenciados a serviço da Casa de Correção a S.M.I. relatando a insuportável situação a que eram submetidos pelo administrador daquela casa e pedindo providências que lhes permitissem viver con dignidade," Rio de Janeiro, 1841; Paul S. Lloyd, *Food and Identity in England, 1540–1640: Eating to Impress* (London: Bloomsbury Academic, 2016), 6–10.

6 Luccock, *Notes,* 358–59; Ebel, *O Rio de Janeiro,* 138; Gustavo Beyer, "Ligeiras notas de viagem do Rio de Janeiro à capitania de São Paulo no

Brasil, no verão de 1813 com algumas notícias sobre a Cidade da Bahia e a Ilha de Tristão da Cunha, entre o Cabo e o Brasil e que há pouco foi ocupada," *Revista do Instituto Histórico* e *Geográfico de São Paulo* 12 (1907): 306; Mariza de Carvalho Soares, "Engenho sim, de açúcar não o engenho de farinha de Frans Post," *Varia Historia* 25, no. 41 (2009): 78–79.

7 Gardner, *Travels*, 11; Renato Leite Marcondes, "O mercado brasileiro do século XIX: uma visão por meio do comércio de cabotagem," *Revista de Economia Política* 32, no. 1 (2012): 156; Larissa Virginia Brown, "Internal Commerce in a Colonial Economy: Rio de Janeiro and its Hinterland, 1790–1822" (PhD diss., University of Virginia, 1986), 148–50; João Luis Ribeiro Fragoso, *Homens de grossa aventura acumulação e hierarquia na praça mercantil do Rio de Janeiro: 1790–1830* (Rio de Janeiro: Civilização Brasileira, 1998), 121–22.

8 Historian Bert J. Barickman found similar trading patterns in vessels departing from Bahia. Bert J. Barickman, *A Bahian Counterpoint: Sugar, Tobacco, Cassava, and Slavery in the Recôncavo, 1780–1860* (Stanford, CA: Stanford University Press, 1998), 51; Nielson Rosa Bezerra, "Escravidão, Farinha e Tráfico Atlântico um novo olhar sobre as relações entre o Rio de Janeiro e Benguela," unpublished manuscript, Rio de Janeiro: Fundação Biblioteca National, Ministério da Cultura (2010): 12–17.

9 Mary Graham, *Journal of a Voyage to Brazil, and Residence There, During Part of the Years 1821, 1822, 1823* (London: Longman, Hurst, Rees, Orme, Brown, and Green, 1824), 160–61; Luís da Câmara Cascudo, *História da alimentação no Brasil*, vol. 1 (São Paulo: Companhia Editorial Nacional, 1967), 94, 101; Luccock, *Notes*, 46.

10 Graham, *Journal*, 127.

11 Ebel, *O Rio de Janeiro,* 60, 163–220; Graham, *Journal,* 127; Brown, "Internal," 73; Renato Leite Marcondes, "Desigualdades regionais brasileiras: comércio marítimo e posse de cativos na década de 1870" (Tese de Livre Docência, Universidade de São Paulo, Ribeirão Preto, FEA-RP, 2006), 67.

12 Carlos Seidler, *História das guerras e revoluções do Brasil de 1825 a 1835* (São Paulo: Companhia Editora Nacional, 1939): 111; Arquivo Geral da Cidade do Rio de Janeiro (hereafter AGCRJ), "Atas da Câmara Municipal," April 30, 1850, 3–9, Códice 17.2.21.

13 Luccock, *Notes*, 45–47; Debret, *Voyage*, 74; AGCRJ, "Atas da Câmara Municipal," June 17, 1851, 17–22, Códice 12.7.2.

14 Debret, *Voyage*, 111; Luccock, *Notes*, 45, 124, 563.

15 Graham, *Journal*, 161–62; Debret, *Voyage*, 73–74, 101–10, vol. 2; Biard, *Dois anos*, 41; Ebel, *O Rio de Janeiro,* 22–23, 175; Brown, "Internal," 153; Luccock, *Notes*, 47; Seidler, *História*, 111; Lisanti, "Sur la nourriture," 532.

16 Robert Walsh, *Notices of Brazil in 1828 and 1829* (London: Frederick Westley and A. H. Davis, 1830), 8; Luís da Câmara Cascudo, *História da alimentação no Brasil*, vol. 2 (São Paulo: Companhia Editorial Nacional, 1967), 309; Ebel, *O Rio de Janeiro,* 69, 98; Graham, *Journal,* 280.

17 Luccock, *Notes*, 119; Iraci del Nero da Costa and Renato Leite Marcondes, "A alimentação no cativeiro: uma coletânea sobre os regimes alimentares dos negros afro-brasileiros," *Revista do Instituto Histórico Geográfico Brasileiro* Ano 162, no. 411 (2001): 199–246; Debret, *Voyage*, vol. 2, 110–11; Jean-Baptiste Alban Imbert, *Manual do fazendeiro: ou Tratado domestico sobre as enfermidades dos negros, generalisado ás necessidades medicas de todas as classes*, t. 2 (Rio de Janeiro: Typographia Nacional, 1839), 364–66.

18 Josepfina Chaia and Luis Lisanti, "O escravo na legislação brasileira (1808–1889)," *Revista de História* XXV, vol. 49, no. 99 (July-September 1974):

242–43; Karasch, *Slave Life*, 138–45; Carlos Eduardo Valencia Villa, *Ao longo daquelas ruas. A economia dos negros livres em Richmond e Rio de Janeiro, 1840–1860* (Jundiaí: Paco Editorial, 2016), 240–41.

19 Karasch, *Slave Life*, 139, 178–84, See Appendix B 384–89; Seidler, *História*, 363–64.

20 Costa and Marcondes, "A alimentação," 199–246; Flores Guzmán, "The Feeding," 22–29.

21 Karasch, *Slave Life*, 142–43; Freyre, *The Masters*, 459–61; Flores Guzmán, "The Feeding," 29.

22 Beyer, "Ligeiras," 281–82.

23 Karasch, *Slave Life,* 140, 178–84; Debret, *Voyage*, vol. 2, 84; Henry Koster, *Travels in Brazil* (London: Longman, Hurst, Rees, Orme, and Brown, 1816), 422–31.

24 Debret, *Voyage*, vol. 2, 40; Gardner, *Travels,* 59; Luccock, *Notes*, 46.

25 Kirsten Schultz, *Tropical Versailles: Empire, Monarchy, and the Portuguese Royal Court in Rio de Janeiro, 1808–1821. New World in the Atlantic World* (New York: Routledge, 2001), 67, 105.

26 José Maria Rodrigues Regadas, "Do regimen das classes abastadas do Rio de Janeiro em seus alimentos e bebidas. Mudanças que nele se tem operado nos últimos quarenta anos. Efeitos do regimen antigo: influência do atual" (medical thesis, Faculdade de Medicina do Rio de Janeiro, Rio de Janeiro: Typographia Imperial e Constitucional de J. Villeneuve e Comp., 1852), 21–25.

27 Ibid., 22–25; Freyre, *The Masters*, 467–68.

28 Francisco Fernandes Padilha, "Qual o regimen alimentar dos pobres no Rio de Janeiro? Que molestias mas commumente grasão entre ellas? Que relações de causalidade se encontrão entre esse regimen e molestias?" (medical thesis, Faculdade de Medicina do Rio de Janeiro, Rio de Janeiro: Typographia Universal de Laemmert, 1853), 13–17; Antonio Corrêa de Sousa Costa, "Qual a alimentação de que usa a classe pobre no Rio de Janeiro e sua influência sobre a mesma" (medical thesis, Faculdade de Medicina do Rio de Janeiro, Rio de Janeiro: Typographia Perseverança, 1865), 33–34.

29 Cristiana Loureiro de Mendonça Couto, *Alimentação no Brasil Imperial* (São Paulo: Educ/FAPESP, 2015), 181–88; *Almanak administrativo, mercantil e industrial da corte e província do Rio de Janeiro para o ano de 1850*, [*Almanak Laemmert*], 409–11.

30 Costa, "Qual a alimentação," 35.

31 Carlos Eduardo Valencia Villa, "Costos de los alimentos y renta de los trabajadores libres en Rio de Janeiro (Brasil) y Richmond (Virginia, EUA) en la primera mitad del siglo XIX," unpublished paper (CLADHE II, Mexico, 2011): 2; Stein, *Vassouras*, 174–78.

32 João D. P. da Silva, "Relatorio sobre a nota ou memoria do Dr. Julio Rodrigues de Moura," *Annaes Brasilienses de Medicina. Jornal da Academia Imperial de Medicina do Rio de Janeiro* 19, no. 1 (June 1867): 44; Manoel da Gama Lobo, "Da Ophtalmia Brasiliana," *Annaes Brasilienses de Medicina. Jornal da Academia Imperial de Medicina do Rio de Janeiro* 17, no. 1 (June 1865): 18.

33 Johann Jakob von Tschudi, *Viagem às províncias do Rio de Janeiro e São Paulo* (São Paulo: Livraria Martins Editora, 1953), 54–55; Louis Couty, *L'esclavage au Brésil* (Paris: Librairie de Guillaumin, 1881), 24–25; Stein, *Vassouras*, 173–79.

34 Stein, *Vassouras,* 78.

35 Marcondes, "Desigualdades," 40–46; Zephyr L. Frank, *Dutra's World: Wealth and Family in Nineteenth-Century Rio de Janeiro* (Albuquerque: University of New Mexico Press, 2004), 77; Herbert S. Klein and Francisco Vidal Luna,

Slavery in Brazil (Cambridge: Cambridge University Press, 2010), 74–75, 178; Zélia Maria Cardoso de Mello, *Metamorfoses da riqueza São Paulo, 1845–1895: Contribuição ao estudo da passagem da economia mercantil-escravista à economia exportadora capitalista* (São Paulo: Hucitec, 1990), 115–17.

36 Imbert, *Manual,* 356–69; Francisco Peixoto de Lacerda Werneck, Barão de Paty do Alferes and Luiz Peixoto de Lacerda Werneck, *Memória sobre a fundação e costeio de uma fazenda na Província do Rio de Janeiro* (Rio de Janeiro: Eduardo & Henrique Laemmert, 1878), 25–29.

37 Costa, "Qual a alimentação," 35; Antonio José de Souza, "Do regimen das classes pobres e dos escravos no Rio de Janeiro em seus alimentos e bebidas. Qual a influência desse regimen sobre a saude?" (medical thesis, Faculdade de Medicina do Rio de Janeiro, Rio de Janeiro: Typographia Univeral de Laemmert, 1851), 29–31.

38 Deborah Neill, "Finding the 'Ideal Diet': Nutrition, Culture, and Dietary Practices in France and French Equatorial Africa, c. 1890s to 1920s," *Food and Foodways* 17, no. 1 (2009): 5–12.

39 Souza, "Do regimen," 31.

40 Kenneth J. Carpenter, "A Short History of Nutritional Science: Part 1 (1785–1885)," *The Journal of Nutrition* 133, no. 3 (March 2003): 638–39.

41 Rachel Laudan, "Power Cuisines, Dietary Determinism and Nutritional Crisis: The Origins of the Globalization of Western Diet," *Interactions: Regional Studies, Global Processes, and Historical Analysis*, Conference Proceedings, Washington DC, Library of Congress February 28 – March 3 (2001), accessed November 25, 2020, http://webdoc.sub.gwdg.de/ebook/p/2005/history_cooperative/www.historycooperative.org/proceedings/interactions/laudan.html.

42 Carpenter, "A Short," Part I, 641.

43 Justus von Liebig, "Letter XXXII," *Familiar Letters on Chemistry: In Its Relations to Physiology, Dietetics, Agriculture, Commerce, and Political Economy* (London: Walton and Maberly, 1859), 440–41.

44 Carpenter, "A Short," Part I, 638–45; Kenneth J. Carpenter, "A Short History of Nutritional Science: Part 2 (1885–1912)," *The Journal of Nutrition* 133, no. 4 (April 2003): 975–76.

45 Kenneth J. Carpenter, "The History of Enthusiasm for Protein," *The Journal of Nutrition* 116, no. 7 (July 1986), 1364–70; Neill, "Finding," 5–10.

46 Couto, *Alimentação no Brasil*, 47–56; Juliana Teixeira Souza, "A autoridade municipal na corte municipal: enfrentamentos e negociações na regulação do comércio de gêneros (1849–1889)" (PhD diss., Universidade de Campinas, 2007), 141.

47 Julyan G. Peard, "Tropical Medicine in Nineteenth-Century Brazil: The Case of the 'Escola Tropicalista Bahiana', 1860–1890," in *Warm Climates and Western Medicine. The Emergence of Tropical Medicine, 1500–1900,* ed. David J. Arnold (Amsterdam: Rodopi, Clio Medica Series, 2003), 115–20; Couto, *Alimentação no Brasil,* 57–61.

48 Costa, "Qual a alimentação," 16, 30–32.

49 Costa, "Qual a alimentação," 40–41; Padilha, "Qual o regimen," 13–17; Couto, *Alimentação no Brasil,* 57–61, 78–116.

50 Costa, "Qual a alimentação," 14–15; Cristiana Loureiro de Mendonça Couto, "The Chemistry of Diet: Medicine, Nutrition, and Staple Foods in Imperial Brazil," *Ambix* 62, no. 4 (2015): 354–59. This view was not unanimous. Francisco F. Padilha stressed that manioc meal "could not be blamed for opilação," for the real culprit of the poor and enslaved nutritional ills was their insufficient food intake, not enough to "repair the forces spent at work." Padilha, "Qual o regimen," 18–19.

51 "Hygiene geral," *Jornal do Agricultor: Princípios Práticos de Economia Rural*, Anno 1, t. 2 (Rio de Janeiro: Dias da Silva Junior, 1880): 374; Jeffrey M. Pilcher, *¡Que Vivan Los Tamales!: Food and the Making of Mexican Identity* (Albuquerque: University of New Mexico Press, 1998), 65, 81; Neill, "Finding," 5; Costa, "Qual a alimentação," 34–39.
52 Freyre, *The Masters*, 468–70.
53 Vaclav Smil, "Eating Meat: Evolution, Patterns, and Consequences," *Population and Development Review* 28, no. 4 (December 2002): 607–10; M. R. Finlay, "Early Marketing of the Theory of Nutrition: The Science and Culture of Liebig's Extract of Meat," in *The Science and Culture of Nutrition, 1840–1940*, ed. Harmke Kamminga and Andrew Cunningham (Amsterdam: Rodopi, Clio Medica Series, 1995), 48.
54 Vincent J. Knapp, "The Democratization of Meat and Protein in Late Eighteenth- and Nineteenth-Century Europe," *The Historian* 59, no. 3 (Spring 1997): 544.
55 Padilha, "Qual o regimen," 14–15.
56 Couto, *Alimentação no Brasil,* 104.
57 Wilson J. Warren, *Meat Makes People Powerful. A Global History of the Modern Era* (Iowa City: University of Iowa Press, 2018), 12–13, 51.
58 Alfredo J. Montoya, *Historia de los saladeros argentinos* (Buenos Aires: Editorial Raigal, 1956), 26–27.
59 Jornal do Commercio, *Retrospecto Commercial do[s] ano[s] 1869–1892* (Rio de Janeiro: Typographia do "Jornal do Commercio," de Rodrigues & C., 1870–1893). A crude estimation based on these data reveals that in 1870, there were more than 35 kilos of charque per capita for the entire population of the Rio de Janeiro province.
60 Brasil, *The Empire of Brazil at the Universal Exhibition of 1876 in Philadelphia* (Rio de Janeiro: Imperial Instituto Artístico, 1876), 266–68. These figures may be overestimated; in 1893, for instance, Rio received approximately 130,000 head of cattle, 13,000 pigs, and 21,000 sheep. See Rio de Janeiro, *Anuario Estatístico do Distrito Federal Ano VI,* 1938 (Rio de Janeiro: Serviço Gráfico do I.B.G.E., 1939), 422.
61 Debret, vol. 2, plate 28.
62 Shane Hamilton, "Analyzing Commodity Chains: Linkages or Restrictions," in *Food Chains: From Farmyard to Shopping Cart,* ed. Warren Belasco and Roger Horowitz (Philadelphia: University of Pennsylvania Press, 2009), 25.

Bibliography

Archives Consulted

Arquivo Geral da Cidade do Rio de Janeiro (cited as AGCRJ)
Biblioteca Nacional, Rio de Janeiro.

Government Documents and Publications

Rio de Janeiro. *Anuario Estatístico do Distrito Federal Ano VI*, 1938. Rio de Janeiro: Serviço Gráfico do I.B.G.E., 1939.

Newspapers and Magazines

Almanak Laemmert (Rio de Janeiro). *Almanak administrativo, mercantil e industrial da corte e província do Rio de Janeiro para o ano de* 1850.

Gama Lobo, Manoel da. "Da Ophthalmia Brasiliana." *Annaes Brasilienses de Medicina. Jornal da Academia Imperial de Medicina do Rio de Janeiro* 17, no. 1 (June 1865): 16–24.

"Hygiene geral." *Jornal do Agricultor: Princípios Práticos de Economia Rural.* Anno 1, t. 2. Rio de Janeiro: Dias da Silva Junior (1880): 374–376.

Jornal do Commercio. *Retrospecto Commercial do[s] ano[s] 1869–1892.* Rio de Janeiro: Typographia do "Jornal do Commercio," de Rodrigues & C., 1870–1893.

Silva, João D. P. da "Relatorio sobre a nota ou memoria do Dr. Julio Rodrigues de Moura," *Annaes Brasilienses de Medicina. Jornal da Academia Imperial de Medicina do Rio de Janeiro* 19, no. 1 (June 1867): 34–50.

Other Primary Sources

Beyer, Gustavo. "Ligeiras notas de viagem do Rio de Janeiro à capitania de São Paulo no Brasil, no verão de 1813 com algumas notícias sobre a Cidade da Bahia e a Ilha de Tristão da Cunha, entre o Cabo e o Brasil e que há pouco foi ocupada." *Revista do Instituto Histórico e Geográfico de São Paulo* 12 (1907): 275–311.

Biard, François Auguste. *Dois anos no Brasil.* Brasília: Senado Federal, 2004.

Binzer, Ina von. *Os meus romanos: Alegrias e tristezas de uma educadora alemã no Brasil.* São Paulo: Editora Paz e Terra, 2004.

Brasil. *The Empire of Brazil at the Universal Exhibition of 1876 in Philadelphia.* Rio de Janeiro: Imperial Instituto Artístico, 1876.

Costa, Antonio Corrêa de Sousa. "Qual a alimentação de que usa a classe pobre no Rio de Janeiro e sua influência sobre a mesma." *Medical Thesis, Faculdade de Medicina do Rio de Janeiro.* Rio de Janeiro: Typographia Perseverança, 1865.

Couty, Louis. *L'esclavage au Brésil.* Paris: Librairie de Guillaumin, 1881.

Debret, Jean Baptiste. *Voyage pittoresque et historique au Brésil ou séjour d'un artiste français au Brésil depuis 1816 jusqu'en 1831 inclusivement.* Paris: Firmin-Didot, 1834.

Ebel, Ernst. *O Rio de Janeiro e seus arredores em 1824.* São Paulo: Editora nacional, 1972.

Ewbank, Thomas. *Life in Brazil.* London: Sampson Low, 1856.

Gardner, George. *Travels in the Interior of Brazil, Principally Through the Northern Provinces and the Gold and Diamond Districts During the Years 1836–41.* London: Reeve Brothers, King William Street Strand, 1846.

Graham, Mary. *Journal of a Voyage to Brazil, and Residence There, During Part of the Years 1821, 1822, 1823.* London: Longman, Hurst, Rees, Orme, Brown, and Green, 1824.

Imbert, Jean-Baptiste Alban. *Manual do fazendeiro: ou Tratado domestico sobre as enfermidades dos negros, generalisado ás necessidades medicas de todas as classes.* T. 2. Rio de Janeiro: Typographia Nacional, 1839.

Koster, Henry. *Travels in Brazil.* London: Longman, Hurst, Rees, Orme, and Brown, 1816.

Liebig, Justus von. "Letter XXXII." *Familiar Letters on Chemistry: In Its Relations to Physiology, Dietetics, Agriculture, Commerce, and Political Economy.* London: Walton and Maberly, 1859.

Luccock, John. *Notes on Rio De Janeiro, and the Southern Parts of Brazil: Taken During a Residence of Ten Years in That Country, from 1808–1818*. London: Printed for Samuel Leigh, 1820.

Padilha, Francisco Fernandes. "Qual o regimen alimentar dos pobres no Rio de Janeiro? Que molestias mas commumente grasão entre ellas? Que relações de causalidade se encontrão entre esse regimen e molestias?" *Medical Thesis, Faculdade de Medicina do Rio de Janeiro*. Rio de Janeiro: Typographia Universal de Laemmert, 1853.

Paty do Alferes, Barão do and de Lacerda Werneck, Luiz Peixoto. *Memória sobre a fundação e costeio de uma fazenda na Província do Rio de Janeiro*. Rio de Janeiro: Eduardo & Henrique Laemmert, 1878.

Regadas, José Maria Rodrigues. "Do regimen das classes abastadas do Rio de Janeiro em seus alimentos e bebidas. Mudanças que nele se tem operado nos últimos quarenta anos. Efeitos do regimen antigo: influência do atual." *Medical Thesis, Faculdade de Medicina do Rio de Janeiro*. Rio de Janeiro: Typographia Imperial e Constitucional de J. Villeneuve e Comp., 1852.

Scully, William. *Brazil Its Provinces and Chief Cities; the Manners & Customs of the People; Agricultural, Commercial, and Other Statistics, Taken from the Latest Official Documents; with a Variety of Useful and Entertaining Knowledge, Both for the Merchant and the Emigrant*. London: Murray & Co, 1866.

Seidler, Carlos. *História das guerras e revoluções do Brasil de 1825 a 1835*. São Paulo: Companhia Editora Nacional, 1939.

Souza, Antonio José de. "Do regimen das classes pobres e dos escravos no Rio de Janeiro em seus alimentos e bebidas. Qual a influência desse regimen sobre a saude?" *Medical Thesis, Faculdade de Medicina do Rio de Janeiro*. Rio de Janeiro: Typographia Universal de Laemmert, 1851.

Tschudi, Johann Jakob von. *Viagem às províncias do Rio de Janeiro e São Paulo*. São Paulo: Livraria Martins Editora, 1953.

Walsh, Robert. *Notices of Brazil in 1828 and 1829*. London: Frederick Westley and A. H. Davis, 1830.

Secondary Sources

Barickman, Bert J. *A Bahian Counterpoint: Sugar, Tobacco, Cassava, and Slavery in the Recôncavo, 1780–1860*. Stanford, CA: Stanford University Press, 1998.

Bezerra, Nielson Rosa. "Escravidão, farinha e tráfico Atlântico um novo olhar sobre as relações entre o Rio de Janeiro e Benguela." Unpublished manuscript. Rio de Janeiro: Fundação Biblioteca Nacional, Ministério da Cultura (2010): 1–62.

Brown, Larissa Virginia. "Internal Commerce in a Colonial Economy: Rio de Janeiro and its Hinterland, 1790–1822." PhD diss., University of Virginia, 1986.

Carpenter, Kenneth J. "The History of Enthusiasm for Protein." *The Journal of Nutrition* 116, no. 7 (July 1986): 1364–1370.

Carpenter, Kenneth J. "A Short History of Nutritional Science: Part 1 (1785–1885)." *The Journal of Nutrition* 133, no. 3 (March 2003a): 638–645.

Carpenter, Kenneth J. "A Short History of Nutritional Science: Part 2 (1885–1912)." *The Journal of Nutrition* 133, no. 4 (April 2003b): 975–984.

Cascudo, Luís da Câmara. *História da alimentação no Brasil*. Vol. 1. São Paulo: Companhia Editorial Nacional, 1967a.

Cascudo, Luís da Câmara. *História da alimentação no Brasil*. Vol. 2. São Paulo: Companhia Editorial Nacional, 1967b.

Chaia, Josepfina, and Luis Lisanti. "O escravo na legislação brasileira (1808–1889)." *Revista de História* XXV, vol. 49, no. 99 (July–September 1974): 241–248.

Costa, Iraci del Nero da, and Renato Leite Marcondes. "A alimentação no cativeiro: uma coletânea sobre os regimes alimentares dos negros afro-brasileiros." *Revista do Instituto Histórico Geográfico Brasileiro* Ano 162, no. 411 (2001): 199–246.

Couto, Cristiana Loureiro de Mendonça. *Alimentação no Brasil Imperial*. São Paulo: Educ/FAPESP, 2015a.

Couto, Cristiana Loureiro de Mendonça. "The Chemistry of Diet: Medicine, Nutrition, and Staple Foods in Imperial Brazil." *Ambix* 62, no. 4 (2015b): 345–362.

Finlay, M. R. "Early Marketing of the Theory of Nutrition: the Science and Culture of Liebig's Extract of Meat." In *The Science and Culture of Nutrition, 1840–1940*, edited by Harmke Kamminga and Andrew Cunningham, 48–74. Amsterdam: Rodopi, Clio Medica, 1995.

Flores Guzmán, Ramiro Alberto. "The Feeding of Slave Population in the United States, the Caribbean, and Brazil: Some Remarks in the State of the Art." *América Latina en la Historia Económica* 20, no. 2 (2013): 3–35.

Fragoso, João Luis Ribeiro. *Homens de grossa aventura acumulação e hierarquia na praça mercantil do Rio de Janeiro: 1790–1830*. Rio de Janeiro: Civilização Brasileira, 1998.

Frank, Zephyr L. *Dutra's World: Wealth and Family in Nineteenth-Century Rio de Janeiro*. Albuquerque: University of New Mexico Press, 2004.

Freyre, Gilberto. *The Masters and the Slaves = Casa-Grande & Senzala: a Study in the Development of Brazilian Civilization*. New York: Alfred A. Knopf, 1971.

Hamilton, Shane. "Analyzing Commodity Chains: Linkages or Restrictions." In *Food Chains: From Farmyard to Shopping Cart*, edited by Warren Belasco and Roger Horowitz, 16–25. Philadelphia: University of Pennsylvania Press, 2009.

Karasch, Mary C. *Slave Life in Rio de Janeiro, 1808–1850*. Princeton: Princeton University Press, 1987.

Klein, Herbert S., and Francisco Vidal Luna. *Slavery in Brazil*. Cambridge: Cambridge University Press, 2010.

Knapp, Vincent J. "The Democratization of Meat and Protein in Late Eighteenth- and Nineteenth-Century Europe." *The Historian* 59, no. 3 (Spring 1997): 541–551.

Laudan, Rachel. "Power Cuisines, Dietary Determinism and Nutritional Crisis: The Origins of the Globalization of Western Diet." *Interactions: Regional Studies, Global Processes, and Historical Analysis*, Conference Proceedings. Library of Congress, Washington DC, February 28–March 3, 2001. Accessed November 25, 2020, http://webdoc.sub.gwdg.de/ebook/p/2005/history_cooperative/www.historycooperative.org/proceedings/interactions/laudan.html.

Lisanti, Luis. "Sur la nourriture des 'Paulistes' entre XVIIIe et XIXe siècles." *Annales. Economies, sociétés, civilisations* 18ᵉ année, no. 3 (1963): 531–540.

Lloyd, Paul S. *Food and Identity in England, 1540–1640: Eating to Impress*. London: Bloomsbury Academic, 2016.

Marcondes, Renato Leite. "Desigualdades regionais brasileiras: comércio marítimo e posse de cativos na década de 1870." *Tese de Livre Docência*, Universidade de São Paulo, Ribeirão Preto, FEA-RP, 2006.

Marcondes, Renato Leite. "O mercado brasileiro do século XIX: uma visão por meio do comércio de cabotagem." *Revista de Economia Política* 32, no. 1 (2012): 142–166.

Mello, Zélia Maria Cardoso de. *Metamorfoses da riqueza São Paulo, 1845–1895: Contribuição ao estudo da passagem da economia mercantil-escravista à economia exportadora capitalista*. São Paulo: Hucitec, 1990.

Montoya, Alfredo J. *Historia de los saladeros argentinos*. Buenos Aires: Editorial Raigal, 1956.

Neill, Deborah. "Finding the 'Ideal Diet': Nutrition, Culture, and Dietary Practices in France and French Equatorial Africa, c. 1890s to 1920s." *Food and Foodways* 17, no. 1 (2009): 1–28.

Peard, Julyan G. "Tropical Medicine in Nineteenth-Century Brazil: The Case of the 'Escola Tropicalista Bahiana', 1860–1890." In *Warm Climates and Western Medicine. The Emergence of Tropical Medicine, 1500–1900*, edited by David J. Arnold, 108–132. Amsterdam: Rodopi, Clio Medica Series, 2003.

Pilcher, Jeffrey M. *¡Que Vivan Los Tamales!: Food and the Making of Mexican Identity*. Albuquerque: University of New Mexico Press, 1998.

Schultz, Kirsten. *Tropical Versailles: Empire, Monarchy, and the Portuguese Royal Court in Rio de Janeiro, 1808–1821. New World in the Atlantic World*. New York: Routledge, 2001.

Smil, Vaclav. "Eating Meat: Evolution, Patterns, and Consequences." *Population and Development Review* 28, no. 4 (December 2002): 599–639.

Soares, Mariza de Carvalho. "Engenho sim, de açúcar não o engenho de farinha de Frans Post." *Varia Historia* 25, no. 41 (2009): 61–83.

Souza, Juliana Teixeira. "A autoridade municipal na corte municipal: enfrentamentos e negociações na regulação do comércio de gêneros (1849–1889)." PhD diss., Universidade de Campinas, 2007.

Stein, Stanley. *Vassouras: A Brazilian Coffee County, 1850–1900. The Roles for Planter and Slave in a Plantation Society*. Princeton: Princeton University Press, 1985.

Trindade, Cláudia Moraes. "Doenças, alimentação e resistência na penitenciária da Bahia, 1861–1865." *História, Ciências, Saúde – Manguinhos* 18, no. 4 (2011): 1073–1093.

Valencia Villa, Carlos Eduardo. "Costos de los alimentos y renta de los trabajadores libres en Rio de Janeiro (Brasil) y Richmond (Virginia, EUA) en la primera mitad del siglo XIX." Conference Proceedings, *CLADHE II*, Mexico, 2011, 1–22.

Valencia Villa, Carlos Eduardo. *Ao longo daquelas ruas. A economia dos negros livres em Richmond e Rio de Janeiro, 1840–1860*. Jundiaí: Paco Editorial, 2016.

Warren, Wilson J. *Meat Makes People Powerful. A Global History of the Modern Era*. Iowa City: University of Iowa Press, 2018.

2 Changing Patterns of Spatial Distribution in Rio de Janeiro's Meat Provisioning System (c. 1850–c. 1880)

> Perhaps no situation, no attention and care, can render a slaughterhouse a pleasant scene; it must, under any management, be a task of difficulty to keep it perfectly clean. Such places ought, therefore, to be hidden from view; but the sole house destined to this purpose in Rio stands in a public road, and is rendered more offensive by the blood and filth issuing from it being allowed to mix with, to discolour and taint the water of the bay. Into that water the offal also is thrown, where it floats about, unless a sufficient number of black people, of the lowest order, be present to seize and wash the entrails as cases for polonies [sic], or for other purposes of a domestic or medicinal nature.[1]

Built in the late eighteenth century, the Santa Luzia slaughterhouse (*matadouro*) was, as the British traveler John Luccock describes in this epigraph, on a public road, just a few blocks from the viceregal palace. It stood behind the Castelo Hill, beside the Santa Luzia church on the beach with the same name.[2] According to Robert Walsh, chaplain to the British embassy in Rio de Janeiro in the 1820s, the abattoir was "not far from the public gardens, and situated on a delightful walk along the sea-shore." Nonetheless, he avers, "The sight and smell of every thing about it are so offensive, that few venture to pass it." Walsh was disgusted not only with the location and odors issuing from the main abattoir in Brazil's capital, but also with the transport conditions of animals and meat within the city. He continues:

> Herds of black cattle ... were killed, and then conveyed on negroes' heads to different stalls in the city. The most disagreeable spectacle I have ever witnessed, is one of these negro butchers with a greasy rag round his waist, and his naked body, covered with blood and gore, perspiring under a raw carcass.[3]

Before the advent of the industrial slaughterhouse or packing companies, meat production and distribution in Rio—and elsewhere in the Atlantic World—did not differ radically from what these travelers described. In the late eighteenth century, the French urban ethnographer Louis-Sébastian Mercier remarked that the rue du Pied-de-Boeuf—the street where cattle slaughtering and meat production in Paris occurred—was the "worst smelling place in the whole world … [with] a number of dirty little alleys that are soaked in the blood of slaughtered animals." In *Great Expectations,* Charles Dickens portrays the Smithfield meat market in London as "a shameful place, being all asmear with filth and fat and blood and foam."[4] If the surroundings and smells of a slaughterhouse were so unpleasant, as those contemporaries keenly exposed, why was it in "public sight"? Processing of this highly perishable foodstuff had to be done in close proximity to consumers because limited technology did not allow for long-distance transportation; thus, a slaughterhouse could not easily "be hidden from view," as Luccock suggests. Hence, the Portuguese expression *carne verde* or raw meat was used to distinguish fresh from preserved meat, with the former having to be "sold within thirty hours after [cattle] slaughtering."[5]

Probably no other foodstuff in the Carioca diet stirred more controversy than fresh meat, in part because its supply was entangled in a mesh of political interests that came under threat as public authorities embraced new economic philosophies and technology became available. The introduction of "free market" practices in the early nineteenth century granted the municipal council (*câmara municipal*) in Rio tools to strengthen its power over the monopolies held by myriad middlemen responsible for provisioning the city. Note that the understanding of "free market," according to Carioca officials, called for government intervention as a means of leveling the playing field for fair competition, which ideally would result in just prices.[6] However, this was a long-term process; as new concerns of a sanitary nature entered the public discourse, and updated shipping methods were introduced, the municipality was gradually able to control all steps of cattle and meat processing, collecting taxes on each.

This chapter examines how those changes shaped meat supplies in the city of Rio de Janeiro. It is organized in three sections: the first studies the institutional arrangements behind the city's fresh meat provision system in the nineteenth century. The latter two utilize butcher shop and slaughterhouse addresses from the *Almanak Laemmert*—a directory of Rio de Janeiro published once a year throughout the nineteenth century—and Geographic Information System (GIS) tools to map those locations in the second half of the 1800s.[7] This methodology yields great insight into a topic that has been seldom documented, revealing that as the municipality built new abattoirs and expanded meat retailing, it could better comply with its provision obligations.

The Santa Luzia Slaughterhouse and the Municipal Monopoly

In a famous late-nineteenth-century naturalistic novel *The Slum* (*O cortiço*), which delves into the daily life of slum-dwellers in Rio, Aluísio Azevedo describes a typical morning as shouting vendors pass by crowded alleyways:

> The bread-seller arrived with a hamper on his head and a high bench tucked beneath his arm ... A cow sadly tinkled from door to door, followed by a muzzled heifer and a man loaded down with milk cans ... For a long time, vendors kept coming and going. Trays of fresh meat, tripe, and offal appeared. Only vegetables were not sold, since there were so many small gardens [at the slum].[8]

This excerpt is revealing for portraying not only how a large number of cariocas had access to certain foodstuffs like bread, milk, and meat but also the conditions of that access. With respect to the provisioning of meat, to guarantee a steady supply of animal protein and by-products from the late eighteenth century to the end of the nineteenth, Rio's authorities tackled the problem on several occasions with the creation, renovation, and regulation of slaughterhouses and butcher shops.[9] In 1777, the Santa Luzia abattoir opened its doors. Even Robert Walsh—quoted earlier—asserts that, in spite of the matadouro's unwholesome setting and the poor quality of its meat, supply was "abundant and constant."[10]

The dilemma, as Walsh presents it, was that while the coexistence of humans and animals in an urban environment seemed unpleasant and posed a serious sanitary risk, livestock were of the essence to city dwellers. The odors and the distasteful scenery of animals herding side by side with humans had to be tolerated, for there were no other means to supply a perishable good to a fast-growing population concentrated in an overcrowded urban center.[11] City officials approached the binary supply/sanitary problem in the following manner: cattle slaughtering and fresh meat retailing in acceptable hygienic conditions had to be conducted in a geographically circumscribed area during the first hours of the day (after which meat was supposed to be salted because it was no longer deemed edible). It is not surprising that the abattoir would be in close proximity to a highly populated area at the city center, which also facilitated inspection by municipal agents.[12]

Nevertheless, it seems that in such a context, supply rather than hygiene was at the forefront of city officials' preoccupations. The Santa Luzia matadouro was located near the beach so animal debris could be discarded directly into the bay, thus creating a series of public sanitary challenges. By the 1820s, municipal regulations dictated how and when to bring herds in the city center and how to dispose of waste from animal slaughter. In 1822, one of these provisions forbade the transit of cattle during the day, stipulating that this could only occur between midnight and 3:00 a.m.; but in 1823, the city council approved a new measure contravening the previous one.[13] During the Old Regime, governments—faced with limited revenues and the difficulty of imposing taxes—commonly ceded or auctioned off contracts, granting individuals exclusive rights to exploit a particular branch of the economy for a certain period of time. Such was the case of cattle and meat provisioning in Rio de Janeiro—viceregal capital in 1763. Given the unpredictability of this venture, the costs, and risks involved, there were contracts throughout the supply network: over livestock brought into the city, over meat production and distribution, and over the use of the matadouro.[14]

In the early 1800s, in this complex provisioning chain, the municipality granted exclusive privileges to two groups: cattle purveyors (*contratadores*) and meat merchants (*marchantes*). The first were traders with enough capital to secure a contract for some years, the second were smaller dealers who could only establish temporary (maybe yearly) agreements. Both, however, provided cattle or meat during a time-framed monopoly, according to predetermined fees paid in advance to the municipality. Typically, the contratator bought herds at raising areas or fairs and introduced them within the city limits. They were also responsible for animal processing. To do so, contratadores rented out buildings for slaughtering, hired the butchers, and allocated meat to the butcher stalls in the urban grid. The marchante acquired herds in the city cattle market, slaughtered them, and distributed carcasses to the urban stalls. The municipal chamber publicly announced contracts for the retailing of meat, specifying its wholesale prices. Based on a system of public auction, the contract was given to highest bidders (*arrematações*). For its part, the local government, during this period, could not initiate new auctions, as long as the population was well served.[15]

There were, however, instances in which state authorities—crown and municipality—intervened in the process to guarantee supply. As the population of Rio increased, especially after 1808, and Brazil gradually transitioned to a constitutional monarchy, members of the municipal council (called *Senado da Câmara*),[16] on several occasions, used the case of the meat provision system to avow their political will as the body that legitimately represented the people. In 1815, during a period of meat shortage, the municipal chamber sought to open the market to new providers, virtually breaking the contract with the original contratador, who appealed to the King Dom João VI alleging that the council had overstepped its authority. Notwithstanding, the council's action was upheld because, as its members claimed, they had the right and obligation to ensure social peace: "Because of meat scarcity ... there is great disorder that begins by some [people] taking meat from other people's hands, and the reasons [given by the contratador] are not good enough."[17]

The dispute between the Senado da Câmara members and contratadores is one of a political economy in transition. The former argued that if only they could bring "thousands of cattle from the captaincy of Mato Grosso" to Rio de Janeiro, the city's meat appetite would be satiated, while the latter quarreled that Rio did not need more than eight hundred heads of cattle per week. This episode, in addition to demonstrating that the municipal chamber, as a body of governance, was asserting its "political power and administrative authority" over certain contratadores, elucidates a real dilemma related to the main issue this chapter is discussing: although Rio might have needed more meat, the limited capacity of the slaughterhouse and its storage facilities far outweighed the chamber's good intentions.[18]

The historiography of early-nineteenth-century Brazil indicates, as did most of the travelers who visited Rio, that the capital city experienced economic growth during that time, a trend boosted by the transference of the Portuguese crown to Rio de Janeiro in 1808. According to Renato Leite Marcondes, the number of cattle (whose origin is difficult to determine) shipped to Rio doubled between 1802 and 1811. Based on his examination of the volume and value of manioc meal, wheat, and salt-beef (*charque*) that arrived in Rio de Janeiro, João Luis Fragoso also emphasizes the internal market dynamism during those decades.[19]

This economic drive is clearly reflected in the construction of two new small abattoirs: one provisional in 1818 in São Diogo and the other, called Matadouro da Cidade Nova, in 1820. On two occasions, the latter was closed for remodeling due to unsanitary conditions before finally being demolished in 1837. These were attempts to increase the capacity of the existing abattoir by building slaughterhouses away from the city center, yet relatively near so as to permit the shipping of meat to areas with high population density. Given this scenario, it is not surprising to find qualitative reports describing meat supplies in Rio oscillating between adequate and scarce in the late 1820s. Originally, the Cidade Nova abattoir had a contract to slaughter approximately 30 herds daily, but in 1821 this number surpassed 90 (except during the Season of Lent); at the same time, Santa Luzia processed more than 120.[20]

In 1823, a decree "abolished the system of arrematações for meat distribution, [established] the free commerce of cattle, and [liberated] meat prices."[21] In that context, "free trade" policies intended to correct the ills of the past, when a few managed cattle supplies. This decree also attempted to give the municipality leverage to regulate cattle trade and meat supply and to tackle unfair competition—thereby significantly reshaping the role of the contratador.[22] Subsequently, several regulations sought to give preference to ranchers over marchantes and to those who offered the herds at the lowest price to the city.[23] However, the new system did not necessarily translate into better provisioning. Further, the reasons behind establishing contracts did not cease to exist after the 1820s.

Contrary to contemporary assumptions, authorities saw "exclusive privileges," as Raymond De Roover put it, as "the lesser of two evils." That is, restrictions on trade were imposed because "the risks were so great that, without a charter granting exclusive privileges, it would have been impossible to attract the necessary capital."[24] The cattle-trailing industry remained a high-cost venture that appealed to few individuals, who expected safe returns. City officials and cattle merchants constantly mentioned the condition of the roads, for instance, to justify meat shortages and high prices, as well as wars and disturbances of a different nature. Given the distances and poor transportation infrastructure, any disruption, natural (rains, forest growth, and river floods) or otherwise (confrontation with natives), continued to affect the provisioning system.[25]

As true as it might be that the law could have opened Rio's meat market to more individuals, there were no major improvements in the livestock industry in Brazil during those years. Moreover, even if dealers were introducing more cattle into Rio's market—and such was the situation given the growing urban need in a vibrant economy—they, along with city officials, had to deal with problems of a different nature as well: lack of pastureland and even water to maintain animals' nutrition needs until they were ready for slaughtering; the nonexistence of cooling facilities to store carcasses after processing; and finally, the threat of public sanitary disarray.[26] Therefore, poor technology posed a far-reaching hurdle to improvement in supply, and that the municipality could not sort out alone.

The strengthening of the municipal council over middlemen was, at best, incremental.[27] More than 70 years after the construction of the Santa Luzia slaughterhouse, a new facility west of the city center opened its doors. There, given urban expansion, private matadouros started to multiply; just in 1833, there were five registered in the area.[28] With the new São Cristóvão abattoir, the local government sought not only to serve this growing population, but also to assume control over meat production and distribution, centralizing cattle slaughtering and meat processing.[29] The next section addresses how this relocation reshaped supplies.

A New Matadouro for Rio de Janeiro and the Advent of the *Açougue Monstro*

Because of Rio's bureaucratic and port functions, the city's residents were accustomed to crossing paths with populations of European and African descent. The coffee economy expansion in the southeast drew upon these political and economic structures accelerating the pace of transformations in the 1850s. As they did, a number of financial institutions, wholesale commercial houses, and manufacturers were established in the city. All of these enterprises demanded a constant supply of laborers; slaves, primarily, worked in all sectors. The termination of the Atlantic slave trade in 1850 boosted the internal slave exchange and attracted a new wave of immigrants from other parts of Brazil and Europe to Rio. Concurrently, its population jumped from 50,000 in 1808 to more than 200,000 in 1850.[30] They were spread across several "urban" and "rural" parishes. The first comprised the Sacramento, São José, Candelária, Santa Rita, Santana, Engenho Velho, Glória, and Lagoa districts. These neighborhoods—also the most populous in the city—housed numerous religious and administrative buildings, import and export trading houses, and small retail and service businesses. The rural parishes were Inhaúma, Irajá, Campo Grande, Jacarepaguá, Guaratiba, Santa Cruz, Ilha do Governador, and Ilha de Paquetá.[31]

To examine fresh meat retailing in 1850s Rio de Janeiro, this section and the following draws upon aspects of central-place theory. In broad strokes, it posits that, in an ideal urban setting, convenience goods (inexpensive, daily necessities, for instance) are retailed throughout the urban grid, near consumers' residences and thus allowing them to make frequent purchases. Shopping goods are costly items (clothing and furniture, for example) that customers obtain occasionally; therefore, they are willing to travel farther to acquire them. In such conditions, sales of shopping goods would cluster in central areas, enabling buyers to compare prices. These concepts developed mostly to analyze free-market societies, but scholars have found them useful for approaching public market economies.[32] The case study here warrants two caveats. First, in nineteenth-century Rio, the city council regulated fresh meat provision (from animal slaughtering to meat distribution). Second, because of spoilage, fresh meat had to be sold quickly; thus, the concentration of butcher shops facilitated inspection and distribution.

Based on these principles, the following discussion addresses the question, how did the spatial distribution of meat retailing evolve in the second half of 1800s Rio? It is impossible to ascribe an increase in consumption to butcher shops expansion. However, the geography of a well-functioned public market could illustrate that the municipality provided access to butcher stalls where population was growing. The maps below present the locations of these facilities in the 1850s, 1860s, 1870s, and 1880s,[33] providing a visual annotation for examining the issues around meat provision in a public market system.

In 1853, the municipal slaughterhouse was moved to the Engenho Velho parish, almost 3.5 km west toward the city center. Concerns over public health and animal circulation in the urban core parishes prompted the building of the São Cristóvão abattoir. The ultimate goal was to move meat processing and their outcomes—foul odors and streets soaked with blood and waste—out of public sight. The marchantes built the facility, which the municipality rented out—a sign that the city council lacked funding to do so—to process the animals that arrived in the Corte (Rio de Janeiro city). Marchantes also owned some pasturelands near the new matadouro, which was close enough to the main butcher stalls in the city center.[34]

Three correlated innovations followed: in 1850, Rio had approximately 30 butcher shops, most of them concentrated in the Rua da Assembléia (da Assembléia Street in Candelária parish, see Figure 2.1), just three years later this number jumped to 70. The expansion occurred toward Santa Rita and Sacramento, two of the most populous parishes in the city. In 1860, in a neighborhood near the matadouro São Cristóvão (later in the Espírito Santo parish), an ice factory, Bailly & Cia, was installed. Finally, another novelty was the creation of so-called monster (gigantic) butcher shops (*açougues monstros*).

Figure 2.1 shows a cluster of butcher stalls in Candelária and São José parishes, in the streets parallel to Rio's main market. On the one hand, such agglomeration might have prompted customers to travel farther to buy meat; but the city was not extended, and because of the prime location of butcher stalls—the city's businesses center—customers could acquire other provisions alongside meat. Likewise, the concentration of butcher stalls facilitated meat distribution and inspection (sanitary and of weights) by the municipality. On the other hand, not all parishes were served equally. Notably, inhabitants in Candelária and north of São José parishes had better access to meat stalls than dwellers in Santana, Santa Rita, and Sacramento, which, in fact, had more concentrated populations. This location trend reveals that the retailing of meat remained, at least until the early years of the 1850s, attuned to the political and commercial center of Rio de Janeiro. In Candelária parish, alongside Rio's major import and export houses, stood the Mercado Novo (where some butcher stalls were located, alongside fish, dry goods, fruits, vegetables, and fowl retailers) as well as general stores (*secos e molhados*) that offered charque, wine, coffee, tobacco, bread, and wheat. Its streets were packed with warehouses advertising cotton, iron, and porcelain, and small shops trading fabric, hats, shoes, and all sorts of clothing items. Its crowded alleys also housed the offices of carpenters, seamstresses, doctors, lawyers, and public translators. Likewise, Candelária was the site of the post office, the customhouse, and the Banco do Brasil.[35]

The urban expansion of Rio after the 1850s resulted in new administrative boundaries. By the 1870s, the city's parishes were identified as follows: urban, old city ([*Cidade Velha*] Candelária, São José, Santa Rita, Sacramento, and Glória); urban, new city ([*Cidade Nova*] Santana, Santo Antonio, and Espírito Santo); suburban (Engenho Velho, Lagoa, São Cristóvão, Gávea, and Engenho Novo); rural (Irajá, Jacarepaguá, Inhaúma, Campo Grande, Santa Cruz), and suburban, islands (Ilha do Governador and Ilha de Paquetá).[36]

Geographical and numerical expansion of butcher stalls from the 1850s to 1870s (illustrated in Figures 2.1 and 2.2) shows that the

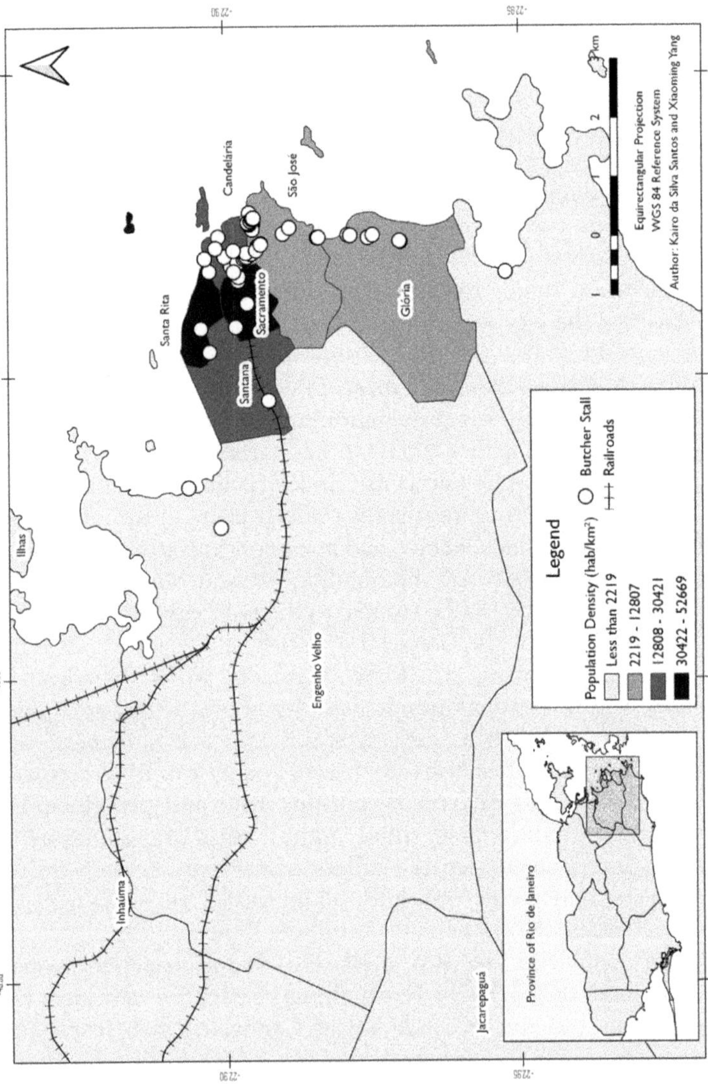

Figure 2.1 Butcher stalls in Rio de Janeiro, 1850s.

Sources: See endnote 33.

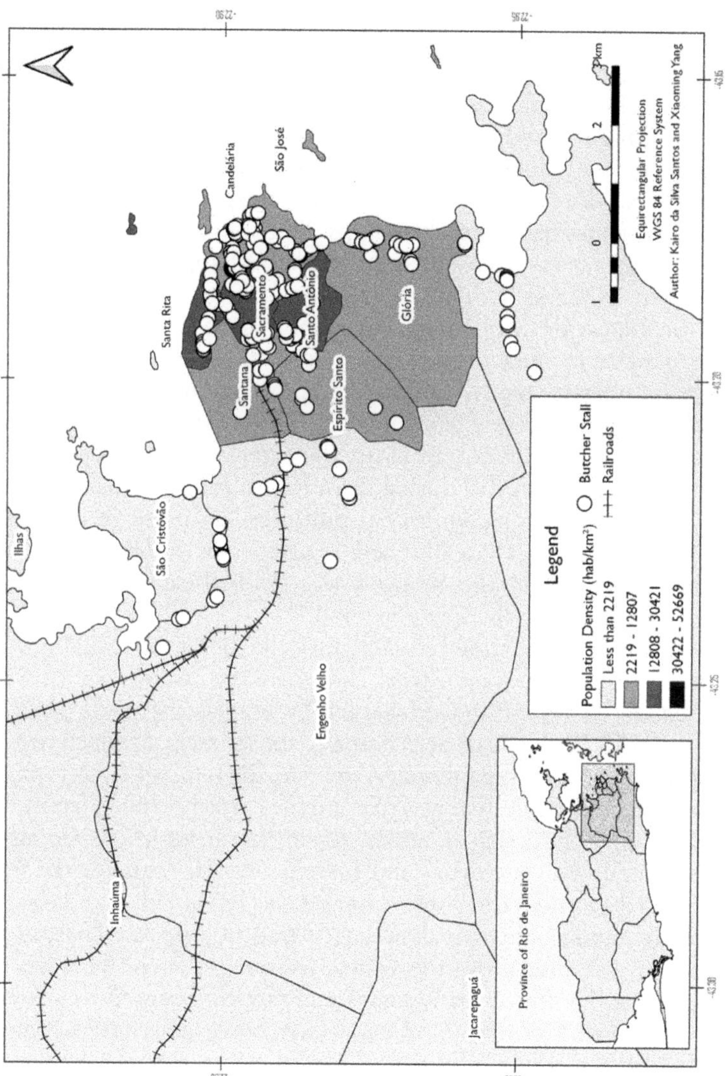

Figure 2.2 Butcher stalls in Rio de Janeiro, 1870s.

Sources: See endnote 33.

majority remained in the city center; however, a significant dispersion occurred over the urban grid toward the west and south zones. This pattern has several implications for meat retailing. First, the increase in the number of butcher shops suggests that consumers could have daily access to a perishable good at walking distance.[37] Indeed, the *Almanak Laemmert* lists roughly as many as eight times more butcher shops in 1870 than it did in 1850. Second, this spatial configuration appeared in areas with a high population density, primarily Cidade Velha but also Cidade Nova. The latter was the site of textile mills, breweries, several small food businesses, and would soon be populated by the poor.[38] Third, from the 1850s to the 1870s, some neighborhoods in Engenho Velho, Santo Antonio, Glória, Espírito Santo, and Lagoa registered a twofold increase in their number of butcher shops. Fourth, whereas in the 1850s in certain western areas each butcher shop served approximately 1,500 inhabitants, in 1870 this quotient dropped by half.

Given the impossibility of harvesting natural ice in Rio de Janeiro, the existence of an ice manufacturer at this time, located near the municipality's abattoir, indicates that it could have been employed in meat transport or preservation, thereby contributing to better supply and storage management. Yet, it is difficult to know the extent to which mechanical refrigeration was used in Rio during those years; probably scarcely and only for industrial and/or commercial purposes—to preserve imported fruit, for instance.[39] The 1866 *Almanak* registers one ice factory belonging to Henrique Leiden, who in 1862 was granted exclusive rights to pursue the venture using the Carré method.[40]

Another feature of mid-nineteenth-century changes in meat supply was the expansion of açougues monstros. They were the result of an association (*sociedade*) of several individuals led by Francisco José de Mello e Souza, who, in 1855 requested permission to the municipal council to add to his leather factory, Companhia de Curtume, the retail of fresh meat in Rio's urban area. His objective was to combine cattle breeding, fattening, and meat retailing. In doing so, Souza—a rancher from Minas Gerais—challenged traditional purveyors and marchantes. He was not the first who attempted to enter Rio's meat market. In 1831, Horácio Messery petitioned the municipality for the construction of a private abattoir to supply Rio with "cattle from the Minas Gerais province," because, as he put it, "[I had] suffered many losses and vexation caused by marchantes in this court."[41] Almost a decade later, some marchantes, "most of them of French origin," formed a similar "corporation." However, according to Jeronimo Teixeira, a city official, "this union … as it exists does greatly diminish the revenues of the câmara [municipal] and the National Treasury by decreasing the number of [cattle] slaughtered."[42] Such petitions and local authorities' responses highlight the complexity behind meat provisioning in Rio de Janeiro. City officials, fearing that associations would inevitably result in monopolies, sought to maintain control over supply by limiting how many purveyors could participate in the market.

As Figure 2.3 illustrates, açougues monstros in Rio de Janeiro were mostly concentrated in the central parishes. But they also served northwest and south of the city center. According to local newspaper announcements, açougues monstros were well kept and clean with "good facilities, luxury, and organization." On some weekdays, queues were so long that "tickets were distributed to clients, who often reached more than one hundred ... free and slave." Apart from their hygienic appeal and organization, what brought customers to açougues monstros were low prices. Because the society's members bought cattle directly from ranchers and because they owned pasturelands (*invernadas*), they could maintain herds in the outskirts of the city until slaughter.[43] By bypassing intermediaries, açougues monstros could offer affordable meat—though some legislators disputed this claim. In 1855, there were approximately 20 açougues monstros in the city. By 1860, this number doubled as they came to control 30 percent of the meat market in Rio de Janeiro, despite objections from other butcher-shop proprietors (*carniceiros*) and constant debate about whether they represented a monopoly. Nevertheless, in 1875, they no longer appeared in the *Almanak* under such a denomination.[44]

The emergence of açougues monstros and the perennial battle between the municipality and marchantes cannot be summarized as a struggle of public versus private interests. Officials also represented cattle raisers, fatteners, merchants, and butchers.[45] However, based on debates at the municipal and national administration levels, authorities appear to have had genuine concern about the fate of ranchers. They considered several ways of sidestepping intermediaries by allowing individuals to acquire cattle directly from raising areas, and by trying to ascertain control over cattle fairs and the processing of viscera.

In 1857, the minister Pedro Araújo Lima (Marquês de Olinda) founded the Official Agency (Agência Oficial), aiming to centralize meat supply by receiving, fattening, and slaughtering cattle from Minas Gerais; marchantes, nevertheless, managed to reach Rio's market, bypassing the Agency. Three years later, Urias Antonio da Silveira signed a similar contract with the municipality, whereby he could purchase herds directly from ranchers in Minas Gerais and Goiás. Often, however, representatives questioned the soundness of such measures, asserting that the câmara municipal had only brought back the contratador with poor results.[46] The solution or, at least, the common practice in late nineteenth century was a combination of both. Breeders (*criadores*), fatteners (*invernistas*), or trail-drivers (*boiadeiros*) could introduce cattle into the municipal slaughterhouse, provided that local authorities recognized (*habilitado*) them as cattle suppliers (*marchantes*). Such was the case of João Vicente Brito Galvão. In 1876, the city council granted him the rights to acquire cattle and supply meat to official butcher stalls (or to those created by him) in

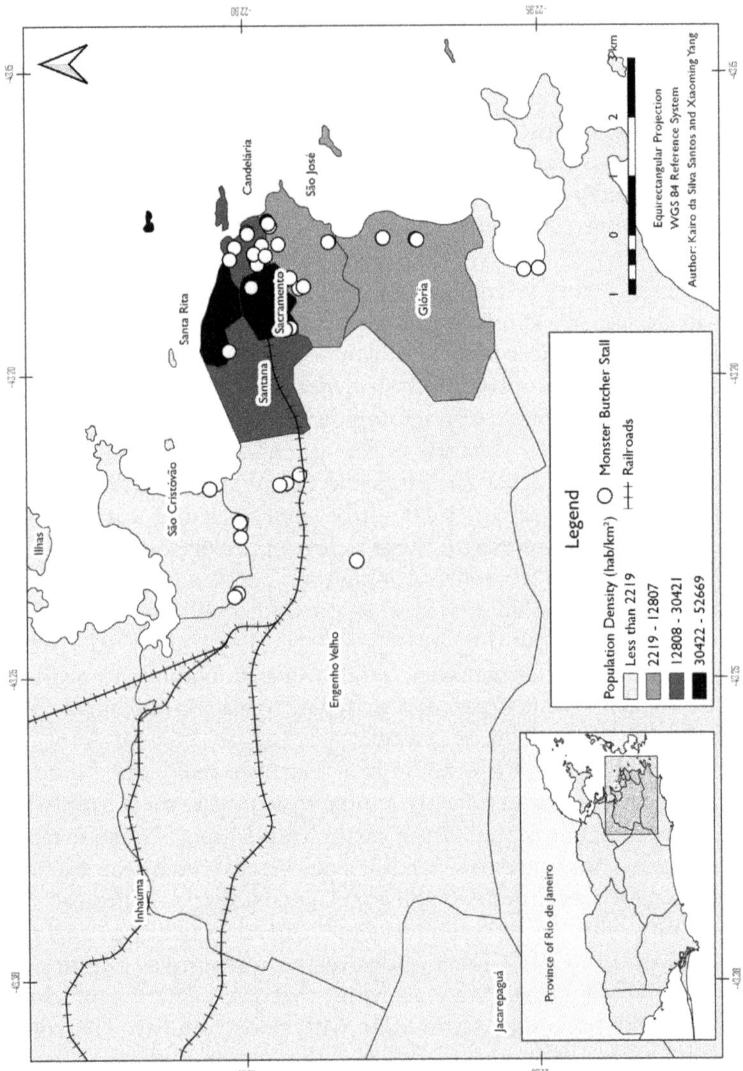

Figure 2.3 Monster butcher stalls in Rio de Janeiro, 1860s.

Sources: See endnote 33.

several Carioca parishes, where he would sell the product slightly above the abattoir's fixed prices.[47]

One unexpected ally that, in fact, empowered the municipality was scientific knowledge about how animal and human health interconnected. In the last quarter of the nineteenth century, arguments in favor of granting the câmara municipal more control over food-safety—for example by centralizing cattle slaughter through an inspected process—gained significant strength. What is more, because consumption of animal proteins became increasingly associated with public welfare, and given meat's perishable condition, to some, it deserved a different status in the free market of commodities, as will be discussed in the next section.[48]

Politicians and intellectuals in Brazil unanimously denounced private monopolies, blaming them for shortages and high prices. Sebastião Ferreira Soares, statistician of the empire, prepared a study on Brazil's agricultural sector, emphasizing that cartels were the major force behind foodstuff price increase in the 1850s.[49] With respect to the provisioning of meat, city officials saw the monopolies as a result of the collusion among middlemen; worse yet, they said, "It is also known that there are cases in which the butcher is also the marchante, the marchante is an invernista, and the invernista is at the same time the cattle raiser." To prevent the formation of such syndicates, the municipality enacted provisions limiting the number of butcher shops because, as one city official put it, "they could be supervised." [50] In July 1867, the Council of State (*conselho do Estado*)—an advisory board to the emperor Pedro II—convened to discuss the new regulatory code for the São Cristóvão matadouro. Most of the counselors (*conselheiros*) voted against the document because of its "anti-free market" tendencies. The conselheiro Joaquim Nabuco best summarizes their mood, explaining that by exercising such overreaching power, the municipality also created new monopolies:

> By trying to avoid a monopoly of a few, we created the monopoly of others; to favor ranchers against marchantes, we invented an artificial competition, ... meanwhile the meat is scarce or expensive ... If the public abattoir does not have the capacity to slaughter all cattle brought to it, it is necessary either to create another public abattoir, or to grant individuals the right to create private slaughterhouses under official inspection.[51]

Although Nabuco's and Ferreira Soares's assessments of foodstuff price increases in Rio de Janeiro conclude with a vehement censure of the ills of monopolies—it is important to remark that they were dialoguing in a milieu in which "free commerce" signified intervention of public power to facilitate competition[52]—both touched upon the technological lag as a deterrent to improving meat provisioning in Brazil's capital city. Ferreira Soares denounced the deplorable conditions of the countryside roads, while Nabuco referred to the municipal abattoir's inadequate slaughtering capacity and even suggested allowing the opening of private facilities to increase meat offerings. In 1881, with the construction of an up-to-date abattoir and the consequent increase in supplies, the city council could follow some of the recommendations the aforementioned authors made. The other one (permitting private citizens to build their own slaughterhouses) would jeopardize the municipality's role as the exclusive body of governance responsible for food safety. If it were to give up this task, who then, city officials might have argued, would protect Cariocas against "fraudulent merchants" or provide the means to supervise methodically and scientifically meat processing? In addressing this question, in the coming years, it was evident that city council members were not willing to relinquish their role as the guardians of public food-safety and much less of the revenues it generated.

From the "Empire of Filth" to a "Majestic Building Complex": The Santa Cruz Slaughterhouse

Describing Rio's meat market in the early 1880s, Christopher C. Andrews—United States consul general to Brazil—avers,

> Beef is brought fresh every morning, and it is generally good. The slaughter of beef-creatures takes place several miles out of the city, under government supervision. The meat is brought into the city on the railroad before evening, and, just before dark, great, heavy, closed wagons, drawn by four mules, go rumbling through the city and deliver beef in quarters at the numerous meat-shops. By ten o'clock in the morning the retailer has generally sold out all of his stock, though after that a few pieces may be seen hanging up at his door.[53]

The above eyewitness account summarizes what city officials expected to achieve when they inaugurated the Santa Cruz matadouro in 1881. The new matadouro location was ideal; since late colonial times, the fields of Santa Cruz—originally a Jesuit Farm, later the Imperial Santa Cruz farm—were the entrance point and resting area of cattle driven from Minas Gerais and São Paulo to Rio de Janeiro. It was situated near the Itá canal, which flows into the Sepetiba Bay. Thus, while the first supplied water to the matadouro and its workers, the latter received, via an open-air canal—along the street later called *Vala do Sangue* (Blood Ditch)—any refuse to be discharged into the ocean. The Santa Cruz slaughterhouse was at approximately 60 km west toward Rio's center. Just after its opening, supplies arrived at the location by maritime commerce, as small boats entered the Itá River with all sorts of merchandise for local grocery stores.[54] In 1884, however, a new railroad station, Matadouro (see Figure 2.4), linked to the Estrada de Ferro D. Pedro II

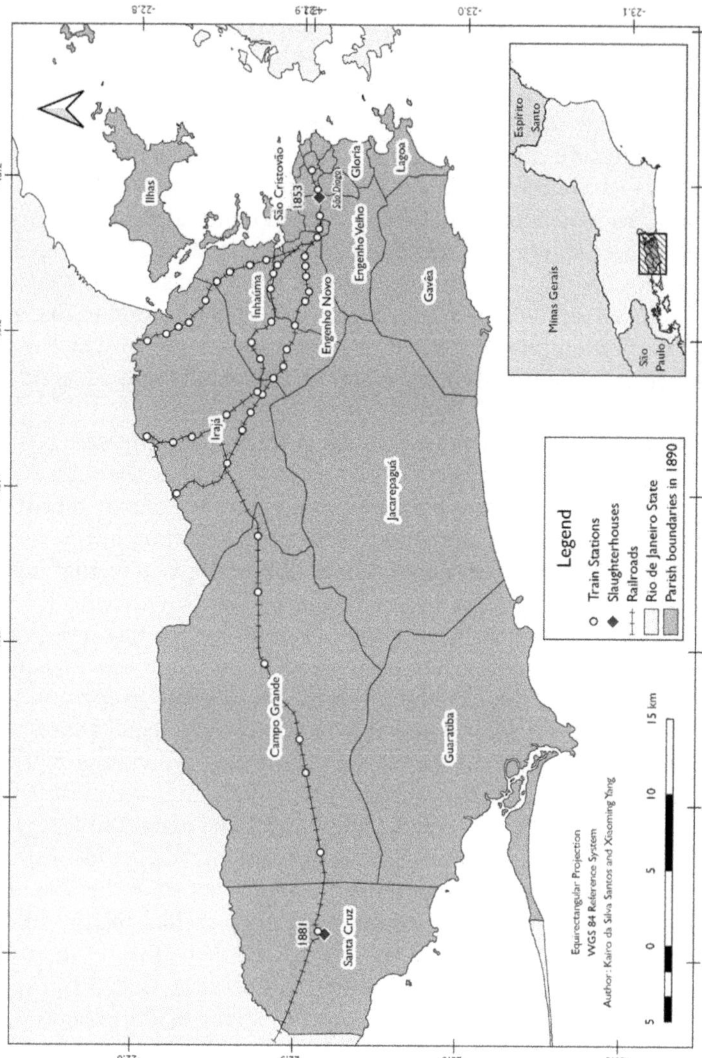

Figure 2.4 Slaughterhouses and railroads in nineteenth-century Rio de Janeiro.

Sources: See endnote 33 and "Estações Ferroviárias do Brasil." Accessed November 7, 2020. www.estacoesferroviarias.com.br/.

(later called Central do Brasil) started to receive cargo and ship meat and offal to the São Diogo station and storehouse in the city center.[55] With this major relocation, the slaughterhouse was definitely removed from public view, leaving behind the "empire of filth" (*império da imundície*), as the São Cristóvão matadouro had become known.[56]

A laudatory book describes the new matadouro as a "majestic building complex." The author stresses, above all, good hygiene and organization. Enclosed by an English-style garden with 420 trees, the abattoir's surroundings resembled the pleasant bucolic scenery of a nineteenth-century farm (*fazenda*). The facility had a barn with a capacity for four hundred animals, buildings for air discharges with scales over which cattle passed after sanitary examination; four rooms for slaughtering; five warehouses for the preparation of viscera, fusion of rejected material, and fabrication of glue and charcoal; plus two pavilions for swine and two for sheep and goat processing. Santa Cruz was so remote from Rio's center that the complex included residencies for its director, doctors, veterinarians, and workers. The first employees settled in 67 houses—some of which were later reserved for schools—where a total of 214 adults and 53 children lived.[57]

Pictures from the aforementioned book present an impressive facility with respect to its size, placidness of the environs, and appearance of its workers—all veterinarians and doctors, for instance, are shown in pristine white lab coats. The author's intention is clear: to associate hygiene with efficiency and both with scientific precision. The matadouro regulations—inspired by the Lisbon's abattoir—meticulously state all steps to be followed: from cattle slaughtering to meat and other by-product processing and transport. Doctors and veterinarians had to inspect all animals that entered the stockyard, the slaughtering process, and the preparation of meat and viscera. While some employees monitored the regular transport of meat and offal by railroad and closely controlled the viscera market, others rigorously accounted for cattle weight. Finally, the code established penalties for those who slaughtered cattle outside the matadouro.[58]

Just after the opening of Santa Cruz, a parliamentary commission visited the new matadouro and prepared a thorough report on the Brazilian cattle and meat industries. The document paints a dismal picture of the country's rural areas. According to the authors, cattlemen were "deprived of all joy … social comfort, [and] mutual aid services that civilization develops and provides." Thus, ranchers were victims of the monopolies, as much as city dwellers were. Since middlemen all along the supply chain were the core problem of the meat provisioning system in Rio, the document stressed the need to strengthen the municipality so it could provide a service of "public utility." What is more, because "only goods that do not deteriorate when not consumed immediately should be governed by the supply and demand principle," the authors conclude with a plea to increase the local government's control over the meat market by limiting the number of cattle slaughtered and establishing municipal butcher shops, where quality and prices were controlled. For the most part, city council members closely followed these suggestions, at least until the 1920s.[59]

As Figure 2.4 shows after Santa Cruz opened its doors, meat processing and transport in Rio de Janeiro had changed considerably since the 1850s. This is evident in the new abattoir's location and its railroad connection to the city's warehouse (in São Diogo) where the majority of butcher stalls stood. With respect to meat transport, although the refrigerator car only arrived in Rio sometime around the 1920s, the railroads allowed meat production to take place away from the city center, and shipment, by rail. Inaugurated in 1858, the Central do Brasil first served parishes in the northwest (1858–1870); in early 1880s, the Mangaratiba line linked the city center with Santa Cruz in the outskirts.[60] Central do Brasil was also the principal line in operation in Rio de Janeiro that bridged the province to Minas Gerais, one of the main purveyors of cattle that arrived in the capital city. The Santa Cruz slaughterhouse stood between the supply area and the consumer market. In 1904, no other major rail line had more stock cars than Central do Brasil, 355 for a 12,622-metric-ton capacity. The second one, part of the *Companhia Mogiana de Estradas de Ferro*, had less than half of that number.[61]

The number of "ice factories and warehouses" in late nineteenth-century Rio de Janeiro did increase, but the use of ice remained sporadic and limited to industrial purposes.[62] Likewise, apparently just one company held exclusive privileges over ice manufacturing. This is not surprising, given that cold air machines were quite expensive and the industry was just in its early stages of development. Because ice was a luxury commodity, consumption of perishable food, including meat, remained a daily affair. For instance, in 1881, Augusto Carlos Grey Tavares and Collatino Marques de Souza requested authorization to establish in the Santa Cruz matadouro (and in railroad cars) a "device capable of maintain cold all meat that has to be shipped to this court." However, the matadouro's interim board of directors denied the petition because "just after slaughtering, meat is shipped ... to the São Diogo warehouse, where it is sold and delivered to different butchers shops ... Therefore, these means of conservation are dispensable."[63] Other contemporary sources corroborate that meat and other perishables were sold immediately after processing. According to an 1890 report prepared by O. H. Dockery, United States consul general in Rio de Janeiro, "Refrigerators are now used in this city to a limited extent [in part because] the supply of articles of food has been for the day only."[64]

Judging by the attention that local newspapers granted the subject of "innovative means to preserve and transport meat," in Rio as in other parts of globe prior to World War I, any attempt to implement refrigeration technology was at most in an experimental stage.[65] By 1915, the municipality declared that it had approximately "30 refrigerated wagons" to ship meat from Santa Cruz to São Diogo. These were, apparently, ordinary boxcars in which spoilage could be delayed by simply placing ice beside the cargo. Actually, Santa Cruz only counted with one so-called refrigerator car. The vehicle was an "ordinary wagon [that] the municipality refurbished according to United States prototypes."[66]

For the aforementioned reasons, after the quarters of meat left São Diogo, they had to be distributed quickly to the city's multiple butcher stalls. Figure 2.5 illustrates that the expansion of meat shops followed the trend cited in the previous section; that is, the majority remained in the business center, near the Mercado Novo and in densely populous districts (some in other markets), accompanying the outward city expansion. In the 1880s, the São José, Santa Rita, Santana, Glória, and Santo Antonio parishes saw an important increase in such facilities. Only Sacramento and Candelária did not undergo a similar pattern, the latter however was losing population toward the end of the century. In concert with this trend, northwest of the city center (broadly encompassing Espírito Santo, Engenho Velho, São Cristóvão, and Engenho Novo parishes) a working-class area that in 1872 concentrated 15 percent of the city's population and in 1890 more than 20 percent also experienced an increment in the number of butcher shops.[67] The same is true for the more affluent south parishes, Glória and Lagoa. Only the outskirt parishes (*subúrbios*) Irajá, Jacarepaguá, Inhaúma, Campo Grande, Guaratiba, and Santa Cruz did not follow a similar trend. These were scarcely populated rural areas with some sugar cane fazendas and factories of sugar, liquor (*aguardente*), bricks, and coal.[68]

Comparing Figures 2.1–2.5 yields a pattern whereby fresh meat sales in Rio de Janeiro concentrated in three centers: Cidade Velha, Cidade Nova, and the city's southern area. In the first, butcher stalls were in close proximity to the main market and other services. Over the period under consideration in this study, Cidade Nova experienced an important population growth. It was also a midway point between the city center and the northern area (including the São Cristóvão parish, which housed several small retail shops, candle and glass factories, and textile mills). Finally, the Glória and Lagoa parishes concentrated an important number of butcher stalls; however, the city center continued to attract most of these facilities. The municipality was keenly aware of these unbalances, which it would seek to redress by legalizing the retailing of meat and offal via mobile butcher stalls (*açougue volante*s).

Despite the increase of butcher stalls in working-class areas, meat and offal peddling was a common activity in Rio, particularly in the suburbs. In 1890, several inventors filed patents for food (including meat) transport apparatuses. Açougues volantes were carts pulled by animals (one, two, or four, depending on their size) with cuts of meat hanging from their ceiling.[69] Promoters of one such pushcart, called the "Vilhalba

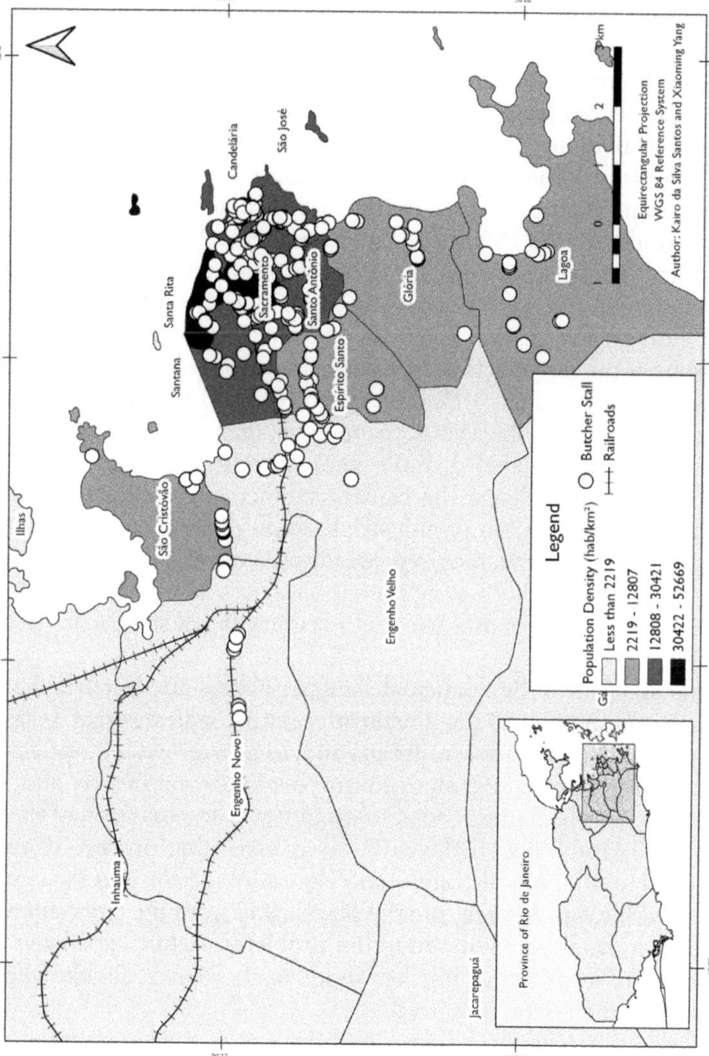

Figure 2.5 Butcher stalls in Rio de Janeiro, 1880s.

Sources: See endnote 33.

system," claimed their invention would "serve mainly the inhabitants of the suburbs where the acquisition of the precious food product is difficult because of the considerable distance ... between buyer ... and ... supplier."[70] As discussed, butcher stalls concentration in the city center or in the most populous parishes had its benefits; but as population growth accelerated, the municipality encountered difficulties in complying with its mandate in the late nineteenth century. Later, meatpacking companies exploited these deficiencies to their benefit.

Certainly, technology—railroads, mainly—helped to eliminate some intermediaries within the city provisioning, which in turn improved meat supply and availability, but before reaching Santa Cruz, cattle had to travel hundreds of kilometers. This supply chain was subject to natural disturbances and political maneuvering. Trying to account for these and other vicissitudes, in the 1890s, the câmara municipal opened Rio's market to all cattle traders (*matança livre*); one year later, it brought back the contractor, signing an agreement with M. Gomes de Oliveira to supply the city with meat for five years.[71] Over this period, Rio's government continued to prohibit the introduction of meat from cattle slaughtered beyond its purview because, as city officials argued, it could not be adequately examined. Ironically, in the 1920s, technology again, allowed "interlopers"—as local officials labeled those who attempted to enter the meat market in Rio—to challenge the câmara municipal's exclusive control over supplies. With promises of industrialized production and up-to-date shipping methods, meatpacking representatives and the federal government saw the municipality's provisioning practices as obsolete symbols of paternalistic economics that twentieth-century Brazil should be rid of.

* * *

A spatial analysis of the municipal slaughterhouses and butcher shops in Rio in the second half of the nineteenth century, indicates that as new technologies were introduced (railroads and, to a lesser extent, refrigeration), the municipality gained more control over the meat market and, as a result, some intermediaries tended to disappear. The expansion of those facilities significantly altered the cattle-meat marketing process, changing its spatial and temporal conditions. The railroads allowed for cattle slaughter and meat processing to take place away from the city center—which, in turn, resolved some sanitation problems—while expansion in the number and locations of butcher shops made meat available where the majority of the population lived.

By focusing on technological improvements as they were reflected on the location trends of slaughterhouses and butcher shops over half a century, this chapter shows that the municipal control of the fresh meat market allowed the city council to fulfill its provisioning obligations. It also argues that shortages and other vicissitudes that Carioca city dwellers confronted from time to time manifested the limitations of the public abattoir system. Because the municipality lacked sufficient refrigerated storage facilities, for instance, it could not plan provisions for longer periods or confront major disturbances in the cattle supply chain. Above all, public officials in Rio did what was possible within the technological framework available to them. That partially explains how fresh meat offerings came to surpass those of salted meat (*charque*) in the early 1900s. Until then, as the next chapter examines, this traditional salt cured meat was the main source of animal proteins to Rio's urban residents.

Notes

1 John Luccock, *Notes on Rio de Janeiro and Southern Parts of Brazil, Taken During a Residence of Ten Years in that Country from 1808 to 1818* (London: Printed for Samuel Leigh, 1820), 43.

2 During the first decades of the twentieth century, most of the landmarks and buildings mentioned here were demolished. Through large-scale public works, the municipal government flattened the Morro do Castelo and filled in the Santa Luzia beach.

3 Robert Walsh, *Notices of Brazil in 1828 and 1829* (London: Frederick Westley and A. H. Davis, 1830), 508.

4 Quoted in Sydney Watts, "The Grande Boucherie, the 'Right' to Meat, and the Growth of Paris," in *Meat, Modernity, and the Rise of the Slaughterhouse,* ed. Paula Young Lee (Durham, NH: University of New Hampshire Press, 2008), 13; Charles Dickens, *Great Expectations*, vol. 1 (Cambridge, UK: Printed at the Riverside Press, 1868), 225.

5 Quoted in Georgia da Costa Tavares, *A atuação dos marchantes no Rio de Janeiro colonial. Estratégias de mercado e redes de sociabilidade no comércio de abastecimento de carne verde 1763–1808* (Rio de Janeiro: Arquivo geral da cidade do Rio de Janeiro, 2012), 17.

6 For a similar approach to the political economy of meat see Kyri Claflin's study about late 1800s-Paris. Kyri Claflin, "La Villette: City of Blood (1867–1914)," in *Meat, Modernity,* 41.

7 The maps in this chapter were produced in collaboration with Dr. Xiaoming Yang from the Geo-Spatial Information Center at California State University, Fresno (Fresno State), students who were awarded the Undergraduate Research Grants at Fresno State, and Kairo da Silva Santos from Universidade Federal do Rio de Janeiro. Erik Steiner from the Spatial History Project at Stanford University graciously provided the metadata (address locator files) and Paulo Márcio Leal de Menezes from Laboratório de Cartografia at Universidade Federal do Rio de Janeiro provided the cartographic bases. I thank them for sharing their work with me.

8 Aluísio Azevedo, *The Slum* (Oxford: Oxford University Press, 2000), 22–23.

9 These objectives were no different from those at play in Paris and Berlin during their slaughterhouse reforms. See Kyri Claflin, "La Villette" and Dorothee Brantz, "Animal Bodies, Human Health, and the Reform of Slaughterhouses in Nineteenth-Century Berlin," in *Meat, Modernity* 41–45, 82–85.

10 Walsh, *Notices of Brazil*, 508.

11 Mary Karasch, "Rio de Janeiro: From Colonial Town to Imperial Capital (1808–1850)," in *Colonial Cities. Essays on Urbanism in a Colonial Context*, ed. Robert Ross and Gerard J. Telkamp (Dordrecht, Netherlands: M. Nijhoff, 1985), 128–29.

12 João Baptista Cortines Laxe and Antonio Joaquim de Macedo Soares, *Regimento das Câmaras municipais ou lei de 1°. De outubro de 1828* (Rio

de Janeiro: B. L. Garnier, 1885), 190–92; Pedro Henrique Pedreira Campos, *Nos caminhos da acumulação. Negócios e poder no abastecimento de carnes verdes para a cidade do Rio de Janeiro (1808–1835)* (São Paulo: Alameda Casa Editorial, 2010), 163; Gergely Baics observed a similar pattern in late-eighteenth-century New York; see Gergely Baics, "Is Access to Food a Public Good? Meat Provisioning in Early New York City, 1790–1820," *Journal of Urban History* 20, no. 10 (2012): 651–54.

13 Campos, *Nos caminhos*, 182.

14 João Luís Fragoso, *Homens de grossa aventura: acumulação e hierarquia na praça mercantil do Rio de Janeiro, 1790–1830* (Rio de Janeiro: Civilização Brasileira, 1998), 324; Rafael Torres Sánchez, "The Failure of the Spanish Crown's Tobacco Tax Monopoly in Catalonia during the Seventeenth Century," Universidad de Navarra, Facultad de Ciencias Económicas y Empresariales, Working paper no. 13/5 (September 2005): 1–3; Raymond De Roover, "Monopoly Theory Prior to Adam Smith: A Revision," *The Quarterly Journal of Economics* 65, no. 4 (November 1951): 495–99.

15 Larissa Virginia Brown, "Internal Commerce in a Colonial Economy: Rio de Janeiro and its Hinterland, 1790–1822" (PhD diss., University of Virginia, 1986), 525–28; Maria de Fátima Silva Gouvêa, "Poder, autoridade e o Senado da Câmara do Rio de Janeiro, ca. 1780–1820," *Tempo* 7, no. 13 (2002): 135–38; Tavares, *A atuação dos marchantes*, 70–77.

16 During the late colonial era, the city's administration was in the hands of the Senado da Câmara. In 1828, the Câmara Municipal da Corte replaced it.

17 Quoted in Gouvêa, "Poder, autoridade," 139.

18 Ibid., 141–50; Campos, *Nos caminhos,* 67–69; Brown, "Internal," 539–40.

19 Renato Leite Marcondes, "Formação da rede regional de abastecimento do Rio de Janeiro: a presença dos negociantes de gado (1801–1811)," *Topoi. Revista de História* 2, no. 2 (2001): 42–49; Maria Theresa Schorer Petrone, "O afluxo de gado a Sorocaba e a importância econômica do caminho do sul na década da independência," *Revista de História* 46, no. 94 (1973): 389–97; Fragoso, *Homens,* 280–82.

20 Campos, *Nos caminhos,* 71.

21 Brasil, *Coleção das leis e decretos do império do Brasil: desde a feliz época da sua indepedência* (Rio de Janeiro: Typographia de P. Plancher-Seignot, 1827), 144–46.

22 Maria Yedda Leite Linhares, *História do abastecimento; uma problemática em questão (1530–1918)* (Brasília: Edições Binagri, 1979), 163; Tavares, *A atuação dos marchantes*, 77; Alcir Lenharo, *As tropas da moderação. O abastecimento da corte na formação política do Brasil, 1808–1842* (Rio de Janeiro: Prefeitura da cidade do Rio de Janeiro, 1992), 39–42.

23 Rio de Janeiro, *Consolidação das Leis e Posturas Municipaes do Districto Federal,* Primeira parte, legislação federal (Rio de Janeiro: Oficinas tipográficas de Paulo Souza & Comp., 1905), 789–92.

24 De Roover, "Monopoly Theory," 509–10; Brown, "Internal," 556.

25 Carlos Eduardo Suprinyak, "Comércio de animais de carga no Brasil imperial: uma análise quantitativa das tropas negociadas nas províncias do Paraná e São Paulo" (master's thesis: Universidade Estadual Paulista, Araraquara, 2006)," 9; Marcondes, "Formação da rede regional," 43–51; Lenharo, *As tropas*, 35.

26 Gouvêa, "Poder, autoridade," 136–37; José Honório Rodrigues, ed., *Atas do conselho de Estado pleno, Terceiro conselho de Estado, 1865–1867*, Brasil, Senado Federal, June 27, 1867, 178, accessed November 25, 2020, www.senado.leg.br/publicacoes/anais/asp/AT_AtasDoConselhoDeEstado.asp.

27 This was certainly the case of Salvador (Bahia), as described by Richard Graham in *Feeding the City. From Street Markets to Liberal Reform in Salvador, Brazil, 1780–1860* (Austin: University of Texas Press, 2010), 191.

28 Campos, *Nos caminhos,* 216–22.
29 The case of London offers a contrast. See Chris Otter, "The Vital City: Public Analysis, Dairies and Slaughterhouses in Nineteenth-Century Britain," *Cultural Geographies* 13, no. 4 (2006): 526–30.
30 Thomas Holloway, "Prefácio: Haddock Lobo e o Recenseamento do Rio de Janeiro de 1849," *Boletim de História Demográfica* Ano XV, no. 50 (2008), accessed October 20, 2020, http://historia_demografica.tripod.com/bhds/bhd50/thrj.pdf; Tarcísio R. Botelho, "População e espaço nacional no Brasil do século XIX," *Cadernos de História* 7, no. 8 (2005): 75–78; Karasch, "Rio de Janeiro," 132–37; Mary Karasch, *Slave Life in Rio de Janeiro, 1808–1850* (Princeton: Princeton University Press, 1987), 66.
31 Holloway, "Prefácio"; Brasil, *Receseamento Geral da Republica dos Estados Unidos do Brazil em 31 de dezembro de 1890, Districto Federal* (Rio de Janeiro: Typ. Leuzinger, 1895), X.
32 This summary does not do justice to the scope of central-place theory. Likewise, this chapter does not present a comparative analysis of convenience and shopping goods locations, nor does it study their degree of cloistering over time. See Brian J. L. Berry, *Geography of Market Centers and Retail Distribution* (Englewood Cliffs, NJ: Prentice-Hall, 1967), 5–8. For a discussion on the theory's evolution see Stephen Brown, "Central Place Theory: Sixty Years on," *Contemporary Marketing History* 6 (1993): 69–73. Recent works on meat retailing are Gergely Baics, "The Geography of Urban Food Retail: Locational Principles of Public Market Provisioning in New York City, 1790–1860," *Urban History* 43 special issue (2016): 4–7; Andrew Robichaud and Erik Steiner, "Trail of Blood. The Movement of San Francisco's Butchertown and the Spatial Transformation of Meat Production, 1849–1901," *The Spatial History Project*, August 2009, accessed November 20, 2020, https://web.stanford.edu/group/spatialhistory/cgi–bin/site/pub.php?id=31; Manel Guàrdia, José Luis Oyón, Sergi Garriga, and Nadia Fava, "Meat Consumption and Nutrition Transition in Barcelona, 1709–1935," *Urban History* 45, no. 2 (2018): 193–94.
33 The method for drawing these maps consisted of collecting butcher stalls' addresses from the *Almanak administrativo, mercantil e industrial do imperio do Brazil [Almanak Laemmert]* (available in Brazilian government documents, *Almanak Laemmert*, 1844–1889, www.crl.edu/node/1225) and converting them into geographic coordinates. These were identified onto Rio's population density maps at the parish level. The latter division was gathered from Kairo da Silva Santos et al., "Evolução da paisagem da cidade do Rio de Janeiro, uma visão cartográfica: aspectos socioespaciais a partir do século XIX," Conference Proceedings, *Anais do V Simpósio Luso-Brasileiro de Cartografia Histórica* (Petrópolis, RJ, 2013): 5–12. The quality of the sources demanded some adjustments. Several addresses were incomplete; others, most likely, were duplicates. These maps show addresses for more than one year in each decade, trying to account for these problems, which in turn, resulted in overestimates. In any case, it is essential to keep in mind that these images provide approximations. Neither the parishes' boundaries nor butcher stalls' locations are precise. The work seeks to show spatial retailing tendencies over time.
34 Edite Moraes da Costa, "Os operários da construção do matadouro público na Imperial Fazenda de Santa Cruz (Rio de Janeiro, 1874–1881)," in *Trabalho Democracia e Direitos, Volume 1, Trabalho livre e escravizado*, ed. Clarice Gontarski Speranza and Micaele Scheer (Porto Alegre, RS: Editora Fi, 2019), 245–48.
35 Francisco Agenor de Noronha Santos, *As freguesias do Rio antigo*, introdução, notas e bibliografia por Paulo Berger (Rio de Janeiro: Edições O Cruzeiro,

1965), 18–23; Patricia Acerbi, "Slave Legacies, Ambivalent Modernity: Street Commerce and the Transition to Free Labor in Rio de Janeiro, 1850–1925" (PhD diss., University of Maryland, 2010), 45–48.

36 Brasil, *Receseamento Geral... 1890,* XLII.

37 O. H. Dockery, "Refrigerators and Food Preservation in Foreign Countries," Report by U.S. consul general in Rio de Janeiro, U.S. Department of State, Consular Reports (Washington: Government Printing Office, 1891), 30–33.

38 Fernanda Mousse Pinto, "A invenção da Cidade Nova do Rio de Janeiro: agentes, personagens e planos" (master's thesis: Universidade Federal do Rio de Janeiro, 2007), 181–82; Patrícia Gomes da Silveira, "Análise das atividades econômicas na Cidade Nova (RJ) oitocentista," *Terra Brasilis (Nova Série)* 4 (2015): 6–8, accessed October 10, 2020, DOI: doi:10.4000/terrabrasilis.1256.

39 During the nineteenth century, Rio de Janeiro also imported natural ice from Boston. Marc W. Herold, "Ice in the Tropics: the Export of 'Crystal Blocks of Yankee Coldness' to India and Brazil," *Revista Espaço Acadêmico* 11, no. 126 (2011): 169–71.

40 Ferdinand Carré was a French inventor who, in 1859, patented an ice-making machine using ammonia as coolant. While other engineers had experimented with air as the refrigerant, ammonia was more efficient because it liquefies at a lower temperature than air. In 1862, at the International Exhibition in London, he presented two apparatuses, one for domestic the other for industrial purposes. Carré's machines were rapidly exported, quickly popularized, and adopted in several countries, at least until the end of the century. *Almanak Laemmert*, 1866, 622; J. F. Nickerson, "The Development of Refrigeration in the United States," *Ice and Refrigeration* 49, nos. 1–6 (July–December 1915): 170; Jonathan Rees, *Refrigeration Nation. A History of Ice, Appliances, and Enterprise in America* (Baltimore, MD: The Johns Hopkins University Press, 2013), 39.

41 Quoted in Lenharo, *As tropas*, 85–86.

42 *Arquivo Geral da Cidade do Rio de Janeiro* (hereafter AGCRJ), Carnes e Matadouros, "[Letter from] Jeronimo Teixeira de [illegible] to Illmos. Srs. Presidente e vereadores da Câmara Municipal," May 25, 1840.

43 Almir El Chaiban Kareh, "Cantando espalharei por toda a parte, Se a tanto me ajudar engenho e arte: Propaganda, técnicas de vendas e consumo no Rio de Janeiro (1850–1870)," *Antropolítica* 21 (2008): 24–26.

44 T. Ottoni, *Annaes do senado do Império do Brazil, Primeiro anno da 12ª legislatura, Sessão de 1864*, vol. 2, Brazil Senado Federal, Secretaria Especial de Editoração e Publicações - Subsecretaria de Anais do Senado Federal, 149–150.

45 Kareh, "Cantando espalharei," 26–27.

46 *Annaes do Parlamento Brazileiro. Câmara dos Senhores Deputados, Sessão de 1882,* vol. 3 (Rio de Janeiro: Typographia Nacional, 1882), 22–25.

47 AGCRJ, "Monopólio celebrado entre a Câmara Municipal com major João Vicente de Brito Galvão para o estabelecimento de açougues municipais," Rio de Janeiro, January 31, 1876.

48 Not surprising, early in the twentieth century, in the city council's administrative chart, the matadouro was subordinated to General Board of Hygiene and Public Assistance (*Diretoria Geral de Hygiene e Assistência Pública*). Rio de Janeiro, *Consolidação das leis e posturas municipaes*, Segunda parte, Legislação districtal, "Condições para o commercio ambulante de miudos de rezes," articles 752–753 (Rio de Janeiro: Oficinas tipográficas de Paula Souza & Comp., 1906), 177–78; Robyn S. Metcalfe, *Meat, Commerce and the City: The London Food Market, 1800–1855* (Perspectives in Economic and Social History) (London: Pickering & Chatto, 2012), 99–112; Lee A. Craig, Barry K.

Goodwin, and Thomas Grennes, "The Effect of Mechanical Refrigeration on Nutrition in the United States," *Social Science History* 28, no. 2 (2004): 332.

49 Sebastião Ferreira Soares, *Notas estatísticas sobre a produção agrícola e a carestia dos gêneros alimentícios no Império do Brasil* (Rio de Janeiro: Typ. Imp. e Const. de J. Villeneuve e Comp.: 1860), 279–89; Linhares, *História do abastecimento,* 22–25.

50 Quoted in Linhares, *História do abastecimento*, 195–97. The Smithfield Market in London labeled as the "world's biggest," confronted similar problems in late eighteenth century. See George Dood, *The Food of London. The Chief Varieties Sources of Supply, Probable Quantities, Modes of Arrival, Processes of Manufacture, Suspected Adulteration and Machinery of Distribution of the Food for a Community of Two Millions and a Half* (London: Longman, Brown, Green and Longmans, 1856), 230.

51 Joaquim Nabuco, Obras Completas de Joaquim Nabuco, vol. 6, *Joaquim Nabuco, um estadista do Império, Nabuco de Araújo*, vol. 4 (São Paulo: Instituto Progresso Editorial, S.A., 1949), 31; Rodrigues, *Atas do conselho,* 181.

52 *Annaes do Parlamento Brazileiro*, 1882, 27.

53 Christopher C. Andrews, *Brazil: its Condition and Prospects* (New York: D. Appleton and Company, 1891), 17.

54 Benedicto de Freitas, *História do matadouro municipal de Santa Cruz* (Rio de Janeiro: Irmãos Pongetti Editores, 1950), 53–75, 135.

55 On the Brazilian railroads, see "Estações Ferroviárias do Brasil," accessed November 7, 2020, www.estacoesferroviarias.com.br/.

56 Freitas, *História do matadouro*, 26–53, 135.

57 Ibid., 53–86.

58 AGCRJ, Matadouro de Santa Cruz, March 20, 1883; "Regulamento para o matadouro público," February 14, 1882, in *Annaes do Parlamento Brazileiro*, 1882, 33–37; Freitas, *História do matadouro,* 64–65.

59 *Annaes do Parlamento Brazileiro*, 1882, 21–28; AGCRJ, Carnes verdes. "Preços das carnes entregues ao consumo público," June 1, 1892.

60 Santos et al., "Evolução," 5–12.

61 William R. Summerhill, "Market Intervention in a Backward Economy: Railway Subsidy in Brazil, 1854–1913," *The Economic History Review*, New Series 51, no. 3 (August 1998), 546–47. See also, "Estações Ferroviárias do Brasil," accessed November 7, 2020, www.estacoesferroviarias.com.br/index.html; Brasil, Ministério da indústria, viação e obras públicas, Diretoria geral de obras e viação, *Estatística das estradas de ferro da união e das fiscalizadas pela união em 31 de dezembro de 1904* (Rio de Janeiro: Imprensa Nacional, 1906), Table 8a.

62 In 1889, an advertisement for the "Empreza brazileira de fabricação de gelo" proudly announced that because its plant "had undergone major improvements ... [it] could supply any quantity of solid and crystalline ice at reasonable prices ... [and it could] produce 10 million kilos [of ice] yearly." *Almanak Laemmert*, 1889, 1902; *Almanak Laemmert*, 1875, 795, and 1882, 286–87.

63 AGCRJ, Mercados de carnes verdes. Carnes e Matadouros, "De Augusto Carlos Grey Tavares e Collatino Marques de Souza à Câmara Municipal da Corte," Rio de Janeiro, August 17, 1881; AGCRJ, Mercados de carnes verdes, Carnes e Matadouros, "From A. Barrozo Pires, Diretoria interina do Matadouro," Rio de Janeiro, April 12, 1882.

64 Dockery, "Refrigerators," 30–33. The consul, David N. Burke, in Salvador (Bahia) stressed the same, pointing out that generally the population was served by ice-carts that passed through the city.

65 *Diario do Commercio*, November 27, 1891; *Gazeta da Tarde*, May 30, 1891. From 1913 to 1914, Brazil's purchases of refrigeration machinery from the

United States increased fivefold; see L. M. Alwyn-Schmidt, "The Trend of the Foreign Situation. Additional Cold Storage Space Required for the Present Day Problem of Feeding Europe—America's Opportunities to Meet This Problem," *Refrigerating World. Incorporating Cold Storage & Ice Trade Journal* 54, no. 1 (February 1919): 22. The case of Rio de Janeiro is not an anomaly; in other parts of the Western hemisphere, mechanical refrigeration remained chiefly limited to industrial uses, brewery and meat processing being the most important ones. Maybe only with the exception of the United States, ice consumption was a twentieth-century phenomenon. Rees, *Refrigeration Nation,* 47–49. See also United States, Department of Commerce, "Ice-Making and Cold Storage Plants in South America," *Trade Information Bulletin* 209 (March 10, 1924): 11–21.

66 AGCRJ, Carnes, "Transportes em vagões frigoríficos," by Luiz Raphael Vieira Souto, June 11, 1915. In the United Sates, the technology used in the first refrigerator cars consisted of placing ice in rail cars, rather than mechanical refrigeration, which was extremely expensive and not entirely reliable, at least until the late nineteenth century. Later, the refrigerator car had "insulation, [and] double walls." The novelty, which allowed packers to transport meat at greater distances, was that "packers built a series of icing stations along the way to refill refrigerators cars when too much of the initial ice placed in the car had melted." See Rees, *Refrigeration Nation,* 88–91.

67 Teresa A. Meade, *Civilizing Rio: Reform and Resistance in a Brazilian City, 1889–1930* (University Park: Pennsylvania State University, 1997), 48–67.

68 Francisco Ferreira da Rosa, *Rio de Janeiro* (Rio de Janeiro: Edição Oficial da Prefeitura, 1905), 64–70; Santos, *As freguesias,* 72–93; Thiago Vinícius Mantuano da Fonseca, "A região portuária do Rio de Janeiro no século XIX: aspectos demográficos e sociais," *Almanack*, Guarulhos, no. 21 (2019): 181–84.

69 Acerbi, "Slave Legacies," 215, Images 27–29, 328–29; *Diário do Commercio*, November 27, 1891.

70 *Gazeta da Tarde*, May 30, 1891.

71 Alvarenga Fonseca, org., *Collecção de Leis Municipaes e Vetos de 1892–1894*, vol. 1, Decreto no. 1 de 9 de janeiro de 1893, "Autorisa o Prefeito a providenciar para o abastecimento do mercado de carne do Districto Federal," 5; Decreto no. 119 de 19 de novembro de 1894, "Autorisa o Prefeito a contractar com M. Gomes de Oliveira o fornecimento de carne verde a população do Districto Federal," (Rio de Janeiro: Typographia do Jornal do Commercio, de Rodrigues & C., 1897), 153–55; Alvarenga Fonseca, org., *Collecção de Leis Municipaes e Vetos de 1895–1896*, vol. 2, Decreto n. 226 de 2 de março de 1896, "Isenta de imposto pelo exercicio de seu commercio a todos os açougueiros que se obrigarem a vender carne verde com lucro de 100 réis em kilo" (Rio de Janeiro: Typographia do Jornal do Commercio, de Rodrigues & C., 1897), 134–35.

Bibliography

Archives Consulted

Arquivo Geral da Cidade do Rio de Janeiro, (cited as AGCRJ)

Government Documents and Publications

Annaes do Parlamento Brazileiro. *Câmara dos Senhores Deputados, Sessão de 1882*. Vol. 3. Rio de Janeiro: Typographia Nacional, 1882.

Brasil. *Coleção das leis e decretos do império do Brasil: desde a feliz época da sua indepedência.* Rio de Janeiro: Typographia de P. Plancher-Seignot, 1827.

Brasil. Ministério da indústria, viação e obras públicas, Diretoria geral de obras e viação. *Estatística das estradas de ferro da união e das fiscalizadas pela união em 31 de dezembro de 1904.* Rio de Janeiro: Imprensa Nacional, 1906.

Brasil. *Receseamento Geral da Republica dos Estados Unidos do Brazil em 31 de dezembro de 1890, Districto Federal.* Rio de Janeiro: Typ. Leuzinger, 1895.

Dockery, O. H. "Refrigerators and Food Preservation in Foreign Countries." Report by U.S. consul general in Rio de Janeiro, U.S. Department of State, Consular Reports. Washington: Government Printing Office, 1891.

Fonseca, Alvarenga, org. *Collecção de Leis Municipaes e Vetos de 1892 – 1894.* Vol. 1. Rio de Janeiro: Typographia do Jornal do Commercio, de Rodrigues & C., 1897a.

Fonseca, Alvarenga, org. *Collecção de Leis Municipaes e Vetos de 1895 – 1896.* Vol. 2. Rio de Janeiro: Typographia do Jornal do Commercio, de Rodrigues & C., 1897b.

Laxe, João Baptista Cortines, and Antonio Joaquim de Macedo Soares. *Regimento das Câmaras municipais ou lei de 1°. De outubro de 1828.* Rio de Janeiro: B. L. Garnier, 1885.

"Regulamento para o matadouro público." February 14, 1882. In *Annaes do Parlamento Brazileiro. Câmara dos Senhores Deputados, Sessão de 1882.* Vol. 3. Rio de Janeiro: Typographia Nacional, 1882.

Rio de Janeiro. *Consolidação das leis e posturas municipaes do Districto Federal.* Primeira parte, legislação federal. Rio de Janeiro: Oficinas tipográficas de Paulo Souza & Comp., 1905.

Rio de Janeiro. *Consolidação das leis e posturas municipaes do Districto Federal.* Segunda parte, legislação districtal. Rio de Janeiro: Oficinas tipográficas de Paula Souza & Comp., 1906.

United States. Department of Commerce. "Ice-Making and Cold Storage Plants in South America." *Trade Information Bulletin* 209 (March 10, 1924), 11–21.

Newspapers and Magazines

Almanak Laemmert (Rio de Janeiro). *Almanak administrativo, mercantil e industrial do imperio do Brazil*

Gazeta da Tarde (Rio de Janeiro)

Alwyn-Schmidt, L. M. "The Trend of the Foreign Situation." Additional Cold Storage Space Required for the Present Day Problem of Feeding Europe—America's Opportunities to Meet This Problem. *Refrigerating World. Incorporating Cold Storage & Ice Trade Journal* 54, no. 1 (February 1919): 21–22.

Nickerson, J. F. "The Development of Refrigeration in the United States." *Ice and Refrigeration* 49, no. 1–6 (July–December 1915): 170–174.

Other Primary Sources

Andrews, Christopher C. *Brazil: Its Condition and Prospects.* New York: D. Appleton and Company, 1891.

Azevedo, Aluísio. *The Slum.* Oxford: Oxford University Press, 2000.

Dickens, Charles. *Great Expectations*. Vol. 1. Cambridge, UK: Printed at the Riverside Press, 1868.

Dood, George. *The Food of London. The Chief Varieties Sources of Supply, Probable Quantities, Modes of Arrival, Processes of Manufacture, Suspected Adulteration and Machinery of Distribution of the Food for a Community of Two Millions and a Half*. London: Longman, Brown, Green and Longmans, 1856.

"Estações Ferroviárias do Brasil." Accessed November 7, 2020. www.estacoesferroviarias.com.br/.

Luccock, John. *Notes on Rio de Janeiro and Southern Parts of Brazil, Taken During a Residence of Ten Years in that Country from 1808 to 1818*. London: Printed for Samuel Leigh, 1820.

Nabuco, Joaquim. Obras Completas de Joaquim Nabuco. Vol. 6. *Joaquim Nabuco, um estadista do Império. Nabuco de Araújo*. Vol. 4. São Paulo: Instituto Progresso Editorial, S.A., 1949.

Ottoni, T. *Annaes do senado do Império do Brazil, Primeiro anno da 12ª legislatura, Sessão de 1864*, vol. 2, Brasil: Senado Federal, Secretaria Especial de Editoração e Publicações - Subsecretaria de Anais do Senado Federal, 1864.

Rodrigues, José Honório, ed. *Atas do conselho de Estado pleno, Terceiro conselho de Estado, 1865–1867*. Brasil: Senado Federal. Accessed November 25, 2020, https://www.senado.leg.br/publicacoes/anais/asp/AT_AtasDoConselhoDeEstado.asp.

Rosa, Francisco Ferreira da. *Rio de Janeiro*. Rio de Janeiro: Edição Oficial da Prefeitura, 1905.

Soares, Sebastião Ferreira. *Notas estatísticas sobre a produção agrícola e a carestia dos gêneros alimentícios no Império do Brasil*. Rio de Janeiro: Typ. Imp. e Const. de J. Villeneuve e Comp., 1860.

Walsh, Robert. *Notices of Brazil in 1828 and 1829*. London: Frederick Westley and A. H. Davis, 1830.

Secondary Sources

Acerbi, Patricia. "Slave Legacies, Ambivalent Modernity: Street Commerce and the Transition to Free Labor in Rio de Janeiro, 1850–1925." PhD diss., University of Maryland, 2010.

Baics, Gergely. "Is Access to Food a Public Good? Meat Provisioning in Early New York City, 1790–1820." *Journal of Urban History* 20, no. 10 (2013): 643–668.

Baics, Gergely. "The Geography of Urban Food Retail: Locational Principles of Public Market Provisioning in New York City, 1790–1860." *Urban History* 43 special issue (2016): 1–19.

Berry, Brian J. L. *Geography of Market Centers and Retail Distribution*. Englewood Cliffs, NJ: Prentice-Hall, 1967.

Botelho, Tarcísio R. "População e espaço nacional no Brasil do século XIX." *Cadernos de História* 7, no. 8 (2005): 67–83.

Brantz, Dorothee. "Animal Bodies, Human Health, and the Reform of Slaughterhouses in Nineteenth-Century Berlin." In *Meat, Modernity, and the Rise of the Slaughterhouse*, edited by Paula Young Lee, 71–85. Durham, NH: University of New Hampshire Press, 2008.

Brown, Larissa Virginia. "Internal Commerce in a Colonial Economy: Rio de Janeiro and its Hinterland, 1790–1822." PhD diss., University of Virginia, 1986.

Brown, Stephen. "Central Place Theory: Sixty Years on." *Contemporary Marketing History* 6 (1993): 69–87.

Campos, Pedro Henrique Pedreira. *Nos caminhos da acumulação. Negócios e poder no abastecimento de carnes verdes para a cidade do Rio de Janeiro (1808–1835)*. São Paulo: Alameda Casa Editorial, 2010.

Claflin, Kyri. "La Villette: City of Blood (1867–1914)." In *Meat, Modernity, and the Rise of the Slaughterhouse*, edited by Paula Young Lee, 27–45. Durham, NH: University of New Hampshire Press, 2008.

Costa, Edite Moraes da. "Os operários da construção do matadouro público na Imperial Fazenda de Santa Cruz (Rio de Janeiro, 1874–1881)." In *Trabalho, Democracia e Direitos, Volume 1, Trabalho livre e escravizado*, edited by Clarice Gontarski Speranza and Micaele Scheer, 245–272. Porto Alegre, RS: Editora Fi, 2019.

Craig, Lee A., Barry K. Goodwin, and Thomas Grennes. "The Effect of Mechanical Refrigeration on Nutrition in the United States." *Social Science History* 28, no. 2 (2004): 325–336.

De Roover, Raymond. "Monopoly Theory Prior to Adam Smith: A Revision." *The Quarterly Journal of Economics* 65, no. 4 (November 1951): 492–524.

Fonseca, Thiago Vinícius Mantuano da. "A região portuária do Rio de Janeiro no século XIX: aspectos demográficos e sociais." *Almanack*, Guarulhos, n. 21 (2019): 166–204.

Fragoso, João Luís. *Homens de grossa aventura: acumulação e hierarquia na praça mercantil do Rio de Janeiro, 1790–1830*. Rio de Janeiro: Civilização Brasileira, 1998.

Freitas, Benedicto de. *História do matadouro municipal de Santa Cruz*. Rio de Janeiro: Irmãos Pongetti Editores, 1950.

Gouvêa, Maria de Fátima Silva. "Poder, autoridade e o Senado da Câmara do Rio de Janeiro, ca. 1780–1820." *Tempo* 7, no. 13 (2002): 111–155.

Graham, Richard. *Feeding the City. From Street Markets to Liberal Reform in Salvador, Brazil, 1780–1860*. Austin: University of Texas Press, 2010.

Guàrdia, Manel, José Luis Oyón, Sergi Garriga, and Nadia Fava. "Meat Consumption and Nutrition Transition in Barcelona, 1709–1935." *Urban History* 45, no. 2 (2018): 193–213.

Herold, Marc W. "Ice in the Tropics: the Export of 'Crystal Blocks of Yankee Coldness' to India and Brazil." *Revista Espaço Acadêmico* 11, no. 126 (2011): 162–177.

Holloway, Thomas. "Prefácio: Haddock Lobo e o Recenseamento do Rio de Janeiro de 1849." *Boletim de História Demográfica* Ano XV, no. 50 (2008). Accessed October 20, 2020, http://historia_demografica.tripod.com/bhds/bhd50/thrj.pdf.

Karasch, Mary. "Rio de Janeiro: From Colonial Town to Imperial Capital (1808–1850)." In *Colonial Cities. Essays on Urbanism in a Colonial Context*, edited by Robert Ross and Gerard J. Telkamp, 123–151. Dordrecht, Netherlands: M. Nijhoff, 1985.

Karasch, Mary. *Slave Life in Rio de Janeiro, 1808–1850*. Princeton: Princeton University Press, 1987.

Kareh, Almir El Chaiban. "Cantando espalharei por toda a parte, Se a tanto me ajudar engenho e arte: Propaganda, técnicas de vendas e consumo no Rio de Janeiro (1850–1870)." *Antropolítica* 21 (2008): 13–49.

Lenharo, Alcir. *As tropas da moderação. O abastecimento da corte na formação política do Brasil, 1808–1842*. Rio de Janeiro: Prefeitura da cidade do Rio de Janeiro, 1992.

Linhares, Maria Yedda Leite. *História do abastecimento; uma problemática em questão (1530–1918)*. Brasília: Edições Binagri, 1979.

Marcondes, Renato Leite. "Formação da rede regional de abastecimento do Rio de Janeiro: a presença dos negociantes de gado (1801–1811)." *Topoi. Revista de História* 2, no. 2 (2001): 41–71.

Meade, Teresa A. *Civilizing Rio: Reform and Resistance in a Brazilian City, 1889–1930*. University Park: Pennsylvania State University, 1997.

Metcalfe, Robyn S. *Meat, Commerce and the City: The London Food Market, 1800–1855*. (Perspectives in Economic and Social History). London: Pickering & Chatto, 2012.

Otter, Chris. "The Vital City: Public Analysis, Dairies and Slaughterhouses in Nineteenth-Century Britain." *Cultural Geographies* 13, no. 4 (2006): 517–537.

Petrone, Maria Theresa Schorer. "O afluxo de gado a Sorocaba e a importância econômica do caminho do sul na década da independência." *Revista de História* 46, no. 94 (1973): 383–404.

Pinto, Fernanda Mousse, "A invenção da Cidade Nova do Rio de Janeiro: agentes, personagens e planos." Master's thesis: Universidade Federal do Rio de Janeiro, 2007.

Rees, Jonathan. *Refrigeration Nation. A History of Ice, Appliances, and Enterprise in America*. Baltimore, MD: The Johns Hopkins University Press, 2013.

Robichaud, Andrew, and Erik Steiner. "Trail of Blood. The Movement of San Francisco's Butchertown and the Spatial Transformation of Meat Production, 1849–1901." *The Spatial History Project*, August 2009. Accessed November 20, 2020. https://web.stanford.edu/group/spatialhistory/cgi–bin/site/pub.php?id=31.

Santos, Francisco Agenor de Noronha. *As freguesias do Rio antigo*, introdução, notas e bibliografia por Paulo Berger. Rio de Janeiro: Edições O Cruzeiro, 1965.

Santos, Kairo da Silva, Raquel Conceição Carvalho, Amanda Biondino Sardella, Alan José Salomão Graça, and Paulo Marcio Leal de Menezes. "*Evolução da paisagem da cidade do Rio de Janeiro, uma visão cartográfica: aspectos socioespaciais a partir do século XIX*." Conference Proceedings. *Anais do V Simpósio Luso-Brasileiro de Cartografia Histórica*. Petrópolis, RJ (2013): 5–12.

Silveira, Patrícia Gomes da. "Análise das atividades econômicas na Cidade Nova (RJ) oitocentista." *Terra Brasilis (Nova Série)* 4 (2015): 1–14. Accessed October 10, 2020. DOI: https://doi.org/10.4000/terrabrasilis.1256.

Summerhill, William R. "Market Intervention in a Backward Economy: Railway Subsidy in Brazil, 1854–1913." *The Economic History Review*, New Series 51, no. 3 (August 1998): 542–568.

Suprinyak, Carlos Eduardo. "Comércio de animais de carga no Brasil imperial: uma análise quantitativa das tropas negociadas nas províncias do Paraná e São Paulo." Master's thesis: Universidade Estadual Paulista, Araraquara, 2006.

Tavares, Georgia da Costa. *A atuação dos marchantes no Rio de Janeiro colonial. Estratégias de mercado e redes de sociabilidade no comércio de abastecimento de carne verde 1763–1808*. Rio de Janeiro: Arquivo geral da cidade do Rio de Janeiro, 2012.

Torres Sánchez, Rafael. "The Failure of the Spanish Crown's Tobacco Tax Monopoly in Catalonia during the Seventeenth Century." Universidad de Navarra, Facultad de Ciencias Económicas y Empresariales, Working paper no. 13/5 (September 2005): 1–25.

Watts, Sydney. "The Grande Boucherie, the 'Right' to Meat, and the Growth of Paris." In *Meat, Modernity, and the Rise of the Slaughterhouse*, edited by Paula Young Lee, 13–26. Durham, NH: University of New Hampshire Press, 2008.

3 Charque for All

Technology, Taste, and Status in Rio de Janeiro (c. 1850–c. 1900)

In 1881, Ina von Binzer traveled from Germany to work as a governess in southeast Brazil. Between that year and 1884, she penned in several letters her experiences in coffee plantations, boarding schools, and wealthy households in Rio de Janeiro and São Paulo. In September, four months after her arrival, she notes

> The Brazilian guest needs no more than a mattress and a wool blanket. He cares not a whit about coziness (not to mention comfort), and the Brazilian host is released from his duties when he gives his guest these basic provisions and lets him partake of his coffee, his black beans, and his dried meat.[1]

Certainly, this was neither Binzer's first encounter with dried meat (*carne seca* or *charque*) nor the last. Like her, foreigners had similar mealtime experiences in Brazil. Collectively, their accounts contradict widespread past and current notions that carne seca was only suitable for the poor and the enslaved. They also reveal that charque was served at almost any dining occasion—in feasts designed to impress as well as in everyday meals—and across the social spectrum.

From the late colonial times until the early 1900s approximately, charque was one of the primary sources of animal protein for *Cariocas* (natives of Rio de Janeiro city). Studies on carne seca output and distribution are abundant and—contrary to those about other subsistence foods—quite thorough.[2] However, little is known about consumption. In discussing charque's commodity network, usually, historians resolve the consumption equation by affirming that it was a staple for the poor and enslaved. Consequently, there has been limited inquiry into charque's place in the eating habits of other social groups. Likewise, because individuals in the lower strata had little or no food choice, charque is deemed an insalubrious and inferior food, incompatible with the elite's taste. Even so, charque continued to be a crucial source of animal protein to all classes of Cariocas far beyond 1888, when slavery was abolished. What is more, before the expansion of the public abattoir, fresh meat was of dubious quality and its supplies unpredictable. Charque, conversely, was abundant and could be stored up to several months. Hospitals, boarding schools, and military outposts all catered using a fair share of carne seca in their commensal meals. While it is true that those individuals could not select their food, there is plenty, although scattered, information that charque was a frequent accompaniment at the table of the gentry as well.

This chapter examines the world of charque consumption from the 1850s to the early 1900s Rio de Janeiro and challenges the assumption that charque was a foodstuff for "unsophisticated" palates. It does so by building upon recent scholarship on foodways and through a close reading of newspaper articles and adverts, cookery books, and postmortem inventories. The first section argues that widespread carne seca consumption was a matter of convenience and habit. The second examines how the medical knowledge of the 1850s and preconceptions about what constituted nutritious food shaped the "ideal diet" discourse of the time. The last one unveils charque's presence in the diet of the affluent Carioca.

Technology: Slave Food, Commensal Food, and Food for the Poor

In an environment with no refrigeration, raw meat must reach the marketplace within hours after the animal slaughtering, as its muscles grow bacteria and mold, and these "metabolize the surface of the meat, discoloring it and producing breakdown products with a foul smell." In tropical regions, where the average temperature varies from 25°C to 30°C, this process accelerates, for "most spoilage organisms ... have their optimum growth temperature within such temperature range." Therefore, without proper preservation control, in those climates "fresh meat has a shelf life of 1 day or less," after which it starts to decompose, and thus is not suitable for human consumption.[3] Before the advent of refrigeration, societies used different techniques to delay meat spoilage. In the Americas, salting was the most popular method utilized until the nineteenth century. Hence, some common names are salted meat or beef, sun-dried meat or beef (*carne de sol*), salt-cured beef, *charque*, *tasajo*, *cecina*, or beef jerky. This work uses the terms, salted meat, salt beef or meat, charque, and carne seca interchangeably, as sources usually do not make any distinction between them.

To sate the Brazilian appetite, charque was produced in the northeast region (where it was known as *carne do Ceará* or *carne de sol*) and in the south (where it was called charque or carne seca) and imported from what the documentation refers to as "La Plata" countries (Argentina and Uruguay). The techniques involved in charque preparation in both regions of Brazil were slightly different; still, lean beef was preferred as it contains less moisture, which reduces decay. During the eighteenth century, the northeast was the leading producing region, particularly in the coastal areas and river mouths, where abundant livestock and the climatic advantages of constant winds and low humidity—and easy access to salt—facilitated the emergence of salted beef-processing plants (*oficinas*). In these oficinas, after killing the animal, workers stripped off its skin and separated flesh from bones; the meat was then cut into quarters. These were soaked in tanks with a brining solution for twenty-four hours and later exposed in trays or suspended in the open to sun dry for one week or more.[4]

Oficinas' markets were in Pernambuco, Bahia, and Rio Grande do Norte, and as far south as Rio de Janeiro and Minas Gerais. To meet such a wide demand, these plants relied on a constant supply of cattle from the northeast's interior. On occasions, they also drew from the local ranches those herds that were destined for urban consumption. Recife, for instance, in the late 1770s witnessed intermittent fresh beef shortages,[5] which authorities in Pernambuco attributed to higher prices that cattle fetched in oficinas than in urban slaughterhouses. Over the last quarter of the eighteenth century and the first of the nineteenth, however, those traditional oficinas lost their position to processing plants in Rio Grande de São Pedro do Sul (later Rio Grande do Sul). The collapse of oficinas was a result of recurrent droughts—which decimated the cattle population—in addition to enormous economic dislocations that followed each event. Sources register quite a few severe droughts in 1777–1779 and 1791–1792; then, in the first decades of the nineteenth century, there were at least four dry periods (1804, 1808–1809, 1816–1817, 1823–1825), each of which resulted in the emigration of landowners, slaves, and livestock to central and southeast Brazil.[6] In 1813, while describing slaves' diet in the Ceará captaincy, the British tradesman Henry Koster summarized the relocation of salted beef-processing plants from north to south Brazil, as follows: "The animal food [of slaves] is generally *carne do Seará* [*sic*],... which comes from Rio Grande do Sul."[7] In 1845–1846, the Ceará province traded a little over 23,000 kilos of charque; in subsequent years, those sales fluctuated dramatically, from 550 kilos in 1847–1848 to none in the next two years. In the early 1850s, available figures reference some recovery, just to register new declines in the following decade.[8]

Despite all of the above data, cattle ranching remained an important economic activity in certain areas of northeast Brazil, in part because of displacements within the region, from the coast to the dry backlands, where, even if the terrain was unsuitable for agriculture, it was—to some degree—appropriate for livestock grazing.[9] Koster, the British traveler, mentioned previously, describes with certain admiration the landscape in this area thusly: "The rapidity of vegetation in Brazil is truly astonishing. Rain in the evening upon good soil will, by sun-rise, have given a greenish tinge to the earth, which is increased, if the rain continues, on the second day, to sprouts of grass of an inch in length; and these on the third day are sufficiently long to be picked up by the half-starved cattle."[10] Ranchers reacted to the mentioned climatic events the best way they could; keenly aware of the droughts' sweeping consequences on their herds, they killed left-over wild animals to prevent them from mixing with superior ones. Others moved farther inland, where they combined livestock raising with cotton production. The latter was cultivated mainly in the arid northeast for export, while the cottonseed supplemented cattle's fodder. The livestock/cotton farm complex provided herds for salted meat production (for local consumption) as well as hides and skins for interprovincial commerce.[11]

In south Brazil, by the mid-1800s, according to detailed accounts from Pelotas (the largest production center in Rio Grande do Sul), charque manufacturing entailed additional steps than those undertaken at oficinas and relied almost entirely on the specialized labor of different groups of slaves. The first group drove the herds from the corrals to the killing floor, a second slaughtered the animals, and yet another skinned and separated their parts. Two highly skilled workers cut the flesh of one animal at a time into large-flat pieces (*mantas*) of approximately 1.5 centimeters thick and 1.5 meters wide. These were transported to a shed where the salting process occurred. The latter entailed, first making parallel incisions in the mantas to help salt penetration and ventilation, and second laying them out in salt beds, stacked against one another. Underneath this pile, a tank collected the drippings turned into the brine, where ribs, tongs, and other trimmings cured. After one or two days, the mantas were placed in the open for drying, which could take up to fifteen days, depending on the weather.[12]

The piles of charque, with no particular packaging (although some accounts referred to charque transported in barrels) were loaded into vessels and shipped to commercial houses, mainly in Rio de Janeiro and the northeast. Other charqueada products, chiefly tallow and leather (manufactured with steam-powered machines) left the plants for national and, occasionally, international markets. Charque reached consumer markets six to twelve months after cattle processing.[13] By the mid-nineteenth century, salt-meat processing plants from Rio Grande do Sul (*charqueadas riograndenses*) achieved what they set out to do: provide a constant supply of animal proteins to urban and rural Brazilians. Although this province could not do so alone, as Chapter 5 reveals.

According to conventional wisdom, charque was a food staple for slaves in Brazil. Not only were they fed with salted meat during the Middle Passage, but also once in American lands, slaves ate carne seca (usually with beans and manioc meal) occasionally or several times over a week, depending on local conditions.[14] Moreover, as the British governess Mary Graham observed in 1820s Rio de Janeiro, charque was also part of the food ration for the poor. Perhaps, "Carne-secca was in much more common use," as John Luccock, Graham's fellow countryman, keenly expressed, because fresh meat was so bad that "nothing but dire necessity

... could induce a person of the least delicacy to taste it." Thus, not even the rich could keep away from charque. Thirty years later, in the same city, the French traveler François Auguste Biard confirmed that salted meat with beans was "the usual dish for poor people and often the higher classes." Abundant anecdotal information signals charque's central place in the Brazilian table across time and ethnic and social lines. In the 1850s, Frenchman Charles Expilly noticed that Indians in the Bahia province ate some sort of salted meat with manioc meal, beans, fried ants, and fish. And it seemed that immigrants had no choice but to incorporate it into their daily meals. In 1859, the governor of Rio de Janeiro reported that European colonists settled in the province had charque as their "ordinary food." The Swiss-American Agassiz couple best summarized the Brazilian relationship with charque and beans; observing the outskirts of Rio de Janeiro province in early 1860 they note, "There is no house so poor that it does not have its beans (*feijões*) [with carne seca], no house so rich as to exclude this homely but most excellent dish, a favorite alike for the high and low [classes]."[15]

These and other sources indicate that Cariocas, regardless of their social standing, consumed salted meat several times a week, if not daily. Although starting in the 1870s, official data show a decline in charque arrivals in Rio de Janeiro (discussed in Chapter 5), by the early 1890s, more than 40,000 metric tons of salted meat entered the city's port.[16] Such estimates are consistent with qualitative sources on Cariocas' eating habits. These data also provide useful information about the broad behavior of this commodity in the urban setting.

Charque was the perfect commensal food. Plantations, military units, hospitals, and boarding schools favored salted meat because of convenience more than price. In 1870, one kilo of charque cost, on average, twice as much as one kilo of beans. Twenty years later the ratio remained similar, although there were important variations on charque pricing according to its origin. In the second half of the nineteenth century, two types of carne seca arrived in Rio. The domestic sort mainly from Rio Grande do Sul and foreign tasajo from "La Plata." At least until the early twentieth century, national charque remained more affordable than the product from Uruguay and Argentina, and even than fresh meat (*carne verde*). However, combined prices for domestic and foreign carne seca were indeed higher than carne verde.[17]

Elevated consumption rates of charque in Rio also related to other attributes of this type of meat. Carne seca supplies—despite the drop in deliveries aforementioned—were predictable.[18] In Brazil, where natural ice was not available and transportation plagued with difficulties, consumers could buy and store large quantities of carne seca. Hence, public institutions (as well as individuals) could better plan routine meals and eventually cope with shortages.[19] In summary, in the face of technological and environmental constraints mentioned previously, charque represented the best alternative to fresh meat.

In rural Rio de Janeiro, contractors used charque allowance as part-payment for wages. In 1860s Petrópolis, freedmen employed in public works received roughly 500 grams of charque daily, except on Sundays and religious holidays. A decade later, criticizing noneconomic incentives for farmworkers, politicians claimed that some received as much as one-third of their wages in carne seca.[20] In urban Rio, salted meat was practically the sole source of animal proteins for asylums, hospitals, and schools; the lower ranks of the army received it as part of their everyday ration as did sailors in the Brazilian navy. In 1858, the newspaper *Brasil Commercial* ran several contractors' announcements seeking freedmen and slave workers, whose daily compensation would be accompanied by meals with manioc meal and carne seca. In the same year, the Santa Isabel Maritime Hospital, the First Cavalry Regiment, and the Imperial School Pedro II announced in the local newspapers that they were accepting bids for food and other supplies. Each included charque in their list of foodstuffs. Judging by one of these postings, not even the Pedro II School students (smartly dressed in fustian vests, ties, and varnished sheepskin shoes) refrained from the common triad of the Brazilian diet: charque, beans, and manioc meal.[21]

An 1890 study on the diet of navy personnel suggested that at sea their ration should include 200 grams of charque three days per week. By the second decade of the twentieth century, charque was still part of the food allocation of other military branches.[22] The inclusion of carne seca in military rations related to its preserving qualities, for acceptable charque could be held in storage for months—imperative in the case of the navy. In addition, such menus convey notions about what an "optimum diet" is thought to be, while reflecting food preferences of rank-and-file; lastly, they are designed to incentivize enlistment.[23] In Brazil, during the transition from the Second Empire (1840–1889) to the First Republic (1889–1930), one could only but wonder if such prospects were realized. Recruitment was difficult; most members enlisted in both the navy and the army, compulsorily or via government-sponsored apprenticeship schools. That in 1910, Cariocas witnessed a major naval uprising (Revolt of the Whip, *Revolta da Chibata*) is only testament to the distance between ideals and tangible actions. Among seamen's grievances, one fellow sailor reckoned, "his comrades revolted [because] food on board was terrible and the abuses unbearable."[24]

Surely, when it came to choices, military men, hospital patients, contract workers, and even boarding school students had little to no control over their diets; therefore, their food intake was not representative and should not be extrapolated to the rest of the society. While public institutions' menus do not correspond to individual diets, they do provide an insight as to the ideal nutritional requirements in a particular historical moment.[25] At the turn of the nineteenth century, although Rio's city council still referred to carne seca as a "foodstuff of primary necessity" alongside bread, rice, and beans, it was apparent that charque was losing its central place in the Carioca plate.[26] Consider, for instance, that in 1895 at Rio's Homeless Shelter (*Asylo de Mendicidade*), the recommended weekly food intake for patients and workers included customary items of the Brazilian diet: rice, beans, sugar, bacon, hominy, bread, coffee, manioc meal, salted cod, 500 grams of charque, and twice the latter amount in carne verde.[27] Not coincidently, in this and other commensal budgets—like the military menus mentioned above—the suggested fresh meat intake was higher than any other food item.

The relocation of salted meat processing plants from north to south Brazil coincided with the preponderance of southeast political elites in the country. After 1808, with the transference of the Portuguese crown to the city of Rio de Janeiro, the local population surged. Cattle, charque, and other food provisions arrived mainly from the provinces of Rio de Janeiro, São Paulo, Minas Gerais, and farther south to supply the new capital of the Portuguese empire.[28] As for fresh meat, by the second half of the nineteenth century, its production and distribution in Rio's urban grid had much improved from the ills travelers described in the early 1800s. Nevertheless, carne verde per capita supplies were still below charque, thus Cariocas continued to rely on salted meat to intake most of their animal protein. However, according to some witnesses, as Rio's dry good stores stocked up with "fashionable foreign food," charque and other "native" foodstuffs started to fall out of favor, particularly with the well-to-do.[29]

Taste: Medical Discourse and Cookery Books

By mid-1800s, there was not a homogeneous voice about the quality and nutritious properties of carne seca. On the contrary, medical journals often decried the meager quantities of it that slaves (in certain plantations of Rio's province) and the militaries received as part of their rations. This pattern changed by the end of the century, when these publications almost invariably characterized carne seca vis-à-vis fresh meat as insalubrious.[30]

Chapter 1 examines several medical theses about Cariocas' eating regimen. It is noteworthy that while some avoid the charque eating topic entirely or tangentially criticize the Brazilian diet of salted meat, beans, and manioc meal, others quote Justus von Liebig's work to validate their propositions. The German chemist contended that after salting, the flesh itself degraded to a "respiratory material." In his words,

> Flesh, by salting, loses in point of nutritive value in consequence of the removal and division … of the salts indispensable to sanguification

> ... Of 3 cwts. of meat, by the full action of salt, 1 cwt. may be rendered useless for the vital process, and converted into an inferior respiratory material.[31]

Alluding to charque and salted cod, the Brazilian physician Antonio Corrêa de Sousa Costa affirms, "the digestibility and the nutritive potency of these substances compared to fresh meat are much lower."[32] That is, charque was deemed a flawed source of animal protein. For reference, contemporary experiments on the Brazilian diet found that for every 100 grams of cooked carne seca and fresh beef the amount of protein is 26.90 and 30 grams, respectively.[33]

Much of the assumption about carne seca's nutritional value was based upon its appearance, preparation method, and alleged primary consumer. Against the mid-nineteenth century backdrop of chemical discoveries, their impact on nutrition knowledge, the increasing correlation between foodways and hygiene, and their importance to public health, charque was less than ideal. Charque's association with slaves, as both their producers and consumers, as well as its processing (perceived as rudimentary) made it a product of a bygone era. In the age of science, charque was antiscience. No wonder public authorities in Brazil interpreted the decline in its consumption alongside beans (*feijoada*)—alluded to in Chapter 1—as a sign of progress.[34]

However, a look into two nineteenth-century cookery books provides a nuanced view on the changing eating habits of Cariocas. The first cookery book published in Brazil in 1840, *Cozinheiro Imperial* (Imperial Cook)—which, according to its editors, aimed at providing up-to-date information on the "culinary sciences"—is based upon a compilation of Portuguese recipes. Although its revised editions included more "authentic" Brazilian dishes (pork and okra stew, for instance) and ingredients (such as manioc meal as a thickening agent), it features several recipes with veal, mutton, lamb, boar, rabbit, turkey, duck, and goose meat, but not a single with charque.[35]

Published perhaps in the 1860s, *Cozinheiro nacional ou coleção das melhores receitas das cozinhas brasileira e européas* (The National Cook or Collection of the Best Recipes of the Brazilian and European Cuisines) had a twofold mission, to "emancipate ... the country from the European tutelage under which it has lived until today" and to reach a broad national and foreign audience. The book assembles Brazilian regional recipes and European ones adapted to autochthonous ingredients. Their editors "employ[ed] a language which, simple in its phrases and word choice, may well reach all ... classes of society."[36] Despite the latter claim, the national readership of *Cozinheiro nacional* was probably a selective one. The book has a chapter on serving and carving etiquette, and a section on suggested kitchen utensils and dinnerware that were geared towards the wealthy class. Nonetheless, *Cozinheiro nacional* shaped a new version of the Brazilian cuisine, which sought to highlight the "regional or ethnic roots" of certain dishes and, by doing so, to elevate their prestige at the national level. It includes a chapter on domestic poultry and several recipes from specific provinces, chiefly from Bahia and Minas Gerais. Finally, contrary to its predecessor, *Cozinheiro nacional* has numerous dishes with Brazilian tubers and roots and quite a few with charque.[37]

In the second half of the nineteenth century, charque moved into the realm of cookbooks alongside feijoada. The latter is an elaborate version of black beans with carne seca and bacon, a common dish in Carioca households since the colonial times. Throughout the nineteenth century, sources reference the presence of feijoada at the Carioca table of rich and poor. Acclaimed as a "national" dish as early as the 1840s, the quality and quantity of the ingredients added to feijoada transformed it into a sophisticated food.[38] Nevertheless, invariably feijoada was reserved for special occasions. For instance, in Rio, it was served at samba festivities (*batucadas*) of poor neighborhoods of the 1830s and in banquets and dinner parties of the 1880s.[39] As feijoada entered nineteenth-century cookbooks, the upper class recast carne seca as a special item, fitting it into their dining practices. Charque was not only the main source of animal proteins for the enslaved and the poor, but also an everyday fare in wealthy households. This reflected long-standing eating habits and preferences across the Carioca social spectrum. The next section discusses the place of charque at the tables of the well off.

Status: Charque with Beans, "The Usual Dish for Poor People and Often the Higher Classes"

A glimpse at the food expenses of José Gomes de Oliveira e Silva—a Carioca whose death in May 1870 triggered the compilation of his assets in a richly documented postmortem estate inventory (*inventário*)—reveals that from mid-1867 to January 1868, his family spent approximately 150 *mil-réis* (or US$ 80.00) at the "Neves & Rodrigues" dry good store (*secos e molhados*).[40] In July 1867, they bought manioc meal, brown sugar, beans, manioc starch (*polvilho*), rice, bacon, and carne seca. In the ensuing months, in addition to various quantities of the items cited earlier, the dry good store delivered corn, coffee, onions, and lard to the Silva family. Together, in the seven-month period covered in this record, they acquired more than 100 kilos in charque.[41] In Brazil, where household ledgers, diaries, and letters were rare, inventários provide detailed information about the quotidian affairs of large segments of the Brazilian society, from landowners, big and small-slaveholders, and street vendors, to shopkeepers, and artisans. This documentation includes evidence about real estate and other possessions of the decedent such as slaves, furniture, books, and clothing. As it was a common practice to buy on credit, some inventários contain lists of foodstuffs (purchased at secos e molhados, bakeries, and butcher shops) and sundry goods (coal, candle, soap, for instance), which the decedent's executor was to settle.[42]

It is important to stress that of over 300 hundred inventories (from 1870 to 1900) consulted at the National Archive in Rio de Janeiro, only approximately a dozen contained invoices, receipts, or lists of assets including foodstuffs. While one could argue that these are few and skewed samples, the fact remains that these documents, as opposed to cookery books for instance, "reveal what was actually eaten."[43] Turning to José, his wife, Justiniana Rosa Gomes de Oliveira, and her stepson, admittedly, one does not know how much of the food items mentioned above they partook of. But neither can one ascertain that the carne seca acquired in this household (or any other, for that matter), only fed their two elderly slaves. Furthermore, when examining food expenses from a diverse poll of inventários (of foreigners, Brazilians, married and single decedents), one finds that charque buying along with manioc meal and beans, emerge as a recurring expenditure over time and across the Carioca social spectrum.

Consider the profile of João Conrado Harster, a German traveling salesman of precious stones and jewels, who died in 1870. The decedent did not possess a house in Rio de Janeiro, but when in the Corte—as Rio's municipality was called—shared one with Anna Jacintha Pereira de Andrade, with whom he fathered two children, Maria Harster and João Conrado Harster. Enclosed in Harster's inventário an invoice from the dry good store, "Joaquim Duarte Estrella," shows that his food purchases mirror those of the Silva family, except for a few wine bottles that he acquired almost daily in early 1870.[44]

Twenty years later, several inventários reveal similar foodstuff spending patterns— perhaps, expenses at dry good stores show more variety—while others include bakery and butcher shop purchases.[45] Examples abound. It is not my intention to extrapolate either the quantity or the frequency of these expenses; however, judging by these accounts, plenty of evidence suggests that upper and middle class Cariocas bought imported wine, cheese, and olive oil alongside beans, rice, manioc meal, and charque. Such was the case of Manoel José Simões, a Portuguese immigrant whose real estate wealth, at the time of his death in 1891, comprised seven houses located north of Rio's city center.[46] He, as other decedents with comparable fortunes, had similar food-spending patterns; acquiring at their local dry good stores a variation of the above listed goods.

In such a scenario, it was only natural that secos e molhados would market special-occasion food (associated with high-ranking individuals) as well as quotidian food. The "José Alves Moreira" store, situated at Travessa do Rosario, offered both types of merchandise to its customers. Its shelves carried a diverse selection of wine and spirits; foreign and national beer; jars of imported jam and capers; Portuguese compotes and olive oil; cans of oysters, sardines, and olives; and French mustard, all alongside carne seca, black beans, and manioc meal.[47] This eclectic selection reflects food habits of late nineteenth-century well-to-do Cariocas. This section suggests that the customer who could afford imported delicacies chose to buy carne seca, perhaps as a substitute for fresh meat or as an ingredient in traditional Brazilian dishes. It was a choice based on prevailing taste.

Louis Couty, French biology professor at the Instituto Politécnico of Rio de Janeiro, published in 1880 what is probably one of the best accounts on charque production and consumption in late nineteenth-century Brazil. Invited by the emperor Pedro II to study national vegetable and animal endowments, Couty traveled to south Brazil, crossing to Argentina and Uruguay to examine yerba mate and charque production. Apart from detailed information on meat-processing techniques, Couty provides keen observations on charque consumption. Contradicting his contemporaries, who insisted that charque was a food for slaves and the poor, he affirms,

> I [do not] believe, as [other] authors ..., [in] the disappearance of saladeiros and carne seca ... when there will be no more slaves in Cuba and Brazil. [T]he eating of carne seca is widespread ... [and] far from being reserved for the poor, this foodstuff is more expensive than fresh meat ... in many regions.[48]

Indeed, it is likely that greater distance from ports made charque less affordable than fresh meat. Therefore, in rural areas, as Couty suggests, "The truth so strange it may seem is that carne seca is mainly eaten by the well-off ... [because] peasants, hicks, and freedmen are too poor ... to consume food as expensive."[49] In 1898, in the city of São Paulo, for instance, the wholesale price for carne verde in the slaughterhouse was 600–700 *réis* (or US$.08) per kilo, while carne seca in the municipal market cost approximately twice that amount.[50] In Rio de Janeiro, as Couty points out in a different study, "carne seca is the most important ... meat consumed by the free population, [it is the] basic food for the craftsman ... [and it is] often eaten several times a week at other tables [even at the wealthy's]."[51] Touching upon the eating habits of the affluent, Couty comments that although carne seca was the basic ingredient for feijoada,

> The prejudices created for the most part by Europeans are such that many people will refuse any quality to a food, which they use often, and [it] is ... very rare that one would serve feijoada to guests. Yet this feijoada is definitely superior to many European dishes poorly imitated. From this viewpoint, ... we can only advise the people of the South to defend their products better, to be themselves and not to sacrifice so readily to the ideas and prejudices of places under different conditions.[52]

The Brazilian government commissioned Couty's research and writings with a goal to promote the country's autochthonous goods (including charque) in Europe, but this and other earlier campaigns did not render the expected results. The French physiologist promised to conduct experiments in his laboratory at the National Museum of Rio de Janeiro, whereby he would feed dogs with charque, meat extract, and carne verde. The goal was to measure the animals' weight daily, ascertaining how they reacted to each type of meat. Couty was confident that through this procedure (which his counterparts in Europe had employed to assess the nutritious value of foodstuffs), he would "arrive at precise conclusions" as to the qualities of these meats. He also planned to send charque samples to soldiers in France to test its acceptability in Europe. Apparently, the French physiologist never conducted these studies—he died prematurely in Rio in 1884—but his first impressions were that charque (at its technological stage) was a food well suited for Brazilians, who were accustomed to it, but not to Europeans. If anything, Couty proposed that in the short-term charque had to improve its color, packaging, and pricing. In the long term, its manufacturers would have to abandon processing based on empirical knowledge and embrace "industrial and scientific preparation."[53]

Contemporary observers shared Couty's assessment that charque's preparation was rather rudimentary. By contrast, consider how the nineteenth-century scientific community discussed a new "meat product," the Liebig's Extract of Meat, whose factory in Fray Bentos (Uruguay) Couty visited. Liebig, mentioned above, was not the first who attempted to create a "beef tea;" but his version—"a thick, dark brown liquid with a powerful beef aroma"—was certainly the most successfully marketed.[54] Its manufacturing entailed a multistep process, requiring "no small amount of labour and machinery." Twenty-four hours after slaughter, the animal's flesh was mechanically minced and evaporated until it converted into pulp. The latter was immersed in large containers with water and steamed over; after one hour, the substance was drained in a colander-like apparatus and its fat removed. The resulting "pure gravy" was steamed once again, this time for approximately eight hours until it reduced into a paste.[55] Liebig described it as "nothing but solid beef-tea—that is, beef-tea from which the water has been evaporated."[56] By 1864, over 1,500 pounds of the Uruguayan manufactured extract arrived in Europe monthly.[57]

Initially, the meat extract was popularized on account of its purported medicinal attributes. The molasses-like liquid, dissolved in water, transformed into an easy-to-digest broth, given to convalescents. Nevertheless, in an 1865 letter to the editor of *The Lancet,* Liebig suggested that because no preservation method available was capable of conserving all meat's nutritious components, the extract was an adequate substitute, particularly for populations that could not afford fresh meat. In the same document, Liebig responds to his detractors, who asserted that the extract had "no nutritive value whatever" and to those who claimed that it could replace meat, upholding that "the truth, as is always the case, lies in the middle."[58] Nineteenth-century scientific journals carried on this debate, publishing results of experiments with the extract (as well as with counterfeit versions and competitors), experts' assessments, and the public's impressions. In 1870, the journal *Scientific American* circulated the accounts of Mr. W. T. Suffolk, a British traveler who described his preferred way to intake the meat extract as "dissolved in hot water as soup." In the absence of hot water, Mr. Suffolk suggests,

> It may be thinly spread upon bread or biscuit and eaten with equal effect. In either way, it gives strength almost immediately, and stands very much in the same relation to ordinary food that petroleum does to coal as a steam-producing fuel, enabling power to be speedily obtained.[59]

Regarding this tonic, health benefits were widely disputed. In 1874, the Borough Hall of Bradford (approximately 200 miles north of London) fined Mr. John Knight, a meat extract seller, for making extravagant claims about its medicinal properties. After an analysis of its contents, Mr. Harris Butterfield, a medical officer of health, declared that the product was, "in his opinion … injurious to health."[60]

These sources reveal the contention between the scientific and lay communities over Liebig's product. Nevertheless, as it fell out of favor with experts, the company attenuated its nutritive claims and turned to cookery. It conducted a worldwide marketing campaign from the mid-nineteenth century onward, publishing cookbooks in Western Europe, Australia, and the Americas—the United States edition is entitled *One Hundred Ways to Use Liebig Company's Extract of Beef A Guide for American Housewives*—and distributing collectible trading cards. Vendors of the extract presented their customers with colorful chromes illustrated with various motifs. In their background are depictions of humankind achievements, quotidian scenes from all corners of the world, portraits of renowned artists and scientists, and representations of historical events. In the front, on the right or left corners, there is a rather large (relative to its backdrop) drawing of the extract's white jar. Captions at the card's top and bottom identify the contextual image and on occasions the extract with the slogan, "The true meat extract Liebig." Scholar Cecilia Molinari de Rennie, who studied the *Inventions of the 19th Century* card-set (a group of six chromes with drawings of technological innovations as the framework and goddess-like women in the front), argues that these images strategically convey notions about progress and industrialization legitimized by neoclassical "symbols of wisdom." They develop a narrative by which the extract was yet another invention of the nineteenth century (alongside the telephone and the telegraph, for instance) within reach of all.[61]

In such a context, no doubt charque represented an antitechnology, unwholesome food. The contrast could not be sharper. Travelers who visited South American meat-processing plants usually stopped at both charqueadas and the facility at Fray Bentos, stressing the technical processes required in the extract's fabrication and the gruesome preparation of carne seca.

> There is something revolting and at the same time captivating in these great charqueadas; [states Herbert H. Smith, a naturalist from the United States who visited Brazil in the 1880s] slaves, half-naked dripping blood; the animals that fight, the floors and gutters running red, the overseer watching over sixty killings per hour ... all combine to form a painting as strange and horrid as can fit into the imagination.[62]

In addition to the imagery associated with the preparation and presentation of charque and the extract, there were also considerations about their nourishing properties. Thomas J. Hutchinson, British consul in Rosario (Argentina) in the 1860s, cited the aforementioned Liebig's study to determine that meat lost 1/3 of its nutritious value with salt.[63] While Liebig affirmed,

> Salted meat but inadequately replaces fresh meat, because in the process of salting a large quantity of the extractive principles of the meat are lost; besides, it is well known that those who live on salt meat for a continuance become subject to different diseases. Dried meat generally means tainted meat scarcely eatable. Extractum Carnis, combined with vegetable albumen, enable us to make up the deficiency; and that combination is the only one at our disposal.[64]

Although by the late nineteenth century most of these claims had been debunked, the meat extract endured as a product of industrialization, an example of scientific cooking. It was most popular in middle-class European households, despite its price.[65] Charque, on the other hand, remained a staple for the poor, as it was the sole source of animal proteins in Brazil's interior, particularly in areas beyond the reach of municipal abattoirs or meatpacking companies (later)—which is to say, the majority of the country, well into the twentieth century. I would argue that this state of affairs, along with charque's failure to find a consumer market in Europe inform past and current views about this meat.

Foreign travelers who visited Brazil during the nineteenth century invariably had some experience with charque eating. Through their writings, we learn that salted meat was a daily food in wealthy households, and that they expressed a range of opinions about this meat. Herbert H.

Smith, for instance, observes that although some foreigners had labeled charque as "rotten and disgusting ..., almost everyone bores it at first, but with a little experience comes the disposition to like it ... It really is a nutritional and tasty [food] when properly prepared." [66] Others were less pliable, like this anonymous author, who relays to potential immigrants to Brazil a provocative picture of it and its consumers, "A man ought not to be obliged to eat carne secca [*sic*] unless he has committed some crime."[67] Judgments such as this carry on implications of taste (frequently charque is described as unsavory, rancid, and dark), but also of status.

As historian Paul S. Lloyd asserts, "Foodways were as much an identity marker as the clothes one wore or the houses one lived in."[68] According to a "racialized" eating/production view, charque was essential to slaves' lives, not only as a staple in their diet but also because they were responsible for its preparation. As one witness put it, "Charque is easy to manipulate, but ... [it entails] hard work, which is appropriate to the intelligence of slaves, the only ones who can bear such heavy labor."[69] Nevertheless, given charque's versatility, gentry and poor had a taste for it, even if for the higher classes it was an "accompaniment," part of the morning or evening food, while for the lower classes it was their sole source of animal protein.[70] The point at issue here is that whereas slaughterhouses were moving from the public view (as Chapter 2 studies), the carne seca chain connected directly to slaves (as producers and consumers). Therefore, to affirm that middle and upper Cariocas savored a charque dish is to blur the line that separates "good" from "bad" taste, and thus rigid hierarchies. Or, as one commentator (in light of the charque price hike in 1886), bluntly put it, "Carne seca avenges its shameful past, it is departing from the slave quarters (*senzalas*) to the palaces, it is no longer the food of the plantations but the ambrosia of the gods."[71]

The assertion that charque was only part of slaves' diet seems to support the conclusion that the decline of the salt-meat industry was ultimately a matter of preference. First, once slavery was abolished, its consumer market "disappeared" and, second, because Europeans' taste was incompatible with such a primitive product.[72] Despite efforts that charque-exporting countries made to find new markets for their product, Europeans, for instance, had rejected salted meat; therefore (some claimed), those who migrated to the Americas followed suit.[73] Such assumptions were definitely in the minds of some policymakers, as they asserted that low salaries, poor education, and, above all, lack of "food worthy of its name" were hindering the prosperity of the Brazilian and foreign proletariat. To right this wrong, in 1889, the newspaper *A Immigração* (The Immigration) recommended to "do whatever it is possible to provide immigrants with their home countries' food," or at least substitute black beans with white ones, as it was (allegedly) done so successfully in the United States westward expansion.[74]

The claim that "refined" people (including immigrants) rejected charque seemed to be based on a rather freighted concept, one that connects the "ideal being" to the "ideal diet."[75] The first one proclaims the superiority of Western features and the second places fresh meat in the center of the meal. There is no documented evidence, one, that immigrants excluded charque from their meals and, two, that rich Cariocas did not partake it.[76] Hence, the contention that charque was only on the plates of slaves and the poor is grounded in status. Likewise, there is plenty (though scattered) evidence that carne seca was on the tables of diverse segments of the Carioca society, including the better-off. The inventários mentioned above reveal as much. In those households, for example, servants prepared with regularity black beans with salted meat—"the favorite accompaniment to any meal."[77] Other sources show its presence in quotidian affairs of the Carioca society. In the early 1880s, the special menu of the *Hotel Bahiano* consisted of "the famous" black bean stew (*feijoada*) and carne seca from Bahia. By the end of the decade, the daily *Gazeta de Notícias* advertised, to possibly few buyers, Spanish knives from Toledo suitable for slicing charque.[78]

There should be no exaggeration; it is clear that, for some, carne seca was their only source of animal proteins while others could choose to have it. This was true in the mid-nineteenth century, as it was in the early twentieth century, as Chapter 5 discusses. A glance at the food intake of free workers in late 1850s Rio de Janeiro corroborates this assertion. In 1856, due to salted meat price increase, fresh meat consumption increased. After 1860, because of anti-inflationary measures, charque offerings returned to normalcy, as did consumption rates.[79] The argument put forth is that until late nineteenth century, charque remained an essential part of the daily fare for destitute and gentry Cariocas. Although in high-end households, it probably changed its status because of preparation and serving environment.

* * *

Because slaves were the primary consumers of charque, historians have treated this processed meat as a unique good, depriving it of a reasonable framework, at least on the consumption end of the commodity chain. This has had several implications. First, in the area of taste, thanks to widespread notions that slaves had meager diets (to be sure, there is plenty of information that the calorie intake of some was insufficient), charque was depicted as an unappetizing and unhealthy food. Despite numerous works that questioned the deprivation picture, traditional views remain. That the poor were the other targeted consumer group only confirmed the "low quality" stigma associated with carne seca. In the same vein, scholars have relied on vivid descriptions by foreign travelers, drawing far-reaching conclusions based on their unpleasant encounters with charque. Although some who visited Brazil made a habit of eating charque and even expressed that it was a better product than that given to soldiers in Europe, these descriptions were cast aside.

Second, in the area of production, if charque was, in fact, a mediocre alternative for beef, cattle used for its processing was of less quality than those channeled to meatpacking or canning plants. Although there is some truth to this assertion, the raw material for tinned meat or the beef extract, for instance, was the same that entered charqueadas. Third, this work argues that because charque did not find a market in Europe—for, in part, it competed with imported frozen and chilled meat, which were certainly better products—underlying the assumptions above, there existed a reputation factor. However, charque crossed all diet and table boundaries in nineteenth-century Rio, most of all as the essential ingredient of feijoada, the Brazilian national dish. Finally, the last element correlates with other factors that shaped Rio's meat market in the late nineteenth century. The decline of charque offerings in Brazil's capital coincided with the strengthening of the municipal abattoir system, thereby with improvement in carne verde supplies. The next chapter focuses on animal husbandry and transportation advances in late nineteenth-century Brazil.

Notes

1 Ina von Binzer, *Os meus romanos: Alegrias e tristezas de uma educadora alemã no Brasil* (São Paulo: Editora Paz e Terra, 2004), 58–59. Linda Lewin will publish a translation of this book into English, *The Joys and Disappointments of a German Governess in Imperial Brazil,* by Ina von Binzer, edited with an introduction by Linda Lewin (Notre Dame, IN: University of Notre Dame Press, 2021). I thank her for sharing this reference.

2 Andrew Sluyter points out that scholars have also overlooked the charque exchange in the Atlantic. His article represents a valuable contribution to the topic, which focuses on the trade between Argentina and Cuba. Andrew Sluyter, "The Hispanic Atlantic's Tasajo Trail," *Latin American Research Review* 45, no. 1 (2010): 98–120.

3 Alan Davidson, *The Oxford Companion to Food* (Oxford: New York: Oxford University Press, 2006), 507; Olusegun A. Olaoye and Iniobong G. Ntuen, "Spoilage and Preservation of Meat: A General Appraisal and Potential of Lactic Acid Bacteria as Biological Preservatives," *International Research Journal of Biotechnology* 2, no. 1 (February 2011): 033–034.

4 Renato Braga, "Um capítulo esquecido da economia pastoril do nordeste," *Revista do Instituto do Ceará, Fortaleza* 61 (1947): 150–51; Leonardo Cândido Rolim, "'Tempo das carnes' no Siará Grande: o mercado das carnes secas na Vila do Aracati (1710–1793)," *Sæculum. Revista de Historia* 29 (2013): 15.

5 Ibid., 151–52; Ibid., 18–20.

6 *Relatório apresentado á Assembléa Legislativa Provincial do Ceará pelo excellentissimo senhor dr. José Bento da Cunha Figueiredo Junior, por occasião da installação da mesma Assembléa no dia 1o de outubro de 1862* (San Luiz: Typ. de B. de Mattos, 1863), 50; Maria Yedda Leite Linhares, *História do abastecimento; uma problemática em questão (1530–1918)* (Brasília: Edições Binagri, 1979), 44–51; Almir Leal de Oliveira, "O comércio das carnes secas do Ceará na segunda metade do século XVIII: as dinâmicas

do mercado colonial," in *Consumo e abastecimento na história*, ed. Maria-Aparecida Lopes, Margarida Maria de Carvalho, and Denise Aparecida Soares Moura (São Paulo: Editora Alameda, 2011), 173–78; Friedrich W. Freise, "The Drought Region of Northeastern Brazil," *Geographical Review* 28, no. 3 (July 1938): 363–78; Ildefonso Albano, *A pecuária no Ceará: notas offerecidas à Primeira Conferencia de Pecuária, organizada no Rio de Janeiro em maio de 1917 pela Sociedade Nacional de Agricultura sob os auspícios do Ministério da Agricultura* (Rio de Janeiro: Imprensa Nacional, 1918), 42.

7 Henry Koster, *Travels in Brazil* (London: Longman, Hurst, Rees, Orme, and Brown, 1816), 432.

8 Albano, *A pecuária no Ceará,* 46–50.

9 Gerald Michael Greenfield, "The Realities of Images: Imperial Brazil and the Great Drought, *Transactions of the American Philosophical Society* 91, no. 1 (2001): 28–29; Albano, *A pecuária no Ceará,* 54.

10 Koster, *Travels in Brazil*, 132.

11 Ibid., 149; Freise, "The Drought," 373; Luiz Cordelio Barbosa, "Cotton in 19th Century Brazil: Dependency and Development" (PhD diss., University of Washington, 1989), 7–10; Thales A. Zamberlan Pereira, "The Rise of the Cotton Trade in Brazil during the Industrial Revolution," (working paper series, N° 2016–09, Department of Economics-FEA/USP, 2016): 5–12.

12 Herbert H. Smith and Karl von den Steinen, *Do Rio de Janeiro a Cuyabá; notas de um naturalista* (São Paulo: Companhia Melhoramentos de São Paulo, 1922), 139–40; Louis Couty, *Le maté et les conserves de viande. Rapport à son excellence monsieur le ministre de l'agriculture et du commerce par le Dr. Louis Couty sur sa mission dans les provinces du Parana, Rio Grande et les États du Sud* (Rio de Janeiro: Typographia Nacional, 1880), 92–107; Jonas M. Vargas, *Os barões do charque e suas fortunas. Um estudo sobre as elites regionais brasleiras a partir de uma análise dos charqueadores de Pelotas* (São Leopoldo, RGS: Oikos Editora, 2016), 95–100.

13 Couty, *Le maté,* 106–7; Stephen Bell, *Campanha Gaúcha: A Brazilian Ranching System, 1850–1920* (Stanford, CA: Stanford University Press, 1998), 70; Vargas, *Os barões do charque*, 101.

14 Oliveira, "O comércio," 178.

15 Maria Graham, *Diário de uma viagem ao Brasil e de uma estada neste país durante parte dos anos 1821, 1822 e 1823* (São Paulo: Companhia editora nacional, 1956), 138; John Luccock, *Notes on Rio de Janeiro and Southern Parts of Brazil, Taken During a Residence of Ten Years in that Country from 1808 to 1818* (London: Printed for Samuel Leigh, 1820), 43; François Auguste Biard, *Dois anos no Brasil* (São Paulo: Companhia editora nacional, 1945), 43; Charles Expilly, *Mulheres e costumes no Brasil* (São Paulo: Companhia editora nacional, 1935), 206; *Relatório do presidente da província do Rio de Janeiro, João de Almeida Pereira* (Nictheroy: Typographya da Patria, de Mora & Miranda, 1859), 27; Louis Agassiz and Elizabeth Agassiz, *A Journey in Brazil* (Boston: The Riverside Press, 1979), 73.

16 Jornal do Commercio, *Retrospecto Commercial do[s] ano[s] 1869–1892* (Rio de Janeiro: Typographia do "Jornal do Commercio," de Rodrigues & C., 1870–1893).

17 Louis Couty, "L'alimentation au Brésil et dan les pays voisins," *Revue d'hygiène et de police sanitaire*, no. 3 (1881): 190.

18 Newspapers in Rio consistently reported on the municipality's efforts to buy cattle as an emergency measure to lower fresh meat prices in the urban market. "Carnes verdes," *Jornal do Commercio*, April 18, 1878; Arquivo Nacional do Rio de Janeiro (hereafter ANRJ), "Inventory of João Conrado Harster, 1870," box 3632, n. 4; ANRJ, "Inventory of Manoel José Simões, 1890," box 3638, n. 21.

19 Mary C. Karasch, *Slave Life in Rio de Janeiro, 1808–1850* (Princeton: Princeton University Press, 1987), 141.
20 *A Pátria. Folha da Província do Rio de Janeiro*, January 12, 1864; *A Pátria* (Echo da Nação) April 5, 1861; *Gazeta de Notícias*, July 30, 1877; Afonso de Alencastro Graça Filho, "Os convênios da carestia: crises, organização e investimentos do comércio de subsistência da Corte (1850–1880)" (master's thesis, Universidade Federal do Rio de Janeiro, 1992), 23–28.
21 *Brasil Commercial*, May 7, 1858; June 13, 1858; July 22, 1858.
22 Sílvia Capanema P. de Almeida, "Corpo, saúde e alimentação na Marinha de Guerra brasileira no período pós-abolição, 1890–1910," *História, Ciências, Saúde - Manguinhos* 19, supl. 1 (2012): 21; *O Pharol*, June 21, 1918.
23 Rachel Duffett, *The Stomach for Fighting: Food and the Soldiers of the Great War* (Manchester: Manchester University Press, 2015), 76–77.
24 *Correio da Manhã*, November 23, 1910; Joseph Love, *The Revolt of the Whip* (Stanford, CA: Stanford University Press, 2012), 21, 22–33. Along with these two demands, sailors threatened to bomb Rio, for higher wages, better working conditions, and in more broad terms, for respect to their "citizen-sailors' rights." Love identifies the latter as a "maximum aspiration" of "lower-class sailors, the majority of them Afro-Brazilians." 30–34, 85, 105.
25 Paul S. Lloyd, *Food and Identity in England, 1540–1640: Eating to Impress* (London: Bloomsbury Academic, 2015), 38–40; Enriqueta Quiroz, *El consumo como problema histórico. Propuestas y debates entre Europa e Hispanoamérica* (México: Instituto de Investigaciones Dr. José María Luis Mora, 2006), 46–47.
26 Alvarenga Fonseca, org., *Collecção de Leis Municipaes e Vetos do primeiro semestre de 1900*, vol. 7, Decreto n. 207 de 12 de junho de 1900, "Providencia sobre as repartições municipais" (Rio de Janeiro: Typographia do Jornal do Commercio, de Rodrigues & C., 1900), 131.
27 Alvarenga Fonseca, org., *Collecção de Leis Municipaes e Vetos de 1895 – 1896*, vol. 2, Decreto 38A de 17 de Dezembro de 1895, "Do regulamento para o asylo de mendicidade" (Rio de Janeiro: Typographia do Jornal do Commercio, de Rodrigues & C., 1897), 340–42.
28 Alcir Lenharo, *As tropas da moderação: o abastecimento da Corte na formação política do Brasil* (Rio de Janeiro: Prefeitura da cidade do Rio de Janeiro, 1992), 33–35.
29 José Maria Rodrigues Regadas, "Do regimen das classes abastadas do Rio de Janeiro em seus alimentos e bebidas. Mudanças que nele se tem operado nos últimos quarenta anos. Efeitos do regimen antigo: influência do atual" (medical thesis, Faculdade de Medicina do Rio de Janeiro, Rio de Janeiro: Typographia Imperial e Constitucional de J. Villeneuve e Comp., 1852), 22.
30 "Epidemia reinante," *Annaes da Academia de Medicina: Publicações Periodicas da Academia Imperial de Medicina* 7, no. 2 (1851): 54; "Projeto de resposta a consulta do governo acerca das origem das enfermidades que afligem os aprendizes menores do arsenal da guerra," *Annaes Brasilienses de Medicina. Jornal da Academia Imperial de Medicina do Rio de Janeiro* 7, no. 7 (1852): 206–09.
31 Justus von Liebig, "Letter XXXII," *Familiar Letters on Chemistry: In Its Relations to Physiology, Dietetics, Agriculture, Commerce, and Political Economy* (London: Walton and Maberly, 1859), 448.
32 Antonio Corrêa de Sousa Costa, "Qual a alimentação de que usa a classe pobre no Rio de Janeiro e sua influência sobre a mesma" (medical thesis, Faculdade de Medicina do Rio de Janeiro, Rio de Janeiro: Typographia Perseverança, 1865), 35. See also Francisco Fernandes Padilha, "Qual o regimen alimentar dos pobres no Rio de Janeiro? Que molestias mas commumente grasão

entre ellas? Que relações de causalidade se encontrão entre esse regimen e molestias?" (medical thesis, Faculdade de Medicina do Rio de Janeiro, Rio de Janeiro: Typographia Universal de Laemmert, 1853), 14.

33 Brasil, *Pesquisa de orçamentos familiares, 2008–2009. Tabelas de composição nutricional dos alimentos consumidos no Brasil* (Rio de Janeiro: Instituto Brasileiro de Geografia e Estatística, 2011), Tabela 1, Energia, macronutrientes e fibra na composição de alimentos por 100 gramas de parte comestível.

34 On the ideal diet see Deborah Neill, "Finding the 'Ideal Diet': Nutrition, Culture, and Dietary Practices in France and French Equatorial Africa, c. 1890s to 1920s," *Food and Foodways* 17, no. 1 (2009): 3–6; Thales A. Zemberlan Pereira, "Was it Uruguay or Coffee? The Causes of the Beef Jerky Industry's decline in Southern Brazil (1850 – 1889)," *Nova Economia* 26, no. 1 (2016): 17; Cristiana Loureiro de Mendonça Couto, "Alimentação no Brasil Imperial: elementos para um estudo de questões dietéticas, químico-médicas e da fisiologia do gosto" (PhD diss., Pontifícia Universidade Católica de São Paulo, 2011), 192.

35 *Cozinheiro imperial ou nova arte do cozinheiro e do copeiro em todos os seus ramos* (Rio de Janeiro: Laemmert 7 C., 1887); Tim Wätzold, *Proclamação da cozinha brasileira como parte do processo de formação da identidade nacional no Império Brasileiro, 1822–1889* (Belo Horizonte: Editora e Gráfica TCS, 2012), 217–40; Cristiana Loureiro de Mendonça Couto, "The Chemistry of Diet: Medicine, Nutrition, and Staple Foods in Imperial Brazil," *Ambix* 62, no. 4 (2015): 359–60; Couto, "Alimentação no Brasil," 145–54.

36 *Cozinheiro nacional, ou coleção das melhores receitas das cozinhas brasileira e europeas* (Rio de Janeiro: Livraria Garnier, n/d), 2–5.

37 Arjun Appadurai, "How to Make a National Cuisine: Cookbooks in Contemporary India," *Comparative Studies in Society and History* 30, no. 1 (1988): 5; Jeffrey M. Pilcher, *¡Que Vivan Los Tamales!: Food and the Making of Mexican Identity* (Albuquerque: University of New Mexico Press, 1998), 48–81; Wätzold, *Proclamação da cozinha brasileira,* 252–72.

38 There is not a single recipe for feijoada, over the nineteenth century the available recipes ask for the inclusion of some or all of the following items: pork loin, pig head, offal, cow's feet, tongue, ham, and sausages. Almir Chaiban El-Kareh, *A vitória da feijoada* (Niterói, RJ: EDUFF, 2012), 117–39.

39 *Gazeta da Tarde*, October 21, 1880; Paul S. Lloyd, "The Changing Status of Offal: A Fashionable Food in England Between 1545 and 1655," *Food, Culture and Society: An International Journal of Multidisciplinary Research* 15, no. 1 (2012): 61–75; Ariza Maria Rocha, "A feijoada no Brasil e o bacalhau em Portugal: a construção da comida como identidade nacional," *Mneme Revista de Humanidades* 15, no. 35 (2014): 235–38.

40 Put into perspective, that quantity amounted to 25 linen pants, 6 table clocks, or the monthly wage of a Captain in the Brazilian army in 1873. John Schulz, *The Financial Crisis of Abolition* (New Haven: Yale University Press, 2008), 135. Converted to U.S. dollars according to Heitor Pinto Moura Filho's study, "Exchange rates of the mil-réis (1795–1913)," *MPRA Paper No. 5210,* University Library of Munich, Germany, (2006): 14–17, accessed November 22, 2020. http://mpra.ub.uni–muenchen.de/5210/.

41 ANRJ, "Inventory of José Gomes de Oliveira, 1870," box 4168, n. 2001.

42 For a description of inventários' structure, see Zephyr Frank, *Dutra's World. Wealth and Family in Nineteenth-Century Rio de Janeiro* (Albuquerque: University of New Mexico Press, 2004) 127–31.

43 Paul S. Lloyd, "Nutritious Foods and Consumption Choices in the Early Modern Period," *Social History of Medicine* 24, no.1 (2011): 163.

44 ANRJ, "Inventory of João Conrado Harster, 1870," box 3642, n. 4.

45 ANRJ, "Inventory of Antônio Joaquim de Araújo Torres, 1890," n. 3247, maço 366; ANRJ, "Inventory of Jacinta Maria da Silva Cunha, 1890," box 3630, n. 19.
46 ANRJ, "Inventory of Manoel José Simões, 1890," box 3638, n. 21.
47 ANRJ, "Inventory of José Alves Moreira, 1890," box 4117, n. 2216.
48 Couty, *Le maté,* 220.
49 Ibid., 200; Luis da Câmara Cascudo, *História da alimentação no Brasil*, vol. 2 (Belo Horizonte: Itatiaia, 1983), 442.
50 *Lavoura e Commercio*, June 23, 1898. Converted to U.S. dollars according to Filho, "Exchange rates," 14–17, accessed November 22, 2020. http://mpra.ub.uni–muenchen.de/5210/.
51 Couty, "L'alimentation au Brésil," 190–91.
52 Ibid., 191.
53 Couty, *Le maté,* 139, 151, 237.
54 M. R. Finlay, "Quackery and Cookery: Justus Von Liebig's Extract of Meat and the Theory of Nutrition in the Victorian Age," *Bulletin of the History of Medicine* 66, no. 3 (1992): 404.
55 Thomas J. Hutchinson, *The Paraná; with Incidents of the Paraguayan War, and South* American *Recollections, from 1861–1868* (London: E. Stanford, 1868), 228–29.
56 Justus von Liebig, "On the Nutritive Value of Extractum Carnis," *The Lancet* 86, no. 2202 (November 1865): 547.
57 Richard Perren, *Taste, Trade and Technology: The Development of the International Meat Industry Since 1840* (Aldershot, UK: Ashgate Publishing, 2006); 45–46.
58 Liebig, "On the Nutritive," 547.
59 "Liebig's Extract of Meat," *Scientific American* 23, no. 5 (July 30, 1870): 72.
60 "Liebig's Liquid Extract of Meat," *The British Medical Journal* 2, no. 722 (October 31, 1874): 565–66.
61 Cecilia Molinari de Rennie, "Art, Science, and Ideology in 19th-century Advertisement for Liebig's Extract of Meat," *HYLE – International Journal for Philosophy of Chemistry* 21, no. 1 (2015): 51.
62 Smith and Steinen, *Do Rio de Janeiro a Cuyabá*, 140.
63 Hutchinson, *The Paraná*, 223.
64 Liebig, "On the Nutritive," 547.
65 Finlay, "Quackery and Cookery," 417.
66 Binzer, *Os meus romanos,* 58–59; Smith and Steinen, *Do Rio de Janeiro a Cuyabá*, 135.
67 *The Rio News*, May 5, 1885.
68 Lloyd, *Food and Identity,* 57.
69 Manoel P. da Silva Ubatuba, "Ligeira notícia do estado da indústria fabril e pastoril na província do Rio Grande do Sul," *Revista Agrícola do Imperial Instituto Fluminense de Agricultura* no. 15 (Rio de Janeiro: Typograhia do Imperial Instituto Artístico, March 1873), 50.
70 Cascudo, *História da alimentação,* 238.
71 *Diario de Notícias*, November 12, 1886; Cascudo, *História da alimentação*, 439.
72 *Propaganda na Europa do mate, do café e da carne secca.* Relatório pelos doutores Couty e engenheiros Luiz Godofredo de Escragnole Taunay e Augusto Carlos da Silva Telles, *Revista Agrícola do Imperial Instituto Fluminense de Agricultura* 14, no. 1 (March 1883): 149–55.
73 Denise Manfredini and Sergio Marley Modesto Monteiro, "Rentabilidade do trabalho escravo no Rio Grande do Sul no século XIX," Conference Proceedings, *Anais do XLII Encontro Nacional de Economia* 020, ANPEC – Associação Nacional dos Centros de Pósgraduação em Economia, 2016, 15; Pereira, "Was it Uruguay or Coffee?" 14.

74 "Divisão da propriedade," *A Immigração. Orgão da Sociedade Central de Immigração* 2, no. 16 (December 1885): 12; "Alimentação dos imigrantes," *A Immigração. Orgão da Sociedade Central de Immigração* 6, n. 58 (June 1889): 7. In a typical contract established between planters and immigrants, in exchange of labor, the former would provide beans, bacon, salt, rice, and charque. *O Pharol*, April 9, 1885.

75 Daniel Bender, Rachel Ankeny, Warren Belasco, Amy Bentley, Elias Mandala, Jeffrey M. Pilcher, and Peter Scholliers, "Eating in Class. Gastronomy, Taste, Nutrition, and Teaching Food History," *Radical History Review* 110 (Spring 2011): 208–12; Rachel Laudan, "Power Cuisines, Dietary Determinism and Nutritional Crisis: The Origins of the Globalization of Western Diet," *Interactions: Regional Studies, Global Processes, and Historical Analysis*, Conference Proceedings, Washington D.C., Library of Congress February 28 - March 3 (2001), Accessed November 25, 2020, http://webdoc.sub.gwdg.de/ebook/p/2005/history_cooperative/www.historycooperative.org/proceedings/interactions/laudan.html; Couto, "The Chemistry of Diet," 357–59.

76 It is likely that immigrants who had access to agricultural and pasture land—where they cultivated corn and beans, for instance, and raised animals—could get away from the standard food allotment in contracts. Likewise, they could produce foods that resembled their homeland fare; however, this is not to say that landless colonists had the luxury to "reject" regular provisions, which included carne seca. Thomas H. Holloway, *Immigrants on the Land. Coffee and Society in São Paulo, 1886–1934* (Chapel Hill: The University of North Carolina Press, 1980), 89–99; Neill, "Finding," 12–22.

77 Sandra Graham, *House and Street. The Domestic World of Servants and Masters in Nineteenth-Century Rio de Janeiro* (New York: Cambridge University Press, 1988), 31.

78 *Gazeta de Notícias*, March 10, 1887; *Gazeta de Notícias*, January 27, 1880.

79 Carlos Eduardo Valencia Villa, "Costos de los alimentos y renta de los trabajadores libres en Rio de Janeiro (Brasil) y Richmond (Virginia, EUA) en la primera mitad del siglo XIX," Conference Proceedings, *CLADHE II*, Mexico (2011): 12–13. In the 1850s, Brazil experienced high inflation, which affected the prices of several food items, including charque. Carlos Eduardo Valencia Villa, *Ao longo daquelas ruas. A economia dos negros livres em Richmond e Rio de Janeiro, 1840–1860* (Jundiaí: Paco Editorial, 2016), 547–49; Juliana Teixeira Souza, "A autoridade municipal na corte municipal: enfrentamentos e negociações na regulação do comércio de gêneros (1849–1889)" (PhD diss., Universidade de Campinas, 2007), 56.

Bibliography

Archives Consulted

Arquivo Nacional do Rio de Janeiro, (cited as ANRJ)

Government Documents and Publications

Brasil. *Pesquisa de orçamentos familiares, 2008–2009. Tabelas de composição nutricional dos alimentos consumidos no Brasil.* Rio de Janeiro: Instituto Brasileiro de Geografia *e Estatística*, 2011.

Fonseca, Alvarenga, org. *Collecção de Leis Municipaes e Vetos de 1895 – 1896*. Vol. 2. Rio de Janeiro: Typographia do Jornal do Commercio, de Rodrigues & C., 1897.

Fonseca, Alvarenga, org. *Collecção de Leis Municipaes e Vetos do primeiro semestre de 1900*. Vol. 7. Rio de Janeiro: Typographia do Jornal do Commercio, de Rodrigues & C., 1900.

Relatório apresentado á Assembléa Legislativa Provincial do Ceará pelo excellentissimo senhor dr. José Bento da Cunha Figueiredo Junior, por occasião da installação da mesma Assembléa no dia 1o de outubro de 1862. San Luiz: Typ. de B. de Mattos, 1863.

Relatório do presidente da província do Rio de Janeiro, João de Almeida Pereira. Nictheroy: Typographya da Patria, de Mora & Miranda, 1859.

Newspapers and Magazines

A Pátria. Folha da Província do Rio de Janeiro
A pátria (Echo da Nação) (Rio de Janeiro)
Brasil Commercial (Rio de Janeiro)
Correio da Manhã (Rio de Janeiro)
Diario de Notícias (Rio de Janeiro)
Gazeta da Tarde (Rio de Janeiro)
Gazeta de Notícias (Rio de Janeiro)
Jornal do Commercio (Rio de Janeiro)
Lavoura e Commercio (São Paulo)
O Pharol (Juiz de Fora)
The Rio News

"Alimentação dos imigrantes." *A Immigração. Orgão da Sociedade Central de Immigração* 6, n. 58 (June 1889): 7.

"Carnes verdes," *Jornal do Commercio*, April 18, 1878.

"Divisão da propriedade." *A Immigração. Orgão da Sociedade Central de Immigração* 2, no. 16 (December 1885): 12.

"Epidemia reinante." *Annaes da Academia de Medicina: Publicações Periodicas da Academia Imperial de Medicina* 7, no. 2 (1851): 53–55.

Jornal do Commercio. *Retrospecto Commercial do[s] ano[s] 1869–1892*. Rio de Janeiro: Typographia do "Jornal do Commercio," de Rodrigues & C., 1870–1893.

Liebig, Justus von. "On the Nutritive Value of Extractum Carnis." *The Lancet* 86, no. 2202 (November 1865): 547.

"Liebig's Extract of Meat." *Scientific American* 23, no. 5 (July 30, 1870): 72.

"Liebig's Liquid Extract of Meat." *The British Medical Journal* 2, no. 722 (October 31, 1874): 565–566.

Ubatuba, Manoel P. da Silva "Ligeira notícia do estado da indústria fabril e pastoril na província do Rio Grande do Sul." *Revista Agrícola do Imperial Instituto Fluminense de Agricultura* no. 15. Rio de Janeiro: Typograhia do Imperial Instituto Artístico (March 1873): 49–52.

Other Primary Sources

Agassiz, Louis, and Elizabeth Agassiz. *A Journey in Brazil*. Boston: The Riverside Press, 1979.

Albano, Ildefonso. *A pecuária no Ceará: notas offerecidas à Primeira Conferencia de Pecuária, organizada no Rio de Janeiro em maio de 1917 pela Sociedade Nacional de Agricultura sob os auspícios do Ministério da Agricultura*. Rio de Janeiro: Imprensa Nacional, 1918.

Biard, François Auguste. *Dois anos no Brasil*. São Paulo: Companhia editora nacional, 1945.

Binzer, Ina von. *Os meus romanos: Alegrias e tristezas de uma educadora alemã no Brasil*. São Paulo: Editora Paz e Terra, 2004.

Costa, Antonio Corrêa de Sousa. "Qual a alimentação de que usa a classe pobre no Rio de Janeiro e sua influência sobre a mesma." Medical Thesis, Faculdade de Medicina do Rio de Janeiro. Rio de Janeiro: Typographia Perseverança, 1865.

Couty, Louis. *Le maté et les conserves de viande. Rapport à son excellence monsieur le ministre de l'agriculture et du commerce par le Dr. Louis Couty sur sa mission dans les provinces du Parana, Rio Grande et les États du Sud*. Rio de Janeiro: Typographia Nacional, 1880.

Couty, Louis. "L'alimentation au Brésil et dan les pays voisins." *Revue d'hygiène et de police sanitaire* 3 (1881): 183–193.

Cozinheiro imperial ou nova arte do cozinheiro e do copeiro em todos os seus ramos. Rio de Janeiro: Laemmert 7 C., 1887.

Cozinheiro nacional, ou coleção das melhores receitas das cozinhas brasileira e europeas. Rio de Janeiro: Livraria Garnier, n.d.

Expilly, Charles. *Mulheres e costumes no Brasil*. São Paulo: Companhia editora nacional, 1935.

Graham, Maria. *Diário de uma viagem ao Brasil e de uma estada neste país durante parte dos anos 1821, 1822 e 1823*. São Paulo: Companhia editora nacional, 1956.

Hutchinson, Thomas J. *The Paraná; with Incidents of the Paraguayan War, and South American Recollections, from 1861–1868*. London: E. Stanford, 1868.

Koster, Henry. *Travels in Brazil*. London: Longman, Hurst, Rees, Orme, and Brown, 1816.

Liebig, Justus von. "Letter XXXII." *Familiar Letters on Chemistry: In Its Relations to Physiology, Dietetics, Agriculture, Commerce, and Political Economy*. London: Walton and Maberly, 1859.

Luccock, John. *Notes on Rio de Janeiro and Southern Parts of Brazil, Taken During a Residence of Ten Years in that Country from 1808 to 1818*. London: Printed for Samuel Leigh, 1820.

Padilha, Francisco Fernandes. "Qual o regimen alimentar dos pobres no Rio de Janeiro? Que molestias mas commumente grasão entre ellas? Que relações de causalidade se encontrão entre esse regimen e molestias?." Medical Thesis, Faculdade de Medicina do Rio de Janeiro. Rio de Janeiro: Typographia Universal de Laemmert, 1853.

"Projeto de resposta a consulta do governo acerca das origem das enfermidades que afligem os aprendizes menores do arsenal da guerra." *Annaes Brasilienses de Medicina. Jornal da Academia Imperial de Medicina do Rio de Janeiro* 7, no. 7 (1852): 206–209.

Propaganda na Europa do mate, do café e da carne secca. Relatório pelos doutores Couty e engenheiros Luis Godofredo de Escragnole Taunay e Augusto Carlos da Silva Telles. *Revista Agrícola do Imperial Instituto Fluminense de Agricultura* 14, no. 1 (March 1883): 145–155.

Regadas, José Maria Rodrigues. "Do regimen das classes abastadas do Rio de Janeiro em seus alimentos e bebidas. Mudanças que nele se tem operado nos últimos quarenta anos. Efeitos do regimen antigo: influência do atual." Medical Thesis, Faculdade de Medicina do Rio de Janeiro. Rio de Janeiro: Typographia Imperial e Constitucional de J. Villeneuve e Comp., 1852.

Smith, Herbert H., and Karl von den Steinen. *Do Rio de Janeiro a Cuyabá; notas de um naturalista.* São Paulo: Companhia Melhoramentos de São Paulo, 1922.

Secondary Sources

Almeida, Sílvia Capanema P. de. "Corpo, saúde e alimentação na Marinha de Guerra brasileira no período pós-abolição, 1890–1910." *História, Ciências, Saúde – Manguinhos* 19 supl. 1 (2012): 15–33.

Appadurai, Arjun. "How to Make a National Cuisine: Cookbooks in Contemporary India." *Comparative Studies in Society and History* 30, no. 1 (1988): 3–24.

Barbosa, Luiz Cordelio. "Cotton in 19th Century Brazil: Dependency and Development." PhD diss., University of Washington, 1989.

Bell, Stephen. *Campanha Gaúcha: A Brazilian Ranching System, 1850–1920.* Stanford, CA: Stanford University Press, 1998.

Bender, Daniel, Rachel Ankeny, Warren Belasco, Amy Bentley, Elias Mandala, Jeffrey M. Pilcher, and Peter Schollier. "Eating in Class. Gastronomy, Taste, Nutrition, and Teaching Food History." *Radical History Review* 110 (Spring 2011): 197–216.

Braga, Renato. "Um capítulo esquecido da economia pastoril do nordeste." *Revista do Instituto do Ceará, Fortaleza* 61 (1947): 149–162.

Cascudo, Luis da Câmara. *História da alimentação no Brasil.* Vol. 2. Belo Horizonte: Itatiaia, 1983.

Couto, Cristiana Loureiro de Mendonça. "Alimentação no Brasil Imperial: elementos para um estudo de questões dietéticas, químico-médicas e da fisiologia do gosto." PhD diss., Pontifícia Universidade Católica de São Paulo, 2011.

Couto, Cristiana Loureiro de Mendonça. "The Chemistry of Diet: Medicine, Nutrition, and Staple Foods in Imperial Brazil." *Ambix* 62, no. 4 (2015): 345–362.

Davidson, Alan. *The Oxford Companion to Food.* Oxford: New York: Oxford University Press, 2006.

Duffett, Rachel. *The Stomach for Fighting: Food and the Soldiers of the Great War.* Manchester: Manchester University Press, 2015.

El-Kareh, Almir Chaiban. *A vitória da feijoada.* Niterói, RJ: EDUFF, 2012.

Finlay, M. R. "Quackery and Cookery: Justus Von Liebig's Extract of Meat and the Theory of Nutrition in the Victorian Age." *Bulletin of the History of Medicine* 66, no. 3 (1992): 404–418.

Frank, Zephyr. *Dutra's World. Wealth and Family in Nineteenth-Century Rio de Janeiro.* Albuquerque: University of New Mexico Press, 2004.

Freise, Friedrich W. "The Drought Region of Northeastern Brazil." *Geographical Review* 28, no. 3 (July 1938): 363–378.

Graça Filho, Afonso de Alencastro. "Os convênios da carestia: crises, organização e investimentos do comércio de subsistência da Corte (1850–1880)." Master's thesis, Universidade Federal do Rio de Janeiro, 1992.

Graham, Sandra. *House and Street. The Domestic World of Servants and Masters in Nineteenth-Century Rio de Janeiro*. New York: Cambridge University Press, 1988.

Greenfield, Gerald Michael. "The Realities of Images: Imperial Brazil and the Great Drought." *Transactions of the American Philosophical Society* 91, no. 1 (2001): 1–148.

Holloway, Thomas H. *Immigrants on the Land. Coffee and Society in São Paulo, 1886–1934*. Chapel Hill: The University of North Carolina Press, 1980.

Karasch, Mary C. *Slave Life in Rio de Janeiro, 1808–1850*. Princeton: Princeton University Press, 1987.

Laudan, Rachel. "*Power Cuisines, Dietary Determinism and Nutritional Crisis: The Origins of the Globalization of Western Diet*." *Interactions: Regional Studies, Global Processes, and Historical Analysis*, Conference Proceedings, Washington, DC, Library of Congress February 28 - March 3 (2001). Accessed November 25, 2020, http://webdoc.sub.gwdg.de/ebook/p/2005/history_cooperative/www.historycooperative.org/proceedings/interactions/laudan.html.

Lenharo, Alcir. *As tropas da moderação: o abastecimento da Corte na formação política do Brasil*. Rio de Janeiro: Prefeitura da cidade do Rio de Janeiro, 1992.

Linhares, Maria Yedda Leite. *História do abastecimento; uma problemática em questão (1530–1918)*. Brasília: Edições Binagri, 1979.

Lloyd, Paul S. "Nutritious Foods and Consumption Choices in the Early Modern Period." *Social History of Medicine* 24, no. 1 (2011): 161–165.

Lloyd, Paul S. "The Changing Status of Offal: A Fashionable Food in England between 1545 and 1655." *Food, Culture and Society: An International Journal of Multidisciplinary Research* 15, no. 1 (2012): 61–75.

Lloyd, Paul S. *Food and Identity in England, 1540–1640: Eating to Impress*. London: Bloomsbury Academic, 2015.

Love, Joseph. *The Revolt of the Whip*. Stanford, CA: Stanford University Press, 2012.

Manfredini, Denise, and Sergio Marley Modesto Monteiro. "Rentabilidade do trabalho escravo no Rio Grande do Sul no século XIX." Conference Proceedings. *Anais do XLII Encontro Nacional de Economia* 020, ANPEC - Associação Nacional dos Centros de Pósgraduação em Economia, 2016.

Moura Filho, Heitor Pinto. "Exchange rates of the mil-réis (1795–1913)." *MPRA Paper No. 5210*. University Library of Munich, Germany (2006): 1–17. Accessed November 22, 2020. http://mpra.ub.uni–muenchen.de/5210/.

Neill, Deborah. "Finding the 'Ideal Diet': Nutrition, Culture, and Dietary Practices in France and French Equatorial Africa, c. 1890s to 1920s." *Food and Foodways* 17, no. 1 (2009): 1–28.

Olaoye, Olusegun A., and Iniobong G. Ntuen. "Spoilage and Preservation of Meat: A General Appraisal and Potential of Lactic Acid Bacteria as Biological Preservatives." *International Research Journal of Biotechnology* 2, no. 1 (February 2011): 033–046.

Oliveira, Almir Leal de. "O comércio das carnes secas do Ceará na segunda metade do século XVIII: as dinâmicas do mercado colonial." In *Consumo e abastecimento na história*, edited by Maria-Aparecida Lopes, Margarida Maria de Carvalho, and Denise Aparecida Soares Moura, 167–188. São Paulo: Editora Alameda, 2011.

Pereira, Thales A. Zamberlan. "The Rise of the Cotton Trade in Brazil during the Industrial Revolution." Working paper series, N° 2016–09, Department of Economics- FEA/USP (2016a): 1–20.

Pereira, Thales A. Zemberlan. "Was it Uruguay or Coffee? The Causes of the Beef Jerky Industry's decline in Southern Brazil (1850 – 1889)." *Nova Economia* 26, no. 1 (2016b): 7–42.

Perren, Richard. *Taste, Trade and Technology: The Development of the International Meat Industry Since 1840*. Aldershot, UK: Ashgate Publishing, 2006.

Pilcher, Jeffrey M. *¡Que Vivan Los Tamales!: Food and the Making of Mexican Identity*. Albuquerque: University of New Mexico Press, 1998.

Quiroz, Enriqueta. *El consumo como problema histórico. Propuestas y debates entre Europa e Hispanoamérica*. México: Instituto de Investigaciones Dr. José María Luis Mora, 2006.

Rennie, Cecilia Molinari de. "Art, Science, and Ideology in 19th-century Advertisement for Liebig's Extract of Meat." *HYLE - International Journal for Philosophy of Chemistry* 21, no. 1 (2015): 39–60.

Rocha, Ariza Maria. "A feijoada no Brasil e o bacalhau em Portugal: a construção da comida como identidade nacional." *Mneme Revista de Humanidades* 15, no. 35 (2014): 224–243.

Rolim, Leonardo Cândido. "'Tempo das carnes' no Siará Grande: o mercado das carnes secas na Vila do Aracati (1710–1793)." *Sæculum. Revista de Historia* 29 (2013): 13–28.

Schulz, John. *The Financial Crisis of Abolition*. New Haven: Yale University Press, 2008.

Sluyter, Andrew. "The Hispanic Atlantic's Tasajo Trail." *Latin American Research Review* 45, no. 1 (2010): 98–120.

Souza, Juliana Teixeira. "A autoridade municipal na corte municipal: enfrentamentos e negociações na regulação do comércio de gêneros (1849–1889)." PhD diss., Universidade de Campinas, 2007.

Valencia Villa, Carlos Eduardo. "Costos de los alimentos y renta de los trabajadores libres en Rio de Janeiro (Brasil) y Richmond (Virginia, EUA) en la primera mitad del siglo XIX." Conference Proceedings, *CLADHE II*, Mexico (2011): 1–22.

Valencia Villa, Carlos Eduardo. *Ao longo daquelas ruas. A economia dos negros livres em Richmond e Rio de Janeiro, 1840–1860*. Jundiaí: Paco Editorial, 2016.

Vargas, Jonas M. *Os barões do charque e suas fortunas. Um estudo sobre as elites regionais brasleiras a partir de uma análise dos charqueadores de Pelotas*. São Leopoldo, RGS: Oikos Editora, 2016.

Wätzold, Tim. *Proclamação da cozinha brasileira como parte do processo de formação da identidade nacional no Império Brasileiro, 1822–1889*. Belo Horizonte: Editora e Gráfica TCS, 2012.

4 Brazil as a Tropical Producer

Improving and Supplying Cattle for Rio de Janeiro (c. 1850–c.1930)

In late nineteenth century, foodstuffs arrived in Rio de Janeiro (then Brazil's capital city) from a variety of national and international providers through a complex transport network. Sugar, coffee, rice, beans, corn, bacon (*toucinho*), manioc meal (*farinha de mandioca*), salted beef (*charque*), and dried and salt-fish were shipped from abroad and from the interior states by mule, river transport, and later rail, as long as it proved cost effective. Although fresh meat (*carne verde*) was processed near the city center, cattle might be raised as far as 1,000 kilometers away from Rio. Thus, the city's meat supply system relied on two economic geographic networks: one related to cattle raising—and fattening—and another to meat provision in the urban grid. Having examined the latter in Chapter 2, the following pages consider the key characteristics of the former. This chapter opens with a description of the main cattle commercial circuits in Brazil as they connected to Rio's urban demand. Over the nineteenth century, the city received matured cattle (on the hoof or via railroads) mainly from the southeast and central-west regions of Brazil; however, starting in early-twentieth century, many of these animals had as their final destination not only Rio's municipal slaughterhouse but also the newly established meatpacking plants (*frigoríficos*) in Rio de Janeiro and São Paulo states. The last section of this chapter examines how the railroads affected these century-old trade networks.

As coffee farming expanded in southeast Brazil, the cattle frontier continued to move west. Indeed, in the 1850s, a small number of animals arriving in fattening pastures of Minas Gerais (also called Minas) and São Paulo originated in the central-west region. During the latter part of the period under consideration in this study (1900–1930), ranchers transformed vast areas of the country's central plateau into pastureland. Far from being an ideal environment for cattle ranching, the region is characterized by a tropical, semi-humid climate and is prone to floods. Further, in the second half of the 1800s, the country's central plateau was the site of intermittent regional and international wars and counterattacks by displaced Indigenous peoples. How, then, under such apparently inhospitable conditions, did cattle ranching flourish? The second part of this chapter addresses this question by examining the particularities of cattle improvement in late-nineteenth-century Brazil. Whereas in most of the Americas, breeders imported northern European cattle for crossbreeding purposes, in certain areas of central-west and southeast Brazil, ranchers turned to zebu, a species native to South Asia.[1] Rooted in practical animal husbandry, farmers improved their herds with a breed suitable to the surroundings. Over the second half of the nineteenth century not only were ranchers in Brazil addressing the needs of Rio de Janeiro's growing urban population, but they also started a process of genetic upgrading that ultimately transformed ranching in tropical environments.

Market Needs and Cattle Supply Areas

In January 1876, by order of the Emperor Pedro II, the British engineer James W. Wells traveled into the northern areas of Brazil. His mission was to evaluate the possibility of establishing communications between the Tocantins and Grande Rivers. When traversing Minas Gerais province,[2] Wells came across a "cattle station" (*retiro*) whose herds were "increasing and multiplying"; however, its owner confessed; "I cannot sell more [cattle] than a limited number in the nearest village." This situation, according to Wells, was common "all over the distant interior of Brazil, [for] there is no market for any production in excess of local demands, except by a long weary and expensive journey to the coast."[3] Surely, cattle drives were "weary" and, in the late 1870s, the city of Rio de Janeiro was the only sizable market in Brazil for beef cattle. In the first decade of the twentieth century, the state of São Paulo emerged as an important marketplace for ranchers from the central-west. Despite the increasing population rates in São Paulo's capital city, by 1900 it had one third of Rio's inhabitants. Hence, the states' livestock acquisitions also related to industrial production destined for out-of-state consumers. These developments altered commercial cattle circuits, generated a lively debate about the best way to improve the *crioulo* cattle,[4] transformed livestock production, and—to a certain extent—the railroad network, all of which contributed to the opening of meatpacking plants in Brazil.

Cattle ranching in pre-industrial economies depended on environmental conditions such as the availability of "free" land, water sources, and native vegetation for grazing. In areas of low population density, cattle were raised on vast plains and then driven by cowhands to fattening pasturelands from which, once matured, they were taken to corrals near consumption centers where they would rest (*lairage*) for a few days before the slaughtering. This process allowed the herds to recuperate some weight and local governments to control the number of animals in the urban meat market.

Until the mid-eighteenth century, cattle that arrived in the city of Rio de Janeiro came from nearby ranches in Campos dos Goitacás and the Santa Cruz Jesuit farm (*fazenda*), both located in the captaincy of Rio de Janeiro. As early as 1770, these areas served as fattening grounds for cattle driven from São Paulo and Minas Gerais.[5] While Campos sent approximately 6,000 to 7,000 herds to Rio annually, during its apogee, Santa Cruz maintained more than 13,000 animals destined for the city. Before reaching the Santa Luzia municipal slaughterhouse, all cattle were placed in lairage at the Campos de São Cristóvão, just about 6 kilometers from the city center.[6] With Rio de Janeiro's urban population increase in late eighteenth century and the development of commercial agriculture in the captaincy, the cattle frontier expanded toward central-west and south Brazil. In fact, by mid-eighteenth century, the Sorocaba fair (in São Paulo, see Figure 4.1) was established to control and tax the entrance of cattle from both regions into Rio de Janeiro.[7]

In early nineteenth century, Cariocas (natives of Rio de Janeiro city) witnessed several spatial transformations related to those economic and demographic changes. While west of the city center became more populated, the fields of Santa Cruz no longer functioned as a raising or fattening area, but as a resting point for cattle destined for urban consumption. Several accounts stress that, depending on Rio's needs, cattle could arrive from south Goiás and Mato Grosso via Minas Gerais. In addition, Rio Grande de São Pedro do Sul (later Rio Grande do Sul, also called Rio Grande) provided mules and charque, while Minas Gerais traded hogs, toucinho, and cheese. In the ensuing decades—despite myriad problems with cattle trailing due to the distances and poor road conditions—south Goiás and Mato Grosso consolidated their positions as providers of beef cattle to fattening grounds in São Paulo and Minas Gerais, while Rio Grande do Sul emerged as the leading national purveyor of charque.[8]

In the 1850s, reports from the Mato Grosso province describe annual trails moving beef cattle to São Paulo and Minas Gerais. In 1856, particularly, the president of Mato Grosso stressed a "notable increment ... in the number of cattle exports."[9] By one account, in 1858, the province sent approximately 17,000 herds to Rio. Four years later, official documentation list taxes from those exchanges as crucial to the local treasury. Despite great regional variance in terms of ranching scale in the province, most of Mato Grosso's production was tied to the needs of southeastern Brazil.[10] In 1857, the foundation of Santana do Paranaíba (where the province's officials collected cattle sale taxes) confirmed this connection. Located on the border of São Paulo and Minas Gerais, the Santana do Paranaíba village was a crossing point on the cattle trail that, starting in south Mato Grosso, followed the Paranaíba River to reach Uberaba in Minas Gerais (see Figure 4.1), ending in Piracicaba (São Paulo).[11] Neither

Figure 4.1 Brazil, c. 1870.

Source: Elaborated based on C. Brockes and C. Held, *Mappa do Imperio do Brazil: augmentado de dados estatisticos e outras correcções resultantes de estudos e melhoramentos recentes* (Rio de Janeiro: H. Laemmert & C., 1883).

the Triple Alliance War (1864–1870)[12] nor concurrent epizootics radically altered this economic trend based on ranching.

What is more, after the war, given the abandonment of ranches in the region, cattle dispersed into the wilderness, where they reproduced naturally. Families of soldiers settled in the area occupied "vacant" lands, thereby displacing Indigenous groups through violence and disease. Postwar, Mato Grosso witnessed population growth and a reboot in the ranching activity. Government incentives also aided the regional economic recovery. When the blockade of the Paraguay River was lifted—which had curtailed local trade for almost five years—communications with Rio de Janeiro resumed and the Corumbá port was free of taxes for import and export for a decade. The imperial administration, clearly concerned with the territory's defense, built forts in the Paraguay River, invested in the construction of a shipyard in Ladario, and reestablished military colonies.[13] Although these incentives were short-lived, and the recovery enthusiasm faded away, they played an important role in the development of cattle ranching in the frontier, particularly in south Mato Grosso.

In the late 1770s, cattle ranching in Goiás became an alternative to the northeastern production, which was intermittently decimated by droughts. First, good pasturelands, natural salt deposits, and abundant water supplies in the eastern region of the captaincy promoted a livestock venture geared mainly toward Bahia, which also reached farther north through the São Francisco River Valley. As Rio de Janeiro became Brazil's leading entrepôt, and the coffee commercial agriculture expanded in the 1850s, beef cattle production in southern Goiás followed suit. The main cattle trail crossed the province to reach the Paraná River, ending in the pasturelands of Minas Gerais. By the 1870s, Goiás was sending there, on average, 18,000 herds annually.[14] As in the case of Mato Grosso, in late 1880s, the governor cited cattle exchange as "the main source of income and the most important industry of the people from Goiás." By the end of the century, the state traded approximately 50,000 to 60,000 cattle annually to Minas Gerais, Rio de Janeiro, and São Paulo.[15]

Since late colonial times, Sorocaba, São Paulo had served as an entrance point for animals driven from central-west and southernmost areas of Brazil. During the first quarter of the nineteenth century, livestock production in the modern state of Rio Grande do Sul found a ready market in the southeast, especially with the development of sugar and, later, commercial coffee farming, along with population increase and its related needs for livestock and by-products for transport, food, and clothing.[16] To drive beef cattle, beasts of burden, and all sorts of goods, drovers used the "caminho do Sul," a trail dating from the 1730s parallel to Brazil's littoral, which started in Sorocaba, crossed over Campos Gerais (now in Paraná state) and ended in the grazing fields of Rio Grande do Sul. Use of this route declined only after the introduction of the railroads at the end of the nineteenth century, when mules were no longer employed as primary means of transportation, and cattle's long journey to consumption markets could be—at least partially—made by rail.[17]

Ample evidence from coastal shipments indicates that, starting in 1800s, Rio Grande de São Pedro do Sul provided a significant amount of charque that arrived in Rio de Janeiro. Although historian Larissa Brown asserts that, by late eighteenth century, "almost one-half of the animals leaving São Paulo for Rio de Janeiro consumption originated in Rio Grande do Sul," the majority of beef cattle that reached Rio's abattoir came from Minas Gerais. Likewise, the author stresses that not only wholesale merchants but also several middling and small dealers who introduced charque in Rio de Janeiro did so in connection with Rio Grande do Sul's vendors.[18] Not all charque that *Riograndenses* (inhabitants of the Rio Grande do Sul province, later state) traded was destined for domestic markets—at least some reached the Caribbean. In any case, data on the province's revenue from 1844 to 1847 show that, on average, Rio Grande collected twice as much taxes on charque exchanges than on cattle, horses, and mules combined.[19]

As for livestock trade, while mules from Rio Grande cut across Paraná and Santa Catarina provinces in the direction of São Paulo—in the 1850s, on average 50,000 beasts of burden passed through Lages (Santa Catarina) annually[20]—there is scant evidence that Rio Grande sent a comparable number of live cattle to either Rio de Janeiro or São Paulo. Chapter 5 expands this argument, but for now it suffices to say that Rio Grande do Sul's livestock raising was concentrated on beasts of burden, while cattle were raised for charque production and linked to ranchers in Argentina and Uruguay. In fact, researchers have underscored that, to supply local salt-beef processing plants (*charqueadas*), the state continuously imported cattle from its neighbors, Argentina, but most importantly, Uruguay. Historian Jonas Vargas contends that in the second half of the nineteenth century, Rio Grande bought approximately 100,000 herds annually from Uruguay. Thus, cattle and charque production in Rio Grande do Sul was subjected to the vagaries of that network.[21]

According to scattered records, in the first decade of the twentieth century, Mato Grosso and Goiás together traded a considerable number of cattle that arrived in the southeast. Although neither the final destination nor the weight of these animals is exactly known, most likely they crossed the fields of Minas Gerais, reaching the fattening grounds of Triângulo Mineiro region (west of Minas) and the slopes of the sierras in Minas, São Paulo, and Rio de Janeiro states.[22] Likewise, some of these herds, which originated in central-west Brazil, were winter-pastured in São Paulo, crossing over to Minas, once matured.

During most of the nineteenth century until World War I, Minas Gerais was a major provider of fattened cattle to Rio de Janeiro. In the 1880s, the director of the state's treasury calculated that Minas traded a little over 130,000 head of cattle annually.[23] In 1904, according to some estimates, the state sent 255,000 units to the Santa Cruz slaughterhouse in Rio. This might be an exaggerated number, for in that year Rio's abattoir slaughtered a little over half that figure. Nevertheless, the fattening grasses of Minas Gerais represented the middle point between central-west Brazil and Rio de Janeiro. In fact, after coffee, cattle exchanges accounted for Minas's second source of revenue, playing a pivotal role in local economies such as the municipalities of Prata, Araguary, and Uberaba, all closely tied to Mato Grosso and Goiás.[24] In 1907, according to the engineer Miguel Arrojado Ribeiro Lisboa, 25,000 cattle left Vacaria (Mato Grosso), 10,000 destined to Paraguay and São Paulo, and the rest trailed via Santana de Paranaíba, ending up in Uberaba.[25]

The other important area for cattle fattening was São Paulo. First, the state's fields served as pasturelands for herds sent to Rio, but in the later years of the nineteenth century, a considerable number of animals brought from the central-west and south regions (particularly from Paraná) of Brazil remained in the state.[26] Some ended up in the city of São Paulo' slaughterhouses, whose population was increasing rapidly,[27] others landed in the state's frigoríficos, where they were processed into frozen or chilled meat, bound for domestic and international markets.

In early twentieth century, how these conditions shaped the quality of Brazilian herds and how they connected to the demands for animal source food in Brazil's capital can be summarized as follows: Minas Gerais and São Paulo functioned mainly as grazing areas where farmers combined agriculture with livestock-raising to satisfy Rio de Janeiro's urban appetite. Situated near the national capital and surrounded by river valleys, Minas Gerais was a gateway from and to Rio de Janeiro. Breeders in the states of Mato Grosso and Goiás, Brazil's central plateau, used the Paraná and Paranaíba River valleys to reach the pasturelands of São Paulo and Minas Gerais. The latter state also produced milk, butter, cheese, and charque for local and regional consumption. One observer calculated that, by 1910, Minas had approximately one hundred dairy factories and twenty-five charqueadas. Given the importance of Minas Gerais and São Paulo to the meat supply system of Brazil's capital, it is not surprising that both came to be at the center of a debate on how to improve the Brazilian crioulo cattle. This controversy is the subject of the next section.

Selecting a Better Breed for the Tropics: The Introduction of Zebu Cattle in Brazil

> Whereas Brazilian cattle, because of their thick skin covered with short and gleaming hair, almost nothing suffers from the sun and insects, Durham cattle, cared for in an open range, show significant degradation. Their whole body is instantly covered in insect bites and ticks. Their hair, initially short and fine, becomes long and scruffy. Their desire to eat diminishes; the animals slim down visibly and a speedy epizootic kills them in a few days.[28]

In the late 1890s, the German scientist Rudolf Endlich embarked on a trip to explore cattle ranching in "the interior of South America." While in Mato Grosso, the botanist witnessed the conditions described above. His observations are particularly revealing for highlighting not only the dismal conditions of recently introduced Durham cattle in the state, but also for what they say about the crioulo breed. Endlich summarizes the disagreement among veterinarians, ranchers, and politicians about cattle raising in late nineteenth-century Brazil. Puzzled by the country's vast expanses of inhabited land and its ranchers' traditional animal husbandry practices, those contemporaries debated how to expand livestock operations in the backlands. While some argued that, if "perfected," the "infected environment" of tropical Brazil could sustain breeding stock from temperate areas of the globe, others advocated the introduction of zebu cattle, an animal from the Indian subcontinent acclimated to the tropics. However, the majority with first-hand ranching experience simply relied on the crioulo and on traditional raising methods, although some eventually started to use the zebu for upgrading.

Brazil clearly had environmental limitations to the introduction of northern European breeds and ranching techniques. Indeed, only a small strip of land—the Campanha Gaúcha—on the border with Uruguay in Rio Grande do Sul shared the richness of the South American pampas' pasturelands. Large portions of Brazil fall into the *Cerrado* biome, a hot, dry savannah ecoregion. Besides the tropical climate, the lack of good roads and fencing (just to name a few difficulties) also hindered development, as experienced in the foreign neighboring ranges. However, it was precisely in these tropical and semitropical regions that cattle ranching, over the second half of the nineteenth century, took hold, mainly to satisfy the needs of Rio de Janeiro's growing urban population.

The allure of the nineteenth-century cattle industry was rooted in two correlated events: the high returns of investments in the livestock business in temperate regions of the Americas and Western Europe; and the certainty that the introduction of advanced ranching techniques was the first step toward increasing production. Ultimately, such developments would result in more meat on workers' tables at lower prices. Thus, observers during that time presumed that countries or regions that relied on traditional ranching practices were incapable of providing meat for the masses—and, to a certain extent, they were. However, taking into consideration the limitations imposed by environment, the technology available to ranchers, and the market needs, the picture that emerges is more complex. Indeed, these contextualizing factors show that, despite all hurdles, fresh meat arrived in Rio de Janeiro in significant quantities—albeit with extreme vacillations.

At the beginning of the twentieth century, Brazilian government officials considered that certain regions of the country had ideal environmental conditions for the development of the livestock industry. With propagandistic fervor, these reports equated the broad extensions of uninhabited territory—where traditional ranching systems prevailed—with the inevitable growth and prosperity of the cattle herds.[29] These optimistic depictions and predictions, notwithstanding, Brazil began experimenting with intensive cattle production and meat industrialization late compared to Uruguay and Argentina. Furthermore, improving the quality of cattle was more complicated than those prognostications envisioned. Tropical and semitropical areas posed serious adaptability challenges to imported pedigree animals. Moreover, any investment in livestock technology required expensive, long-term commitments, which only a small group of livestock raisers could take on.[30]

Two common, yet contrary, themes appear in contemporary accounts of cattle ranching in nineteenth-century Brazil. On the one hand, critics stress basic impediments: heat, humidity, epizootics, and a poor transport system; some authors, on the other hand, highlight the country's vast expanses of land and low population density as prerequisites for the development of the modern cattle industry. The first line of argument is rooted in travelers' accounts of the Brazilian hinterlands, whereas the second stems mainly from government officials and potential national and foreign investors. The latter position reflects, in part, the optimism of ranching prosperity in temperate areas of the continent, including the Argentinean Pampas, which, in fact, bears no similarity to most of Brazil's tropical environs. Therefore, the storyline that has emerged and perpetuated is one of backwardness. In summary, despite Brazil's large uninhabited areas, the cattle industry was hindered not necessarily as a consequence of environmental challenges—as there was a firm conviction that nature could be perfected—but because ranchers and government authorities lacked the entrepreneurial impulse to tackle them.[31]

Is it possible to reconcile these apparently contradictory narratives? Moreover, given that both are partially correct, how did cattle production, under such circumstances, adapt to the increasing needs of Rio de Janeiro, and later São Paulo? While the historiographical lens tends to emphasize the study of processes by which humans change and disrupt their environment in the pursuit of economic ventures, Tyler Priest suggests shifting this equation by considering "the impact of the natural environment on business." The case of ranching in most of Brazil, that is the central-southeast area, provides such an opportunity.[32] There, precisely because of the environment, neither the European breeding stock nor the techniques of cattlemen in nearby Argentina and Uruguay could be easily transplanted. Thus, by attempting to find an animal adequate to the tropical environs, like the zebu,[33] ranchers were not committing a "gross error"—as Eduardo Cotrim, a renowned Carioca veterinarian and rancher, put it—but rather making a rational decision based on local conditions and obstacles. Those obstacles, according to historian Robert

W. Wilcox, along with "specific measures taken to overcome barriers ... ultimately established a precedent for tropical ranching."[34]

Over the second half of the nineteenth century, most cattle that arrived in Rio de Janeiro were raised and fattened in central-west and southeast Brazil, roughly in the Cerrado ecoregion.[35] It encompasses several areas of transition, shifting from trees and shrubs, grassland (*campo limpo*), and riparian forests. Given its vegetation diversity and extreme climatic events, such as droughts and floods, some Cerrado areas were not entirely suitable for either agriculture or livestock raising. The flat lands, however, enjoyed a regular rainfall pattern that intensified in the summer months (December–March), thus sustaining legumes and grasses with highly nutritious sources of forage.[36] Campo limpo (grassland)—the best vegetation for cattle—was common in "isolated areas ... and banks of rivers," such as Campos da Vacaria (south Mato Grosso) and the Paraná River Valley (which extends from south São Paulo to north Paraná), the Mato Grosso plateau, the Triângulo Mineiro, and south Goiás.[37] In early-twentieth century, scholars observed great variance in stocking density throughout the region; for instance, while the Paraná River basin had an estimated carrying capacity of one animal per six hectares, similar rangeland in Campos da Vacaria (which had better natural pasturelands) could sustain twice as many cattle.[38]

The grazing fields of southernmost Brazil provided even better livestock forage. In the early twentieth century, the zoologist Hermann von Ihering calculated a stocking rate of approximately one animal per hectare there. A temperate climate and undulating topography characterized the open plains (*Campanha Gaúcha*) in Rio Grande do Sul, where grasses and legumes combined with rivers and streams to produce the best natural forage in the country.[39] These conditions explain why, by early twentieth century, very few ranchers were experimenting with alfalfa, which Eduardo Cotrim described as the "best known fodder."[40]

In most Brazilian pasturelands, crioulo cattle predominated. These were small, short-legged, sharp-horned animals, "weighing on an average not more than 400 lbs. when dressed."[41] Although they had low meat yield, the crioulo were well adapted to the Cerrado ecoregion. Their thick skin and short hair protected them from the thorny vegetation, insects, and sun, making them more "resistant to the elements than fine races."[42] Aside from the crioulo, other "national" races roamed in central and southeast Brazil: Caracu, Junqueira, Curraleira, China, Mocha, and Franqueira. These races were not the result of controlled selection, but rather of natural breeding in an unfenced range over the years. Nonetheless, in his early twentieth-century assessments, Eduardo Cotrim postulates that these national races could only be improved if crossbred with European herds, because they were "descendants from the *Bos Taurus* ... the domestic bovine of the western civilization to which we belong by origin, character, and customs." As for the zebu, Cotrim continues, only time would prove that this "Hindu idol worshiped by Brazilian ranchers is incapable of improvement."[43]

In his lengthy study entitled *A fazenda moderna* (The Modern Farm) Cotrim sought to convince fellow ranchers that European breeds could not only adapt to Brazilian environs—provided that it was "purged of parasites"—but, in fact, flourish. Hence, he suggests introducing cattle breeds to each state of Brazil, according to its range, natural forage, means of transport, and market conditions. To the pasturelands of Minas Gerais, Goiás, and São Paulo, Cotrim recommends Angus, Devon, and Hereford. In Mato Grosso, all of cited races, including Durham, would adapt well, especially in Campos de Vacaria. The prairies of Paraná and Santa Catarina states were ideal for mixed races, and eventually Hereford and Angus, while Rio Grande do Sul had optimum conditions for all races.[44]

However, according to Rudolf Endlich, European breeds did not adapt easily to the tropical and semitropical climate of central-west Brazil. As a result, and contrary to experiences in temperate areas of the continent, these imported animals were, in fact, severely affected by heat, humidity, and cattle ticks.[45] What is more, any attempt to improve livestock quality required decades to bear fruit. Hence, during the nineteenth century, the only noticeable development in that direction was the introduction of the zebu in Minas Gerais and Rio de Janeiro in the 1870s. The resulting crossbred—as long as accompanied by better management pursued over generations—was reliable, resistant to disease and drought, and fit for long trail drives.[46]

It is not exactly clear when, but scattered records indicate that, by the early 1870s, ranchers in Rio de Janeiro were experimenting with zebu. One such farmer was Henrique Hermeto Carneiro Leão (Barão do Paraná). In 1873, while visiting the London Zoo, the Carioca landowner, saw "a zebu couple" that had been brought into the city as a gift to Queen Victoria. Recognizing in these animals similar qualities—resistance to droughts, ticks, and fortitude—to grazing bulls that he had observed in the pasturelands of Minas Gerais and Rio de Janeiro, he imported a calf from London, which arrived at his family's fazenda in Sapucaia (Rio de Janeiro province) in 1875. Two years later, by his recommendation, Accacio de Souza Brandão, a rancher in Cantagalo (Rio de Janeiro province), bought another calf from the same zebu couple. Soon after, says the barão, such was the local "enthusiasm" for his crossbreds that London commercial houses began to introduce "dozens of Zebus from India" in Brazil.[47]

Again, although the chronology of purchases and the geographical distribution of zebu are not clear, apparently from Rio those animals reached the pasturelands of Minas Gerais, arriving in the central plateau in the later years of the nineteenth century. In the early stages of this process, private ranchers carried out and financed the acquisition of zebu cattle. One such entrepreneur was Teófilo de Godoy, who in 1893 traveled to India, initiating a series of purchases that, by 1914, had reached 2,000 cattle, most of which arrived in the pasturelands of Minas Gerais. By 1911, zebu specimens appeared at the state's livestock fairs; six years later, they had a guaranteed place in national expositions. By then, however, state (particularly Minas Gerais) and federal governments began to provide some subsidies for purebred cattle purchases. Systematic imports of zebu started in the early twentieth century; by some accounts, between 1904 and 1921 *Mineiro* and *Fluminense* (inhabitants of the states of Minas Gerais and Rio de Janeiro) ranchers acquired more than 5,000 herds.[48]

According to Endlich, the zebu's size was comparable to the Shorthorn's; however, their most important characteristics were their "resistance against climatic influences of hot countries" and ability to travel great distances. By no means was there consensus on the zebu.[49] As early as 1907, Miguel Arrojado Ribeiro Lisboa and Eduardo Cotrim stressed that, in such an environment, even the zebu degenerated over time. Cotrim observed that in the Mesopotamia Argentina (Entre Ríos and Corrientes provinces), ranchers would "never ... recommend the Zebu." Thus, he argued, with "courage to confront biases against the introduction of breeding stock and constant rational processes of cattle improvement," Argentines in those provinces had overcome difficulties, augmenting and improving their herds. To those in Brazil who had introduced the zebu because of their suitability to the environs, Cotrim responded that, rather than "seeking the adequate animal to the environment," it is indispensable to "purge" the "infected environment"—for instance, with disinfecting baths and better forage.[50]

Given that most, if not all, cattle in Brazil were raised in unfenced pasturelands, and far from main roads, rounding them up—two requirements for proper dipping, for instance—was of utmost difficulty.[51] Those in favor of the zebu pointed to precisely these obstacles, plus the inclemency of tropical diseases as deterrents to the introduction of European breeds in Brazil. The major point of contention, though, was the claim that the zebu crossbred eventually degenerated. However, these were, according to Barão do Paraná, "mere theories," and these theories, he continues, were "the greatest enemy of the zebu," because after more than "twenty years of experience ... [he affirms] the zebu is not only capable of strengthening but even to regenerate any national or foreign race."[52]

In 1916, during the first Livestock Conference in the São Paulo state, Antônio da Silva Prado[53] also appealed to ranchers' experiences to convince his audience that the zebu could be used in zones "where it is impossible to provide forage other than hard native grasses."[54] The conference's 12-point conclusion summarized this regional divide, suggesting that, whereas zebu and crioulo cattle were suitable for the pasturelands of Mato Grosso and Minas Gerais,[55] European breeds were more appropriate to São Paulo's. It is important to stress the following. First, these perceptions were based on the zebu's external appearance and disseminated when European purebreds were the standard animals for breeding purposes. Second, the example of a successful cattle operation in South America was in temperate areas of Argentina and Uruguay, not in Brazil. Third, in Europe, there was indeed a preference for crossbred European animals, whose meat was "tender interlaced with fat deposits"; zebu meat, by comparison, was "drier," "leaner," and "potentially tougher when cooked."[56]

The experiences of two cattlemen, J. Nogueira Itagyba in Minas Gerais and Fernand Ruffier in Paraná, illustrate the disagreements over the zebu. In his *Manual prático de criação de gado no Brazil* (Practical Manual of Livestock Production in Brazil), Ruffier defines the zebu as "a splendid working ox [suitable] to warm and poor regions" given their challenging environment and technological lag. Nevertheless, he avers, "The zebu is a heresy that will have to disappear as the livestock industry progresses." Therefore, its use was temporary, an "intermediate" phase in the development of the national livestock industry.[57] On the other side of spectrum, Itagyba, a lawyer, self-proclaimed "orchardman and cattleman by choice," and owner of a "bucolic farm," acknowledges the structural hurdles of ranching in Brazil for which only the zebu was fit. According to Itagyba, 30 years after its introduction (particularly in the Triângulo Mineiro region), the zebu became the preferred breed by cattlemen and merchants alike, because "the so called refined and civilized races, after long trails in the backlands (on the hoof or by rail), arrive at fairs and slaughterhouses dispirited and injured." With great sarcasm, he questions zebu's opponents, for their "key argument is that Europeans had not introduced it in the old continent. Hence, one concludes, had the zebu roamed the streets of Paris, Berlin, or London, it would be [judged in Brazil as] the ideal breeding stock."[58]

In his article, Itagyba describes in great length his misfortune with European races (which he had acquired following instructions of Manuals of Veterinary), revealing how those animals had succumbed to droughts and foot-and-mouth disease. In one of these events, Itagyba witnessed the loss of 60 percent of his calves; in another, only a handful of zebu crossbred animals had survived. After these experiences and several visits to farms in the Triângulo Mineiro, he replaced European with zebu cattle: "The immediate result … [he stresses] is that I did not lose a single herd after the 1915 eight-month drought."[59]

Between 1917 and early 1920s, similarly impassioned debates crowded the pages of major newspapers in Brazil, most notably from São Paulo. In this short period, while a group of farmers instituted the Herd Book Zebu Association, in 1918, Great Britain banned the imports of frozen beef from Brazil on account of its lean and tough characteristics. Two years later, the Brazilian government, in what seemed to be a validation of its British counterpart's measure, prohibited the introduction of zebu in the country. Certainly, this action was also a response to the detection, in the late 1910s, of rinderpest in a lot of imported zebu bulls in São Paulo.[60] But such an act could not halt a process that had been taking place, particularly in the Cerrado, since the 1870s. Indeed, while significant imports of zebu only resumed in the 1950s, by the 1920s, Brazilian ranchers had developed a national zebu breed: the Indubrasil. In 1922, the winner of the IV National Livestock Exposition was a zebu specimen, owned (ironically) by a *Paulista* (from São Paulo state) farmer. By the 1930s, "the suitability debate had been resolved in favor of the Zebu"—the intervention of the federal government with the foundation of experimental ranches and the creation of a zebu registry facilitated this outcome.[61]

The discussion of the zebu extended to southernmost Brazil and was expressed in similar terms in the agricultural publications of Rio Grande do Sul. Zebu cattle were in the north part of the state, but scarcely in the Campanha Gaúcha, the only region in Brazil that had natural conditions for raising the high-quality animals that the refrigeration industry required. By 1914, just one county in the state "had adopted the zebu." Riograndesenses continuously imported criollo cattle from Argentina and Uruguay, while at the same time introducing Herford and Shorthorn; by 1918 "at least 37 percent of the regional herd" was crosses of British breeds. However, in relation to their neighbors, these efforts came late. While pure pedigree animals had arrived in Argentina as early as the 1850s, with results in the local herds two decades later, in Rio Grande scattered records suggest that they were only systematically introduced at the beginning of the twentieth century.[62]

Considered in the broader context of ranching modernization in the Americas from mid-to-late-nineteenth century, not a single region of Brazil, including Rio Grande do Sul, underwent transformations similar to those in certain areas of neighboring Argentina or Uruguay. Cattle raising remained widespread throughout the country, with no indication that ranchers used fencing for crossbreeding or improved feeding. Nevertheless, the introduction of zebu could be seen as a sign of modernization, a unique modernization for sure, but one aligned with the local environment and market conditions. Such an improvement is reflected not only in the increment of herds, but also in the value of crossbred animals. For instance, in 1902 Goiás, a zebu-cross cattle could cost twice as much as a crioulo. Itagyba, the cattleman mentioned above, observed a similar ratio in transactions in the interior of Minas Gerais and at the Santa Cruz slaughterhouse in Rio de Janeiro.[63]

Although the controversy over the zebu was an internal affair, and Cotrim's "provocations"—mentioned earlier—had the domestic audience in mind, it was inspired by debates in Europe and geared toward external buyers. By appealing to Brazilian "western civilization" roots, he was indicating to importers in Europe—mostly in Great Britain— that Brazil and São Paulo in particular would meet their quality standards. With an eye toward European markets, cattle associations, rural magazines, and bulletins, not only in São Paulo but elsewhere in the country, also displayed the same mistrust of the zebu. Nevertheless, the sudden surge of Brazil's frozen meat exports due to World War I was only possible because, years before, the adoption of the zebu in the central plateau and in the southeast, along with the expansion of the railroad grid and the introduction of meatpacking companies, allowed fat cattle from these regions to reach the frigoríficos and, from there, Brazil's coast. As Antônio da Silva Prado (who had intimate knowledge and interests in these three sectors) put it in 1916: "Without the Zebu, Brazil would not be exporting meat nor would it be doing so soon. Almost all cattle being slaughtered for beef exports are zebu mestizo."[64] Having considered the importance of the zebu in the development of the Brazilian livestock industry, the next section focuses on how the railroads transformed cattle shipping in the country.

Driving Livestock to Markets: The Railways Disrupt Cattle Trails

In the early twentieth century, traditional livestock breeding and trailing operations in Brazil faced prospects of modernization, for its "vast expanses of pasturage available ... for cattle-raising"[65] began to attract the attention of national and foreign investors. As in other areas of the Americas, the introduction of technology to improve livestock production—as part of economic development and its stimuli, whose roots can be traced back to Great Britain and the United States—prompted changes, albeit very slowly, in the conditions described above, and challenged actors linked to long-established ranching and trading networks. This section describes how transport technology boosted trade and began to affect those along this supply chain.

The circulation patterns of cattle required a series of intermediaries, whose interests and livelihood were threatened by the advent of the railroads. Before the arrival of this new transportation technology, breeders would typically sell their animals to trail drivers who herded them on the hoof for several months to pasturelands for fattening. There, cattle were kept in winter pasturage until they reached a size suitable for sale. Depending on the extent of technology involved, this process could last up to a full year, at which point the herds would be sold again, this time to merchants at local fairs. Those dealers then transported the cattle to suburban corrals, where they rested for a few days to replenish their natural properties and control supplies within the limits of the urban market. Their long journey finally ended at the municipal abattoir. In the case of Rio de Janeiro, the local governments oversaw the meat retailing process, determining consumer prices through a system of annual public auctions.[66]

A major but incremental change in those commercial cattle circuits took place after the introduction of the railroad; however, the traditional production areas described above were not simply replaced by new ones. Rather, some entered a phase of expansion due, in part, to the advances in animal husbandry in remote raising areas, the increasing market needs in Rio de Janeiro and São Paulo, and the expansion of the railway network. By early twentieth century, although trailers continued to drive yearlings to fattening areas, the foundation of railhead towns allowed a small number—increasing over the years—of matured cattle to be sent by rail either to slaughterhouses in Rio de Janeiro or to recently established packing houses in the southeast. However, because the rail lines did not always follow fattening zones in this process, some areas were forced to yield their primacy to those located near train stations or to those created to such an end.[67]

Given that the cost of hauling cattle to consumer markets was determined not only by driving expenses but also, most importantly, by "the value of the meat and fat lost through shrinkage in transit,"[68] with the railroads, fatteners and merchants could better protect their investment. Roughly estimating, by the early 1910s, a yearling steer in Mato Grosso was valued at about 40 to 45 *mil-réis* (US$13 to $14.50), while mature cattle sold in Minas Gerais fetched twice that amount.[69] Not surprisingly, several rail stations crossed fattening grounds in Minas. In addition, to facilitate trade and to collect taxes more efficiently, state governments created cattle fairs. By the 1890s, ranchers in south Minas Gerais, from the municipalities of Bom Sucesso, Lavras, Pitangui, Itapecerica, Abaeté, Campo Bello, Formiga, and Turvo negotiated their cattle at the Três Corações official fair, transporting them through the rail services of *Estrada de Ferro Minas e Rio* to Rio de Janeiro and São Paulo states. Benfica (Minas Gerais) was the official fair and entrepôt for ranchers in central and north Minas Gerais, linking the municipalities of Curvello, Silva Xavier, and Sete Lagoas to São Paulo via the *Estrada de Ferro Central do Brasil* (see Figure 4.2).[70]

Some of these cattle fairs were short-lived, as with Três Corações in south Minas Gerais. Soon after the railroad Estrada de Ferro Minas e Rio reached the municipality of Três Corações do Rio Verde in 1884, the state government created the fair. The objective was to concentrate fattened cattle in the area and ship them directly to the Santa Cruz slaughterhouse in Rio via the new railroad. The first concession was given to Belchior Pimenta Abreu, who was responsible for organizing the fair, to maintain the pasturelands and to promote cattle expositions. Between 1902 and 1914, the number of herds negotiated in Três Corações increased almost twofold; in the same period, animal cargo in the Estrada de Ferro Minas e

Figure 4.2 Selected railroad lines in Brazil, c. 1930.

Source: Moacir M. F. Silva, "Geografia das estradas de ferro brasileiras em seu primeiro centenário (1854–1954)," in *I Centenário das ferrovias brasileiras* (Rio de Janeiro: IBGE, 1954), 3–6.

Rio jumped from a little over 2,000 herds in 1884 to more than 100,000 in 1908. Technological developments contributed to the fair's demise. When São Paulo opened its first packing company, ranchers could send cattle directly from fattening grounds to the frigoríficos, and from there to domestic or international markets. By the 1920s, Minas had closed several cattle fairs.[71] A similar fate befell the Sorocaba fair in São Paulo, described in 1885 by an observer as "run-down" business.[72]

The pace of transport innovation was, of course, uneven throughout the country; furthermore, the savings mentioned above depended upon hauling costs and the region in which cattle were raised. In 1898, ranchers from Rio Verde, Rio Bonito, and Jataí municipalities (in south Goiás) regularly moved their fattened cattle (four to five year old) along a "sluggish and arduous almost 60 day-long journey" to the Passos cattle fair in Minas Gerais. After trailing more than 600 kilometers, the animals were fattened on pasture, for a period of four to eight months (in Minas Gerais); once matured, they were walked up to the Santa Cruz matadouro in Rio or to São Paulo. In spite of all expenses, in 1898, a commentator in the newspaper *Lavoura e Commercio* insisted (with optimism) that this was still a "profitable business."[73]

With an eye toward strengthening the mining and food sectors, the federal government charged low rates for use of its lines. In 1919, for instance, the railroad *Estrada Federal Noroeste do Brasil* (see Figure 4.2), which connected São Paulo and Mato Grosso, offered a 50 percent discount on freight rates, depending on the weight and quantity of the animals shipped.[74] In spite of such incentives, which amounts to a subsidy (given the nature of railroad cattle shipping, stock cars always returned empty from their destination back to their point of origin),[75] a considerable number of herds made their journey on the hoof or, when coming from central Brazil, by raft. In Goiás, even after the introduction of the railway *Estrada de Ferro de Goiás* (see Figure 4.2) in 1893, the vast majority of animals continued to be "walked" out of the state, mainly because they were lean animals to be fattened somewhere else. After 1893, however, a small fraction of mature cattle from Goiás reached the meatpacking plants in São Paulo by rail.[76]

While most cattle were still driven on the hoof from grazing lands to the main train stations—indeed, "exotic grasses" were cultivated near the tracks to feed the animals[77]—the railways helped reduce shipping costs, expand cattle production areas, and integrate markets. Ultimately, this method resulted in time- and feed-savings and, most importantly, lessened the deterioration of animal quality during the journey. The rail lines represented a major transport improvement—though imperfect, as they did not reach several areas of Brazil and were, in fact, poorly interconnected.[78] Observing the case of Mato Grosso, historian Zephyr Frank affirms that although the railroads did not integrate the state's market, they did "lower the transport costs of the frontier's products."[79]

The opening of the road *Estrada Mato Grosso-São Paulo* in late 1906 offers an example of how the railroads impacted cattle drives. The Campos de Vacaria was one of the most productive cattle ranges in south Mato Grosso. In 1908, after several failed attempts to establish a direct connection between this area and São Paulo, a consortium later called

Companhia Viação de São Paulo-Mato Grosso began to oversee a new road. Starting in Porto Alegre (MT), steers were herded east, crossed the Paraná River by raft and reached Indiana (SP)—a fattening station, from which, once matured, cattle were once again driven to the state's pasturelands and/or meatpacking houses. To feed the herds along the trail, the company established a series of lodges (*pousos*), with grasses for livestock and accommodations for trail drivers. After 1917, sections of the road itself along with some of its ancillary structure became obsolete; for, in that year, the *Estrada de Ferro Sorocabana* reached Indiana (see Figure 4.2), where ranchers embarked cattle destined for São Paulo.[80]

Another way to assess the impact of the railroads is to consider the volume of cattle transported by rail. Cargo records from the Brazilian railroads reveal that, from the 1890s to the early years of the twentieth century, the Estrada de Ferro Minas e Rio shipped approximately 70,000 head of cattle per annum.[81] The transit of "animals" on the Estrada de Ferro Central do Brazil railway, which in 1898 extended from Rio de Janeiro all the way across the state to the municipality of Três Rios in Minas Gerais, increased from 9,000 metric tons in 1885 to 90,000 in 1905. In the same period, data from the *Companhia Mogiana de Estradas de Ferro*—which ran from São Paulo to Minas Gerais (See Figure 4.2)—show that animal cargo rose from 2,000 units in 1887 to more than 60,000 in 1905.[82] In mid-1910s, cattle shipment grew in units, thanks in part to wartime demands. Starting in 1916, Mogiana's livestock cargo surpassed 100,000 units, reaching 140,000 three years later.[83] From 1908 to 1920, the railway *Viação Férrea do Rio Grande do Sul* (see Figure 4.2), which combined all state lines in 1905, shipped approximately 70,000–80,000 head of cattle annually.[84]

Although these data do not provide details as to the kinds of animals transported, or their final destination, probably, in the case of São Paulo, Minas Gerais, or Rio de Janeiro, the cattle shipped were destined to satisfy the needs of urban centers in the southeast and to supply meatpacking companies in the region. In Rio Grande do Sul, the track length and extension of rail lines over the years indicate improved links between cattle raising areas and charqueadas. They also show direct connections to Uruguay, whose railroad system and better port facilities were used to transship charque from Rio Grande do Sul to other regions of Brazil.

An analysis of national data on total livestock (excluding horses) shipping weight shows that from the early twentieth century to 1922, animal cargo grew at an annual rate of approximately 7 percent (see Figure 4.3). These years were selected based on the availability and organization of the sources—after 1922, it is not possible to differentiate the types of animal transported consistently. The sudden surge after 1914 is clearly related to World War I, as is the dip in 1919. Throughout this period, additional figures reveal three tendencies: first, cattle traffic accounted for 85–90 percent (depending on the year) of total freight, while combined shipments

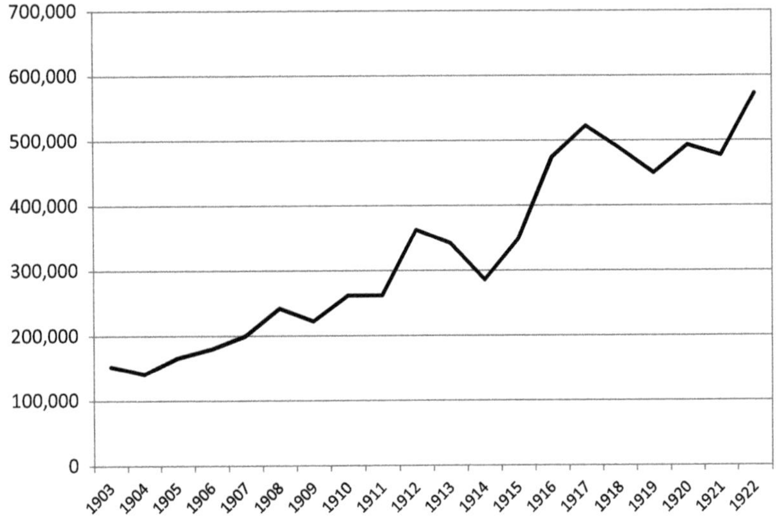

Figure 4.3 Total livestock cargo in Brazil (metric tons), 1903–1922.

Sources: Brasil, Ministério da indústria, viação e obras públicas, Directoria geral de obras e viação, *Estatística das estradas de ferro da união e das fiscalizadas pela união em 31 de dezembro de 1903–1922* (Rio de Janeiro: Imprensa Nacional, 1905–1925): Table 13. Data from the years 1906 and 1907 are estimates.

of goats and pigs represented the remainder; second, the Central do Brasil and Minas e Rio lines (in the southeast) transported the vast majority of animals that circulated in Brazil,[85] including goats and pigs, although these were more evenly distributed among rail lines; and third, while from 1903 to 1910 the aforementioned lines transported more than 80 percent of total national cattle cargo, by the end of the decade, their share had decreased to 63 percent. Cattle cargo of the Viação Férrea do Rio Grande do Sul surged, rivaling with that of Minas Gerais's railroads. However, the most noticeable trend relates to the activity of the lines from São Paulo: Sorocabana, Mogiana, particularly the Companhia Paulista. In 1917, the last of the three hauled almost similar weight as Central do Brasil, but in 1920, Companhia Paulista alone transported more cattle than Central do Brasil.[86]

Because the development of the modern meat chain depended on technological improvements in transport and refrigeration (which connected cattle supply areas to packing plants, and these to consumer markets), the dramatic increase in the Paulista cattle shipment underscores the contribution of the rail network to the nascent frigorífico industry in São Paulo.[87] For instance, in 1909, the Paulista opened its Barretos station; three years later, the Companhia Frigorífica e Pastoril (1913) initiated operations in the same town. Soon, other national and foreign investors established meatpacking companies in Brazil. In 1917, the state of Rio de Janeiro inaugurated its first packing plant—although as Chapter 6 examines, it encountered several barriers to enter Rio's market. What is more, while superficially it might seem that this growth only benefited the export sector (given the spike in frozen meat remittances between 1916 and 1919), new frigoríficos output was also geared toward the needs of an emergent working and middle class in Rio de Janeiro and São Paulo. In particular, after World War I, packers—faced with diminished European demand—focused their attention inward to densely populated areas in the country.[88]

* * *

During the nineteenth century, noticeable changes occurred in Brazil as a result of the development of commercial coffee farming and related urbanization and industrialization, particularly in the southeast. With respect to ranching, as early as the 1850s, cattle breeding areas started to move westward, into the country's central plateau. In the meantime, the extension of the railroad grid lowered transport costs and allowed mature cattle to reach urban markets and packing plants more efficiently. These developments were no different from those seen in other meat-producing countries, including Argentina and Uruguay, whose ranching modernization, for the most part, entailed (but was not limited to) the following steps: expansion of pasturelands, internal transport advancement, and imports of British (mainly) purebred stock to improve the quality of local herds. When it came to the third step, Brazil, unlike its aforementioned neighbors, pursued an unconventional path, as certain areas of the country adopted the zebu for upgrading. This innovation, although controversial, enabled ranchers to satisfy domestic and, eventually, European needs. Likewise, it set the stage for livestock production in tropical environments during the twentieth century. The next chapter addresses how these and other technological advances transformed fresh meat offerings in Rio de Janeiro.

Notes

1 According to current classification, cattle of European (*Bos taurus*) and Indian origin (*Bos indicus*) are two distinct species; they probably have a common ancestor, *Bos primigenius*, but developed in different regions. Zebu cattle have a distinct shoulder hump and long ears. Robert W. Wilcox, *Cattle in the Backlands: Mato Grosso and the Evolution of Ranching in the Brazilian Tropics* (Austin: University of Texas Press, 2017), 200.

2 In the colonial era, Portuguese America was subdivided into "captaincies"; during the Brazilian Empire (1822–1889) these were converted into "provinces." They were renamed "states" with the advent of the Republic in 1889.

3 James W. Wells, *Exploring and Travelling Three Thousand Miles Through Brazil from Rio de Janeiro to Maranhão, with an Appendix Containing Statistics and Observations on Climate, Railways, Central Sugar Factories, Mining, Commerce, and Finance, the Past, Present, and Future, and Physical*

Geography of Brazil (London: Sampson Low, Marston, Searle, & Rivington, 1886), 369–70.

4 Crioulo cattle (*criollo* in Spanish) are mixed-blood cattle of Iberian-origin brought to the Americas.

5 Manuel Martins do Couto Reis, "Memorias de Santa Cruz," *Revista do Instituto Histórico e Geográfico do Brasil* 5, no. 18 (Rio de Janeiro: Typographia universal de Laemmert & C., 1885): 187.

6 Larissa Virginia Brown, "Internal Commerce in a Colonial Economy: Rio de Janeiro and its Hinterland, 1790–1822" (PhD diss., University of Virginia, 1986), 479–81.

7 Maria Theresa Schorer Petrone, "O afluxo de gado a Sorocaba e a importância econômica do caminho do sul na década da independência," *Revista de História* 46, no. 94 (1973): 392.

8 Brown, "Internal Commerce," 653.

9 Nineteenth-century Brazilian sources used the word "exports" interchangeably referring to interprovincial trade and international commerce.

10 *Relatorio do presidente da provincia de Mato Grosso, o chefe de divisão Augusto Leverger, na abertura da sessão ordinaria da Assembléa Legislativa Provincial em 4 de dezembro de 1856* (Cuiabá, Typ. do Echo Cuiabano, 1856), 8; Wilcox, *Cattle in the Backlands,* 35–45.

11 Domingos Sávio da Cunha Garcia, "Mato Grosso (1850–1889). Uma província na fronteira do Império" (master's thesis, Universidade de Campinas, 2001), 24–42.

12 The Triple Alliance War, also known as the Paraguayan War, is South America's bloodiest war, and saw Brazil, Argentina, and Uruguay pitted against Paraguay. Its root causes lay in the fragmentation of the Viceroyalty of the Río de La Plata (which roughly encompassed most of today's Argentina and regions of Bolivia, Paraguay, and Uruguay) and geopolitics of the newly independent states. Brazil feared that Argentina's expansion (the second-largest country on the subcontinent) would threaten its power in South America and limit free navigation on the Paraguay River, which provided a major access route to Mato Grosso. Paraguay feared Brazilian and Argentinean expansionism, while attempting to maintain independence from both countries. Brazil, for its part, repeatedly meddled in Uruguay's internal affairs; in 1864, it backed a political faction favorable to Brazilian interests. Later that year, Paraguay invaded Mato Grosso and petitioned Argentina to cross its territory to attack Brazilian troops in Rio Grande do Sul and Uruguay. Argentina did not concede; in response, in March 1865 Paraguay declared war against Argentina. Two months later, Argentina, Brazil, and Uruguay allied against Paraguay and signed the Treaty of Triple Alliance. The costs of the war were devastating, particularly for Paraguay. It lost territories to its South American neighbors (Mato Grosso enlarged its territory at the expense of Paraguay), and approximately 50 percent of the Paraguayan population died from combat, hunger, and epidemics. Boris Fausto, *História do Brasil* (São Paulo: EDUSP, 1995), 208–17.

13 Paulo Marcos Esselin, *A pecuária bovina no processo de ocupação e desenvolvimento econômico do Pantanal Sul-Mato-Grossense (1830 – 1910)* (Dourados: Editora da Universidade Federal de Dourados, 2011), 236–59.

14 David McCreery, *Frontier Goiás, 1822–1889* (Stanford, CA: Stanford University Press, 2006), 148.

15 *Relatorio apresentado á Assembléa Legislativa Provincial de Goyaz á 8 de abril de 1886 pelo exm. presidente da provincia,* dr. Guilherme Francisco Cruz (Goyaz: Typ. Provincial, 1886), 14; *Mensagem dirigida a Camara Legislativa*

de Goiás pelo governador do estado Major Dr. Rodolpho Gustavo da Paixão (Goiaz: Typ. Perseverança de Tocantins e Aranha, 1891), 34.

16 Brown, *Internal*, 490–93.

17 It is important to stress that beasts of burden continued to link production areas in the interior to nearby ports and rail stations, from which goods were carried to their final destination. Carlos Eduardo Suprinyak, "Comércio de animais de carga no Brasil imperial: uma análise quantitativa das tropas negociadas nas províncias do Paraná e São Paulo" (master's thesis, Universidade Estadual Paulista, Araraquara, 2006), 5–8; Herbert S. Klein, "The Supply of Mules to Central Brazil: The Sorocaba Market, 1825–1880," *Agricultural History* 64, no. 4 (1990): 1–25; Renato Leite Marcondes, "Formação da rede regional de abastecimento do Rio de Janeiro: a presença dos negociantes de gado (1801–1811)," *Topoi. Revista de História* 2, n. 2 (2001): 42–48; Petrone, "O afluxo de gado," 385–86.

18 Brown, *Internal*, 492–513, see tables 7.2, 513, 7.3, 514, 590–91, 9.4, 636–42, and 9.5, 643.

19 *Relatório do presidente da província de São Pedro do Rio Grande do Sul, o senador conselheiro Manoel Antonio Galvão, na abertura da Assembléa Legislativa Provincial em 5 de outubro de 1847, acompanhado do orçamento da receita e despesa para o anno de 1847 a 1848* (Porto Alegre: Typographia de Argos, de J. C. Barreto, 1847), 49.

20 *Relatório do presidente da província de Santa Catarina Francisco Carlos de Araújo Brusque apresentado a Assembléia legislativa Provincial* (Rio de Janeiro: Typographia do Correio Mercantil, 1860), 33.

21 Stephen Bell, *Campanha Gaúcha: A Brazilian Ranching System, 1850–1920* (Stanford, CA: Stanford University Press, 1998), 80; Jonas Vargas, "Abastecendo plantations. A inserção do charque fabricado em Pelotas (RS) no comércio atlântico das carnes e a sua concorrência com os produtores platinos (século XIX)," *História (São Paulo)* 33, no. 2 (2014): 541, accessed November 28, 2020, DOI: 10.1590/1980-436920140002000025.

22 N. de S., "A indústria em Minas Gerais," *Annuario de Minas Gerais. Estatística, história, chorographia, finanças, variedades, biographia, literatura, indicações*, ano 1 (Belo Horizonte, 1906), 111; Diôres Santos Abreu, "Comunicações entre o sul de Mato Grosso e o sudoeste de São Paulo. O comércio de gado," *Revista de História* 53, no. 105 (1976): 198.

23 Quoted in Cristiano Corte Restitutti, "As fronteiras da província: rotas de comércio interprovincial, Minas Gerais, 1839–1884" (master's thesis, Universidade Estadual Paulista, Araraquara, 2006), 261. This work presents an impressively detailed account about Minas Gerais interprovincial commerce.

24 N. de S., "A indústria em Minas Gerais," 99, 111.

25 Miguel Arrojado Ribeiro Lisboa, *Oeste de São Paulo-Sul de Mato Grosso* (Rio de Janeiro: Typ. do "Jornal do comercio," de Rodrigues & C., 1909), 145.

26 Restitutti, "As fronteiras," 193.

27 In 1900, the city of São Paulo had almost four times more inhabitants than it had counted one decade earlier. Brasil, Instituto Brasileiro de Geografia e Estatística, "População nos Censos Demográficos, segundo os municípios das capitais – 1872/2010," accessed November 11, 2020, https://censo2010.ibge.gov.br/sinopse/index.php?dados=6.

28 Rudolf Endlich, "A criação do gado vaccum nas partes interiores da América do Sul," *Boletim da agricultura* 3, no. 12 (1902): 813–14.

29 See Brasil, *Annuario Estatístico do Brazil, 1°. Ano (1908–1912)*, vol. 2 (Rio de Janeiro: Typographia da Estatística, 1917), IV–XIV; Roberto C. Simonsen,

The Meat & Cattle Industry of Brazil; Its Importance to Anglo-Brazilian Commerce (London: Industrial Publicity Service, 1919), 2–5.

30 Richard Perren, *Taste, Trade and Technology: The Development of the International Meat Industry Since 1840* (Aldershot, UK: Ashgate Publishing, 2006), 33; David Zimmerman, "Live Cattle Export Trade between United States and Great Britain, 1868–1885," *Agricultural History* 36, no. 1 (1962): 47–52; John Walton, "Pedigree and the National Cattle Herd *circa* 1750–1950," *The Agricultural History Review* 34, no. 2 (1986): 149–170; Carmen Sesto, "The Vanguard Landowners of Buenos Aires: A New Production Model, 1856–1900," *Hispanic American Historical Review* 82, no. 4 (2002): 721–23.

31 Rodolfo Waehneldt, "Exploração da província de Mato Grosso," *Revista do Instituto Histórico, Geográphico e Ethnográphico do Brasil*, t. 27, v. 28 (1864): 205–06.

32 Tyler Priest, "Extraction Not Creation: The History of Offshore Petroleum in the Gulf of Mexico," *Enterprise & Society* 8, no. 2 (2007): 230.

33 Zebu cattle is more resistant to ticks, carrying only "10 to 20% of the number of ticks found on other cattle." See Claire Storm, *Making Catfish Bait our of Government Boys. The Fight Against Cattle Ticks and the Transformation of the Yeoman South* (Athens, GA: University of Georgia Press, 2009), 209.

34 Eduardo Cotrim, "Indústria pecuária. Problemas da indústria pecuária na República Argentina e estudo comparativo com o Brasil," in *Memória apresentada ao Exmo. Sr. dr. Pedro de Toledo, ministro da agricultura, indústria e commercio* (Rio de Janeiro: Typographia do Serviço de Estatística, 1912), 171; Robert W. Wilcox, "Ranching and Market Access in the Backlands: Mato Grosso, Brazil, ca. 1900–1940s," *La Historia Crítica*, no. 51 (September–December 2013): 73.

35 Brasil, *Annuario Estatístico do Brazil, 1°. Ano (1908–1912)*, XI.

36 Robert W. Wilcox, "'The Law of the Least Effort': Cattle Ranching and the Environment in the Savanna of Mato Grosso, Brazil, 1900–1980," *Environmental History* 4, no. 3 (1999): 339–43; "Campo cerrado," *Revista Brasileira de Geografia* 2, no. 3 (1940): 478; Fernando Segadas Vianna, "Os diferentes tipos de vegetação do Brasil e sua possibilidade de explotação e utilização," *Revista Brasileira de Geografia* 26, no. 2 (1964): 241–42.

37 Maria Thereza Schorer Petrone, "As áreas de criação de gado," in *História geral da civilização brasileira*, t. 1, v. 2, ed. Sérgio Buarque de Holanda (Rio de Janeiro: Editora Bertrand Brasil, 1993), 218–27; Vianna, "Os diferentes," 242–44.

38 Vianna, "Os diferentes," 241–44; Hermann von Ihering, "A distribuição de campos de mattas no Brazil," *Revista do Museu Paulista* 7 (1907): 137–38; Miguel Arrojado Ribeiro Lisboa, "Industria Pastoril em Mato Grosso," *Almanaque Brasileiro Garnier* (1911): 160–66.

39 In addition, animals in the region were less prone to disease than in tropical and semitropical regions of Brazil. Ihering, "A distribuição," 138; Leo Waibel, *Capítulos de geografia tropical e do Brasil* (Rio de Janeiro: Serviço gráfico do Instituto Brasileiro de Geografia e Estatística, 1958), 9–13; "Campos de criação do Rio Grande do Sul," *Revista Brasileira de Geografia* 2, no. 2 (1940): 262; Maria da Glória de Carvalho Campos, "Notas para um estudo da distribuição do rebanho bovino no Brasil meridional," *Revista Brasileira de Geografia* 17, no. 3 (1955): 334–39; Bertha K. Becker, "Expansão do mercado urbano e transformação da economia pastoril," *Revista Brasileira de Geografia* 28, no. 4 (1966): 297–330.

40 Eduardo Cotrim, *A fazenda moderna. Guia do criador de gado bovino no Brasil* (Bruxellas: Typographia V. Verteneuil & L. Desmet, 1913), 113.

41 *Arquivo Geral da Cidade do Rio de Janeiro*, Carnes e Matadouros, "Demonstração discriminada do gado bovino abatido no matadouro de Santa Cruz por nossa conta nos anos de 1893–1896," by Manuel José da Costa [illegible], May 14, 1900; J. C. Oakenfull, *Brazil in 1911* (Frome, UK: Printed by Butler & Tanner, 1912), 240.
42 Endlich, "A criação," 813.
43 Cotrim, *A fazenda moderna,* 135.
44 Ibid., 225–26.
45 Endlich, "A criação," 813–15; McCreery, *Frontier Goiás,* 134. See the experiences of Percival Farquhar in Brazil: Charles A. Gauld, *The Last Titan. Percival Farquhar, American Entrepreneur in Latin America* (Stanford, CA: Institute of Hispanic American and Luso-Brazilian Studies, 1964), 218–27.
46 Robert W. Wilcox, "Ranching Modernization in Tropical Brazil: Foreign Investment and Environment in Mato Grosso, 1900–1950," *Agricultural History* 82, no. 3 (2008): 375–78.
47 "O cruzado zebú," *Boletim da agricultura* 5, no. 8 (August 1904): 366–67. This is certainly one of many stories that integrate the narrative of the adoption of zebu cattle in Brazil. See Joana Medrado, "Do pastoreio à pecuária. A invenção da modernização rural nos sertões do Brasil Central" (PhD diss., Universidade Federal Flumense, 2013), 101.
48 Robert W. Wilcox, "Zebu's Elbows: Cattle Breeding and the Environment in Central Brazil, 1890–1960," in *Territories, Commodities and Knowledges: Latin American Environmental History in the Nineteenth and Twentieth Centuries*, ed. Christian Brannstorm (London: Institute for the Study of the Americas, 2004), 223–25; Medrado, *Do pastoreio à pecuária,* 106–40.
49 Endlich, "A criação," 744–45.
50 Wilcox, "Ranching Modernization," 376; Lisboa, *Oeste*, 153; Cotrim, *A indústria pecuária*, 19, 165–71; Lisboa, "Indústria Pastoril," 157.
51 Storm, *Making Catfish*, 3–5.
52 "O cruzado zebú," 367.
53 Antônio da Silva Prado was a prominent a Paulista coffee planter and politician with interests in railroad ventures; he also founded the first packinghouse in the state of São Paulo.
54 Antônio da Silva Prado, "Congresso de Pecuária," *O criador paulista* 11, no. 10 (October 1916): 275–78.
55 According to some estimates, by the 1910s, approximately 50 percent of the cattle population in Uberaba (Minas Gerais) was crosses of zebu. *Annuario de Minas Gerais. Chorographia do estado, história, estatística, variedades, letras, bibliographia*, ano 5 (Belo Horizonte, 1913), 874.
56 Shawn Van Ausdal, "Reimagining the Tropical Beef Frontier and the Nation in Early Twentieth-Century Colombia," in *Trading Environments. Frontiers, Commercial Knowledge, and Environmental Transformation, 1750–1990*, ed. Gordon M. Winder and Andreas Dix (New York: Routledge, 2016), 171–72; Wilcox, *Cattle in the Backlands*, 213.
57 Fernando Ruffier, *Manual prático de criação de gado no Brazil* (São Paulo: Empreza Editora de 'Chácaras e Quintaes,' 1918), 65. Relevant to this discussion is this manual's cover, which bears no semblance to the Brazilian farming landscape: it portrays a fenced property, with a wooden barn in the background, and a farmer wearing a pair of denim overall surrounded by dairy cows. Likewise, is important to be aware that Ruffier had farming experience in France, Great Britain, Mexico, and the United States.
58 *O Pharol*, January 9, 1916; February 3, 1916.
59 Ibid., February 3, 1916.

60 This measure, however, should certainly be seen in a broader context. After World War I, given meat (canned or otherwise) overproduction and low prices of the high quality variety, there was little appetite for the Brazilian low-grade product. Perren, *Taste, Trade and Technology*, 130; Van Ausdal, "Reimagining," 181.

61 Wilcox, "Zebu's Elbows," 233–34, see also Medrado, "Do pastoreio à pecuária," 157–58. Similar debates occurred in Colombia, see Shawn Van Ausdal, "Productivity Gains and the Limits of Tropical Ranching in Colombia, 1850–1950," *Agricultural History* 86, no. 3 (Summer 2012): 10–13.

62 Moreover, any genetic improvement should be accompanied by fencing and cultivated pastures, which only occurred systematically in Rio Grande do Sul after World War I. Wilcox, "Ranching and Modernization," 375–78; Sesto, "The Vanguard," 724; Bell, *Campanha Gaúcha*, 110–15; Waibel, *Capítulos*, 9–30.

63 *Mensagem enviada ao congresso na abertura da segunda sessão da legislatura pelo presidente do estado Dr. José Xavier de Almeida* (Goyaz: Typ. do 'Goyaz', 1902), 39; *O Pharol*, February 3, 1916.

64 Prado, "Congresso de Pecuária," 275–78; Wilcox, "Ranching and Market," 91.

65 This assessment appeared in the *Latin-American Yearbook*, paraphrasing a report by the Brazilian Railway Company published in 1912; *Latin-American Yearbook for Investors and Merchants for 1918* (New York: Criterion Newspaper Syndicate, 1918), 87.

66 See Klein, "The Supply of Mules," 6–7; Schmidt, "Tropas e Tropeiros," 105–06; Clarence F. Jones, "A fazenda Miranda em Mato Grosso," *Revista Brasileira de Geografia* 12, no. 3 (1950): 363–68.

67 Alexandre Macchione Saes and Elton Rodrigo Rosa, "Mercado Pontual: Atuação Estatal na Formação da Feira de Gado de Três Corações (1900–1920)," *Estudos Econômicos* 43, no. 4 (2013): 754–57; Abreu, "Comunicações," 210; Steven Topik, *The Political Economy of the Brazilian State, 1889–1930* (Austin: University of Texas Press, 1987), 115–18.

68 J. Colin Crossley and Robert Greenhill, "The River Plate Beef Trade," in *Business Imperialism, 1840–1930: An Inquiry Based on British Experience in Latin America*, ed. D. C. M. Platt (Oxford: Clarendon Press, 1977), 288–89.

69 Wilcox, *Cattle in the Backlands*, 261, endnote 14; *Annuario Estatístico Illustrado do estado de Minas Gerais*, ano 4 (Belo Horizonte, 1911), 285.

70 Moacir M. F. Silva, "Um guia ferroviário brasileiro do fim do século XIX," *Revista Brasileira de Geografia* 16, no. 2 (1954): 253–58.

71 Saes and Rosa, "Mercado," 757–68.

72 José Francisco de Oliveira, "A viação férrea e os engenhos centrais," *Revista de Estradas de Ferro* 1, no. 11 (November 1885): 167.

73 *Lavoura e commercio*, April 7, 1898.

74 For an analysis about the disputes between railroad companies and ranchers over high freight rates in the 1930s and 1940s see Paulo Roberto Cimó Queiroz, *Uma ferrovia entre dois mundos: A E. F. Noroeste do Brasil na primeira metade do século XX* (Bauru, Campo Grande: EDUSC/Editora da UFMS, 2004), 272–83; William R. Summerhill, *Order Against Progress: Government, Foreign Investment, and Railroads in Brazil, 1854–1913* (Stanford, CA: Stanford University Press, 2003), 85–98.

75 Steven Topik, *The Political Economy*, 111–20.

76 Paulo Roberto de Oliveira, "Um caminho voltado para dentro: o circuito goiano e o comércio entre Goiás e São Paulo na Primeira República" (PhD diss., Universidade de São Paulo, 2013), 105, 181–83.

77 Warren Dean, "The Brazilian Economy, 1870–1930," in *The Cambridge History of Latin America*, ed. Leslie Bethell, *The Cambridge History of Latin America* 5 (Cambridge: Cambridge University Press, 1986), 711.

78 Scholar Richard Perren observed a similar pattern in Australia and New Zealand. See Perren, *Taste, Trade and Technology*, 19–23.
79 Zephyr L. Frank, "Exports and Inequality: Evidence from the Brazilian Frontier, 1870–1937," *The Journal of Economic History* 61, no. 1 (March 2001): 43.
80 Abreu, "Comunicações," 197–214.
81 Brasil, Ministério da indústria, viação e obras públicas, Diretoria general de obras e viação, *Estatística das estradas de ferro da união e das fiscalizadas pela união em 31 de dezembro de 1903–1922*, Table 13 (Rio de Janeiro: Imprensa Nacional, 1905–1925); Bruno Nascimento Campos, "Tropas de aço: Os primeiros impactos da Minas and Rio Railway sobre a economia de abastecimento do sul de Minas (1884–1902)," *Cultura Histórica & Patrimônio* 1, no. 1 (2012): 102.
82 *The Brazilian Year Book 1908* (Rio de Janeiro: Offices of the Brazilian Year Book, 1908), 607–17.
83 Saes and Rosa, "Mercado," 767; Rodrigo Fontanari, Alexandre Macchione Saes, and Paulo Roberto de Oliveira, "Transporte ferroviário e economia regional em São Paulo: comércio de café e gado pela Cia. Mogiana E. F. (1900–1920)," Conference Proceedings, *XXXIII Encontro da Associação Portuguesa de História Económica e Social* (Aphes), *Estado, Sociedade e Mercados Num Mundo Global* (2013): 11–12.
84 Brasil, Ministério da indústria, viação e obras públicas, ..., *Estatística das estradas de ferro da união e das fiscalizadas pela união em 31 de dezembro de 1908–1920,* Table 13 (Rio de Janeiro: Imprensa Nacional, 1910–1924); Bell, *Campanha Gaúcha*, 142–48; Suprinyak, "Comércio de animais," 5–8.
85 This is not surprising, considering that in terms of traffic and cargo, these were the most important lines in the country. Topik, *The Political Economy*, 97; Marcel Pereira da Silva, "De gado a café: as ferrovias no Sul de Minas Gerais, (1874–1910)" (master's thesis, Universidade de São Paulo, 2012), 147–56.
86 Flávio A. M. de Saes, *As ferrovias de São Paulo, 1870–1940* (São Paulo: Editora Hucitec, 1981), 117–20; Oliveira, "Um caminho," 159.
87 For a historiographical discussion on the role that the expansion of the railroad grid played in the economic development of late nineteenth-century Brazil, see William Summerhill, "Transport Improvements and Economic Growth in Brazil and Mexico," in *How Latin American Fell Behind. Essays on the Economic Histories of Brazil and Mexico, 1800–1914,* ed. Stephen Haber (Stanford, CA: Stanford University Press, 1997), 93–117.
88 The case of Brazil is consistent with other experiences. For Spain, see Miguel Muñoz Rubio, "El transporte ferroviario de ganado y el mercado entre 1848 y 1913," *Historia Agraria: Revista de Agricultura e Historia Rural* 67 (December 2015): 101–03.

Bibliography

Archives Consulted

Arquivo Geral da Cidade do Rio de Janeiro, (cited as AGCRJ)

Government Documents and Publications

Brasil. *Annuario Estatístico do Brazil, 1°. Ano (1908–1912)*. Vol. 2. Rio de Janeiro: Typographia da Estatística, 1917.

Brasil. Ministério da indústria, viação e obras públicas, Diretoria general de obras e viação, *Estatística das estradas de ferro da união e das fiscalizadas pela união em 31 de dezembro de 1903–1922*. Rio de Janeiro: Imprensa Nacional, 1905–1925.

Brasil. Instituto Brasileiro de Geografia e Estatística. "População nos Censos Demográficos, segundo os municípios das capitais - 1872/2010." Accessed November 11, 2020, https://censo2010.ibge.gov.br/sinopse/index.php?dados=6.

Mensagem dirigida a Camara Legislativa de Goiás pelo governador do estado Major Dr. Rodolpho Gustavo da Paixão. Goiaz: Typ. Perseverança de Tocantins e Aranha, 1891.

Mensagem enviada ao congresso na abertura da segunda sessão da legislatura pelo presidente do estado Dr. José Xavier de Almeida. Goyaz: Typ. do 'Goyaz', 1902.

Relatorio apresentado á Assembléa Legislativa Provincial de Goyaz á 8 de abril de 1886 pelo exm. presidente da provincia, dr. Guilherme Francisco Cruz. Goyaz: Typ. Provincial, 1886.

Relatorio do presidente da provincia de Mato Grosso, o chefe de divisão Augusto Leverger, na abertura da sessão ordinaria da Assembléa Legislativa Provincial em 4 de dezembro de 1856. Cuiabá: Typ. do Echo Cuiabano, 1856.

Relatório do presidente da província de Santa Catarina Francisco Carlos de Araújo Brusque apresentado a Assembléia legislativa Provincial. Rio de Janeiro: Typographia do Correio Mercantil, 1860.

Relatório do presidente da província de São Pedro do Rio Grande do Sul, o senador conselheiro Manoel Antonio Galvão, na abertura da Assembléa Legislativa Provincial em 5 de outubro de 1847, acompanhado do orçamento da receita e despesa para o anno de 1847 a 1848. Porto Alegre: Typographia de Argos, de J. C. Barreto, 1847.

Newspapers and Magazines

Lavoura e commercio (São Paulo)
O *Pharol* (Juiz de Fora)

Other Primary Sources

Annuario Estatístico Illustrado do estado de Minas Gerais. Ano 4. Belo Horizonte, 1911.

Annuario de Minas Gerais. Chorographia do estado, história, estatística, variedades, letras, bibliographia. Ano 5. Belo Horizonte, 1913.

Brockes, C., and C. Held. *Mappa do Imperio do Brazil: augmentado de dados estatisticos e outras correcções resultantes de estudos e melhoramentos recentes*. Rio de Janeiro: H. Laemmert & C., 1883.

Cotrim, Eduardo. "Indústria pecuária. Problemas da indústria pecuária na República Argentina e estudo comparativo com o Brasil." *In Memória apresentada ao Exmo. Sr. dr. Pedro de Toledo, ministro da agricultura, indústria e commercio*. Rio de Janeiro: Typographia do Serviço de Estatística, 1912.

Cotrim, Eduardo. *A fazenda moderna. Guia do criador de gado bovino no Brasil.* Bruxellas: Typographia V. Verteneuil & L. Desmet, 1913.

Endlich, Rudolf. "A criação do gado vaccum nas partes interiores da América do Sul." *Boletim da agricultura* 3, no. 1 (1902): 740–749, 810–821.

Ihering, Hermann von. "A distribuição de campos de mattas no Brazil." *Revista do Museu Paulista* 7 (1907): 125–157.

Latin-American Yearbook for Investors and Merchants for 1918. New York: Criterion Newspaper Syndicate, 1918.

Lisboa, Miguel Arrojado Ribeiro. *Oeste de São Paulo-Sul de Mato Grosso.* Rio de Janeiro: Typ. do "Jornal do comercio," de Rodrigues & C., 1909.

Lisboa, Miguel Arrojado Ribeiro. "Indústria Pastoril em Mato Grosso." *Almanaque Brasileiro Garnier* (1911): 153–179.

Oakenfull, J. C. *Brazil in 1911.* Frome, UK: Printed by Butler & Tanner, 1912.

"O cruzado zebú." *Boletim da agricultura* 5, no. 8 (August 1904): 365–368.

Oliveira, José Francisco de. "A viação férrea e os engenhos centrais." *Revista de Estradas de Ferro* 1, no. 11 (November 1885): 167–170.

Prado, Antônio da Silva. "Congresso de Pecuária." *O criador paulista* 11, no. 10 (October 1916): 271–279.

Reis, Manuel Martins do Couto. "Memorias de Santa Cruz." *Revista do Instituto Histórico e Geográfico do Brasil* 5, no. 18. Rio de Janeiro: Typographia universal de Laemmert & C., (1885): 154–199.

Ruffier, Fernando. *Manual prático de criação de gado no Brazil.* São Paulo: Empreza Editora de 'Chácaras e Quintaes', 1918.

Simonsen, Roberto C. *The Meat & Cattle Industry of Brazil; Its Importance to Anglo-Brazilian Commerce.* London: Industrial Publicity Service, 1919.

de S., N. "A indústria em Minas Gerais." In *Annuario de Minas Gerais. Estatística, história, chorographia, finanças, variedades, biographia, literatura, indicações.* Ano 1. Belo Horizonte, 1906.

The Brazilian Year Book 1908. Rio de Janeiro: Offices of the Brazilian Year Book, 1908.

Waehneldt, Rodolfo. "Exploração da província de Mato Grosso." *Revista do Instituto Histórico, Geográphico e Ethnográphico do Brasil.* T. 27. V. 28 (1864): 193–229.

Wells, James W. *Exploring and Travelling Three Thousand Miles Through Brazil from Rio de Janeiro to Maranhão, with an Appendix Containing Statistics and Observations on Climate, Railways, Central Sugar Factories, Mining, Commerce, and Finance, the Past, Present, and Future, and Physical Geography of Brazil.* London: Sampson Low, Marston, Searle, & Rivington, 1886.

Secondary Sources

Abreu, Diôres Santos. "Comunicações entre o sul de Mato Grosso e o sudoeste de São Paulo. O comércio de gado." *Revista de História* 53, no. 105 (1976): 191–214.

Becker, Bertha K. "Expansão do mercado urbano e transformação da economia pastoril." *Revista Brasileira de Geografia* 28, no. 4 (1966): 297–328.

Bell, Stephen. *Campanha Gaúcha: A Brazilian Ranching System, 1850–1920.* Stanford, CA: Stanford University Press, 1998.

Brown, Larissa Virginia. "Internal Commerce in a Colonial Economy: Rio de Janeiro and its Hinterland, 1790–1822." PhD diss., University of Virginia, 1986.

"Campo cerrado." *Revista Brasileira de Geografia* 2, no. 3 (1940a): 478–479.

Campos, Bruno Nascimento. "Tropas de aço: Os primeiros impactos da Minas and Rio Railway sobre a economia de abastecimento do sul de Minas (1884–1902)." *Cultura Histórica & Patrimônio* 1, no. 1 (2012): 91–107.

"Campos de criação do Rio Grande do Sul." *Revista Brasileira de Geografia* 2, no. 2 (1940b): 262–263.

Campos, Maria da Glória de Carvalho. "Notas para um estudo da distribuição do rebanho bovino no Brasil meridional." *Revista Brasileira de Geografia* 17, no. 3 (1955): 33–42.

Crossley, J. Colin, and Robert Greenhill. "The River Plate Beef Trade." In *Business Imperialism, 1840–1930: an Inquiry Based on British Experience in Latin America* edited by D.C.M. Platt, 284–334. Oxford: Clarendon Press, 1977.

Dean, Warren. "The Brazilian Economy, 1870–1930." In *The Cambridge History of Latin America 5*, edited by Leslie Bethell, 683–724. Cambridge: Cambridge University Press, 1986.

Esselin, Paulo Marcos. *A pecuária bovina no processo de ocupação e desenvolvimento econômico do Pantanal Sul-Mato-Grossense (1830–1910).* Dourados: Editora da Universidade Federal de Dourados, 2011.

Fausto, Boris. *História do Brasil.* São Paulo: EDUSP, 1995.

Fontanari, Rodrigo, Alexandre Macchione Saes, and Paulo Roberto de Oliveira. "Transporte ferroviário e economia regional em São Paulo: comércio de café e gado pela Cia. Mogiana E.F. (1900–1920)." Conference Proceedings *XXXIII, Encontro da Associação Portuguesa de História Económica e Social* (Aphes), *Estado, Sociedade e Mercados Num Mundo Global* (2013): 1–22.

Frank, Zephyr L. "Exports and Inequality: Evidence from the Brazilian Frontier, 1870–1937." *The Journal of Economic History* 61, no. 1 (March 2001): 37–58.

Garcia, Domingos Sávio da Cunha. "Mato Grosso (1850–1889). Uma província na fronteira do Império." Master's thesis: Universidade de Campinas, 2001.

Gauld, Charles A. *The Last Titan. Percival Farquhar, American Entrepreneur in Latin America.* Stanford, CA: Institute of Hispanic American and Luso-Brazilian Studies, 1964.

Jones, Clarence F. "A fazenda Miranda em Mato Grosso." *Revista Brasileira de Geografia* 12, no. 3 (1950): 353–370.

Klein, Herbert S. "The Supply of Mules to Central Brazil: The Sorocaba Market, 1825–1880." *Agricultural History* 64, no. 4 (1990): 1–25.

Marcondes, Renato Leite. "Formação da rede regional de abastecimento do Rio de Janeiro: a presença dos negociantes de gado (1801–1811)." *Topoi. Revista de História* 2, no. 2 (2001): 41–72.

McCreery, David. *Frontier Goiás, 1822–1889.* Stanford, CA: Stanford University Press, 2006.

Medrado, Joana. "Do pastoreio à pecuária. A invenção da modernização rural nos sertões do Brasil Central." PhD diss., Universidade Federal Fluminense, 2013.

Muñoz Rubio, Miguel. "El transporte ferroviario de ganado y el mercado entre 1848 y 1913." *Historia Agraria: Revista de Agricultura e Historia Rural* 67 (December 2015): 79–109.

Oliveira, Paulo Roberto de. "Um caminho voltado para dentro: o circuito goiano e o comércio entre Goiás e São Paulo na Primeira República." PhD diss., Universidade de São Paulo, 2013.

Perren, Richard. *Taste, Trade and Technology: The Development of the International Meat Industry Since 1840*. Aldershot, UK: Ashgate Publishing, 2006.

Petrone, Maria Theresa Schorer. "O afluxo de gado a Sorocaba e a importância econômica do caminho do sul na década da independência." *Revista de História* 46, no. 94 (1973): 383–406.

Petrone, Maria Thereza Schorer. "As áreas de criação de gado." In *História geral da civilização brasileira*. T. 1, V. 2, edited by Sérgio Buarque de Holanda, 218–258. Rio de Janeiro: Editora Bertrand Brasil, 1993.

Priest, Tyler. "Extraction Not Creation: The History of Offshore Petroleum in the Gulf of Mexico." *Enterprise & Society* 8, no. 2 (2007): 227–267.

Queiroz, Paulo Roberto Cimó. *Uma ferrovia entre dois mundos: A E. F. Noroeste do Brasil na primeira metade do século XX*. Bauru, Campo Grande: EDUSC/ Editora da UFMS, 2004.

Restitutti, Cristiano Corte. "As fronteiras da província: rotas de comércio interprovincial, Minas Gerais, 1839–1884." Master's thesis, Universidade Estadual Paulista, Araraquara, 2006.

Saes, Alexandre Macchione, and Elton Rodrigo Rosa. "Mercado Pontual: Atuação Estatal na Formação da Feira de Gado de Três Corações (1900–1920)." *Estudos Econômicos* 43, no. 4 (2013): 745–772.

Saes, Flávio A. M. de. *As ferrovias de São Paulo, 1870–1940*. São Paulo: Editora Hucitec, 1981.

Sesto, Carmen. "The Vanguard Landowners of Buenos Aires: A New Production Model, 1856–1900." *Hispanic American Historical Review* 82, no. 4 (2002): 719–754.

Silva, Marcel Pereira da. "De gado a café: as ferrovias no Sul de Minas Gerais, (1874–1910)." Master's thesis, Universidade de São Paulo, 2012.

Silva, Moacir M. F. "Um guia ferroviário brasileiro do fim do século XIX." *Revista Brasileira de Geografia* 16, no. 2 (1954a): 252–266.

Silva, Moacir M. F. "Geografia das estradas de ferro brasileiras em seu primeiro centenário (1854–1954)." In *I Centenário das ferrovias brasileiras*, 1–85. Rio de Janeiro: IBGE, 1954b.

Storm, Claire. *Making Catfish Bait our of Government Boys. The Fight Against Cattle Ticks and the Transformation of the Yeoman South*. Athens, GA: University of Georgia Press, 2009.

Summerhill, William. "Transport Improvements and Economic Growth in Brazil and Mexico." In *How Latin America Fell Behind: Essays on the Economic Histories of Brazil and Mexico, 1800–1914*, edited by Stephen H. Haber, 93–117. Stanford, CA: Stanford University Press, 1997.

Summerhill, William. *Order Against Progress: Government, Foreign Investment, and Railroads in Brazil, 1854–1913*. Stanford, CA: Stanford University Press, 2003.

Suprinyak, Carlos Eduardo. "Comércio de animais de carga no Brasil imperial: uma análise quantitativa das tropas negociadas nas províncias do Paraná e São Paulo." Master's thesis, Universidade Estadual Paulista, Araraquara, 2006.

Topik, Steven. *The Political Economy of the Brazilian State, 1889–1930*. Austin: University of Texas Press, 1987.

Van Ausdal, Shawn. "Productivity Gains and the Limits of Tropical Ranching in Colombia, 1850–1950." *Agricultural History* 86, no. 3 (Summer 2012): 1–32.

Van Ausdal, Shawn. "Reimagining the Tropical Beef Frontier and the Nation in Early Twentieth-Century Colombia." In *Trading Environments. Frontiers, Commercial*

Knowledge, and Environmental Transformation, 1750–1990, edited by Gordon M. Winder and Andreas Dix, 166–192. New York: Routledge, 2016.

Vargas, Jonas. "Abastecendo plantations. A inserção do charque fabricado em Pelotas (RS) no comércio atlântico das carnes e a sua concorrência com os produtores platinos (século XIX)." *História (São Paulo)* 33, no. 2 (2014): 540–566. Accessed November 28, 2020, DOI: 10.1590/1980-436920140002000025.

Vianna, Fernando Segadas. "Os diferentes tipos de vegetação do Brasil e sua possibilidade de explotação e utilização." *Revista Brasileira de Geografia* 26, no. 2 (1964): 231–244.

Waibel, Leo. *Capítulos de geografia tropical e do Brasil.* Rio de Janeiro: Serviço Gráfico do Instituto Brasileiro de Geografia e Estatística, 1958.

Walton, John. "Pedigree and the National Cattle Herd *circa* 1750–1950." *The Agricultural History Review* 34, no. 2 (1986): 149–170.

Wilcox, Robert W. "'The Law of the Least Effort': Cattle Ranching and the Environment in the Savanna of Mato Grosso, Brazil, 1900–1980." *Environmental History* 4, no. 3 (1999): 338–368.

Wilcox, Robert W. "Zebu's Elbows: Cattle Breeding and the Environment in Central Brazil, 1890–1960." In *Territories, Commodities and Knowledges: Latin American Environmental History in the Nineteenth and Twentieth Centuries*, edited by Christian Brannstorm, 218–246. London: Institute for the Study of the Americas, 2004.

Wilcox, Robert W. "Ranching Modernization in Tropical Brazil: Foreign Investment and Environment in Mato Grosso, 1900–1950." *Agricultural History* 82, no. 3 (2008): 366–392.

Wilcox, Robert W. "Ranching and Market Access in the Backlands: Mato Grosso, Brazil, ca. 1900–1940s." *La Historia Crítica*, no. 51 (September–December 2013): 71–96.

Wilcox, Robert W. *Cattle in the Backlands. Mato Grosso and the Evolution of Ranching in the Brazilian Tropics*. Austin: University of Texas Press, 2017.

Zimmerman, David. "Live Cattle Export Trade Between United States and Great Britain, 1868–1885." *Agricultural History* 36, no. 1 (1962): 46–52.

5 The Public Abattoir Banishes Charque from the Carioca Table (c. 1890–c. 1910)

This chapter presents a comprehensive overview of the salt-meat (*carne seca* or *charque*) chain as it evolved for Rio de Janeiro. In the late 1800s, charque deliveries to the city declined considerably. Alternatively, Cariocas could turn to fresh meat (*carne verde*), which had become more accessible and almost as affordable as charque in the early 1900s. This chapter focuses on south-to-south connections to understand the decline in salted meat offerings in Rio. It examines developments in its leading suppliers: Argentina and Uruguay. As both began to channel most of their livestock to meatpacking companies, cattle flow to salt-meat processing plants diminished vis-à-vis refrigerated meat output deemed for exports. It is not surprising that, just before World War I, Argentinean and Uruguayan salted meat sales to Rio de Janeiro practically ceased. Rio Grande do Sul, the only national charque producer of sizeable importance, could not keep up with domestic needs, although it continued to supply Brazil's northeast region.

Despite the importance of charque in the Carioca diet laid out in Chapter 3, from the last decades of the nineteenth century until 1914, it virtually disappeared from the shelves of dry good stores (*secos e molhados*) in Rio de Janeiro. This chapter argues that this phenomenon related to local developments as much as transnational ones. At the dawn of the twentieth century, the strengthening of Rio's public abattoir system resulted in predictable fresh meat supplies, which provided Cariocas with a better alternative than carne seca. Simultaneously, Rio's leading purveyors of charque, Argentina and Uruguay, and to a lesser extent Rio Grande do Sul (also called Rio Grande), began to industrialize their meat production to attend demands in northern Europe. Such a shift in the transatlantic meat market effectively diverged South American cattle destined for salt-meat processing plants towards meatpacking companies. This is a story about how changes in the global livestock economy and in meat consumption practices shaped charque and fresh meat offerings in Rio de Janeiro.

At different stages and scales, livestock and meat production in the South American grasslands (encompassing the eastern Argentinean plains and the Campos in Uruguay and Rio Grande do Sul) underwent radical transformations that ended up affecting the supplies of salted meat in Rio and elsewhere in the Americas. In the context of the industrial revolution, the increasing need for meat at the urban centers of the north hemisphere created a market that was supplied initially by the United States and later by Argentina. In the second half of the nineteenth century, both countries began to improve their cattle to comply with meatpacking industry requirements. When freezing and chilling technology allowed meat to be transported over great distances (while maintaining good appearance and nutritious value), traditional cattle production and meat preservation techniques were phased out or relocated to less competitive areas; such was the case of the salt-pork industry in the United States and the charque processing plants in South America. In short, dried and salted meats were victims of the refrigeration industry.[1]

Considered in a global perspective, whereas in early twentieth-century London, an "apprentice … could batten on beef steak from Queensland and Argentina,"[2] in Rio de Janeiro, carne seca (*tasajo* in Spanish) from "La Plata" region (Argentina and Uruguay) became a rarity. This is not to say that the needs of the center subordinated those of the periphery. In fact, in Rio, the local government alongside private entrepreneurs—although by different means—tried to provide "meat for the masses." Brazilian officials, meat packers, and physicians—like their counterparts in Europe and the United States—promoted the "hygienic" and highly nutritive fresh meat while demoting charque, deemed archaic and unpalatable.[3] Caught in the middle of this transition, Cariocas saw the offerings of charque decline while those of carne verde alone—although constant and up to certain point more affordable than the former—could not keep up with their animal protein demands.

At the national level, late nineteenth-century Brazil experienced dramatic structural changes. The expansion of coffee plantations in Rio de Janeiro and later São Paulo, coupled with the end of the Transatlantic Slave Trade in 1850 prompted a massive flow of slaves from north Brazil to the southeast. Fearing labor scarcity and inspired by racial ideologies, growers from São Paulo—which by the 1890s replaced Rio as the leading coffee producing state—early on experimented with waged European workers. They also subsidized some of the transport costs of those immigrants, whose numbers spiked after 1888 when the Gold Law abolished slavery.[4] One year later, the militaries overthrew the emperor Pedro II, concluding several decades of centralized monarchical government. The transition from monarchy to republic was peaceful. However, in the economic arena, the need to increase money supply for wages along with "encouragement of stock market frauds, … giveaway of public lands, and overpriced contracts … to transport immigrants" created a market bubble in 1890. In 1891, high inflation and currency devaluation ensued.[5] In the 1890s, international coffee prices followed a downward pattern, complicating, even more, the scenario mentioned before. The first republican governments had to confront the crisis while dealing with increasing regionalism.[6] It took more than a decade for the country's economy to recuperate. With favorable coffee prices and the transition from slave to wage labor complete, the first decade of the twentieth century witnessed economic growth, albeit regionally and socially uneven.[7]

The starting point of this chapter is an overview of the meat market in Brazil's capital from the 1890s to 1914; it reveals how fresh meat replaced charque as the primary source of animal proteins to Cariocas. Then, it describes changes in livestock and salt-meat production in Rio's main international providers: Argentina and Uruguay. Because Rio's urban market is at the core of this study, the aim is to trace developments in its supply areas back to the streets and tables of Brazil's most important city. The last section examines the crisis of salt-meat processing plants or factories (*charqueadas*) in Rio Grande do Sul in light of early-twentieth-century economic trends and eating habits. As technological improvements signaled the end of traditional methods of meat preservation, authorities in Rio started to frame charque as an unhygienic and old-fashioned staple. Such a food of the past, they claimed, was ultimately hindering the progress of poor Brazilians and the country as a whole.

The Apogee of the Public Abattoir System and the Demise of Charque

In 1913, A. D. Melvin, chief of the United States Bureau of Animal Industry, published a study entitled *The South American Meat Industry*. The work examines ranching and meatpacking operations in Argentina, Paraguay, Uruguay, and Brazil. In his assessment about the latter, Melvin highlights the low quality of its cattle compared to those in neighboring nations, the preference of Brazilian ranchers for zebu cattle, and the incidence of tropical animal disease in the country's pasturelands. While describing Rio de Janeiro's meat market, Melvin notes, "The municipality owns the abattoir and employs the butchers and the inspectors. Rio de Janeiro has a fine municipal abattoir, recently completed, at which all of the slaughtering for the city is done."[8] The research conducted in this book endorses this observation. Indeed, with the opening of the Santa Cruz slaughterhouse (*matadouro*) in 1881, the municipality could better control livestock and meat supplies, oversee sanitary conditions of meat processing and delivering, and supervise butcher stalls. Altogether, those changes allowed the local government to further its fresh meat provisioning obligations.

As Chapter 2 examines, strengthening the municipal abattoir system was a long-term undertaking, stretching well over the second half of the nineteenth century. Such an improvement was visible in the construction of new slaughterhouses and the expansion of butcher stalls, which made fresh meat available where the population was growing. This is not a minor detail; given the lack of household ice appliances, customers had access to a perishable good within walking distance. What is more, as the next pages demonstrate, fresh meat became as affordable as carne seca by the early twentieth century.

As part of the industrialization and urbanization that Rio de Janeiro underwent during the late nineteenth century, the city government regularly recorded and published data on all manner of structural changes in urban life, including information on housing construction, the extension of public transportation and communication services, and statistics on livestock slaughtered at the municipal abattoir (see Figure 5.1). Although they do not speak to the amount of meat that actually reached the tables of Cariocas, the official livestock figures do provide a reasonable estimate of local per capita consumption, for they were gathered on the basis of the taxes collected on each animal slaughtered at Santa Cruz—tariffs that were a crucial source of income for the municipality. In addition, the patterns of meat availability in Rio are consistent with those observed in other cities with similar technological features, which show a much higher rate of fresh meat consumption in the urban setting than in rural areas. The erratic behavior of beef availability—and its downward tendency—should not overshadow the fact that, throughout this period,

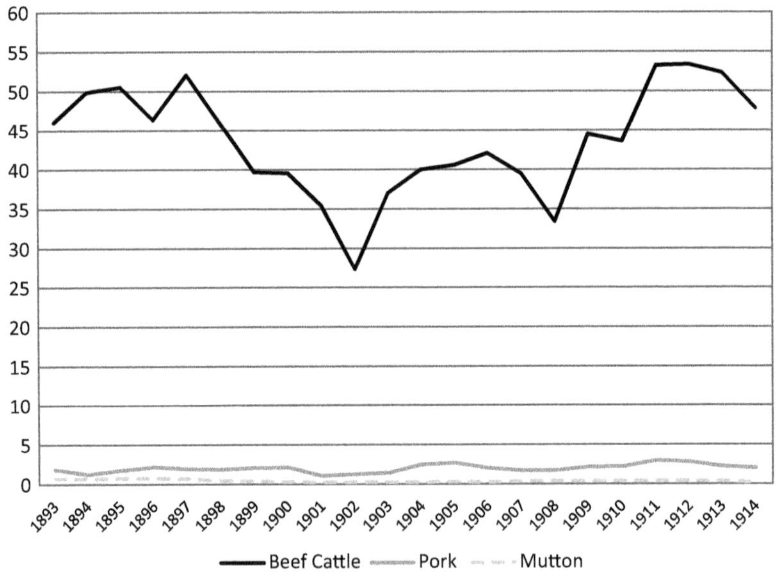

Figure 5.1 Available per capita meat supply for Rio de Janeiro (kilograms), 1893–1914.

Sources: Brasil, *Annuario Estatístico do Brazil 1° Anno (1908–1912)*, vol. 2. Economia e Finanças (Rio de Janeiro: Typographia da Estatística, 1917), 138; Rio de Janeiro, *Anuário Estatístico do Distrito Federal Ano IX*, 1941 (Rio de Janeiro: Publicação do Departamento de Geografia e Estatística, 1942), 298.

beef maintained its rank as the main source of animal proteins available in Rio's matadouro.

An analysis of Figure 5.1 reveals the following two main findings: first, the quantities of beef in the municipal slaughterhouse exceeded, by far, those of other types of meat (pork and mutton). Second, beef available per capita experienced irregular cyclical tendencies, with significant downturns in 1902 and 1908. The conditions that led to these decreases are discussed further down. With respect to prices, wholesale data from the same source demonstrate that beef was also the cheapest kind of fresh meat available in Rio's urban grid. For instance, from 1910 to 1912, a kilo of pork oscillated between 600 and 1.1 *mil-réis*, mutton 1-to-1.7, and beef between 400 and 800.

The data presented in Figure 5.1 do not presume to contend that beef was accessible to everyone but, rather, to point out that given the circumstances in which the Santa Cruz abattoir was set up to function, it did improve supply conditions by centralizing the slaughter of cattle under an inspected process that made beef both more plentiful and comparatively cheaper than pork or mutton meat. Ultimately, these changes made it possible to manage meat supplies and maintain predictable prices. Nevertheless, given the extensive nature of stock raising and the technological lag in Brazil, its provisioning system was constantly subject to natural disasters and political maneuvering. What is more, the new system ended up fomenting monopoly practices, because arrangements between suppliers and city officials made the municipality more dependent upon revenue from the local abattoir and taxes collected on each animal brought to slaughter.[9] Any disruption, natural or otherwise, thus affected the provisioning system, resulting in shortages and social upheaval, as elucidated below.

In 1902, editorialists at the *Jornal do Commercio* described in dismay what they called a city in turmoil (*cidade em alvoroto*), as they reported on a popular riot protesting an order by Rio's municipal chamber to confiscate and dispose of meat from cattle slaughtered outside the city. In 1901, purveyors from the rural communities of Maruhy and Maxambomba, supported by a federal mandate, had begun to introduce their meat into Rio's market. However, just a few months later, the city's mayor, Joaquim Xavier da Silveira Júnior, alleged that the central government's permit had opened the doors of his city and the shelves of its butcher shops to unauthorized, uninspected meat. Consequently, he ordered that all such "alien product"—as any meat processed outside the Santa Cruz slaughterhouse was called—be seized. On May 23, 1902, approximately three metric tons of meat were impounded from markets in the city center and subsequently burned. Despite opposition from butchers, altercations in the downtown area, and a judicial appeal from cattle suppliers, city officials continued to carry out confiscations in the parishes of Santana and Candelária, safeguarded by local police.

By then, however, municipal staff and law enforcement agents were facing formidable resistance from butchers and consumers alike, both clearly concerned over shortages. For several days, mobs burned meat transportation carts, looted butcher shops, destroyed streetlights, and damaged streetcars. In Praça da Harmonia, "two small dynamite bombs" were detonated. Shortly thereafter, the unrest spread to Morro da Pedra do Sal, where residents armed with stones, empty bottles, clubs, guns, and knives confronted the police. The riot ended a week later with several military policemen (*praças*) injured and a good number of rioters incarcerated. By the end of that year, the amount of meat available per capita in Rio fell to its lowest level since 1893.[10]

Then, in 1906, floods in Rio de Janeiro and Minas Gerais compromised farming and ranching production and interrupted the flow of trade between the two states. Two years later, carne verde output in the city of Rio fell by 4,000 metric tons. Clearly, two structural problems intermittently affected meat supplies in Rio de Janeiro: political deliberations over the city government's right to maintain its monopoly, and the irregular fluctuations to which traditional livestock production and marketing were subject. Yet, fresh meat provisions surpassed charque supplies in the early 1900s.[11]

Figure 5.2 illustrates available per-capita charque and carne verde in Rio de Janeiro. It is important to stress that these are mere estimates of what actually reached the urban dining table. This is particularly true

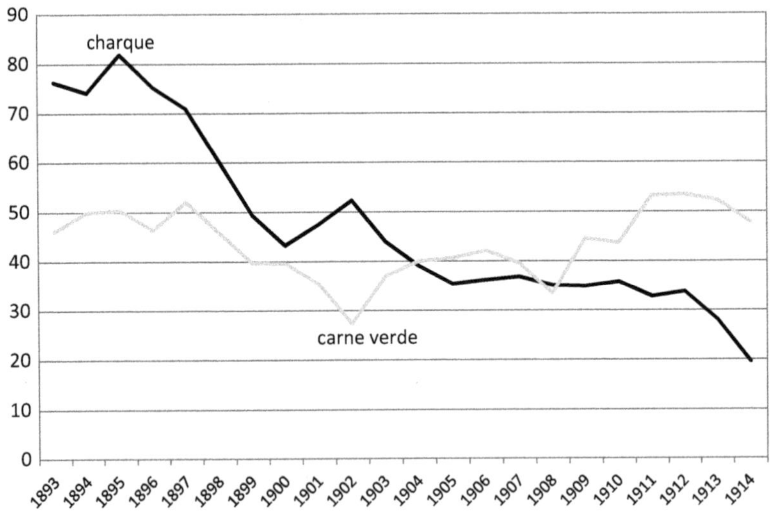

Figure 5.2 Available per capita charque and carne verde supply for Rio de Janeiro (kilograms), 1893–1914.

Sources: See Figure 5.1 and Jornal do Commercio, *Retrospecto Commercial do[s] ano[s] 1893–1914* (Rio de Janeiro: "Jornal do Commercio," de Rodrigues & C., 1894–1915).

in the case of charque, as the source does not differentiate what might have been transshipped from the city of Rio to the state's interior. What is more, contrary to fresh meat, charque did not require immediate consumption, as it could be stored for several months with no deterioration. In any case, these figures provide a framework to consider the offerings of these goods in Brazil's most populated city.

According to Figure 5.2, starting in 1895, there is a decline in per-capita charque and carne verde supply in Rio. In the case of charque, this was not a new phenomenon; such a trend began, at least, in the 1870s. As discussed above, carne verde supplies also fluctuated considerably. Notwithstanding these events, fresh meat offerings recovered, maintaining in 1914 rates similar to those observed at the beginning of the series. Conversely, charque supplies continued to decline, reaching in the same year slightly less than 20 kilos per city dweller. Simply put, whereas in 1893, there were roughly twice as much charque available per head as carne verde in Rio de Janeiro, in 1914, the proportions were inverse. How did contemporaries react to this shifting pattern?

On the one hand, except for a few articles that charque dealers published in the local newspapers, there was practically no public outcry over the steady decline in carne seca offerings in Rio de Janeiro. On the other hand, whenever carne verde provisions dropped, there were heated discussions in the press. Occasionally, local disturbances (or outright rebellion mentioned before) accompanied these debates. In the political economy of both types of meat, two critical elements were at play. While customers knew that the municipality had no power over charque production, they did fathom the local government's role in the fresh meat market. Likewise, as charque offerings continue to decline in Rio's urban market, locals could alternatively turn to carne verde, which as Table 5.1 shows, became more accessible and with prices comparable to those of salted meat. Such a possibility strengthened a shared framework between urban residents and public officials, whereby the latter were only fulfilling agreed-on provision duties.

Since the 1880s, scattered records, including newspaper clippings, called attention about rising charque prices in Rio. In 1881, a commentator from *Gazeta de Notícias* observed, "*Charqueadores* [owners of salt-meat factories] should convince themselves that charque is not a food for the rich but for the poor classes, if its prices go up ... consumption will decline."[12] It is probably that charqueadores themselves were not responsible, but the victims of several events that had been affecting their business negatively since the 1850s. Additionally, price data show that, starting in the 1890s, charque began to lose its place as the most convenient source of animal proteins to Cariocas.

Table 5.1 shows indices of wholesale prices for carne verde, national charque, and foreign charque, from 1893 to 1912. It is important to stress that these data are far from perfect. First, traditionally "foreign" charque

Table 5.1 Wholesale price index numbers for carne verde, national charque, and foreign charque (per kilogram), 1893–1912 (1912 = 100)

Years	*Carne verde*	*National charque*	*Foreign charque*
1893	124	51	130
1894	111	41	109
1895	150	30	96
1896	123	48	120
1897	125	61	120
1898	138	101	126
1899	144	94	124
1900	124	51	139
1901	119	66	109
1902	103	65	67
1903	99	53	71
1904	98	73	75
1905	89	73	74
1906	88	72	74
1907	88	80	78
1908	92	86	86
1909	91	84	83
1910	84	70	87
1911	100	77	85
1912	100	100	100

Source: Brasil, *Annuario Estatístico do Brazil 1° Anno (1908 – 1912)*, vol. 2. Economia e Finanças (Rio de Janeiro: Typographia da Estatística, 1917), 139.

(from Argentina and Uruguay) was more expensive than the national variety as a function of quality and of high tariffs, which the Brazilian government imposed on imported charque. Second, the sources (although not consistently for all years in the series) provide "minimal" and "maximum" prices. The prices used in Table 5.1 represent averages. Lastly, in the 1890s, Brazil underwent an acute economic crisis. As a result, high inflation, financial disarray, increasing debt, and exchange depreciation characterized the first decade of the Republican government.

The years 1893 to 1899 witnessed wholesale price increases for charque (national and imported) and carne verde, which is consistent with the high inflation scenario of the young republic.[13] In 1900, prices for the three commodities began a downward trend, again consistent with the deflation that marked the early 1900s. While in 1893, a kilo of national charque cost approximately 400 *réis*, foreign 1.2 *mil-réis*, and carne verde 1.0 *mil-réis* (which is to say that, in 1893, for 2.5 kilos of national charque, Cariocas bought one of carne verde), in 1912 there was no such gap, each costing roughly 800 *réis* a kilo (or US$.25). According to a study that Léo de Affonseca Junior (director of Commercial Statistics of the Ministry of Finance in 1919) prepared about the cost of living in Rio de Janeiro, from 1893 to 1914 carne verde's retail prices increased by about 12.5 percent, whereas charque's (regardless of origin) surpassed 150 percent.[14] A lengthy report published by the financial newspaper *Jornal do Commercio* in 1913 corroborates these data, revealing that charque's retail prices (national and foreign) were higher than carne verde's in that year. The same newspaper reports that, in 1914, one kilo of charque cost almost twice as much as one kilo of fresh meat; such a trend continued with small variations at least until 1930.[15]

During the 1890s, other foodstuffs followed a pattern similar to that observed in the cases of charque and carne verde. Prices for national rice, American lard, black beans, bacon (from Minas Gerais), and manioc meal experienced an upward movement, starting in 1893. They picked up one year later, declined slightly in 1895–1896, and sustained this trend in 1898–1900, depending on the commodity. Manioc meal, for instance, fetched high prices until 1900. In 1903–1905, other food items underwent a new moderate price increase, remaining stable after the latter year until World War I.[16]

The literature on Brazilian wages concurs that in the late 1890s, skilled and unskilled workers saw a decline in their purchase power thanks, in part, to the high inflation aforementioned. In Rio de Janeiro, according to figures by historian Eulalia Maria Lahmeyer Lobo, wages for vegetable street vendor, doorman, barber, and bricklayer rose slightly from 1893 to 1898; then remained flat until 1905–1906, when they fell to start recovering three or four years later. In the first hike-cycle (1893), most likely, wage increment did not offset food price increase. Salaries did rise in the first decade of the 1900s (except for a small dip in 1905–1906) until World War I, but workers had to face new food price increases again in 1903–1905. Taking into account housing expenses, it is apparent that at the turn of the twentieth century, a family's survival in urban Rio depended on the work of several of its members, including children.[17]

This panorama lends itself to two significant observations about Rio's meat market during the transition from charque to carne verde. According to ideal contemporaneous dietary parameters, Rio's city officials could provide an adequate (from the sanitary and price viewpoints) source of animal proteins to Cariocas. However, the income of the targeted consumer group fell short of everyone's expectations. In the 1880s, as Christopher C. Andrews, United States consul general to Brazil in Rio de Janeiro put it, "The majority of the people live hand to mouth."[18] They certainly continued to do so in the 1910s. In such circumstances, it is difficult to evaluate how city dwellers perceived the improvement in fresh meat supplies/prices vis-à-vis the drop in charque provisions. If anything, in the early 1910s, low and middling-income groups demanded even more intervention from the municipality in the meat market, for they continued to conceive of meat as a food of "first necessity." Indeed, when disruptions of any sort affected supplies, these actors asked for more, not less intervention from municipal authorities.

In 1901, the weekly *The Rio News* published an alarming prediction about Brazil's economy on account of diminishing meat intake in Rio, "The meat consumption per capita is considered by political economists one of the best tests of the prosperity of a community. Subject to this test, the prosperity of the city of Rio de Janeiro ... shows a remarkable decline in the last two years."[19] From 1898 to 1900, the reduction in fresh meat consumption was 25 percent and charque 24 percent. The anonymous article stresses that a drop in meat consumption could have serious repercussions, for when people forgo meat, they also

> deprive themselves of many other articles. This means a decrease in trade and in business profits. Failures result and banks, becoming alarmed, withhold assistance from business men, thus ... increasing the number of failures. In consequence, ... public health deteriorates and labouring capacity diminishes. The accumulation of wealth is retarded and enterprise ceases to find a stimulus for developing the resources of the country.[20]

The author concludes by making a veiled reference to Brazil's economic woes in the aftermath of the Encilhamento. However, moving forward, the crisis consolidated the transition from slave to free labor force, industrial expansion for mass consumption, investments in public works, and the baking system. Notably, such developments were concentrated in southeast Brazil, deepening regional differences and economic inequalities.[21]

This chapter contends that the strengthening of the municipal abattoir system, which contributed to the substitution of charque for fresh meat, was yet another sign of the times. This, in part, because municipal supplies had become more predictable, and carne verde's prices, relative to charque's, made the latter uncompetitive. Such a development, which occurred during the heyday of the municipal control over the meat market, had the following implications: first, fresh meat's availability played a significant role in the multicausal falling in charque consumption in Rio de Janeiro. Second, the traditional abattoir proved, at least for a while, effective—although, with downturns—and that speaks to the principles behind fresh meat provisioning in late nineteenth-century Rio de Janeiro. As discussed, city dwellers' reacted violently to the 1902 and 1908 drops in carne verde supplies. On both occasions, Cariocas demanded municipal intervention to restore regular provisions.

The political economy of the public market, often classified by the historiography as paternalistic, does not appropriately characterize Rio's meat market. The centralization of meat production allowed the municipality to manage cattle introduction in the urban grid (which prevented waste in the face of limited refrigerated facilities), to establish sanitary regulations for cattle slaughtering and meat distribution, and to set up prices.

It was a system anchored in "old and new regime theories about market unit and good urban provisioning."[22] It is undeniable that city officials were concerned with revenue brought about the services they offered, but they seemed to be genuinely interested in maintaining adequate supply; when they did not, public opinion (sometimes violently) raised the alarm over the municipality's failing its essential duties. Contemporaries regularly reported on the "carne verde question"; in their newspaper writings, one learns of a common understanding that meat was a public good under the local government's purview.[23] No such understanding existed for the provision of charque—although also considered a food of prime necessity—and even when its supplies plummeted, very few voiced their concern, which is yet another indication that the fresh meat market was functioning relatively well. City officials and other witnesses carefully distinguished between those goods that should be in the free market of commodities and those that should not, like fresh meat. The latter, they claimed, because of spoilage had to be processed and distributed in the city perimeter, exclusively by the municipality.

Over time, substitute products threatened charque's place in the Carioca diet, which is to say that a good with similar or better characteristics, offered at comparable prices, would replace it easily.[24] International developments as much as local ones explain the substitution that was taking place in late nineteenth-century Rio. Cariocas in the meat marketplace could choose charque or carne verde as their prices became comparable. Admittedly, this was a "choice of sorts," for in the early 1910s there were fewer animal products available in Rio than in the late 1890s. Likewise, meat prices increased at a higher rate than wages went up. Still, as Brazil entered the twentieth century, its capital city managed to maintain adequate supplies when it came to the item most identified with public welfare. This is one vital reason that should account for charque's decline in Rio de Janeiro.

Until recently, the historiography interpreted these developments almost exclusively because of significant differences in the workforce of salted meat factories.[25] Since the Brazilian charque industry relied on slave labor, it was deemed inefficient vis-à-vis its peers in South America. Current studies challenge this hypothesis (discussed in the last section of this chapter). What seems to be missing from this equation is that, in the global meat market, governments and investors in Europe and the Americas actively stimulated fresh meat consumption, supporting the livestock-producing complex, from farming to chilling processing plants on both sides of the Atlantic.[26] As a result, pasturelands in the South American grasslands, for instance, geared livestock output toward meat packing companies, negatively affecting the supply to salt-meat processing plants (*saladeros* in Spanish). Data from late-nineteenth-century Rio corroborate this misfortune.

In October 1917, the *Jornal do Commercio* published several articles on food price increases in Rio de Janeiro. The accounts include observations on the basic staples of the Brazilian diet: charque, rice, manioc meal, beans, maize, and sugar. By themselves, their conclusions are not surprising, what happened in Rio occurred in other parts of the globe as a result of World War I. However, as an importer of a merchant house in Rio explained in 1918, the war alone could not account for the charque price hike, as high tariffs on imports also played a part.[27] Moreover, as Figure 5.2 shows, carne seca entrances in Brazil's capital city began to drop several decades before the conflict.[28]

The next section addresses the conditions behind this steady decline by looking at Brazil's international providers, Argentina and Uruguay. While in both countries the meatpacking industry displaced some saladeros, the Brazilian government levied tariffs on imported charque aiming to protect national producers. This move would explain the high prices identified by the *Jornal do Commercio* and, most likely, the increased demand for other sources of animal proteins, such as carne verde in Rio.[29]

The Decline of the Saladero Industry in Argentina and Uruguay

> The relationship between any Brazilian municipality with any of the neighboring Republic [Argentina] is of narrower interest than those between our cities and states: and not only with Argentina, but with the United States, and to a lesser degree with all the other countries that export food products [to Brazil]. Certainly, there is no exaggeration to say that there is not, in the whole extent of our territory, a district, a village, a farm, where [locals] do not eat the Argentinean salt beef and flour, [...]; meat and bread—the first, the elementary, the indispensable foodstuffs of present-day people.[30]

Although the author of this quotation, Alberto Torres, a renowned Brazilian politician and intellectual, is more concerned with the status of Brazilian federalism—materialized in 1891 with a new republican constitution—than with its food supply network, his comments on the country's dependence on imported charque was partially correct. Torres was partially correct because, by the early twentieth century, Argentina was no longer the largest exporter of charque to Brazil and Rio de Janeiro. As Figure 5.3 illustrates, since the latter years of the nineteenth century, Uruguay was the leading seller of salt beef to Rio de Janeiro—that is, until 1906, when Rio Grande do Sul replaced both countries. This section examines the conditions that explain this radical change for Argentina and Uruguay; the next focuses on Rio Grande do Sul.

Figure 5.3 shows the quantities of charque from Rio Grande do Sul, Argentina, and Uruguay that arrived in Rio de Janeiro from 1872 until

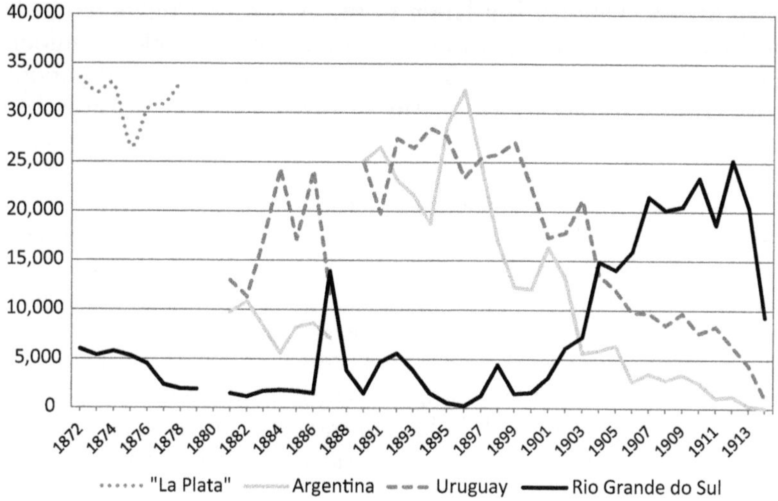

Figure 5.3 Rio de Janeiro charque imports from "La Plata," Argentina, Uruguay, and Rio Grande do Sul (metric tons), 1872–1914.

Source: *Jornal do Commercio, Retrospecto Commercial do[s] ano[s] 1872–1914* (Rio de Janeiro: Typographia do "Jornal do Commercio," de Rodrigues & C., 1873–1915).

1914. Between 1872 and 1878, sources name remittances from Argentina and Uruguay as "La Plata," reason for which they are shown as such. It is important to stress that some charque cargo did not remain in Rio. Roughly, 10 to 20 percent of the total (depending on the year) was transshipped to ports in Bahia, Pernambuco, and, occasionally, Cuba; another amount was sent to Rio's province. From 1872 until 1906 approximately, Uruguay and Argentina were the chief providers of charque that arrived in Rio, with a clear dominance of the former over Buenos Aires, except in 1891 and 1896 (note that the 1887 extraordinary increase in Rio Grande's remittances relates to the closing of La Plata ports from March to July of that year). After 1889, Uruguay alone dominated tasajo exports to Rio, only to be partly supplanted by Rio Grande do Sul in the early twentieth century. In 1893 Rio's imports of charque amounted to 48,000 metric tons; in 1914, those purchases did not reach 1,100 metric tons.[31] The story behind these numbers reveals how the livestock and by-product industries in the South American Pampas changed over the last decades of the nineteenth century, as they furthered their linkages to international markets.

In the nineteenth century, throughout the South American Pampa, the expansion of ranching and correlated industries followed a somewhat similar process. Initially, herdsmen and their animals occupied vast expanses of "uninhabited" land as needed, taking advantage of natural endowments: lush grasslands and abundant water sources. In the so-called free grass era, national legislation to secure property rights resulted in the displacement or outright war against Indigenous peoples. Traditional open-range livestock grazing shaped this phase. In a second period, a select group of ranchers—primarily in sheep and later in cattle herding and in collaboration with their Northern European counterparts—began to introduce modern husbandry techniques. These usually entailed natural selection of better specimens, installation of fences, water wells and other equipment, and genetic upgrading with imported purebred animals. Finally, better communication systems allowed pastoral industries to channel their goods (domestically and overseas) more efficiently. Overall, while the price of animals increased, competition from commercial agriculture did the same for land. Both had harmful consequences for traditional salt meat factories, which thrived during the first phase. As livestock improvement took hold, and transport of perishable products became more affordable, saladeros relocated to less expensive areas, and meatpacking plants were implemented.[32]

The description above comes with several caveats. First, the expansion of the cattle frontier was risky—as several ranching schemes failed—and brought about large as well as and medium-size properties. Second, developments in animal husbandry were not linear, and above all, they were regional rather than national. Often, in a country, ranching operations, productivity level, and market integration varied in scope and over time. Third, as internal frontiers closed, cattlemen and saladeros looked elsewhere for affordable land and animals; in doing so, they regularly moved beyond national political boundaries. In pastoral regions such as the Mexico–U.S. border and the South American pampas, shared ecological endowments and integrated animal production cycles allowed calves to relocate for fattening, while mature cattle did the same to avoid droughts and circumvent wars, for instance. Breeders also acquired animals (purebred, crossbred, and *criollos*[33]) and rented pasturelands abroad. On occasions, ranchers themselves purchased properties on both sides of borders. In short, extensive and intensive ranching, improved and non-improved animals, saladeros and meatpacking plants (*frigoríficos*) coexisted within national boundaries. Furthermore, stockmen and saladeristas used international mobility to avoid tariffs, to protect their assets from the elements, or simply to complement their operations.[34]

As the livestock and meat processing industries modernized, the export portfolio of pastoral regions also diversified to include aside from traditional commodities (wool, tasajo, hides, skins, and tallow) frozen and chilled mutton and beef.[35] Consider the case of Argentina, where the saladero business expanded rapidly after 1810—just when the country started its war for independence from Spain—prompted by the opening of its markets, occupation of Indigenous people's lands, and increasing international demand. In 1825, for instance, the Buenos Aires province had 20 salting factories that processed, on average, 70,000 head of cattle annually; by the 1850s, the latter number had jumped almost fivefold.[36] Hides and tallow were destined to England and France, while salt meat arrived mainly in Brazil and Cuba. Argentina's internal market for fresh meat was also of remarkable importance. In 1857, for instance, approximately 150,000 herds were slaughtered in the Buenos Aires province for local consumption, which roughly comes to one head of cattle per two inhabitants.[37]

Just as the number of saladeros in nineteenth-century Argentina picked, the arrival of capitalism in the South American grasslands rearranged the livestock industry and its by-products. Ecologically, improvement started at the Humid Pampa that had exceptional soil and grasses. One of the best-documented cases in the country is that of the Buenos Aires province. There, historians have shown that, over the course of the nineteenth century, big, middling and small cattlemen (*estancieros*) combined and prioritized, according to national and international demands, cattle raising (for hides, skins, tallow, and tasajo production), sheep rearing (for wool and mutton processing), and sheep and cattle raising again (for refrigerated meat processing).[38] Such a process was not the simple result of "availability of huge areas of natural pasture suitable for fattening freezing-grade cattle," or "speedy," as J. Colin Crossley and Robert Greenhill have characterized it.[39] Historian Carmen Sesto argues that starting in the 1850s, a "vanguard" of landowners who—contrary to the traditional assumption about the agrarian elites in nineteenth-century Latin America—"modernize[d] their systems of production and administration, and made risky investments." Substitution of criollo animals with purebred livestock began as early as 1856, when a small number of proprietors in close contact with their British counterparts in sheep farming, exchanged not only animals but also, knowledge and technology on "pedigree selection and breeding." A second step, which entailed the creation of breeding zones, introduction of wire fences, and water wells, followed the expansion of grazing areas. By the 1880s, the vanguard was producing purebred animals, whose quality was comparable to those in Great Britain. Lastly, the introduction of machinery spurred by international demand completed the long cycle of development of the *bonaerense* (from the province of Buenos Aires) cattle industry.[40]

Other elements, such as increasing domestic needs—in 1915, for instance, whereas Argentinean farms (*estancias*) slaughtered almost 40 percent of cattle for meat exports, the remainder was destined for home consumption—and the extension of railroads also accounted for the development of Argentina's pastoral industry. First, steamboat transport via the Paraná and Uruguay rivers (both flowing to Río de la Plata) connected the Litoral Region to port facilities. Later, major railways linked the Pampa pasturelands to the Buenos Aires port, from where goods reached European shores mostly or were transshipped to ports in Montevideo and Colonia (Uruguay). Although, initially, Argentina's rail grid concentrated in the eastern provinces and converged primarily in the country's capital, between 1884 and 1900, rail millage increased fourfold, and from the latter year to 1915, it doubled in size. Such a transport network undoubtedly benefited the export sector; it also cemented national economic and political integration.[41]

While Argentina's institutional framework incentivized stock-raising, not all provinces in the Pampa followed the bonaerense archetype. The current historiography stresses different rhythms in the country's pastoral expansion. For instance, Roberto Schmit sustains that notwithstanding improvements that stockmen in Entre Ríos province introduced in the 1840s, they did not result in productivity levels similar to those observed in the bonaerense plains by the end of the century. Local ecology (high humidity made animals prone to epizootics, increased chances of mortality while grasses of inferior quality and the undulated terrain complicated animal control) and distance from markets hindered ranchers from Entre Ríos after the 1860s. Likewise, it took longer for animal genetic upgrading to produce tangible results.[42] According to one account, in the latter decades of the century, whereas a little over 17 percent of the herds in Entre Ríos were crossbred or purebred, in the early 1900s, criollo cattle represented only 8 percent of the stock of the Buenos Aires province.[43]

Saladeros' location patterns changed according to the development of the livestock industry across South America. While the tasajo industry practically vanished from the Buenos Aires province, it found renewed life in Entre Ríos and western Uruguay. Later, northern Paraguay and Mato Grosso (Brazil) entered the new saladero business.[44] In 1893, for example, more than 300,000 herds arrived at salt meat factories in the province of Buenos Aires; by 1907, there was not a single head.[45] These data relate to broad livestock improvements as much as to the introduction of frigoríficos in Argentina. In the 1880s, four freezing plants began to operate in the Buenos Aires province, processing mutton and lamb primarily to Great Britain. In the lapse from 1880 to 1920, these exports never exceeded 120,000 tons annually. In 1903, frozen beef remittances, which started with modest amounts in the late 1890s, surpassed those of mutton and incremented dramatically, reaching more than 300,000 tons in 1913. Indeed, frozen beef represented only 0.03 percent of Argentine exports total value in the 1885–1889 period, jumped to 5 percent in 1900–1904 and doubled its share in 1900–1913.[46]

In this context, competition for land—for instance, from grain production—and cattle bound to the chilled/frozen meat industry increased.[47] In the case of processed meat, the raw material—at least initially—for saladeros and frigoríficos was the same. Although the processing of chilled meat required high-grade steers, mixed or low-grade animals were utilized in the fabrication of frozen or canned meat, the product that Argentina and Uruguay first exported in significant numbers.[48] Later, looking for the best animals they could acquire, frigoríficos sidestepped local animal fairs, paying in advance or purchasing cattle directly from estanceiros, thereby monopolizing the cattle market. Even though saladeros reacted by relocating their operations to affordable areas and by forming interest groups, they could not compete with frigoríficos over improved and non-improved cattle. After all, frigoríficos could pay better prices for cattle given the higher value-added to their product compared to charque.[49]

According to Alfredo Montoya's classic study on Argentinean saladeros, another reason for this decline was the increasing exports of live cattle. Between 1880 and 1899, these remittances roughly augmented threefold; the main destinations of those animals were Uruguay and Brazil, while a small number reached Great Britain. However, the latter commerce practically ended by 1900 due to an outbreak of foot-and-mouth disease and the consequent closing of British ports to live animals, which, in turn, incentivized chilled meat trading.[50]

It is important to underscore that livestock upgrading in Argentina went *pari passu* with the "discrediting" of tasajo. Several speeches before the powerful Sociedad Rural Argentina—founded in the 1860s to promote the interests of agrarian elite vis-à-vis the state—reveal as much. In 1866, Miguel Puiggari, a chemistry professor, suggested that given tasajo's "poor quality, unpleasant appearance, and undesirable sanitary condition ... [it] should be substituted with [a product] that is in harmony with food science ... and industrial advances." In a well-rehearsed racialized narrative, a contributor to the Sociedad asserted that, unlike the British, the "sad and disgraced" tasajo eater had no choice but to consume it. Another commentator went further, stating that Europeans simply "do not want it [charque] at any price," for they only had it in times of famine.[51] More than 50 years later, and in a similar tone, Ricardo Pillado, director of the Argentinean department of Agriculture, summarizes the situation of chilled meat versus charque in certain areas of South America as follows:

> The tasajo industry is so primitive, so rudimentary, and so modest in its yields that it no longer fits in the progress of the present age. Today, fresh beef from improved cattle is offered to world consumption by packing companies ... according to the exigencies of the European market, for the tables of the most civilized nations, a situation well different from that in the past, when meat from the Argentinean Pampas fed the Negroes working in sugar mills in Cuba or in coffee plantations in Brazil.[52]

Setting aside Pillado's prejudices—some of which Chapter 3 addresses—he also predicted that the saladero industry was bound to disappear. At the regional level, we know that rather than "disappear," salt-meat processing plants relocated within Argentina and beyond its borders. However, moving to a national scale, his predictions seem correct. Although during the 1890s Argentina's international remittances of tasajo increased—mainly because it was supplying regions where the United States was no longer exporting salted pork—by 1913, carne seca represented only 0.1 percent in the total value of Argentine overseas sales; when in 1890 it had accounted for nearly 5 percent. In the same lapse of time, while in 1890, Argentina sent 43,481 metric tons of tasajo to Brazil, by 1913, this number reduced to almost 4,000 metric tons.[53] The saladero was an industry of a bygone era; the evolution of Argentina's position in the transatlantic meat market reveals as much.

The linkages between the United States and Argentina as suppliers of salted pork and beef to similar markets replicated itself when it came to chilled/frozen meat. In the 1880s, the United States emerged as the first exporter of chilled meat to Great Britain. In 1884, United States authorities asserted, "We virtually monopolize the trade of the United Kingdom in foreign fresh beef."[54] Indeed, from 1881 until 1900, the United States was practically the only exporter of chilled beef that arrived at Great Britain's ports. However, its market share had been diminishing: 60 percent of the total weight from 1881 to 1885, 80 percent in 1881–1895, 57 percent in 1901–1905, to just about 25 percent in 1906–1910. The drastic decline in the last period related to the emergence of Argentina's beef industry, as its exports accounted for half of the British imports. In 1911–1915, Argentina sent almost 100 percent of chilled meat introduced in Great Britain. It should be noted that, during World War I, the United States occupied its first position again, but this position was short-lived, linked to the war emergency. By the 1920s, the United States was no longer an exporter of meat but a net importer, because of increasing internal demand.[55]

Uruguay entered the international processed meat business later than Argentina, and its share of the global market was smaller. In the South American context, however, Uruguay was an essential player for Brazil's live cattle and charque markets. Uruguayan saladeros exported to Cuba and Brazil; both absorbed practically the entire Uruguayan production. In the early nineteenth century, there were approximately seven salt-meat processing plants in the region of Montevideo; in the 1850s, sources registered more than 20.[56] On average, from 1867 to 1891, Brazil imported 230,960 metric tons annually from Uruguay; what is more, over this period, while the exports to Cuba declined, those to Brazil increased. Between 1909 and 1913, 53 percent of Uruguayan tasajo arrived in Brazilian ports of Rio de Janeiro, Salvador, and Recife.[57]

In Uruguay, such dependence on its closest neighbor prompted heated debates; most notably, Uruguayans sought to find new markets for tasajo. The discussion could be traced back to the early 1860s, when—given charque's overproduction and low prices—a delegation from Club Nacional[58] suggested reaching out to Great Britain, where large amounts of bacon from United States was consumed. Two decades later, producers considered Italy and Spain as possible markets. Once again, in the early twentieth century, Uruguayan interests—with the help of their diplomatic service—tried to channel tasajo to Europe and Africa, but none of these efforts bore fruit.[59] Brazil remained one of the primary recipients of Uruguayan tasajo. Additionally, in South America, the industry confronted several difficulties by the end of the century.

Uruguayan saladeros competed with their counterparts in Argentina and Rio Grande do Sul over criollo cattle, while tasajo from these three sources reached similar consumer markets. Brazilian protectionism also represented a serious obstacle to saladeros in Uruguay (See Table 5.2). From 1860 to 1882, charque Platino entered Brazil duty-free, but by the late 1880s, the federal government levied a 20 percent tariff on these imports.[60] According to Magdalena Bertino and Julio Millot, in 1887, for instance, Uruguay was unable to export 70 percent of its tasajo production, in part because of Brazilian protectionism. Consequently, some saladeros moved primarily to Rio Grande do Sul (on the border with Uruguay), but also to Mato Grosso. In 1904, there were at least six saladeros of Uruguayan capital in Brazil. In fact, according to some studies, the boom that the Brazilian salt meat industry experienced during those years was related in part to those businesses, as they "were modern facilities ... some had their own electric power plant." In Mato Grosso, for instance, the charqueada Miranda, which in 1907 slaughtered 5,000 herds, had a capacity for 20,000.[61]

Table 5.2 Brazilian import tariffs (percent per kilo or unit) on charque, fresh or refrigerated meat, and live cattle, 1857–1914

	Charque	*Fresh or refrigerated meat*	*Live cattle*
Years	*(kilo)*	*(kilo)*	*(unit)*
1857	15	30	5
1860	free	free	free
1869	free	free	free
1874	10	free	free
1882	free	free	free
1887	20	20	10
1889	20	20	15
1897	20	30	15
1900	20	30	15
1911	20	30	15
1914	40	30	20

Sources: Brasil, *Tarifa das Alfândegas do Império do Brasil, 1857–1887* (Rio de Janeiro: Typographia Nacional, 1857–1887), several pages; Brasil, *Tarifa das Alfândegas, 1889–1914* (Rio de Janeiro: Typographia Nacional, 1889–1914), several pages.

Another source of competition came from canning and meat-extract plants. The most notable was the Liebig's Extract of Meat Company that started operations in 1865 in Villa Independencia (later, Fray Bentos, the city that grew out of its development) in the Uruguayan Litoral. The firm had its port and estancias. In the 1880s, during the production season, it processed 100 animals daily. Alongside meat extract, it manufactured smoked tongues, bone meal, dried blood, and guano, which reached European markets primarily. Although the Liebig's company utilized advanced technology, it relied entirely on criollo cattle. Indeed, it almost monopolized the cattle market in Uruguay's Litoral region. According to Richard Perren, "the advantage of producing it [meat extract] in Uruguay was that the country had large numbers of poor unimproved cattle that would never have found a sale in London as fresh meat." However, criollo cattle was the raw material for frozen meat production; hence in the early 1900s, Liebig's firm found itself competing with frigoríficos as well. As a result, it bought or rented pasturelands in Entre Ríos y Corrientes (in Argentina's northeast region) and later relocated to the coast.[62] Much like saladeros, Liebig's meat extract company could not compete with frigoríficos, while Uruguay's transition to improved cattle was well underway.

Historians identify as early as the 1860s the first stage of livestock and ranching upgrading in Uruguay. Such initial developments entailed: the combination of sheep with cattle raising (this measure, within a ranching unit, resulted in optimization of pasturelands and diversification of risks), imports of purebred animals, use of fences (which allows for better farming management), expansion of the cattle frontier, where herds grazed over natural forage, and better property rights. Together, these advances gave birth to modern ranching in Uruguay, which in the last quarter of the nineteenth century was fully engaged to external markets for wool and frozen/chilled beef.[63] Although there are no definitive figures as to the level of mixing with purebred animals in Uruguay; meat yield from the country's cattle increased from 161 kilos for the years 1882–1886 to 243 kilos in 1905–1913. By the 1930s, the criollo accounted for only a small fraction of total cattle population in Uruguay.[64] Historian María Inés Moraes has shown that, between 1870 and 1913, Uruguay's livestock production grew at an annual rate of 3 percent. As the author further explains, such a performance—given Uruguay's limited capacity to incorporate new pasturelands—was the result of technological improvements rather than of the expansion of the ranching frontier, as was the case in Argentina, Canada, Australia, and the United States.[65]

Uruguay's processed meat exports reflect such developments. First, as historian Thales A. Zamberlan Pereira has shown, in the 1850s, Great Britain's imports of Uruguayan beef extract and other preserved meat increased significantly, from almost irrelevant figures in 1871 to more than 50,000 cwt (hundredweight) in 1889. Second, starting in the 1860s until the first decade of the twentieth century, tasajo exports experienced a two-fold weight decline, averaging in the 1911–1914 period less than 8 percent of Uruguay's total overseas sales. Third, the value of refrigerated meat remittances, on the other hand, which in 1912 represented only 3 percent of total Uruguay's exports, reached 15 two years later. Although Uruguay saw the installation of its first frigorífico in 1902, production surged later in the decade.[66]

While Argentina and Uruguay were leaving behind the saladero business,[67] there emerged an opportunity for Rio Grande do Sul to tap into the charque consumer market in Brazil. However, in Rio de Janeiro (the main single urban market for national and international charque) politicians, journalists, and physicians started to raise the alarm over charque's quality, hygienic properties, and deleterious effects on the "Brazilian race." In 1918, given that supervision of charqueadas was practically nonexistent, government officials alleged that workers exposed to sick animals had skin ulcerations; worse yet, consumption of such a charque had resulted in deaths by an intestinal infection.[68] Indeed, since the late 1800s, some voices in Rio's major newspapers favored waging a "crusade against charque."[69] The next section discusses how charqueadores *Riograndenses* (from Rio Grande do Sul) reacted to these and other challenges, as the end of slavery only seemed to deprive them of both consumers and labor force.

Rio Grande do Sul in a "Crusade against Charque"

During most of the nineteenth century, two animal-derived commodities, charque and hides, dominated the economy of Rio Grande do Sul, with a clear preeminence of the former. Salt- meat processing plants were an essential industry not only to the state but also to Brazil's manufacturing sector. With the decline of salted meat factories in northeast Brazil, Rio Grande emerged as the main production center in the country, although intrinsically linked to the livestock industry in neighboring countries. Uruguay and Argentina provided the bulk of charque consumed in Brazil (which competed with domestic output) and a vital number of herds that continuously supplied charqueadas Riograndenses. These, in turn, via Rio Grande's ports or on occasion through Uruguay, given its superior infrastructure, sold charque to the northeast and Rio de Janeiro. What is more, while the presence of Brazilian ranchers in Uruguay could be traced back to the early 1800s, over the latter period under consideration in this study, Uruguayan entrepreneurs crossed the border in the opposite direction to establish their saladeros and avoid Brazilian duties.[70]

As in the case of the international borders of United States in the late 1800s, the South American Pampas functioned as an economic unit centered on livestock raising for the production of fresh, salted, chilled, and frozen meat for local, regional, and external markets (on both sides of the Atlantic). In the northern and southern hemispheres of the

American continent, common natural endowments allowed grazing bulls to roam across borders, integrating livestock production cycles. This resulted not only in the exchange of commodities but also of knowledge (in terms of animal husbandry practices and meat processing techniques). Nevertheless, throughout this period, tariffs and politics intervened with enough clout to improve and/or halt trade.[71]

One way to appreciate this proposition is to consider—in light of the last section's description on the saladero industry in Argentina and Uruguay—charque flow in South America during the nineteenth century. Roughly speaking, from the 1800s to 1850s, whereas half of Rio Grande do Sul's output arrived in the provinces of Bahia and Pernambuco, Rio de Janeiro got the other half. It is probably that these were entrance points of the product, from where it was later redistributed to the interior. According to Pedro Cezar Dutra Fonseca, in "1861 two commodities, charque and hides corresponded to three-fourths of all Rio Grande do Sul's sales."[72] Argentina and Uruguay were the other two leading providers of charque that reached the tables of north and south Brazil.

In the second half of the century, focusing specifically on remittances to Rio de Janeiro, Jonas M. Vargas shows that combined charque sales from Montevideo and Buenos Aires followed an upward tendency, from 5,000 metric tons in 1850 to more than 30,000 in the 1880s, while Rio Grande do Sul's sales decreased from a little below 15,000 in 1850 to less than 2,000 in 1886.[73] As for the province's deals with other Brazilian ports, although this downward tendency is verified (particularly after the 1870s), it is noteworthy that Rio Grande do Sul continued to be a vital supplier to northeast Brazil. Nevertheless, this decline illustrates the main problems that charqueadas Riograndenses confronted in the late nineteenth century. The result was the closing of processing plants in certain municipalities (mostly in Pelotas, the principal center of production near Rio Grande's coast) and the opening of new plants in the province's interior, on the border with Uruguay (*fronteira* region), and in other states of Brazil.[74]

As Figure 5.3 illustrates, after a steep decline from 1894 to 1896—most likely due to the Federalist revolution[75]—starting in 1906 until 1914, charque remittances from Grande do Sul to Rio de Janeiro surpassed those of Argentina and Uruguay. Such figures indicate that, as the latter countries transitioned to the refrigerated industry, Rio Grande do Sul became practically the sole provider of charque to Rio, notwithstanding with limited amounts. It is essential to underscore that Figure 5.3 does not account for two elements. Some riograndense charque entered Brazil via Uruguayan ports; this was a common practice given the latter's better port facilities. In addition, beginning in 1908, Paraguay, Mato Grosso, São Paulo, and Minas Gerais also appear in the statistics as sellers of charque that arrived in Rio.

Salt-meat factories in Rio Grande do Sul began to experience striking changes by the 1850s. First, the end of slave trafficking posed a severe threat to the continuous flow of laborers, and second, the importation of superior quality tasajo from La Plata into Brazil augmented competition for consumer markets. In 1851, after Brazil's invasion of Uruguay, both countries signed up a commercial treaty, which provided ideal conditions for charqueadores Riograndenses: a 25 percent tariff on Uruguayan charque imported via Brazilian ports and the free exchange of cattle between both countries.[76] Such generous terms favored Riograndenses enormously by making domestic charque more affordable, vis-à-vis La Plata's, while guaranteeing that charqueadas would have access to Uruguayan herds, without which they could not survive. However, this was a temporary measure; less than a decade later, the federal government lifted tariffs on charque and other commodities from Uruguay. In the late 1880s, once again, Brazil levied a 20 percent tariff on imported charque and 15 percent on live cattle, as Table 5.2 illustrates.[77] The protectionism trend (which affected other items such as rice, potato, beans, codfish, wheat flour, and sugar, for instance) continued, at least until the first decade of the twentieth century.[78]

The extent to which tariffs intervened in the regional charque trade and their overall impact in the countries involved is a complex matter beyond the scope of this study.[79] In this instance, duties that the Brazilian state levied on charque affected prices for national charque and provoked major domestic divisions. Whereas Riograndenses saw higher taxes as fundamental to the prosperity of their industry, such restrictions were contrary to almost any other region and interest groups in Brazil.[80]

In any case, tariff protection could not halt the demise of the traditional charqueada. Apart from the problems mentioned above, the end of slavery, the emergence of the frigorífico industry, and overall government intervention in favor of the latter shaped the destiny of old salt-meat factories. Few topics in regional historiography have been the subject of more controversy than the collapse of charqueadas Riograndenses. In his seminal work, Fernando Henrique Cardoso argues that Brazilian salt-meat processing plants were less productive and had higher costs than the ones in La Plata, in part because of their reliance on enslaved workers.[81] Several authors have shown that slave labor in charqueadas Riograndenses was highly specialized. What is more, after 1850, with the end of the transatlantic slave trade, charqueadores adopted several measures to maximize productivity. In Pelotas, for instance, this is reflected in the increment of male slaves in charqueadas and a greater diversity of occupations in a single processing plant.[82]

There is no doubt that the end of slavery represented a major blow to the charqueada industry, not only because of the loss in workforce but also thanks to the decline in slave prices. In fact, in the early 1880s, knowing that abolition was imminent, proprietors in Rio Grande do Sul issued a record number of manumissions, including conditional ones, which required slaves to perform services to a master or a third person as a contracted worker (*contratado*) for a period up to seven years.[83] In addition to these and other developments described above, it is important to view the fall of charqueadas in Rio Grande do Sul in a broad perspective. First, albeit late, Riograndenses, like their Argentinean and Uruguayan counterparts, started to transition to the freezing industry, which might have affected cattle supplies to charqueadas.[84] Second, after a period of steady decline, from the 1890s until 1913, charque sales, in fact, increased. This explains why although carne seca Riograndense vanished from the Carioca market, it continued to reach the tables of northeasters. What is more, given that, at least until the early 1930s, charque continued to be the primary commodity in the state, it is imperative to consider the transformation toward the industrial salt-meat complex as intrinsic to the fall of the traditional ones.[85]

The crisis of the slave-labor based charqueada opened the door to its modernization. By the end of the nineteenth century, Rio Grande do Sul's border region with Uruguay witnessed the emergence of new charqueadas. These plants relied on a free work force, had a greater degree of labor organization, and were equipped with steam engines. Apart from canned beef and meat extract, their output included nonedible animal by-products, such as soap and candle. It is noteworthy that, like their counterparts in the freezing industry, these new charqueadores sought to improve the quality of their herds by importing purebred animals from Argentina, Uruguay, and Great Britain. Such was the case of charqueadas in the Quaraí and Bagé municipalities, both on the border with Uruguay.[86] Even Pelotas, which closed dozens of plants over the second half of the nineteenth century, registered 11 charqueadas in 1900. Therefore, it is not surprising that in 1906, for instance, charque represented more than 50 percent of the total state's revenue on sales of livestock and by-products. In fact, amid sharp fluctuations, Rio Grande's salt meat sales rose from 25,000 metric tons in 1890 to 64,000 in 1913.[87]

These figures underscore not only the continued importance of charque to Rio Grande's economy but also to northeast Brazil, which from the late 1860s onward received, on average, 80 percent of Rio Grande's charque sales. In Rio de Janeiro, however, as charque supplies dwindled (with prices comparable to those of carne verde), consumers could turn to a better product given not only improvement in fresh meat supplies (described earlier), but also their increased earning capacity. The latter as a result of the transition from slave to waged labor, urbanization, and industrialization; altogether, these events motivated new eating habits and stimulated the internal market.[88] This economic setting, in light of the debate over the ideal animal protein, intake represented yet another setback to charque.

As Sarah Milov points out, commodities do not exist in an ideal form apart from state policy.[89] The making of fresh meat as vital to the well-being of Cariocas—and ultimately to all Brazilians—is articulated in so many words and actions of the federal and state governments. The first, although lacking a specific industrial program, since the late 1880s until the early 1910s embraced protectionist policies, levying a 20 percent tariff on charque and 30 percent on refrigerated meat, a measure designed to boost the domestic meatpacking sector. As for the state level, in September 1902, the governor of Rio de Janeiro Quintino Bocaiuva expressed the importance of animal protein intake as a matter of economics and hygiene. In his words, "The meat consumption question is not one of a commercial nature; it is a hygiene issue and a social issue, especially in our country where natural population growth is scarce and scarcer yet is the supply of immigrants."[90]

Like Governor Bocaiuva, several physicians and journalists expressed their opinion about meat consumption in a similar tone: while fresh beef was associated with good nutrition (and thus the right step in moving Brazil to a path of industrialization and modernization), charque was tied to slavery and a past that the republic wanted to forget, but most of all because it was deemed unhygienic, therefore responsible for disease and low population growth. The two sides of the debate were clearly defined; on the one hand, charque was labeled as a "poison" to the less fortunate—by an anonymous author in *Gazeta de Notícias,* who also stressed it was accountable for "blood impoverishment." On the other, traders and importers of charque in Rio declared that, because of its low price and storage capacity, it was "was a unique and irreplaceable food for the working classes."[91]

By the early twentieth century, more voices emerged against charque's consumption and in favor of fresh meat. In 1917, a commentator in *O Pharol* criticized the informal dressing code in Rio, speculating on the climatologic causes of disease and low development: "Who knows if the Brazilian sadness (*tristeza*) is climatologic? The absurd diet of beans and carne seca [in a country where] the temperature can reach thirty degrees Celsius or higher can explain all neurosis, even suicides."[92] To be sure, a diet that relied heavily on charque could lead to all sorts of maladies, most notably beriberi, a disease associated with the lack of thiamine. Large segments of the 1800s-Brazilian society, particularly those who did not have control over their diets: slaves, soldiers, and children were thiamine deficient.[93] Notwithstanding, what seems to be at play is a racial consumption divide. Charque was not the right food for Brazilians who, in addition to being poorly fed, did not "have the appearance and vigor" of the population in La Plata countries.[94]

The person who best summarized and predicted the future of charque consumption in Brazil was one with intimate knowledge about its role in the country's economy. In 1908, Carlos Barbosa Gonçalves, the governor of Rio Grande do Sul, affirmed that charque would continue to be on the table of individuals in the states of Bahia and Pernambuco, particularly in remote rural areas, where the population access to carne verde was limited. Hence, the local industry would continue to prosper and, indeed, it did, at least until the 1930s.[95]

* * *

The reasons behind charque's disappearance from the Carioca dinner table are manifold. The historiography has pointed to the end of slavery, competition with La Plata output, and alterations in consumer preference, among others. This chapter ponders the role that transnational and local developments played in this process. Given that Argentina and Uruguay were, until the late nineteenth century, the main suppliers of salt-meat to Brazil, improvements in their livestock and refrigeration industries (which connected to demands in Great Britain) compromised cattle flow to saladeros and, thus, tasajo production. In the domestic arena, it was apparent that Rio Grande do Sul alone could not keep up with needs in Rio. Nevertheless, while charque practically vanished from the local dry goods stores, salt-meat continued to be the chief source of animal proteins to consumers in the northeast. Charqueadores Riograndenses were able to comply with such a demand—thanks to modernization—as a response to the challenges mentioned above. Finally, in spite of the dramatic drop in charque offerings in Rio, neither politicians nor the press heralded a public outcry over the topic. They did engage in a different debate, one that entailed the making of fresh meat as the ideal commodity and of charque as an outdated, unhygienic food. Their argument benefited from the fact that, at least for a while, the municipal slaughterhouse was able to provide city dwellers with the "right" kind of animal proteins. However, in the aftermath of World War I, just as it was done with charque a few years earlier, proponents of the refrigeration technology began to recast the abattoir system as antiquated and unsanitary, framing frigoríficos as the panacea for the hungry masses. The next chapter examines the latter topic.

Notes

1 Jimmy M. Skaggs, *Prime Cut. Livestock Raising and Meatpacking in the United States. 1607–1983* (College Station: Texas A&M University Press, 1986), 74; Steve C. Gordon, "From Slaughterhouse to Soap-Boiler: Cincinnati's Meat Packing Industry, Changing Technologies, and the Rise of Mass Production, 1825–1870," *The Journal of the Society for Industrial Archeology* 16, no. 1 (1990): 64–66.

2 James Critchell and Joseph Raymond, *History of the Frozen Meat Trade. An Account of the Development and Present Day Methods of Preparation, Transport, and Marketing of Frozen and Chilled Meats* (London: Constable & Company, 1912), 317. Current research on the nineteenth-century British diet presents a more complex picture than these quotations suggest, showing—for instance—that meat intake varied significantly in the working class.

See Rachel Duffett, *The Stomach for Fighting: Food and the Soldiers of the Great War* (Manchester: Manchester University Press, 2015), 43–47.

3 Maria Yedda Leite Linhares, *História do abastecimento; uma problemática em questão (1530–1918)* (Brasília: Edições Binagri, 1979), 206–07.

4 In the late nineteenth century, a series of laws sought to emancipate slaves gradually. In 1871, the "Law of the Free Womb" freed all children born to slave mothers, although minors remained—with few exceptions—under the authority of their mother's masters until they were 21. The law also called for the creation of a Manumission Fund. In 1885, new legislation established that all slaves over 65 years old were to be free. In the 1880s, as the abolitionist cause gained force, slaves engaged in open acts of resistance. In São Paulo, for instance, they fled plantations in considerable numbers, while other states abolished the system entirely. The most recent survey in English about slavery in Brazil is Herbert S. Klein and Francisco Vidal Luna, *Slavery in Brazil* (Cambridge: Cambridge University Press, 2010), 74–75. See also, Katia M. de Queirós Mattoso, *To Be a Slave in Brazil, 1550–1888* (New Brunswick, NJ: Rutgers University Press, 1986), Chapter 7; Maria Helena P. T. Machado, "Slavery and Social Movements in Nineteenth-Century Brazil: Slave Strategies and Abolition in São Paulo," *Review (Fernand Braudel Center)* 34, no. 1/2, (2011): 163–91; Leslie Bethell, "The Decline and Fall of Slavery in Nineteenth Century Brazil," *Transactions of the Royal Historical Society* 1 (1991): 71–88.

5 This economic crisis became known as *Encilhamento* (girthing). John Schulz has argued that the market bubble was a direct consequence of the abolition of slavery in 1888. John Schulz, *The Financial Crisis of Abolition* (New Haven: Yale University Press, 2008), 7–8.

6 The most notable threat to Brazil's geographic integrity was the costly and bloody Federalist Revolution in Rio Grande do Sul, which lasted from 1893 to 1895. The civil war, over the level of political autonomy in the state vis-à-vis the national government, pitted federalists against republicans. Whereas the latter supported the second Republican president, Floriano Peixoto, and the state's governor, Julio Castilhos, the former group favored a parliamentary system of government. Given federalists' connections with Brazilian ranchers (*estancieiros*) settled in Uruguay and with traditional Imperial elites, republicans labeled their opponents "monarchists and separatists." Joseph L. Love, *Rio Grande Do Sul and Brazilian Regionalism 1882–1930* (Stanford, CA: Stanford University Press, 1971), chapter 3.

7 Francisco Vidal Luna and Herbert S. Klein, *The Economic and Social History of Brazil Since 1889* (Cambridge: Cambridge University Press, 2014), 34–47; Nathaniel H. Leff, "Economic Development in Brazil, 1822–1913," in *How Latin America Fell Behind: Essays on the Economic Histories of Brazil and Mexico, 1800–1914*, ed. Stephen H. Haber (Stanford, CA: Stanford University Press, 1997), 37–40.

8 A. D. Melvin, "The South American Meat Industry," in *Yearbook of the United States Department of Agriculture* (Washington: Government Printing Office, 1913), 361.

9 In 1904, those revenues amounted to almost the same sum that the city council (*prefeitura)* collected from sanitary fees. Francisco Pereira Passos, *Mensagem do Prefeito de Districto Federal lida na sessão do Conselho Municipal de 2 de abril de 1904 e 1 de setembro de 1904* (Rio de Janeiro: Typographia da "Gazeta de Noticias," 1904), 23; 65–66.

10 *Jornal do Commercio*, October 5, 1901; May 3, 23, 26, 30, 31, 1902.

11 *Jornal do Commercio*, February 10, 1906.

12 *Gazeta de Notícias*, February 28, 1880; June 10, 1881.

13 Luna and Klein, *The Economic,* 39–42.
14 Brasil, *Annuario Estatístico do Brazil, 1° Ano,* vol. 2 *(1908–1912),* 139. Converted to U.S. dollars according to Heitor Pinto Moura Filho's study, "Exchange rates of the mil-réis (1795–1913)," *MPRA Paper No. 5210,* University Library of Munich, Germany (2006): 14–17, accessed November 22, 2020. http://mpra.ub.uni–muenchen.de/5210/; Léo de Affonseca Junior, *O custo da vida na cidade do Rio de Janeiro* (Rio de Janeiro: Imprensa Nacional, 1920), 13. In her classic study on price evolution in Rio, Eulalia Maria Lahmeyer Lobo states that from 1898 until World War I, prices for all foodstuffs experienced a downward trend "except for charque and bacon." Eulália Maria Lahmeyer Lobo, et al., "Evolução dos preços e do padrão de vida no Rio de Janeiro, 1820–1930 – resultados preliminares," *Revista Brasileira de Economia* 25, no. 4 (October–December 1971): 249.
15 Jornal do Commercio, *Retrospecto Commercial de 1912* (Rio de Janeiro: Typographia do "Jornal do Commercio," de Rodrigues & C., 1913), 56; Jornal do Commercio, *Retrospecto Commercial de 1930* (Rio de Janeiro: Typographia do "Jornal do Commercio," de Rodrigues & C., 1931), 152.
16 Eulália Maria Lahmeyer Lobo, *História do Rio de Janeiro: do capital comercial ao capital industrial e financeiro,* vol. 2 (Rio de Janeiro: Inst. Brasileiro de Mercado de Capitais – IBMEC, 1978), 803–05; 812–13; Luis A. Catão, "A new wholesale price index for Brazil during the period 1870–1913," *Revista Brasileira de Economia* 46, n. 4 (1992): 519–33; 526–27.
17 Lobo, "Evolução," 251; Luna and Klein, *The Economic*, 38–40. For the case of São Paulo see, Molly C. Ball, "Prices, Wages, and the Cost of Living in Old Republic São Paulo: 1891–1930," *Research in Economic History* 34, Emerald Publishing Limited (2018): 22–23.
18 Christopher C. Andrews, *Brazil: its Condition and Prospects* (New York: D. Appleton and Company, 1891), 17.
19 "Meat Consumption," *The Rio News*, February 26, 1901.
20 Ibid.
21 Schultz, *The Financial*, 134; Luna and Klein, *The Economic*, 79–81.
22 Kyri Claflin, "La Villette: City of Blood (1867–1914)," in *Meat, Modernity, and the Rise of the Slaughterhouse,* ed. Paula Young Lee (Durham, NH: University of New Hampshire Press, 2008), 41. For a different take on the municipality's role on food provisioning, consider the case of late nineteenth-century London. There, the city council's foremost obligation rested in the sanitary realm, not necessarily on price control. Chris Otter, "The Vital City: Public Analysis, Dairies and Slaughterhouses in Nineteenth-Century Britain," *Cultural Geographies* 13 (2006): 526–29.
23 *Jornal do Commercio*, October 5, 1901; May 3, 23, 26, 30, 31, 1902; February 10, 1906; See *Correio da Manhã*, January 22, 1903; February 02, 03, 04, 05, 06, 10, 11, 12, 13, 26, 28, 1903; March 02, 03, 04, 05, 06, 07, 08, 09, 10, 11, 1903.
24 Thales A. Zamberlan Pereira, "Was it Uruguay or Coffee? The Causes of the Beef Jerky Industry's Decline in Southern Brazil (1850 – 1889)," *Nova Economia* 26, no. 1 (2016): 13–14; Denise Manfredini and Sergio Marley Modesto Monteiro, "Rentabilidade do trabalho escravo no Rio Grande do Sul no século XIX," *Anais do XLII Encontro Nacional de Economia* (Proceedings of the 42nd Brazilian Economics Meeting) 020, ANPEC – Associação Nacional dos Centros de Pósgraduação em Economia (2014): 15. The case of Barcelona (Spain) offers an interesting parallel; there, fresh meat substituted for salted cod in the urban market in the early twentieth century. Manel Guàrdia, José Luis Oyón, Sergi Garriga, and Nadia Fava, "Meat

Consumption and Nutrition Transition in Barcelona, 1709–1935," *Urban History* 45, no. 2 (2018): 203.

25 One paper published recently situates the charque supply crisis in Brazil in a broader, South-American context, although the author does not consider developments in Brazilian urban markets. Pereira, "Was it Uruguay or Coffee?."

26 Richard Perren, *Taste, Trade and Technology: The Development of the International Meat Industry Since 1840* (Aldershot, UK: Ashgate Publishing, 2006), 114–29.

27 *Jornal do Commercio*, October 2, 1917; Rio de Janeiro, *Anuário Estatístico do Distrito Federal Ano IX*, 1941 (Rio de Janeiro: Publicação do Departamento de Geografia e Estatística, 1942), 298; Roberto C. Simonsen, *The Meat & Cattle Industry of Brazil; Its Importance to Anglo-Brazilian Commerce* (London: Industrial Publicity Service, 1919), 2–5; *Gazeta de Notícias*, May 29, 1918.

28 *Jornal do Commercio*, October 2, 1917.

29 "Jerked-Beef versus Refrigerated Meat," *Refrigerating World* 56, no. 6 (1921): 32; Susana Bleil de Souza, "Charqueadas i instal.lacions frigorífiques a la frontera gautxa: el trànsit pel port de Montevideo a principis del segle XX," *Recerques: història, economia, cultura* 45–46 (2002–2003): 89, accessed November 21, 2020, www.raco.cat/index.php/Recerques/article/view/140210.

30 Alberto Torres, *A organização nacional; Primeira parte – A Constituição* (São Paulo: Companhia Editora Nacional, 1938), 216–17.

31 Affonseca Junior, *O custo da vida*, 6.

32 This brief summary derives mostly from my studies on ranching and commercial livestock circuits in North and South America. For broad, regionally diverse studies on the topic see Maria-Aparecida Lopes and Paolo Riguzzi, "Borders, Trade, and Politics: Exchange between the United States and Mexican Cattle Industries, 1870–1947," *The Hispanic American Historical Review* 92, no. 4 (November 2012): 603–35; Roberto Schmit, "Estancias y estancieros en Entre Ríos durante el siglo XIX, (1840 y 1880)," *Mundo Agrario* 16, no. 31 (2015) 1–24, accessed November 22, 2020, www.mundoagrario.unlp.edu.ar/article/view/MAv16n31a01/6634; Hilda Sabato, *Agrarian Capitalism and the World Market: Buenos Aires in the Pastoral Age, 1840–1890* (Albuquerque: University of New Mexico Press, 1990); Stephen Bell, *Campanha Gaúcha: A Brazilian Ranching System, 1850–1920* (Stanford, CA: Stanford University Press, 1998); David H. Breen, *The Canadian Prairie West and the Ranching Frontier, 1874–1924* (Toronto: Univ. of Toronto Press, 1983); Robert Wilcox, *Cattle in the Backlands. Mato Grosso and the Evolution of Ranching in the Brazilian Tropics* (Austin: University of Texas Press, 2017).

33 Criollo (*crioulo* in Portuguese) cattle are mixed-blood bovines of Iberian origin brought to the Americas.

34 Rachel St. John, "Divided Ranges: Trans-border Ranches and the Creation of National Space along the Western Mexico-U.S. Border," in *Bridging National Borders in North America: Transnational and Comparative Histories*, ed. Benjamin H. Johnson and Andrew R. Graybill (Durham, NC: Duke University Press, 2010), 128–33; Carla Menegat, "Os brasileiros e suas estâncias no Estado Oriental do Uruguai (1845–1852): perspectivas de análise," Conference Proceedings, *Anais Eletrônicos XXVII Simpósio Nacional de História ANPUH* (Natal: UFRN/ANPUH, 2013), 5–10; Maria-Aparecida Lopes, "Carne para 'las masas hambrientas.' Interconexiones del comercio de ganado vacuno en el Atlántico Norte, 1884–1914," in *Mercados en común. Estudios sobre conexiones transnacionales, negocios y diplomacia en las*

Américas (siglos XIX y XX), ed. Maria-Aparecida Lopes and María Cecilia Zuleta (México: El Colegio de México, 2016): 79–117; Kristin Hoganson, "Meat in the Middle: Converging Borderlands in the U.S. Midwest, 1865–1900," *Journal of American History* 98, no. 4 (January 2012): 1039–48.

35 Eduardo José Miguez, "La expansión agraria de la Pampa húmeda (1850–1914). Tendencias recientes de su análisis histórico," *Anuario IEHS* 1 (1986): 95; Agustina Rayes, "Sobreviviendo en el cambio. Las exportaciones argentinas de lanas y cueros en tiempos de cereales y frigoríficos, 1890–1913," *Quinto Sol* 18, no. 1 (January–June 2014): 2–12, accessed November 22, 2020, https://cerac.unlpam.edu.ar/index.php/quintosol/article/view/836/1568.

36 Jonathan C. Brown, "Dynamics and Autonomy of a Traditional Marketing System: Buenos Aires, 1810–1860," *The Hispanic American Historical Review* 56, no. 4 (November 1976): 620–22; Julio Djenderedjian, *Historia del capitalismo agrario pampeano. La agricultura pampeana en la primera mitad del siglo XIX,* t. 4 (Buenos Aires: Siglo Veintiuno Editores Argentina – Editorial de Belgrano, 2008), 139.

37 Rolf Sternberg, "Occupance of the Humid Pampa 1856–1914," *Revista Geográfica*, no. 76 (June 1972): 98; Brown, "Dynamics," 621–22.

38 Sternberg, "Occupance," 70–71; Sabato, *Agrarian Capitalism*, 159.

39 J. Colin Crossley and Robert Greenhill, "The River Plate Beef Trade," *Business Imperialism, 1840–1930: An Inquiry Based on British Experience in Latin America,* ed. D.C.M. Platt (Oxford: Clarendon Press, 1977), 294.

40 Carmen Sesto, "The Vanguard Landowners of Buenos Aires: A New Production Model, 1856–1900," *Hispanic American Historical Review* 82, no. 4 (November 2002): 720–34.

41 Peter H. Smith, *Politics and Beef in Argentina: Patterns of Conflict and Change* (New York: Columbia University Press, 1969), 38; Andrés M. Regalsky and Elena Salerno, "Argentina," in *Historia mínima de la expansión ferroviaria en América Latina*, ed. Sandra Kuntz Ficker (México: El Colegio de México, 2015), 296–309; Perren, *Taste, Trade and Technology*, 21–25.

42 Schmit, "Estancias," 19; Julio Djenderedjian, "Expansión agrícola y colonización en Entre Ríos, 1850–1890," *Desarrollo Económico* 47, no. 188 (January–March 2008): 602; Roberto Schmit and Julio Djenderedjian, "La empresa rural en el largo plazo. Cambios en la explotación de una gran estancia rioplatense entre el orden colonial y el nacimiento del capitalismo, 1780–1870," *Boletín del Instituto de Historia Argentina y Americana "Dr. Emilio Ravignani"* Tercera serie, no. 29 (1st semester 2006): 43–44.

43 Alfredo Montoya, *Historia de los saladeros argentinos* (Buenos Aires: Raigal, 1956), 97–100.

44 Crossley and Greenhill, "River Plate Beef Trade," 296; Rodolfo Leyes, "Del saladero a la fábrica de extracto de carne: Transformaciones de los procesos de trabajo en la industria de la carne, Entre Ríos, 1864–1935," *Trabajo y Sociedad* 26 (2016): 344–46.

45 Ricardo Pillado, *Estudio sobre el comercio argentino con las naciones limítrofes* (Buenos Aires: Imprenta de J. Kidd y Cía, 1910), 76.

46 Crossley and Greenhill, "River Plate Beef Trade," 291–96; Pillado, *Estudio*, 76; Jorge G. Fodor, Arturo A. O'Connell, and Mario R. dos Santos, "La Argentina y la economía atlántica en la primera mitad del siglo XX," *Desarrollo Económico* 13, no. 49 (April–June 1973): 11–12; E. G. Jones, "The Argentine Refrigerated Meat Industry," *Economica* 26 (June 1929): 164–65; Agustina Rayes, "Destinadas a un destino: Los inicios de las exportaciones argentinas de carnes frigoríficas, 1883–1913," *Estudios Interdisciplinarios de América Latina y El Caribe* 26, no. 1 (2015): 23; Smith, *Politics*, 36.

47 Competition for land also came from grain production, mainly wheat. See Djenderedian, *La agricultura pampeana,* 139.
48 For instance, between 1901 and 1903, Argentina exported 10 to 20 times more frozen than chilled meat to Great Britain. Jones, "The Argentine," 165.
49 Magdalena Bertino and Julio Millot, *Historia Económica del Uruguay, Tomo II, Parte II: 1860–1910* (Montevideo: Fundación de Cultura Universitaria, 1996), 143–55; Crossley and Greenhill, "River Plate Beef Trade," 66; Fodor, O'Connell, and Santos, "La Argentina y la economía," 12.
50 Montoya, *Historia,* 97–100; Djenderedjian, "Expansión agrícola," 602; Arturo A. O'Connell, "La fiebre aftosa, el embargo sanitario norteamericano contra las importaciones de carne y el triángulo Argentina-Gran Bretaña-Estados Unidos en el período entre las dos guerras mundiales," *Desarrollo Económico* 26, no. 1 (April–June 1986): 31.
51 Miguel Puiggari, "Discurso sobre la conservación de las carnes alimenticias bajo el punto de vista científico y económico," *Anales de la Sociedad Rural Argentina. Revista Pastoril y Agrícola,* no. 2 (October 31, 1866): 48; A. Estrada, "Lectura sobre la conservación de las carnes," *Anales de la Sociedad Rural Argentina. Revista Pastoril y Agrícola,* no. 1 (September 30, 1866): 26–28; N. I., "La antigua estancia concluyó," *Anales de la Sociedad Rural Argentina. Revista Pastoril y Agrícola,* no. 8 (April 15, 1867): 255; Hilda Sabato, *Agrarian Capitalism,* 163–64.
52 Pillado, *Estudio,* 75.
53 Agustina Rayes, "En las puertas del Dorado. Las exportaciones argentinas, 1890–1913" (PhD diss., Universidad Torcuato Di Tella, Buenos Aires, 2013), 208–11; Skaggs, *Prime Cut,* 37; J. Alden Bower, "A Survey of the Beef Cattle Industry in the United States, Argentina, Canada and Australia from 1890 to 1914" (master's thesis, University of Wisconsin-Madison, 1915), 98–101.
54 T. F. Bayard, *Cattle and Dairy Farming,* United States Consular Reports, part 1 (Washington: Government Printing Office, 1888), 7–8.
55 Crossley and Greenhill, "River Plate Beef Trade," 292; Rayes, "Destinadas a un destino," 24.
56 José Pedro Barrán and Benjamín Nahum, *Historia rural del Uruguay moderno,* vol. 1 part 1, (Montevideo: Ediciones de la Banda Oriental, 1967), 48.
57 Eduardo Acevedo, *Notas y apuntes: contribución al estudio de la historia económica y financiera de la república oriental del Uruguay* (Montevideo: Imp. y encuadernación "El siglo ilustrado," 1903), 15–16; Clarence F. Jones, "The Trade of Uruguay," *Economic Geography* 3, no. 3 (July 1927): 367; Bertino and Millot, *Historia Económica del Uruguay*, 151.
58 An association founded in 1860 whose mission was to "watch over the moral and material progress of the republic." Barrán and Nahum, *Historia rural,* 130.
59 Acevedo, *Notas y apuntes*, 15–21; Barrán and Nahum, *Historia rural*, 130–32.
60 Brasil, *Tarifas das Alfândegas do Império do Brasil, 1857–1887* (Rio de Janeiro: Typographia Nacional, 1857–1887), several pages; Brasil, *Tarifa das Alfândegas, 1889–1914* (Rio de Janeiro: Typographia Nacional, 1889–1914), several pages; Barrán and Nahum, *Historia rural*, 93.
61 Raúl Jacob, *Cruzando la frontera* (Montevideo: Editorial Arpoador, 2004), 35–36; Miguel Arrojado Ribeiro Lisboa, *Oeste de São Paulo-Sul de Mato Grosso* (Rio de Janeiro: Typ. do "Jornal do comercio," de Rodrigues & C., 1909), 157–58; Fernanda Codevilla Soares, "Santa Thereza. Um estudo sobre as charqueadas da fronteira Brasil-Uruguay" (master's thesis, Universidade Federal de Santa Maria, 2006), 50–54; Bertino and Millot, *Historia Económica del Uruguay*, 153.

62 Crossley and Greenhill, "River Plate Beef Trade," 294–96; Bertino and Millot, *Historia Económica del Uruguay*, 144, 177–80; Perren, *Taste, Trade and Technology*, 46–47.
63 María Inés Moraes, "El capitalismo pastor. Dinámica tecnológica e institucional de la ganadería uruguaya entre 1870–1930," *Historia Agraria. Revista de Agricultura e Historia Rural*, no. 29 (2003): 19–21.
64 Magdalena Bertino and Héctor Tajam, *La ganadería en el Uruguay, 1911–1943*, unpublished manuscript, D.T. 3/00 (March 2000): 17–21.
65 Moraes, "El capitalismo pastor," 19–20; Jones, "Trade of Uruguay," 368.
66 Pereira, "Was it Uruguay or Coffee?," 18; Bertino and Millot, *Historia Económica del Uruguay*, 138–41.
67 However, gradually, in 1908, for instance, Uruguay registered only one frigorífico and 16 salt meat-processing plants. Bertino and Millot, *Historia Económica del Uruguay*, 138–41.
68 Jornal do Commercio, *Retrospecto Comercial de 1918* (Rio de Janeiro: Typographia do "Jornal do Commercio," de Rodrigues, & C., 1919), 318.
69 *Gazeta de Notícias*, April 12, 1892.
70 Luís Augusto Ebling Farinatti, "Confins meridionais: famílias de elite e sociedade agrária na Fronteira Sul do Brasil (1825–1865)" (PhD diss., Universidade Federal do Rio de Janeiro, 2007), 64–66; Jonas M. Vargas, *Os barões do charque e suas fortunas. Um estudo sobre as elites regionais brasleiras a partir de uma análise dos charqueadores de Pelotas* (São Leopoldo, RGS: Oikos Editora, 2016), 157; Alfredo Varela, *Rio Grande do Sul: descripção physica, histórica e económica* (Pelotas: Livraria Universal, 1897), 461–62, vol. 1; Menegat, "Os brasileiros," 5–10.
71 Lopes, "Carne para," 79–117; Farinatti, "Confins meridionais," 72.
72 Pedro Cezar Dutra Fonseca, "A transição capitalista no Rio Grande do Sul: a economia gaúcha na primeira república," *Estudos Econômicos* 15, no. 2 (May–August, 1985): 264.
73 Vargas, *Os barões do charque*, 209–12.
74 For instance, in the year 1862–1863 charqueadas in Pelotas slaughtered a little more than 350,000 herds; five years later, this number jumped to almost 450,000, only to decline to approximately 242,000 in 1880–1881. *Annuario da Província do Rio Grande do Sul (RS) para o ano de 1885* (Porto Alegre: Editores Gundlach & Cia., Livreiros, 1884), 240–41.
75 See endnote 6. Susana Bleil de Souza, "Fronteira, poder político e articulações comerciais no Brasil meridional do final do século XIX,"*Anuario IEHS 23* (2008): 305–33.
76 Farinatti, "Confins meridionais," 77.
77 *Diario do Rio de Janeiro*, April 1, 1860; Barrán and Nahum, *Historia rural*, 93; Pereira, "Was it Uruguay or Coffee?," 11.
78 Jornal do Commercio, *Retrospecto Commercial de 1912* (Rio de Janeiro: Typographia do "Jornal do Commercio," de Rodrigues & C. 1913), 8–20.
79 For an excellent discussion on the topic, see Souza, "Fronteira," 305–33.
80 Sandra Jatahy Pesavento, "Trabalho livre e orden burguesa. Rio Grande do Sul – 1870–1900," *Revista História* 120 (January–July 1989): 143; Sandra Jatahy Pesavento, *República velha gaúcha: charqueadas, frigoríficos, criadores* (Porto Alegre, RS, Brasil: Editora Movimento, em convênio com o Instituto Estadual do Livro, Departamento de Cultura, Secretaria de Cultura, Desporto e Turismo, RS, 1980), 43–45.
81 Fernando Henrique Cardoso, *Capitalismo e escravidão no Brasil meridional. O negro na sociedade escravocrata do Rio Grande do Sul* (São Paulo: DIFEL, 1962), 186–205.

82 Bruno Stelmach Pessi, "O fim do tráfico e a organização do trabalho nas charqueadas pelotenses: ofícios e avaliação dos escravos arrolados nos inventários de charqueadores," *Aedos. Revista do corpo discente do Programa de Pós-graduação em história da UFRGS* 2, no. 4 (2009): 159–62, accessed November 11, 2020, https://seer.ufrgs.br/index.php/aedos/article/viewFile/11190/6898; Vargas, *Os barões do charque*, 118–32; Jonas M. Vargas, "Das charqueadas para os cafezais? O comércio de escravos envolvendo as charqueadas de Pelotas (RS) entre as décadas de 1850 e 1880," *V Encontro Escravidão e liberdade no Brasil meridional*, unpublished manuscript (May 2011): 1–19. On productivity, see Manfredini and Monteiro, "Rentablidade," 8–14; Leonardo M. Monastério, "FHC errou? A economia da escravidão no Brasil meridional," *História e Economia Revista Interdisciplinar. Brazilian Business School* 1, no. 1 (São Paulo: Terra Comunicação Editorial, 2005): 13–28.

83 Graciela Bonassa Garcia, "Terra, trabalho e propriedade: a estrutura agrária da campanha rio-grandense nas décadas finais do período imperial (1870–1890)" (PhD diss., Universidade Federal Fluminense, 2010), 128–36; Maria Angelica Zubaran, "Slaves and *Contratados*: The Politics of Freedom in Rio Grande do Sul, Brazil, 1865–1888," (PhD diss., State University of New York at Stony Brook, 1998), 139, 151–65.

84 Bell, *Campanha Gaúcha*, 110–14.

85 Vargas, *Os barões do charque*, 198; Pesavento, *República Velha*, 37.

86 Soares, "Santa Thereza," 55–58, 74–75; Márcia Solange Volkmer, "'Onde começa ou termina o território pátrio.' Os estrategistas da fronteira: empresários uruguaios, política e a indústria do charque no extremo oeste do Rio Grande do Sul (Quaraí 1893–1928)" (master's thesis, Universidade do Vale do Rio dos Sinos, 2007), 49, 108, 144–46.

87 Vargas, "Das charqueadas para os cafezais?," 15; *Mensagem enviada a assembléia dos representantes do estado do Rio Grande do Sul, pelo presidente Antonio Augusto Borges de Medeiros* (Porto Alegre: Officinas Typographicas d' 'A Federação', 1907), 29; Ester J. B. Gutierrez, *Negros, charqueadas & olarias: um estudo sobre o espaço pelotense* (Pelotas: Editora UFPeL, 2001), 83–88; Pesavento, *República Velha*, 37.

88 Luna and Klein, *The Economic*, 70–81; Vargas, *Os barões do charque*, 208–10.

89 Sarah Milov, "Promoting Agriculture: Farmers, the State, and Checkoff Marketing, 1935–2005," *Business History Review* 90, no. 3 (2016): 507.

90 *Mensagem apresentada a assembleia legislativa em 20 de setembro de 1902 pelo presidente do Estado Q. Bocaiuva* (Rio de Janeiro: Typographia do Jornal do Commercio de Rodrigues & C., 1902), 104.

91 *Gazeta de Notícias*, April 12, 1892; *Gazeta de Notícias*, June 15, 1890; *Gazeta de Notícias*, August 27, 1890.

92 Sara Bovilyg, "Notas do Rio," *O Pharol*, January 23, 1917.

93 The salting and drying by sunlight exposition practically kill thiamine in meat, a vitamin that helps the body to transform food into energy; a thiamine-deficient mother whose child's only source of food is breastmilk lacks an essential vitamin to survive. Kenneth F. Kiple, "The Nutritional Link with Slave Infant and Child Mortality in Brazil," *The Hispanic American Historical Review* 69, no. 4 (November 1989): 687–88.

94 *Gazeta de Notícias*, April 12, 1892. In early 1800s, United States-cured and dried beef was considered "unpalatable and low." See Emily Pawley, "The Point of Perfection Cattle Portraiture, Bloodlines, and the Meaning of Breeding, 1760–1860," *Journal of the Early Republic* 36 (2016): 54.

95 *Mensagem enviada a assembléia dos representantes do estado do Rio Grande do Sul, pelo presidente Carlos Barbosa Gonçalves 1908* (Porto Alegre: Officinas Graphicas da 'Livraria do Globo,' 1908), 41–43.

Bibliography

Government Documents and Publications

Annuario da Província do Rio Grande do Sul (RS) para o ano de 1885. Porto Alegre: Editores Gundlach & Cia., Livreiros, 1884.

Bayard, T. F. *Cattle and Dairy Farming*, United States Consular Reports. Part 1. Washington: Government Printing Office, 1888.

Brasil. *Annuario Estatístico do Brazil 1° Anno (1908 – 1912)*. Vol. 2. Economia e Finanças. Rio de Janeiro: Typographia da Estatística, 1917.

Brasil. *Tarifas das Alfândegas do Império do Brasil, 1857–1887*. Rio de Janeiro: Typographia Nacional, 1857–1887.

Brasil. *Tarifa das Alfândegas, 1889–1914*. Rio de Janeiro: Typographia Nacional, 1889–1914.

Mensagem apresentada a assembléia legislativa em 20 de setembro de 1902 pelo presidente do Estado Q. Bocaiuva. Rio de Janeiro: Typographia do Jornal do Commercio de Rodrigues & C., 1902.

Mensagem enviada a assembléia dos representantes do estado do Rio Grande do Sul, pelo presidente Antonio Augusto Borges de Medeiros. Porto Alegre: Officinas Typographicas d' 'A Federação', 1907.

Mensagem enviada a assembléia dos representantes do estado do Rio Grande do Sul, pelo presidente Carlos Barbosa Gonçalves 1908. Porto Alegre: Officinas Graphicas da 'Livraria do Globo', 1908.

Passos, Francisco Pereira. *Mensagem do Prefeito de Districto Federal lida na sessão do Conselho Municipal de 2 de abril de 1904 e 1 de setembro de 1904*. Rio de Janeiro: Typographia da "Gazeta de Noticias", 1904.

Rio de Janeiro. *Anuário Estatístico do Distrito Federal Ano IX*, 1941. Rio de Janeiro: Publicação do Departamento de Geografia e Estatística, 1942.

Newspapers and Magazines

Correio da Manhã (Rio de Janeiro)
Diario do Rio de Janeiro
Gazeta de Notícias (Rio de Janeiro)
Jornal do Commercio (Rio de Janeiro)

Bovilyg, Sara. "Notas do Rio." *O Pharol* (Juiz de Fora). January 23, 1917.

Estrada, A. "Lectura sobre la conservación de las carnes." *Anales de la Sociedad Rural Argentina. Revista Pastoril y Agrícola* no. 1 (September 30, 1866): 26–28.

"Jerked-Beef versus Refrigerated Meat." *Refrigerating World* 56, no. 6 (1921): 32–33.

Jornal do Commercio. *Retrospecto Commercial do[s] ano[s] 1872–1914, 1918, 1930*. Rio de Janeiro: Typographia do "Jornal do Commercio," de Rodrigues & C., 1873–1915, 1919, 1931.

"Meat Consumption." *The Rio News*, February 26, 1901.
N. I. "La antigua estancia concluyó." *Anales de la Sociedad Rural Argentina. Revista Pastoril y Agrícola* no. 8 (April 15, 1867): 255–256.
Puiggari, Miguel. "Discurso sobre la conservación de las carnes alimenticias bajo el punto de vista científico y económico." *Anales de la Sociedad Rural Argentina. Revista Pastoril y Agrícola*, no. 2 (October 31, 1866): 35–53.

Other Primary Sources

Acevedo, Eduardo. *Notas y apuntes: contribución al estudio de la historia económica y financiera de la república oriental del Uruguay*. Montevideo: Imp. y encuadernación "El siglo ilustrado", 1903.
Affonseca Junior, *Léo de. O custo da vida na cidade do Rio de Janeiro*. Rio de Janeiro: Imprensa Nacional, 1920.
Andrews, Christopher C. *Brazil: its Condition and Prospects*. New York: D. Appleton and Company, 1891.
Critchell, James, and Joseph Raymond. *History of the Frozen Meat Trade. An Account of the Development and Present Day Methods of Preparation, Transport, and Marketing of Frozen and Chilled Meats*. London: Constable & Company, 1912.
Lisboa, Miguel Arrojado Ribeiro. *Oeste de São Paulo-Sul de Mato Grosso*. Rio de Janeiro: Typ. do "Jornal do comercio," de Rodrigues & C., 1909.
Pillado, Ricardo. *Estudio sobre el comercio argentino con las naciones limítrofes*. Buenos Aires: Imprenta de J. Kidd y Cía, 1910.
Simonsen, Roberto C. *The Meat & Cattle Industry of Brazil; Its Importance to Anglo-Brazilian Commerce*. London: Industrial Publicity Service, 1919.
Torres, Alberto. *A organização nacional; Primeira parte - A Constituição*. São Paulo: Companhia Editora Nacional, 1938.
Varela, Alfredo. *Rio Grande do Sul: descripção physica, histórica e económica*. Pelotas: Livraria Universal, 1897.

Secondary Sources

Ball, Molly C. "Prices, Wages, and the Cost of Living in Old Republic São Paulo: 1891–1930." *Research in Economic History* 34, Emerald Publishing Limited (2018): 1–34.
Barrán, José Pedro, and Benjamín Nahum. *Historia rural del Uruguay moderno*. V. 1 Part 1. Montevideo: Ediciones de la Banda Oriental, 1967.
Bell, Stephen. *Campanha Gaúcha: A Brazilian Ranching System, 1850–1920*. Stanford, CA: Stanford University Press, 1998.
Bertino, Magdalena, and Julio Millot. *Historia Económica del Uruguay, Tomo II Parte II: 1860–1910*. Montevideo: Fundación de Cultura Universitaria, 1996.
Bertino, Magdalena, and Héctor Tajam. *La ganadería en el Uruguay, 1911–1943*. Unpublished manuscript, D.T. 3/00 (2000): 1–38.
Bethell, Leslie. "The Decline and Fall of Slavery in Nineteenth Century Brazil." *Transactions of the Royal Historical Society* 1 (1991): 71–88.
Bower, J. Alden. "A Survey of the Beef Cattle Industry in the United States, Argentina, Canada and Australia from 1890 to 1914." Master's thesis, University of Wisconsin-Madison, 1915.

Breen, David H. *The Canadian Prairie West and the Ranching Frontier, 1874–1924*. Toronto: University of Toronto Press, 1983.

Brown, Jonathan C. "Dynamics and Autonomy of a Traditional Marketing System: Buenos Aires, 1810–1860." *The Hispanic American Historical Review* 56, no. 4 (November 1976): 605–629.

Cardoso, Fernando Henrique. *Capitalismo e escravidão no Brasil meridional. O negro na sociedade escravocrata do Rio Grande do Sul*. São Paulo: DIFEL, 1962.

Catão, Luis A. "A new wholesale price index for Brazil during the period 1870–1913." *Revista Brasileira de Economia* 46, no. 4 (1992): 519–534.

Claflin, Kyri. "La Villette: City of Blood (1867–1914)." In *Meat, Modernity, and the Rise of the Slaughterhouse*, edited by Paula Young Lee, 27–45. Durham, NH: University of New Hampshire Press, 2008.

Crossley, J. Colin, and Robert Greenhill. "The River Plate Beef Trade." In *Business Imperialism, 1840–1930: an Inquiry Based on British Experience in Latin America* edited by D.C.M. Platt, 284–334. Oxford: Clarendon Press, 1977.

Djenderedjian, Julio. *Historia del capitalismo agrario pampeano. La agricultura pampeana en la primera mitad del siglo XIX*. T. 4. Buenos Aires: Siglo Veintiuno Editores Argentina – Editorial de Belgrano, 2008a.

Djenderedjian, Julio. "Expansión agrícola y colonización en Entre Ríos, 1850–1890." *Desarrollo Económico* 47, no. 188 (January–March 2008b): 577–606.

Duffett, Rachel. *The Stomach for Fighting: Food and the Soldiers of the Great War*. Manchester: Manchester University Press, 2015.

Farinatti, Luís Augusto Ebling. "Confins meridionais: famílias de elite e sociedade agrária na Fronteira Sul do Brasil (1825–1865)." PhD diss., Universidade Federal do Rio de Janeiro, 2007.

Fodor, Jorge G., Arturo A. O'Connell, and Mario R. dos Santos. "La Argentina y la economía atlántica en la primera mitad del siglo XX." *Desarrollo Económico* 13, no. 49 (April–June 1973): 3–65.

Fonseca, Pedro Cezar Dutra. "A transição capitalista no Rio Grande do Sul: a economia gaúcha na primeira república." *Estudos Econômicos* 15, no. 2 (May–August 1985): 263–289.

Garcia, Graciela Bonassa. "Terra, trabalho e propriedade: a estrutura agrária da campanha rio-grandense nas décadas finais do período imperial (1870–1890)." PhD diss., Universidade Federal Fluminense, 2010.

Gordon, Steve C. "From Slaughterhouse to Soap-Boiler: Cincinnati's Meat Packing Industry, Changing Technologies, and the Rise of Mass Production, 1825–1870." *The Journal of the Society for Industrial Archeology* 16, no. 1 (1990): 55–67.

Guàrdia, Manel, José Luis Oyón, Sergi Garriga, and Nadia Fava. "Meat Consumption and Nutrition Transition in Barcelona, 1709–1935." *Urban History* 45, no. 2 (2018): 193–213.

Gutierrez, Ester J. B. *Negros, charqueadas & olarias: um estudo sobre o espaço pelotense*. Pelotas: Editora UFPeL, 2001.

Hoganson, Kristin. "Meat in the Middle: Converging Borderlands in the U.S. Midwest, 1865–1900." *Journal of American History* 98, no. 4 (January 2012): 1025–1051.

Jacob, Raúl. *Cruzando la frontera*. Montevideo: Editorial Arpoador, 2004.

Jones, Clarence F. "The Trade of Uruguay." *Economic Geography* 3, no. 3 (July 1927): 361–381.

Jones, E. G. "The Argentine Refrigerated Meat Industry." *Economica* 26 (June 1929): 156–172.

Kiple, Kenneth F. "The Nutritional Link with Slave Infant and Child Mortality in Brazil." *The Hispanic American Historical Review* 69, no. 4 (November 1989): 677–690.

Klein, Herbert S., and Francisco Vidal Luna. *Slavery in Brazil*. Cambridge: Cambridge University Press, 2010.

Leff, Nathaniel H. "Economic Development in Brazil, 1822–1913." In *How Latin America Fell Behind: Essays on the Economic Histories of Brazil and Mexico, 1800–1914*, edited by Stephen H. Haber, 34–64. Stanford, CA: Stanford University Press, 1997.

Leyes, Rodolfo. "Del saladero a la fábrica de extracto de carne: Transformaciones de los procesos de trabajo en la industria de la carne, Entre Ríos, 1864–1935." *Trabajo y Sociedad* 26 (2016): 341–359.

Linhares, Maria Yedda Leite. *História do abastecimento; uma problemática em questão (1530–1918)*. Brasília: Edições Binagri, 1979.

Lobo, Eulália Maria Lahmeyer, Lucena Barbosa Madureira, Octavio Canavarros, Zakia Feres, and Sonia Gonçalves. "Evolução dos preços e do padrão de vida no Rio de Janeiro, 1820–1930 - resultados preliminares." *Revista Brasileira de Economia* 25, no. 4 (October–December 1971): 235–265.

Lobo, Eulália Maria Lahmeyer. *História do Rio de Janeiro: do capital comercial ao capital industrial e financeiro*. Vol. 2. Rio de Janeiro: Inst. Brasileiro de Mercado de Capitais - IBMEC, 1978.

Lopes, Maria-Aparecida, and Paolo Riguzzi, "Borders, Trade, and Politics: Exchange between the United States and Mexican Cattle Industries, 1870–1947." *The Hispanic American Historical Review* 92, no. 4 (November 2012): 603–635.

Lopes, Maria-Aparecida. "Carne para 'las masas hambrientas.' Interconexiones del comercio de ganado vacuno en el Atlántico Norte, 1884–1914." In *Mercados en común. Estudios sobre conexiones transnacionales, negocios y diplomacia en las Américas (siglos XIX y XX)*, edited by Maria-Aparecida Lopes and María Cecilia Zuleta, 81–119. México: El Colegio de México, 2016.

Love, Joseph L. *Rio Grande Do Sul and Brazilian Regionalism 1882–1930*. Stanford, CA: Stanford University Press, 1971.

Luna, Francisco Vidal, and Herbert S. Klein. *The Economic and Social History of Brazil Since 1889*. Cambridge: Cambridge University Press, 2014.

Machado, Maria Helena P. T. "Slavery and Social Movements in Nineteenth-Century Brazil: Slave Strategies and Abolition in São Paulo." *Review (Fernand Braudel Center)* 34, no. 1/2, (2011): 163–191.

Manfredini, Denise, and Sergio Marley Modesto Monteiro. "*Rentabilidade do trabalho escravo no Rio Grande do Sul no século XIX*." *Anais do XLII Encontro Nacional de Economia* (Proceedings of the 42nd Brazilian Economics Meeting) 020, ANPEC - Associação Nacional dos Centros de Pósgraduação em Economia (2014): 1–17.

Mattoso, Katia M. de Queirós. *To Be a Slave in Brazil, 1550–1888*. New Brunswick, NJ: Rutgers University Press, 1986.

Melvin, A. D. "The South American Meat Industry." In *Yearbook of the United States Department of Agriculture*. Washington: Government Printing Office, 1913.

Menegat, Carla. "Os brasileiros e suas estâncias no Estado Oriental do Uruguai (1845–1852): perspectivas de análise." Conference Proceedings, *Anais Eletrônicos XXVII Simpósio Nacional de História ANPUH*. Natal: UFRN/ANPUH (2013): 1–18.
Miguez, Eduardo José. "La expansión agraria de la Pampa húmeda (1850–1914). Tendencias recientes de su análisis histórico." *Anuario IEHS* 1 (1986): 89–119.
Milov, Sarah. "Promoting Agriculture: Farmers, the State, and Checkoff Marketing, 1935–2005." *Business History Review* 90, no. 3 (2016): 505–536.
Monastério, Leonardo M., "FHC errou? A economia da escravidão no Brasil meridional." In *História e Economia Revista Interdisciplinar. Brazilian Business School* 1, n. 1. São Paulo: Terra Comunicação Editorial (2005): 13–28.
Montoya, Alfredo. *Historia de los saladeros argentinos*. Buenos Aires: Raigal, 1956.
Moraes, María Inés. "El capitalismo pastor. Dinámica tecnológica e institucional de la ganadería uruguaya entre 1870–1930." *Historia Agraria. Revista de Agricultura e Historia Rural*, no. 29 (2003): 13–44.
Moura Filho, Heitor Pinto. "Exchange rates of the mil-réis (1795–1913)." *MPRA Paper No. 5210*. University Library of Munich, Germany (2006): 1–17. Accessed November 22, 2020. http://mpra.ub.uni–muenchen.de/5210/.
O'Connell, Arturo A. "La fiebre aftosa, el embargo sanitario norteamericano contra las importaciones de carne y el triángulo Argentina-Gran Bretaña-Estados Unidos en el período entre las dos guerras mundiales." *Desarrollo Económico* 26, no. 1 (April–June 1986): 21–50.
Otter, Chris. "The Vital City: Public Analysis, Dairies and Slaughterhouses in Nineteenth-Century Britain." *Cultural Geographies* 13, no. 4 (2006): 517–537.
Pawley, Emily. "The Point of Perfection Cattle Portraiture, Bloodlines, and the Meaning of Breeding, 1760–1860." *Journal of the Early Republic* 36 (2016): 37–72.
Pereira, Thales A. Zamberlan. "Was it Uruguay or Coffee? The Causes of the Beef Jerky Industry's Decline in Southern Brazil (1850–1889)." *Nova Economia* 26, no. 1 (2016): 7–42.
Perren, Richard. *Taste, Trade and Technology: The Development of the International Meat Industry Since 1840*. Aldershot, UK: Ashgate Publishing, 2006.
Pesavento, Sandra Jatahy. *República velha gaúcha: charqueadas, frigoríficos, criadores*. Porto Alegre, RS: Editora Movimento, em convênio com o Instituto Estadual do Livro, Departamento de Cultura, Secretaria de Cultura, Desporto e Turismo, RS, 1980.
Pesavento, Sandra Jatahy. "Trabalho livre e orden burguesa. Rio Grande do Sul - 1870–1900." *Revista História* 120 (January–July 1989): 135–151.
Pessi, Bruno Stelmach. "O fim do tráfico e a organização do trabalho nas charqueadas pelotenses: ofícios e avaliação dos escravos arrolados nos inventários de charqueadores." *Aedos. Revista do corpo discente do Programa de Pós-graduação em história da UFRGS* 2, no. 4 (2009): 157–168. Accessed November 11, 2020, https://seer.ufrgs.br/index.php/aedos/article/viewFile/11190/6898.
Rayes, Agustina. "En las puertas del Dorado. Las exportaciones argentinas, 1890–1913." PhD diss., Universidad Torcuato Di Tella, Buenos Aires, 2013.
Rayes, Agustina. "Sobreviviendo en el cambio. Las exportaciones argentinas de lanas y cueros en tiempos de cereales y frigoríficos, 1890–1913." *Quinto Sol* 18, no. 1 (Jan–Jun 2014): 2–22. Accessed November 22, 2020, https://cerac.unlpam.edu.ar/index.php/quintosol/article/view/836/1568.

Rayes, Agustina. "Destinadas a un destino: Los inicios de las exportaciones argentinas de carnes frigoríficas, 1883–1913." *Estudios Interdisciplinarios de América Latina y El Caribe* 26, no. 1 (2015): 7–30.

Regalsky, Andrés M., and Elena Salerno. "Argentina." In *Historia mínima de la expansión ferroviaria en América Latina*, edited by Sandra Kuntz Ficker, 281–316. México: El Colegio de México, 2015.

Sabato, Hilda. *Agrarian Capitalism and the World Market: Buenos Aires in the Pastoral Age, 1840–1890*. Albuquerque: University of New Mexico Press, 1990.

Schmit, Roberto, and Julio Djenderedjian. "La empresa rural en el largo plazo. Cambios en la explotación de una gran estancia rioplatense entre el orden colonial y el nacimiento del capitalismo, 1780–1870." *Boletín del Instituto de Historia Argentina y Americana "Dr. Emilio Ravignani"* Tercera serie, no. 29 (1st semester 2006): 7–49.

Schmit, Roberto. "Estancias y estancieros en Entre Ríos durante el siglo XIX, (1840 y 1880)." *Mundo Agrario* 16, no. 31 (2015): 1–24. Accessed November 22, 2020, www.mundoagrario.unlp.edu.ar/article/view/MAv16n31a01/6634.

Schulz, John. *The Financial Crisis of Abolition*. New Haven: Yale University Press, 2008.

Sesto, Carmen. "The Vanguard Landowners of Buenos Aires: A New Production Model, 1856–1900." *Hispanic American Historical Review* 82, no. 4 (November 2002): 719–754.

Skaggs, Jimmy M. *Prime Cut. Livestock Raising and Meatpacking in the United States. 1607–1983*. College Station: Texas A&M University Press, 1986.

Smith, Peter H. *Politics and Beef in Argentina: Patterns of Conflict and Change*. New York: Columbia University Press, 1969.

Soares, Fernanda Codevilla. "Santa Thereza. Um estudo sobre as charqueadas da fronteira Brasil-Uruguay." Master's thesis, Universidade Federal de Santa Maria, 2006.

Souza, Susana Bleil de. "Charqueadas i instal.lacions frigorífiques a la frontera gautxa: el trànsit pel port de Montevideo a principis del segle XX." *Recerques: història, economia, cultura* 45–46 (2002–2003): 73–89. Accessed November 21, 2020, https://www.raco.cat/index.php/Recerques/article/view/140210.

Souza, Susana Bleil de. "Fronteira, poder político e articulações comerciais no Brasil meridional do final do século XIX."*Anuario IEHS* 23 (2008): 305–333.

St. John, Rachel. "Divided Ranges: Trans-border Ranches and the Creation of National Space along the Western Mexico-U.S. Border." In *Bridging National Borders in North America: Transnational and Comparative Histories*, edited by Benjamin H. Johnson and Andrew R. Graybill, 116–140. Durham, NC: Duke University Press, 2010.

Sternberg, Rolf. "Occupance of the Humid Pampa 1856–1914." *Revista Geográfica*, no. 76 (June 1972): 61–102.

Vargas, Jonas M. "Das charqueadas para os cafezais? O comércio de escravos envolvendo as charqueadas de Pelotas (RS) entre as décadas de 1850 e 1880." *V Encontro Escravidão e liberdade no Brasil meridional*. Unpublished manuscript (May 2011): 1–19.

Vargas, Jonas M. *Os barões do charque e suas fortunas. Um estudo sobre as elites regionais brasleiras a partir de uma análise dos charqueadores de Pelotas*. São Leopoldo, RGS: Oikos Editora, 2016.

Volkmer, Márcia Solange. "'Onde começa ou termina o território pátrio'. Os estrategistas da fronteira: empresários uruguaios, política e a indústria

do charque no extremo oeste do Rio Grande do Sul (Quaraí 1893–1928)." Master's thesis, Universidade do Vale do Rio dos Sinos, 2007.
Wilcox, Robert W. *Cattle in the Backlands. Mato Grosso and the Evolution of Ranching in the Brazilian Tropics*. Austin: University of Texas Press, 2017.
Zubaran, Maria Angelica. "Slaves and *Contratados*: The Politics of Freedom in Rio Grande do Sul, Brazil, 1865–1888." PhD diss., State University of New York at Stony Brook, 1998.

6 Meatpacking Companies and a New Politics of Provision in Rio de Janeiro (c.1910–c.1930)

The early twentieth century witnessed a renewed interest in meat-eating (beef, in particular) in the Western world. Surely, debates over the benefits of animal-derived food predate the 1900s; however, refrigeration technology, which made it possible to transport and store perishables faster and safer, reinforced the notion that meat was the ideal source of proteins to the masses. A wide array of actors, including food manufacturers, national governments, and policymakers—although lacking sound scientific support—associated meat intake with high productivity;[1] hence, the push to replace public abattoirs with meatpacking companies on both sides of the Atlantic. Meatpackers contended that their technological innovation would make their product affordable and available in larger quantities and in good sanitary conditions for urban workers. For their part, national governments (sometimes at odds with their local counterparts) promoted industrialization to rid municipalities of old slaughterhouses and traditional food supply monopolies. As this chapter discusses, both sectors confronted a series of obstacles to realizing their ambitions.

In the case of Rio de Janeiro, on the one hand, since the colonial times, meat provisioning was one of the municipal government's essential duties, and it did not relinquish such a role lightly. On the other hand, although the working class was the prime target for the mass-produced meat that packing plants offered, the actual increase in consumption depended upon a series of conditions, chiefly, improvement in workers' wages. Therefore, the transition toward refrigerated meat, not only in Brazil but also elsewhere, was more complicated than envisioned by its early promoters. In the previous chapters, this book has discussed the stories behind the provision of fresh and salt-meat (*carne verde* and *carne seca*) to Rio de Janeiro, the main urban center of nineteenth-century Brazil. This chapter furthers this discussion in light of newly implemented meatpacking companies in the country. The goal is to describe the conditions under which private actors created those meatpacking companies and ponder their immediate consequences in Rio de Janeiro. The first section describes the onset of meat industrialization in Brazil; the second examines how it challenged the municipal abattoir system. Lastly, the chapter considers the role that packinghouses played in the urban meat market from the 1920s to the 1930s.

The Arrival of Meatpacking Companies in Brazil

During the last decades of the nineteenth century and the first of the twentieth, Brazil experienced an upsurge in industrial output, most notably in consumer and intermediate goods, and in the textile, transport, and food-processing sectors. World War I (WWI), indeed, created unexpected demand for processed meat and other animal-derived products. Brazil only met such a demand thanks to industrial development that occurred before the war. Likewise, the introduction of the electrical grid and imports of cold equipment occurred prior to 1914. This early industrial push was associated with the export boom of agricultural commodities (coffee, in particular), as it stimulated the production of machinery to process and transport such goods. Revenues from those exports fostered the internal market for consumer goods and the banking system, while the government utilized export duty revenues to overhaul public works. Once the war ended, limited availability of machinery and growing internal demand for consumer non-durables, intermediate inputs, construction goods, and metalworking machinery prompted a new wave of industrialization subsidized by the government.[2] Scholars still debate the level of protectionism before and after the war.[3]

The emergence of meatpacking plants in Brazil was the direct result of domestic entrepreneurship and foreign investment. Incentives that the federal and state governments conceded also played a part in launching meat industrialization. In 1910, the federal government opened public bidding for the construction of experimental slaughterhouses (*matadouros modelos*) and meatpacking (*frigoríficos*) plants. As expressed in the decree, the goal was to channel Brazil's animal-derived foods to external markets, reduce food degeneration waste, and improve public health. To achieve such objectives, the government proposed the installation of matadouros modelos, "equipped with refrigerated chambers and [microbiology laboratories] in … Minas [Gerais], São Paulo, and Rio de Janeiro." It also sponsored the foundation of a federal sanitary service for the inspection of animals and perishable foods, and the construction of cold chambers in Brazil's main ports, centers of meat production, and vessels and railroad cars.[4]

Apart from subsidizing transport and storage facilities, the federal administration exempted construction material and cold-related equipment from import duty and gave preferential treatment to meat shipping via federal railways. The government was also directly involved in the area of livestock upgrading. It established experimental ranches (*fazendas modelos*) that sought to improve the *crioulo* cattle (descendant from Iberian bovine breeds) and manage native forage in stock-raising areas. In 1907, it offered incentives for the importation of purebred animals and, two years later, established a genealogic registration service (herdbook) for breeding stock. The decree acknowledges Brazil's tardiness, compared to its closest neighbors, to modernize its national herd and related industry. It also foresees that improvement in the sector would boost foreign sales of animal source foods and domestic consumption of perishables.[5] States provided tax incentives to foreign and national investors as well. São Paulo, for instance, exempted packing plants "from export taxes for up to 10 years." Later, Rio Grande do Sul and Minas Gerais followed its example.[6]

Three phases characterize the beginnings of meat industrialization in Brazil. From the 1910s to the 1920s, national and well-known conglomerates such as Anglo, Swift, Armour, and Wilson launched the first processing plants in the states of São Paulo, Rio de Janeiro, Rio Grande do Sul, Minas Gerais, and Paraná. By the early 1920s, ten companies were operating in the country. Brazilian interests controlled half of these plants. However, production capacity at foreign-owned plants was two to three times higher than at national ones. A crisis in the sector in the 1920s—related to overproduction and low external demand after WWI—gave birth to a second phase, when British and United States syndicates bought the majority of domestic-owned plants. In the last stage, Brazilian firms acquired these companies, coming to dominate the sector in the 1940s and 1950s.[7]

In the 1930s, Brazil's southwest and south regions housed all packinghouses in the country. They were located near the pasturelands of Mato Grosso, Goiás, Minas Gerais, São Paulo, Rio Grande do Sul, and Rio de Janeiro, where a system of railroads connected raising and fattening grounds in these states to the main urban centers and ports in Brazil's coast (see Figure 6.1).

The origins of the meat industrialization in Brazil are intertwined with the coffee plantation interests in São Paulo, hence the state's leadership in this first phase. In the late nineteenth century, São Paulo and neighboring areas had large stocks of cattle, a growing urban population that constituted a relatively vibrant consumer market, and a web of railroad and port structures that facilitated internal and external trade. Additionally, as the productivity of their exhausted coffee plantations declined, *Paulistas* (natives of São Paulo state) began to look for other sectors to diversify their investments.[8] Thus, it is not surprising that the first concession for a frigorífico in Brazil was granted to a prominent coffee planter with ample interests in railroads and exports, Antônio da Silva Prado. In 1910, Prado and Alexandre Siciliano, an Italian immigrant, founded the *Companhia Frigorífica e Pastoril de Barretos* (linked to the *Estrada de Ferro Companhia Paulista*, which Prado partly owned).

According to a company's advert, Barretos's grasslands were an ideal location for a packing plant given its proximity to the pasturelands of

Figure 6.1 Meatpacking companies in Brazil, c. 1930.

Source: Elaborated based on Wilson Suzigan, *Indústria brasileira: origem e desenvolvimento* (São Paulo: Hucitec, 2000), 356.

north and northeast Minas Gerais, south Goiás, the Pantanal region, and south Mato Grosso. Most cattle continued to be driven from raising to fattening grounds on the hoof, but the extension of the Paulista Railway would allow animals to make at least part of this journey via rails. Likewise, Paulista's refrigerator cars would transport processed meat from Barretos to storehouses in the cities of Campinas and São

Paulo and the port of Santos. As a result, stresses the advert, the company would save in transport cost, reduce herds' weight loss by approximately 15 kilos,[9] and offer "good quality, flavorful meat ... at reduced prices."[10] Frigorífico Barretos opened its doors in 1913 and began to distribute meat to a handful of butcher shops in the central market of São Paulo city. In April, the newspaper *Correio Paulistano* chronicled the following verdict based on meat samples from Barretos: "Housewives find this meat of superior appearance and quality [and it is ideal] for domestic consumption; our palate deems it excellent, [we give it] our best compliment." Soon after, butcher shops in several municipalities in the state of São Paulo were carrying meat from Barretos, reportedly at lower prices.[11]

Despite such good reviews, the frigorífico encountered multiple problems. As in Rio de Janeiro, some cities in São Paulo did not allow "outside" meat into their market; second, São Paulo city did not have sufficient structure to store foodstuffs coming from Barretos. What is more, as it was common in Brazil during those years, company owners recognized that their "meat's quality is less than desirable," blaming such an appraisal on the domestic animals' inferiority. Thus, frigorífico Barretos initially focused on supplying the Paulista market and considered that exports could be possible only after improvement in the local herds.[12] Chapter 4 provides a context for this debate.

In 1913 and 1914, a discussion over the quality of industrial beef filled the pages of several periodicals in São Paulo. The newspaper *A Gazeta* claimed that the product from Barretos, which it called "artificial meat" (*carne artificial*), was of "objectionable salubrious properties." The daily alleged that the company had processed animals infected with foot-and-mouth disease and urged the sanitary service to intervene in the "infamous meatpacking" plant because customers had suffered "gastric discomfort." In 1914, the Society of Medicine and Surgery of São Paulo (*Sociedade de Medicina e Cirurgia de São Paulo*) attributed the controversy to the fact that even "cultured people" did not understand cold technology, particularly the difference between frozen and chilled meat. Concluding, "Scientifically refrigerated meats can be delivered to the public without risk to their health, for they are indeed hygienic, tasty, and easy to digest."[13]

These debates notwithstanding, meatpacking plants continued to arrive in Brazil. In 1915, Continental Products Company began operations in Osasco (São Paulo). It was part of the Matador Land and Cattle Company, a subsidiary of the Chicago-based Schwarzschild & Sulzberger Company, until 1917 when Wilson and Company acquired it. Continental's main target market seemed to be overseas. Linked to the Sorocabana railway, shortly after its inauguration, Matador was exporting to the United States. In 1918, the Companhia Frigorífica Santos opened its doors in the port city with the same name. Three years later, investors from the United States inaugurated the Companhia Armour do Brasil in São Paulo city.

This plant was, by all accounts, the largest yet in the state. According to its advert in *Correio Paulistano*, it could process 2,000 animals daily. In 1929, a new small frigorífico (with a slaughtering capacity of 300 herds per day) opened its doors in Cruzeiro, about 200 kilometers northeast from the state capital. In the 1920s, Frigorífico Anglo bought the Santos and Barretos plants.[14]

Out of the 12 packinghouses installed in Brazil before 1930, São Paulo housed five. Such infrastructure was geared toward urban centers like São Paulo and Rio de Janeiro and foreign markets. By the end of that decade, those plants were regularly sending their products to Europe and the United States, while frozen meat became the state's second export product, the first was coffee.[15]

After São Paulo, Rio Grande do Sul had the most plants in Brazil.[16] Companhia Armour do Brasil opened its doors in 1917 in Livramento, on the border with Uruguay. In 1919, two other companies started operations in the state, Companhia Swift do Brasil in Rio Grande city and Companhia Frigorífica de Pelotas in Pelotas. The first two could process 1,200 and 1,000 herds respectively per day, and the last 450. Companhia Armour do Brasil was also a salt-meat factory (*charqueada*), so was Companhia Swift do Brasil.[17] The state government via a syndicate of ranchers (*União dos Criadores*) managed the Pelotas plant, the only nationally owned in Rio Grande do Sul. Like the frigoríficos in São Paulo, those in Rio Grande do Sul managed the early-1920 crisis by consolidating. For instance, in 1921, the frigorífico Anglo bought the Pelotas plant. Another outcome of the crisis in the state was a decline in refrigerated meat production and a resurgence in salted meat output.[18]

In the early twentieth century, Rio de Janeiro's city council (*prefeitura*) authorized, though reluctantly, the construction of a private slaughterhouse within its limits, the matadouro da Penha. Indeed, until its approval in 1902, the facility had its meat confiscated and was temporarily shut down on several occasions. Finally, the prefeitura allowed the plant to function under the inspection of the General Director of Hygiene (*Director Geral de Hygiene*). The matadouro da Penha processed only a small fraction of the meat distributed in Rio, although its share incremented over the years. It would take more than a decade for a new private meatpacking company to enter the city's meat market.[19]

In 1917, the Anglo-Brazilian Meat Company began to operate in the matadouro de Santa Cruz, processing 500 herds daily.[20] In the same year, British investors installed the Frigorífico Anglo, Sociedade Anônima Frigorífico Anglo (also called Matadouro or Frigorífico Mendes) in Mendes (Rio de Janeiro state). However, the agreement with the Anglo-Brazilian ceased two years later, as the local government contended that it had exclusive rights to supply the city. The short life of the first arrangement and the location of the latter plant—more than 100 kilometers northwest of the federal district—illustrate some of the controversies associated with meat industrialization in Rio, and to a certain extent in Brazil during those years. Such a controversy pitted promoters of frigoríficos against city officials. It also generated a vigorous debate: over the nature of industrialized meat (vis-à-vis carne verde); over the role of local and federal governments to tax, supervise, and distribute both products; and, ultimately, over the political economy that both layers of public administration sponsored. In so many words, Alexandre Bernardino de Moura, a legal advisor to Brazil's Ministry of Agriculture, described the situation in 1910:

> The municipalities are exercising the function of regulating the production and trade of "raw meat" very legitimately given that it spoils quickly and cannot be consumed beyond these localities' limits. While the [federal] government intends to regulate the production and trade of a type of meat that does not decompose and, as such, is subject to the principle of free competition and general commercial laws.[21]

As Chapter 2 examines, during the second half of the nineteenth century, Rio's city council contended that because of its spoilage factor, fresh meat should be under its exclusive purview. However, as foreign and national companies continued to multiply in the early twentieth century, their representatives, alongside the federal government, claimed that such a characterization was a pretext that the municipality used to monopolize meat production and distribution. A similar discussion occurred in the city of São Paulo. In 1916, council members debated whether the frigoríficos of Barretos and Osasco should be taxed, by whom, and by how much. They also considered which institution should carry on sanitary inspections.[22] The next section addresses how this dispute played out in 1920s-Rio de Janeiro.

Struggles over an "Old, Nasty, and Inconvenient Monopoly," the Municipal Retreat from its Meat Supply Obligations

In 1942, a farmer from Rio Grande do Sul petitioned the federal government to convert the feedlots of the matadouro de Santa Cruz into rice fields. The Minister of Finance, Artur de Sousa Costa, denied the request, arguing that those feedlots (where up to 160,000 head of cattle rested before slaughter) were essential to the supply of Rio de Janeiro city. In his assessment, however, President Getúlio Vargas displayed striking contrast with Costa.[23] In doing so, he conveyed a new understanding behind meat provision in the city:

> [It is] erroneous and retrograde [to maintain] these feedlots [in Santa Cruz]. These lands must be divided into lots and colonized … by

> horticulturists, whose cooperatives should cultivate vegetables and grains to supply the markets of this capital and contribute to reducing the cost of living. [As for] cattle, [they] must be slaughtered outside [the city] and its byproducts transported by meatpacking [companies].[24]

To be sure, Vargas was only confirming a reality. By the 1940s, the matadouro Santa Cruz's production contributed only a small fraction of what reached consumers' tables in Rio, and without feedlots, it could not function. Indeed, if meat could be transported from outside, there was no need to maintain a slaughterhouse within the city's perimeter. The president's assessment was yet another example that the political and economic reasons behind the municipal abattoir system had faded. The next pages examine the initial stages of its demise.

The previous chapters argue that, amid difficulties in the late nineteenth century, Rio's municipality seemed to manage fresh meat supplies and maintain predictable prices. After 1917, though, increasing demand, higher prices, and threats from whom city officials characterized as interlopers made the local government's position more difficult. However, the solution to the "carne verde question"—as the financial daily *Jornal do Commercio* labeled the meat supply crisis in 1917—did not entail a simple choice between traditional or modern animal handling and meat processing.[25] WWI provided Brazil with a chance to boost its refrigerated meat exports. Extraordinary circumstances obliged Europeans to lower their standards, which in turn opened a channel for Brazilian sales of low-grade frozen beef. Almost two months after the war began, *Jornal do Commercio* characterized the timing as "more than opportune" for the national livestock and by-products industry, as it coincided with the crisis in the salt-meat factory (*charqueadas*) business and the expansion in meatpacking plants. As a sign of the unexpected opportunity, the port in Santos, where most of Brazil's meat would embark for overseas markets, did not have appropriate storage facilities. Provisionally, companies utilized vessels with cold rooms.[26] Records show that remittances of frozen meat jumped from just 1 ton in 1914 to 66,000 metric tons in three years, while the value of livestock and byproducts shipments that represented only 6 percent of all Brazilian exports in 1913 doubled by 1919.[27]

The wave of exports was so intense that, in 1918, the secretary of agriculture cautioned about a shortage of herds for the domestic market and prohibited the slaughter of breeding stock. He also expressed deep concern that government agents only inspected meatpacking plants and slaughterhouses, and not charqueadas spread throughout the country. The upsurge in processed meat remittances, once again, provoked debate over the quality of the Brazilian livestock and by-products. In 1918, João Romero, a representative of Swift in Brazil, repeated a common claim that the zebu meat was difficult to freeze, for it was dry, tasteless, and—worse yet—poor in fat, which is why it deteriorated quickly. He observed that even in India ["the region of origin of the zebu"], Swift only had meat extract plants but not chilled and frozen ones, because the "zebu meat is not suitable for refrigeration." Nevertheless, continues Romero,

> there is … no breed to choose from; every animal goes as long as it is … in a condition of being slaughtered. Zebu crossed cattle are now well accepted because of their average weight and for the simple reason that Europeans, especially the demanding British … given the extraordinary meat shortage, accept everything, and pay very well.[28]

Such pressure over the local herds is visible in Figure 6.2, which shows per capita fresh beef cattle consumption in Rio de Janeiro from 1912 to 1938. Supplies began to decline in 1916, plummeting four years later to their lowest level since the early 1910s; they remained erratic until 1925 and followed an upward trajectory in the subsequent decade. It is important to note that these figures do not account for meatpacking companies' deliveries to Rio after WWI, but particularly in the 1920s, they may have contributed chilled and frozen meat to the city's market.[29] The next section examines the mid-1920s to the mid-1930s in more detail. As for the 1916–1925 period, until the latter years, Rio de Janeiro relied mostly

Figure 6.2 Available per capita fresh beef cattle (carne verde) supply for Rio de Janeiro (kilograms), 1912–1938.

Source: Rio de Janeiro, *Anuário Estatístico do Distrito Federal Ano IX*, 1941 (Rio de Janeiro: Publicação do Departamento de Geografia e Estatística, 1942), 298.

on the Santa Cruz and Penha slaughterhouses; hence, the city council was responsible for maintaining provisions and curb costs. According to this mandate, in 1917, Mayor Amaro Cavalcanti Soares de Brito established maximum meat prices. The measure sparked confrontations with purveyors.[30] Earlier that year, the Association of Fresh Meat Retailers (*Sociedade União Protectora dos Retalhistas de Carne Verde*) convened to address the shortages, concluding that "excessive exports of frozen meat" was the culprit for price hikes, but insisting that the municipal monopoly complicated their business.[31]

In 1918, the federal government went further and created the Commission of Public Food Supply (*Commissariado da Alimentação Pública*) to intervene in the market, curb speculation, and fix prices. It was, according to A. B. Ramalho Ortigão, a representative from the Commercial Association of Rio de Janeiro (*Associação Comercial do Rio de Janeiro*), a measure designed to prevent violent acts such as the burning down of stores and shops, as had occurred in Juiz de Fora (Minas Gerais) and Petrópolis (Rio de Janeiro). Alongside the price of meat, the cost of other basic foodstuffs in the Brazilian diet spiked, including rice, beans, manioc meal, corn meal, wheat flour, codfish, lard, coffee, and milk. For some goods, such an upsurge was a direct consequence of exports. Consider, for instance, that salted meat sales, which in 1914 did not exceed 150 metric tons, jumped to more than 8,000 in 1917; in the latter year, the remittances of beans surpassed 90,000 tons, three years before it was a little over 300.[32]

The disruption in the domestic supply was also a matter of escalating transport costs. Interstate coastal shipments, for instance, were suddenly diverted to long-distance trips, railroad repair came to a halt given the difficulty of importing mechanical parts, and coal prices reached historical highs.[33]

A. B. Ramalho Ortigão, mentioned previously, authored a detailed study on the Commissariado's work. He presents a lengthy defense of the state's intervention in the economy and credits the agency for slowing down foodstuff costs. Comparing prices before and after the Commission's existence, the author concludes that, between July 1914 and July 1918, there was a hike of approximately 100 percent (i.e., 78 percent in charque and more than 200 percent in manioc meal). In contrast, from July (when the Commissariado began to operate) to December 1918, those increases did not surpass 30 percent.[34] Nonetheless, to workers in Rio, these policies did not provide immediate respite, as their wages stagnated. In fact, scholars had registered a surge in strike activity and rallies in Rio and São Paulo for better working conditions and higher salaries.[35]

Other actors, like small business associations in Rio, accused the Commissariado of playing favorites. While these groups recognized the real lack of cattle in the market—so much that they suggested halting all meat exports and closing butcher stalls at least two days per week—they alleged that the Commissariado supplied butcher shops in the city center first, distributing to those in the outskirts only "half of their regular provisions." Worse yet, these organizations contended that the frigorífico Mendes had become the de facto meat supplier to the city, allocating frozen meat destined initially for exports, to urban consumers who were not accustomed to such a product.[36]

The latter claim, in particular, resonates with a broader debate over the nature of the meat supply system in Rio de Janeiro. First, as a private entity, the frigorífico Mendes had no right to become the sole provider to the city, for this was a long-standing municipal privilege. Second, as in other places, the population was indeed suspicious of industrial meat when first introduced in Rio. These arguments were in the long list of grievances that Rio's city council had against meatpacking companies in the 1920s. When European demand for imported foods collapsed at the end of WWI, and Brazil could no longer export "third-grade" beef, meatpackers turned their attention to the domestic market. As Earl R. Downes argues, "In the long term, [... the] cattle and beef sector found that the internal market held the true solution to their quest for a market."[37] Thus, pressure on the monopoly of municipal slaughterhouses stirred up, as did the fight to control Rio de Janeiro's meat provisioning system.

In 1917, frigorífico Mendes initiated operations in the state of Rio de Janeiro, delivering the by-product of three hundred herds to the city of Rio daily. Local officials sanctioned (*habilitaram*) the meatpacking plant as a cattle supplier (*marchante*), that is, as a purveyor of fresh (not chilled or frozen) meat to the city. The transaction was reminiscent of mid-nineteenth century operations, under the conditions discussed in Chapter 2.[38] Then, in 1925, the company petitioned the prefeitura to increment its quota up to 1,800 animals, together with a definitive provision contract. The municipality denied that request on the premise that the "license is annual[.] [It] is not perpetual ... in order not to harm the slaughterhouse of Santa Cruz, where it is necessary to maintain regular daily service."[39] When the dispute reached other government levels, officials discarded the city council's arguments as obsolete and inconvenient. Antônio Geremario Telles Dantas, municipal director of economy, asserted that the population's initial disapproval of refrigerated meat was a "temporary and cost-dependent condition" that was bound to change:

> The consumption of "alien meat" grows each day, though one can say with certainty that the use of refrigerated meat has not become a habit of our population. It is also true that people generally prefer fresh meat, but this is a time-dependent condition ... Thus, the only slaughterhouse in Rio to survive with oppressive measures against alien meat actually [did so] while there was a monopoly. When the Brazilian Meat Packing Co. was able through the judiciary to crack the city tax barrier, the slaughterhouse suffered its first telling blow.

> Thinking about restoring that old, nasty, and inconvenient monopoly is a mere illusion, in the face of which this statement supports the financial interests of the prefeitura.[40]

In their petition, frigorífico Mendes's representatives explained that meat consumption, especially on the outskirts of the city (*subúrbios*), had been augmented, mainly because of their product's low price and good quality, plus the company's "efficiency in distribution."[41] It is true, though, that Mendes increased its beef cattle deliveries to Rio.[42] However, despite Dantas's efforts and good omens for the packers, meat industrialization brought about predicaments anew. What is more, as late as the mid-1920s, popular media sided with the municipality. The press in Rio accused frigorífico Mendes of attempting to distribute "rotten meat" in the city, consistently characterizing their representatives as "greedy" people who, "in their eagerness to profit," had little concern about the population's well-being.[43] Some news sources questioned the municipality's monopoly over meat supplies but defended the city government's role in maintaining a reserve of cattle for domestic needs. They also accused foreign packers of depleting the Brazilian pasturelands so they could deliver beef to European markets. In 1924, an editorial in *Gazeta de Notícias* asked rhetorically, "Would they care if Brazil is to be without the necessary cattle to feed its populations?" The response was an enthusiastic call to arms: "We are in an imperative duty to defend ourselves at all costs, using all weapons within our reach."[44]

To consumers' and municipal officials' ears, such a plea only validated the municipal monopoly. It is not surprising that, at least until the 1930s, the prefeitura's monopoly remained all the more suitable—which is not to suggest that city officials rejected free-market policies, for they were well aware that those economic principles supported the arguments of the federal government and meatpacking companies. It seems as though they had an understanding of liberalism that observed the law of supply and demand, but reserved a crucial role for the government, so its agents could regulate the marketplace and supervise meat quality. In 1906, a city administrator in Rio summarized the city's views on meat provision as follows: "Meat is a special good … It is a good not subject, like others, to the law of supply and demand, irrespective of municipal intervention."[45] In the 1920s, the nature and extent of this "municipal intervention" were what set local officers at odds with authorities at the state and federal levels.

For their part, meatpackers capitalized on this struggle using the judicial system, as in the case of the matadouro Mendes. Vested interests—of cattle suppliers, city officials, and, ultimately, consumers—explain why the demise of Santa Cruz was a long-term, politically charged process. While the municipality might have used urban residents' preferences as an excuse to defend its interests, city administrations had historically protected meat-purchasing customers against intermediaries and outsiders—interlopers, in their words. Over the second half of the nineteenth century, but particularly after the establishment of matadouro de Santa Cruz in the 1880s, the city council had better means of regulating cattle commerce and processing and fresh meat retailing. What is more, before the introduction of railroads and refrigeration, the municipality acted as a guarantor that this highly perishable staple would reach Rio's butcher stalls in good condition. For a while, Santa Cruz represented the pinnacle of these policies and city dwellers, among others, expected the municipality to carry them on.

By the 1920s, however, new technologies had widened the marketing of meat, which threatened the municipality's supervisory duty. Thus, the old supply system, alongside meat purveyors, cattle merchants, and city officials, came to be identified as vestiges of paternalistic policies. Additionally, Santa Cruz's antiquated production practices and inadequate facilities evidenced that it could not keep up with population growth. Finally, as the city council barred intermediaries in the meat provision system, it created a series of obstacles that hindered any improvement in the supply network. In this context, some saw meat industrialization as the ultimate solution to improve the diet of *Carioca* (native of the city of Rio de Janeiro) workers, although it alone could not accomplish such an ambitious goal.

Meatpacking Companies in the Age of New Food Policies

Does better technology equate to better supplies? This section addresses this question by extending the analysis period until the late 1930s. It does so partly because packinghouses' deliveries to Rio de Janeiro only became of significance in that decade. This approach sheds light on the role that industrialization—and a new politics of provision that accompanied it—played in furnishing an item of utmost importance to the urban table.

Conventional wisdom dictates that as cities replaced outdated abattoirs with meatpacking plants, meat supplies improved. That is, provision became more predictable and wholesome meat widely accessible, particularly to the working class. However, it took years, if not decades, for such outcomes to take hold, and they usually occurred in conjunction with other structural changes. Consider the case of the United States. In 1905, a governmental official ranked the country "high in the scale of meat-consuming nations of the world" because of the "the vastness of [our] ... highly developed [meat] industries ... [and] the comparative cheapness of our meat-food products."[46] Still, at the dawn of the twentieth century, the working-class in the United States spent approximately half of their income on food. In Great Britain, "meat was a rare commodity" at the table of low-income workers. What is more, often, governments refrained from their meat provision obligations brought about food scares and labor exploitation.[47] Finally, these countries' experiences reveal that increase in meat supplies went hand-in-hand with better provisions of other nutrient-dense foods (like dairy products), with the expansion of refrigeration (which made perishables more accessible), and with improvement in household income.[48]

As the previous section examines, the supply of fresh meat to Rio de Janeiro underwent recurring fluctuations. Nonetheless, for the most part, from 1912 to 1938, per capita provisions oscillated between 40 and 50 kilos, except for the years 1917–1927. This cycle relates to WWI. As discussed earlier, the war had a twofold impact on the livestock/meat complex in Brazil. On the one hand, it accelerated the development of the meatpacking industry; on the other, it radically curtailed beef availability for domestic consumption. It took almost a decade for rations to restore to prewar levels. Per capita supplies fell slightly in the early 1930s and remained stable for the rest of the decade.[49] By then, packing companies had been slowly taking center stage in the meat supply system of Rio de Janeiro—first as purveyors of fresh meat and later of the chilled or frozen type.[50]

Figure 6.3 illustrates total fresh meat available for consumption in Rio de Janeiro between 1925 and 1937, as provided by the matadouros of Santa Cruz and Penha, and plants located outside the city's boundaries.[51] According to an observer, to guarantee the delivery of wholesome fresh beef to Rio's storehouses, these facilities processed the animals and shipped (via rails) the by-product immediately after killing. Federal agents thoroughly oversaw these processes. A group of veterinarians inspected the herds when they arrived at slaughterhouses, others examined the carcasses, and yet another crew ascertained the final product's quality before it reached Rio's butcher stores.[52] As Figure 6.3 shows, in the first year of the series, the matadouros of Santa Cruz and Penha supplied the overwhelming majority of meat distributed in Rio. However, by the end of the period, outside purveyors allocated nearly 70 percent. It is not possible to identify all these external plants; in any case, it is evident that the municipal facility (Santa Cruz) no longer could keep up with the city's growing demand.[53]

Note that apart from the purveyors registered in Figure 6.3, industrial plants had been delivering refrigerated meat to Rio de Janeiro, particularly after WWI. In 1927, a witness affirmed, "Besides the supply of absolutely fresh-killed meat, Rio receives also quite an amount of chilled and frozen meat. These chilled meats come from the big meat-packing plants from Sao Paulo, the Armour Co., and the Continental Products Co., and from the Anglo Frigorifico's plants at Barretos."[54] The author stressed that, at that juncture, restaurants and hotels were the primary buyers of these processed products. There is no reason to believe that, in the 1930s, only customers at these public venues partook of refrigerated meat. Additional data show that Santa Cruz's output remained

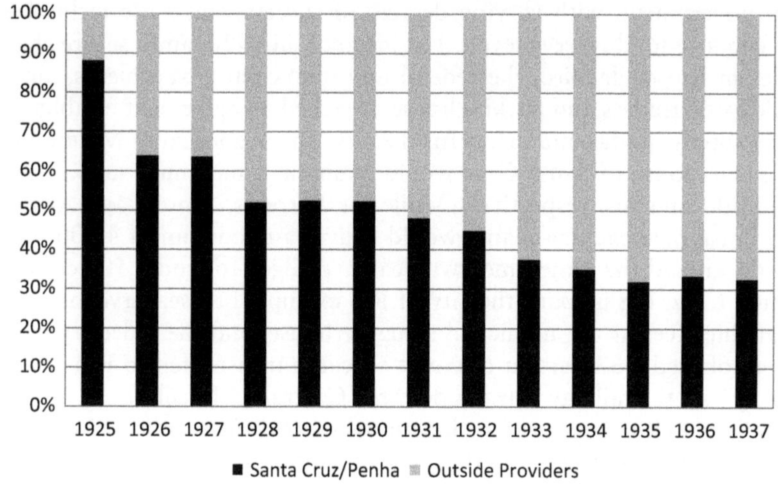

Figure 6.3 Fresh meat (carne verde) providers to Rio de Janeiro, 1925–1937.

Sources: Rio de Janeiro, *Anuário Estatístico do Distrito Federal Ano VI*, 1938 (Rio de Janeiro: Serviço do Gráfico do IBGE, 1939), 70, 219, 427; Brasil, Instituto Brasileiro de Geografia e Estatística, *Repertório Estatístico do Brasil, Quadros Retrospectivos no. 1. Separata do Anuário Estatístico do Brasil – 1939/1940* (Rio de Janeiro: Serviço Gráfico do Departamento de Geografia e Estatística, 1941), 95.

unchanged; that is, in 1937, the municipal plant slaughtered almost the same number of herds it did in the 1890s. What is more, per the municipality's estimations, between 1930 and 1937 the city's "taxes on meat not coming from Santa Cruz" doubled.[55]

Therefore, the local government only maintained adequate meat supplies because it had opened the city to "interlopers." At first, these purveyors provided "absolutely fresh-killed meat," as mentioned previously. Still, it was only a matter of time for cold technology to displace the abattoir system and with it the municipality's role in surveying meat production and distribution in the urban perimeter. In 1925, one headline in *Gazeta de Notícias* read, "The lack of meat in the city ... The crisis that threatened that primary food item is, fortunately, being averted. Yesterday, enough cattle arrived in Santa Cruz to supply the city."[56] News like this was not as common in 1930s Rio, in part because Santa Cruz no longer played a central role in provisioning the city and frigoríficos had more capacity to store and manage supplies.

Market integration via meatpacking and transportation technology in the south and southeast regions of Brazil gave the actors involved in the meat supply chain better tools to cope with cyclical crisis that the industry was prey to. As a result, the meat trade had the potential to become a year-round endeavor. Ranchers, cattle purveyors, retailers, and the government, with varying degrees of success, could use technology to enhance food reserve levels. For instance, in 1920, amid severe shortages in Rio de Janeiro, the federal and municipal governments, alongside cattle traders and packinghouses, reached an agreement establishing beef supply quotas and prices for the city. The frigorífico of Mendes and the matadouro of Santa Cruz would maintain a minimum stock of 800 and 500 animals, respectively, while the Barretos, Santos, and Armour do Brasil meatpacking plants would deliver a maximum of 4,000 herds to the city. At the same time, two dealers pledged to send 2,500 cattle to Santa Cruz. For its part, the city of Rio exempted these purveyors from slaughter fees at the municipal slaughterhouse, and the federal government offered a 33 percent discount on cattle transported to Rio "exclusively" via the railway Estrada de Ferro Central do Brasil.[57]

It is not clear how or if such actions reduced the scarcity. Either way, these arrangements were all the more difficult in settings lagging in transport and meat production technology. Consider the case of Mexico City. In the 1930s–1940s, it solely relied on the municipal abattoir; hence, local administrators had limited leeway to cope with natural cyclical events and unexpected shocks, like epizootics or wars. What is more, in traditional meat production systems, the largest expense falls on the weight loss and deterioration that animals suffer as they travel from fattening pasturelands to cities for processing. In 1942, according to estimations of Armando J. de Mendoza, a representative of a Cincinnati processing plant in Mexico, each head of cattle that arrived in Mexico City's central slaughterhouse lost approximately 40 kilos during transit. Such waste, continues Mendoza, drains the "national economy, and raises the price of meat introduced"[58] in the city.

However, better storage and faster shipping are only two elements on the long road to expanding and guaranteeing animal proteins to all.[59] In a broad sense, low-income Cariocas did not experience several other purported outcomes of meat industrialization. First, the innovation occurred in a setting where the provision of other animal foodstuffs (milk, eggs, poultry, or fish) remained unchanged. Thus, Cariocas continued to rely on fresh meat as they had decades before. Second, in the 1920s, crises of a different nature overshadowed any advance in supplies. At least until 1925, provisions were recovering from the worldwide conflict. In the late 1930s, despite the government's proclaimed concern for the poor, working-class wages did not improve.[60] As a result, over that decade, most Rio's residents achieved—when they did—dietary requirement by relying on starches and sugar.

In 1946, the federal government published a study on the Brazilian cost of living. Tracing the conditions in Rio de Janeiro back to 1912, it shows a food basket for a "middle-class" Carioca family split into primary and supplementary items. The first included rice, sugar, olive oil, codfish, lard, potatoes, coffee, fresh and salt-meat, onions, tea, manioc meal, wheat flour, beans, milk, condensed milk, butter, matte, maize, bread, and bacon. Supplementary foodstuffs were collard greens, lettuce, okra, chayote squash, cabbage, banana, oranges, tomatoes, papaya, fish, and eggs. Current research estimates that the food basket for the poor only consisted of meat, milk, beans, corn, manioc meal, bread, sugar, potato, and lard.[61] Studies show that in the late 1930s, Cariocas sought significant quantities of low-cost, energy-rich foodstuffs: manioc meal and beans, for instance. Likewise, they consumed impressive amounts of sugar and wheat flour, most likely as bakery goods: bread, cookies, and cakes. In the late 1930s, annual per capita supplies of sugar and wheat flour were almost 55 and 70 kilos respectively.[62]

Simultaneously, Rio's poor residents had scant access to protective foods (those containing vitamins and minerals that prevent malnutrition) such as milk and eggs. In the 1930s, Cariocas' apparent consumption of the former did not reach 130 milliliters per day. In the early 1940s, on average, they did not intake more than two dozen eggs annually. Government dietary guidelines established that the individual milk allowance should have been three times that amount and that of eggs four times higher, depending on age.[63] Regular consumption of these foodstuffs was all the more difficult because access to refrigeration remained spotty and uneven. As early as 1918, the press in Rio refers to ice as an item of primary necessity. "The most modest worker," printed the daily *Gazeta de Notícias*, "should have in his house a box with sawdust and an ice block, which would allow him to preserve his meat, fish, and the milk for his young son."[64] However, in 1940, half of Carioca households had no electricity. Probably, some relied on such a rudimentary "icebox" to preserve their food. Others resorted to centuries-old practices, visiting the market daily or buying perishables from street vendors who hawked fish, poultry, eggs, offal, fruits, and vegetables in the streets of Rio de Janeiro.[65] Still, others walked to their local butcher stall to acquire a staple whose provisions had remained fairly predictable.

Compared to other animal-derived foods, one kilo of beef cattle was more affordable than the same amount of salted, pork, mutton, or poultry meat, or one dozen eggs. On average, beef was cheaper than fish, with few exceptions, sardines being one. In 1937, the annual per capita fish intake was only nine kilos; beef cattle was four times that amount. As for other staple foods, fixed prices at the formal street market (*feira livre*) reveal that one kilo of beef could buy 2.5 kilos of beans or 3 kilos of manioc meal.[66] These are prices consistent with those from decades earlier, signaling that after all, there were no substitutes that Rio's residents could not turn to. For instance, poultry provisions increased dramatically in subsequent decades, but in 1930s city's statistics, they are practically irrelevant.[67]

Studies on Cariocas' well-being in the late 1930s present a grim picture. Historian John J. Crocitti estimates that in 1938, "approximately

70 percent of workers earned monthly salaries less than the cost of a sample diet for an average family of four."[68] If one accounts for housing—Rio was one of the most expensive cities in Brazil, it is apparent that several members of such a household had to work to keep afloat. Current scholarship reveals that after 1935, a decline in real wages coupled with inflation eroded the purchasing power of the Brazilian labor force. For Rio de Janeiro, Thales Augusto Zamberlan Pereira's examination on welfare ratios, which measures "how many consumption baskets a labourer could afford with a daily wage,"[69] shows a deterioration in the livelihood of skilled workers. As for unskilled workers, in 1937 Rio, they spent almost 60 percent of their income on foodstuff.[70] In São Paulo, the landscape was no different. A well-known survey conducted in 1934 put monthly food costs for *Paulistano* (from the city of São Paulo) laborers at 50 percent. Indeed, "as would be expected, the lower the income the greater the proportion spent on food."[71] In 1937, Paulistanos, like their Carioca counterparts, devoted approximately 60 percent of their wages to acquiring groceries. In light of these findings, scholars have cautioned to "view the 1930s as a 'golden age' in terms of working class nutrition."[72]

These studies conclude that there was more rice, manioc meal, bread, and sugar than milk or meat at the working-class table. Even under these circumstances, fresh beef cattle (not salted meat) provided Cariocas some animal protein. Surely, only modest amounts of this staple were within reach of poor dwellers in Rio, but they were indeed meaningful compared to meat provisions in other Brazilian cities. What is more, beef cattle remained—as was the case in the late nineteenth century—one of the most affordable animal source foods in Rio's marketplace. No wonder Cariocas continued to look for meat; between 1940 and 1945, beef cattle consumption (including offal) accounted for approximately 80 percent of animal protein intake in Rio de Janeiro.[73]

Analysis of how meatpacking plants shaped meat supplies in Rio before World War II reveals a mixed picture, as more packinghouses' deliveries did not translate into more meat at the Carioca table. However, without this technology, supplies were indeed at the mercy of cyclical crises, human-made or not. (Mexico City in the 1930s, mentioned above, reveals as much). Between the 1870s and the 1920s, the population in Rio increased fourfold. Naturally, the municipality struggled to carry on its meat purveyor mandate, while other urban issues, housing, for instance, seemed more threatening to the city's stability. On the other hand, no government oversight over provisions could have dire consequences for consumers and workers. As the United States case illustrates, when left to their own devices, meatpacking plants displaced small cattle purveyors and butchers, concentrated resources, and created private monopolies. It took direct government intervention to tame their appetite for more control. The expansion of animal-derived foods to urban populations was a multilayered, gradual process harnessed by structural developments.

In their absence, meatpacking companies' pledge to deliver wholesome, affordable meat to Cariocas was nothing but an empty promise.

* * *

In late nineteenth-century Rio de Janeiro, the establishment of the Santa Cruz municipal slaughterhouse aimed to remedy the anarchy of clandestine slaughtering of animals for human consumption. To this end, it encompassed a whole series of sanitary measures and price controls. For a time, this system kept the capital city relatively well-provisioned, as the figures on per capita rates of beef consumption illustrate. By the early twentieth century, though, pressure from emerging interest groups linked to meatpacking industries threatened the municipal slaughterhouse monopoly. Sponsors of this new technology promised that cost reduction and increased productivity would eventually lower meat prices for urban consumers. In light of those challenges, city officials, and other actors involved in the supply chain of beef cattle resorted to political maneuverings to combat industrialized slaughterhouse meddling in their traditional operations. Despite their momentary success in barring "alien meat" from the urban market, by the early 1940s, frigoríficos had become the de facto purveyors to the city.

With respect to the impact of meatpacking on the urban provisioning system, Rio de Janeiro's meat supply data reveal no significant changes, either in per capita beef rations or in prices. Finally, the meatpackers' claim that industrial efficiency would lead to higher meat consumption is undermined by the experience of meat industrialization first adopters. Such experience shows that technological advances alone cannot alter consumption patterns, as only an accompanying improvement in income distribution is capable of promoting such a change. Consequently, the limited modernization occurred in a historical context when the purchasing power of the poor remained largely unchanged, even while the modern twentieth-century state emerged as the national arbiter of wages for the working and middle classes.

Notes

1 Vaclav Smil, "Eating Meat: Evolution, Patterns, and Consequences," *Population and Development Review* 28, no. 4 (December 2002): 609; Rachel Laudan, "Power Cuisines, Dietary Determinism and Nutritional Crisis: The Origins of the Globalization of Western Diet," *Interactions: Regional Studies, Global Processes, and Historical Analysis,* Conference Proceedings. Library of Congress, Washington DC, February 28 – March 3, 2001. Accessed November 25, 2020, http://webdoc.sub.gwdg.de/ebook/p/2005/history_cooperative/www.historycooperative.org/proceedings/interactions/laudan.html; Deborah Neill, "Finding the 'Ideal Diet': Nutrition, Culture, and Dietary Practices in France and French Equatorial Africa, c. 1890s to 1920s," *Food and Foodways* 17, no. 1 (2009): 3.

2 Wilson Suzigan, *Indústria brasileira: origem e desenvolvimento* (São Paulo: Hucitec, 2000), 143, 354–79; Flávio A. M. de Saes, "A controvérsia sobre a

industrialização na Primeira República," *Estudos Avançados* 3, no. 4 (1989): 20–39; Winston Fritsch, "Apogeu e crise na primeira república," in *A ordem do progresso: Cem anos de política econômica republicana, 1889–1989*, ed. Marcelo de Paiva Abreu, Dionísio Dias Carneiro Netto, Gustavo Henrique Barroso Franco, and Winston Fritsch (Rio de Janeiro: Editora Campus, 1994), 42–43; Helio Jaguaribe, *Economic and Political Development. A Theoretical Approach and a Brazilian Case Study* (Cambridge: Harvard University Press, 1968), 106–10.

3 This debate is beyond the scope of this chapter; for a new perspective, see Stephen Haber, "Development Strategy or Endogenous Process? The Industrialization of Latin America," Working Paper No. 269, Stanford, CA, (2005): 1–86; Bill Albert and Paul Henderson, *South America and the First World War: The Impact of the War on Brazil, Argentina, Peru, and Chile* (Cambridge: Cambridge University Press, 2002), 186; Suzigan, *Indústria*, 143.

4 Brasil, Senado Federal, Decreto n. 7.945, April 7, 1910, "Estabelece bases de concurrencia para matadouros modelos e entrepostos frigoríficos destinados á conservação e transporte de productos nacionaes estrangeiros, mediante favores e condições," accessed November 20, 2020, www.camara.leg.br/; Brasil, Ministério da Agricultura, "Relatorio apresentado ao presidente dos Estados Unidos do Brazil pelo ministro de estado da Agricultura, industria e commercio Rodolpho Nogueira da Rocha Miranda no anno de 1910," vol. 1 (Rio de Janeiro: Oficinas da directoria geral de estatística, 1910), 81–89.

5 Ibid.; Brasil, Senado Federal, Decreto n. 7.778, December 30, 1909, "Dá regulamento ao serviço de registro genealógico de animaes," accessed November 20, 2020, www.camara.leg.br/.

6 Joseph L. Love, *São Paulo in the Brazilian Federation 1889–1937* (Stanford, CA: Stanford University Press, 1980), 258; Earl Richard Downes, "The Seeds of Influence: 'Brazil's 'Essentially Agricultural' Old Republic and the United States, 1910–1930" (PhD diss., University of Texas at Austin, 1980), 165–66; Benedicto de Freitas, *História do matadouro municipal de Santa Cruz* (Rio de Janeiro: Irmãos Pongetti Editores, 1950), 111–16.

7 Armen Mamigonian, "Notas sobre os frigoríficos do Brasil Central Pecuário," *Boletim Paulista de Geografia*, no. 51 (1976): 9–12; Miguel Gimenes Benites, "Os frigoríficos da grande São Paulo e arredores: estudo geográfico" (master's thesis, Universidade de São Paulo, 1978), 2–4; Suzigan, *Indústria*, 352–61; Warren Dean observes this behavior in other sectors of São Paulo's economy. Warren Dean, *The Industrialization of São Paulo* (Austin: The University of Texas Press, 1969), 111–12.

8 See Wilson Suzigan and Tamás Szmrecsányi, "Os investimentos estrangeiros no início da industrialização do Brasil," in *História econômica da primeira república: coletânea de textos apresentados no I Congresso Brasileiro de História Econômica*, setembro de 1993, ed. Sérgio S. Silva and Tamás Szmrecsányi (São Paulo: Editora Hucitec/FAPESP/ABPHE, 1996), 267–69; Stephen Bell, *Campanha Gaúcha: A Brazilian Ranching System, 1850–1920* (Stanford, CA: Stanford University Press, 1998), 136–55; Downes, "Seeds of Influence," 160–61; Richard Graham, *Britain and the Onset of Modernization in Brazil 1850–1914* (Cambridge: Cambridge University Press, 1968), 196–97; Flávio A. M. de Saes, "Estradas de ferro e diversificação da atividade econômica na expansão cafeeira em São Paulo, 1870–1900," in *História econômica da independência e do império*, ed. Tamás Szmrecsányi and José Roberto do Amaral Lapa (São Paulo: Edusp/Imprensa Oficial/Editora Hucitec, 2002), 177–96.

9 When animals were driven from raising to fattening grounds and again from these pasturelands to cities for processing, they lost considerable body weight.

By transporting herds via rails, packers could save up transport costs, which depended on the number of cattle shipped and on freight rates. Most importantly, they protected the animals from arduous trails that resulted in injuries and shrinkage in weight.

10 *Correio Paulistano*, March 24, 1910; April 6, 1914.

11 *Correio Paulistano*, April 18, 1913; August 31, 1913.

12 *Correio Paulistano*, March 24, 1910.

13 *Correio Paulistano*, April 2, 1913; January 16, 1914; *A Gazeta*, January 7, 1914.

14 Humberto Perinelli Neto, "Nos quintais do Brasil: homens, pecuária, complexo cafeeiro e modernidade – Barretos (1854/1931)" (PhD diss., Universidade Estadual Paulista, Franca, 2009), 232–33; *Correio Paulistano*, December 24, 1914; June 29, 1915; July 5, 1915; January 7, 1921; June 26, 1929.

15 São Paulo, "Mensagem apresentada ao congresso legislativo, na 2ª sessão da 14ª legislatura, em 14 de julho de 1929, pelo Doutor Julio Prestes de Albuquerque, presidente do estado de São Paulo" (n.p., n.d.), 31–32; Suzigan, *Indústria*, 356.

16 In late 1880s, the Brazilian Extract of Meat & Hide Factory started operations in Rio Grande do Sul for the production of meat extract and canned foodstuffs. A. W. Bennett, "Diplomatic and Consular Reports on Trade and Finance, Brazil, Report for the year 1889–1890 on the Trade of Rio Grande do Sul," United Kingdom, Foreign office, 1890, Annual Series, no. 702 (London: Harrison and Sons, 1890), 9; W. M. Pearce, *The Matador Land and Cattle Company* (Norman: University of Oklahoma Press, 1964), 128–29; Simon G. Hanson, "The Farquhar Syndicate in South America," *The Hispanic American Historical Review* 17, no. 3 (1937): 317.

17 Another important aspect of the Brazilian meat industry is that some of those processing plants' output included chilled and frozen meat as well as charque, a product that such a technology envisioned replacing.

18 "A creação do Instituto de Carnes sul rio-grandense," *A Federação. Órgam do Partido Republicano*, October 8, 1935; Bell, *Campanha Gaúcha*, 154–55.

19 *Gazeta de Notícias*, January 4, 1900; December 25, 1901; "Decreto no. 2056, de 16 de Dezembro de 1918," Antonio José da Silva Brandão, in *Collecção de Leis Municipaes e Vetos do ano de 1918*, vol. 42, org. J. B. Horta Barbosa (Rio de Janeiro: Typ. do Jornal do Commercio, de Rodriguez & C., 1919), 95.

20 Initially, the company only processed refrigerated meat for exports, and it had limited authorization to supply the city. To confront WWI shortages, Rio's Mayor Amaro Cavalcanti Soares de Brito temporarily suspended free slaughtering (*matanças livres*) in Santa Cruz and granted exclusive rights to the Anglo-Brazilian to use the matadouro, thus sidestepping cattle suppliers (*marchantes*). The agreement came under fire; local newspapers hotly debated whether the Anglo had legal right to serve the city and accused the company of distributing "rotten meat" in the marketplace. Marchantes, for their part, appealed to the city's treasury department, reminding the mayor that "the Santa Cruz slaughterhouse is a public establishment, it is not a private entity, ... it is an institution under the municipal domain." Another point of contention was that cattle stocks had diminished dramatically in Brazil, and competition between the Anglo-Brazilian and marchantes for the same raw material had resulted in higher meat prices. The company's view—reproduced here by Richard P. Momsen, vice-consul of the United States in Rio de Janeiro—was that the "slaughterhouse at Santa Cruz was placed in the control of special workmen brought from foreign countries" to improve

meat and other animal by-products production. However, "better quality meat for export to Europe was obtainable in other countries at a lower cost." Richard P. Momsen, "Activities of an Anglo-Brazilian Meat Company," in *Commerce Reports, Daily Consular and Trade Reports*, no. 164 (Washington: Government Printing Press, 1918), 179. *Gazeta de Notícias*, July 1, 1917; "A carne," October 2, 1917; "A carne," October 5, 1917; "Carnes verdes," *Jornal do Commercio*, September 13, 1917; September 25, 1917.

21 "A questão dos matadouros modelos," *O Paiz*, May 13, 1910.

22 *Correio Paulistano*, March 21, 1916.

23 Getúlio Vargas became president of Brazil through a coup d'état in 1930. He governed as provisional ruler until 1934, when indirect elections allowed him to remain in power for three more years. In 1937, Vargas staged a new coup d'état and inaugurated the *Estado Novo* (New State), which gave him authority to rule by decree; he resigned in 1945. In 1951, democratic elections brought Vargas back to the presidency; he governed Brazil up to 1954, when he committed suicide.

24 *Correio da Manhã*, February 27, 1942.

25 *Jornal do Commercio*, October 2, 1917.

26 Leo Waibel, *Capítulos de geografia tropical e do Brasil* (Rio de Janeiro: Serviço gráfico do Instituto Brasileiro de Geografia e Estatística, 1958), 28–30; quoted in *Correio Paulistano,* September 29, 1914; *Correio Paulistano*, September 18, 1915; October 18, 1915.

27 Brasil, Ministério da Agricultura, "Relatorio apresentado ao presidente dos Estados Unidos do Brasil pelo ministro de estado da agricultura, industria e commercio, Dr. João Gonçalves Pereira Lima. Anno de 1918," vol. 1 (Rio de Janeiro: Typographia da directoria geral de estatisica), 186–88; Brasil, Ministério da Agricultura, "Relatorio apresentado ao presidente dos Estados Unidos do Brasil pelo ministro de estado dos negócios da agricultura, industria e commercio, Dr. Ildefonso Simões Lopes. [Ano de 1920]" (Rio de Janeiro: Papelaria e typographia Villas Boas e C., 1921), 52; Rio de Janeiro, *Anuário Estatístico do Distrito Federal Ano IX*, 1941 (Rio de Janeiro: Publicação do Departamento de Geografia e Estatística, 1942), 298; "Meat Packing in South America," *Refrigerating World. Incorporating Cold Storage & Ice Trade Journal* 54, no. 1 (1919): 24.

28 *Correio Paulistano*, February 14, 1918.

29 "Feeding Rio de Janeiro," *Bulletin of the Pan American Union* 61, no. 10 (Washington: Government Printing Office, 1927): 979.

30 A study on Rio's cost of living shows a remarkable upsurge in food, clothing, and fuel prices between 1914 and 1919. Léo de Affonseca Junior, *O custo da vida na cidade do Rio de Janeiro* (Rio de Janeiro: Imprensa Nacional, 1920), 11–12. Likewise, in Argentina, this process coincided with increasing beef prices thanks to the expansion in exports. See Peter H. Smith, *Politics and Beef in Argentina. Patterns of Conflict and Change* (New York: Columbia University Press, 1969), 74–75; *Jornal do Commercio*, October 2, 1917; Roberto C. Simonsen, *The Meat & Cattle Industry of Brazil; Its Importance to Anglo-Brazilian Commerce* (London: Industrial Publicity Service, 1919), 2–5, *Gazeta de Notícias*, August 11, 1917; August 19, 1917.

31 *Gazeta de Notícias*, May 19, 1917.

32 A. B. Ramalho Ortigão, *O anno commercial econômico y financeiro de 1918* (Rio de Janeiro: Typografia Bersnard Frères, 1919), 275–362, 466–83.

33 Albert and Henderson, *South America*, 91; Ortigão, *O anno commercial*, 293.

34 Ortigão, *O anno commercial*, 293.

35 This is not to suggest causality between the cost of living and strikes. Indeed, labor movements in Brazil gained traction during the prewar boom, but they reached a zenith in the 1917–1920 period. These years witnessed the formation of industrial unions and the occurrence of general strikes in São Paulo and Rio de Janeiro. Francisco Vidal Luna and Herbert S. Klein, *The Economic and Social History of Brazil Since 1889* (Cambridge: Cambridge University Press, 2014), 76–77; Fritsch, "Apogeu," 45–46; Eulália Maria Lahmeyer Lobo, *História do Rio de Janeiro: do capital comercial ao capital industrial e financeiro,* vol. 2 (Rio de Janeiro: Instituto Brasileiro de Mercado de Capitais – IBMEC, 1978), 521–29.

36 "O problema da carne verde," *Correio da Manhã*, September 28, 1918.

37 Downes, "Seeds of Influence," 479.

38 Arquivo Geral da Cidade do Rio de Janeiro (hereafter AGCRJ), "[Letter from] Sociedade Anônima Frigorífico Anglo ao Exmo. Sr. Prefeito do Distrito Federal," September 14, 1925.

39 Ibid., AGCRJ, "[Reply from Antonio de Souza Pereira Botafogo, diretor geral da diretoria de abastecimento e fomento agrícola]," October 17, 1927; Downes, "Seeds of Influence," 476–79.

40 AGCRJ, "Parecer do diretor geral da fazenda, Dr. Geremario Telles Dantas, sobre uma proposta apresentada em 1928, tendo por fundamento o decreto no. 3932 de 12/01/1927," emphasis added, n.d.

41 AGCRJ, "Memorial apresentado pela Companhia Armour of Brasil corporation," December 14, 1926.

42 Brasil, Ministério da Agricultura, *Relatório dos trabalhos da superintendência do abastecimento durante o anno de 1922* (Rio de Janeiro: Imprensa Nacional, 1923), 46–47.

43 "Carne podre para a população," *Gazeta de Notícias*, December 18, 1919.

44 *Gazeta de Notícias*, December 13, 1924.

45 Rio de Janeiro, *Consolidação das leis e posturas municipaes,* Segunda parte, legislação districtal (Rio de Janeiro: Oficinas tipográficas de Paula Souza & Comp., 1906), 478.

46 John Roberts, "Annual Production of Animals for Food and Per Capita Consumption of Meat in the United States," United States Department of Agriculture, Twenty-Second Annual Report of the Bureau of Animal Industry for the Year 1905 (Washington: Government Printing Office, 1907), 282.

47 Rachel Duffett, *The Stomach for Fighting: Food and the Soldiers of the Great War* (Manchester: Manchester University Press, 2015), 43–47. In his famous novel *The Jungle*, Upton Sinclair describes the brutal and unsanitary means by which laborers processed animals in Chicago's industrial meat complex. The work, published for the first time in 1906, provoked a public outcry, prompting congressional investigations and subsequent regulations that sought to improve meat handling and break up packers' monopolies. Upton Sinclair, *The Jungle*, Minneapolis: Lerner Publishing Group, 1971. ProQuest Ebook Central. A recent view on these developments maintains that the Pure Food and Drug Act and the Federal Meat Inspection Act normalized the industry's main traits. For consumers, as long as they could count on cheap and sanitary meat, the plight of workers resonated little with them. See Joshua Specht, *Red Meat Republic: A Hoof-to-Table History of How Beef Changed America* (Princeton: Princeton University Press, 2019), 215–17. In 1920s Rio de Janeiro, newspapers consistently denounced the unwholesome state of the Matadouro de Mendes. *Gazeta de Notícias*, August 5, 1928; March 29, 1929.

48 In the United States, the average household only replaced pork—historically, the least expensive cut of meat—with beef cattle in the 1950s. Katherine

Leonard Turner, *How the Other Half Ate: A History of Working-Class Meals at the Turn of the Century* (Berkeley: University of California Press, 2014), 1–18; Lee A. Craig, Barry K. Goodwin, and Thomas Grennes, "The Effect of Mechanical Refrigeration on Nutrition in the United States," *Social Science History* 28, no. 2 (2004): 325–36; Manel Guàrdia, José Luis Oyón, Sergi Garriga, and Nadia Fava, "Meat Consumption and Nutrition Transition in Barcelona, 1709–1935," *Urban History* 45, no. 2 (2018): 193–94.

49 Rio de Janeiro, *Anuário Estatístico do Distrito Federal Ano IX*, 1941, 298; Rio de Janeiro, *Anuário Estatístico do Distrito Federal Ano X*, 1946 (Rio de Janeiro: Publicação do Departamento de Geografia e Estatística, 1947), 163–64, vol. II, Estatística Econômica.

50 Local government data only register chilled and frozen meat (*carnes frigorificadas*) deliveries to the city in the 1940s; however, scattered sources reveal their presence in Rio after World War I. Rio de Janeiro, *Anuário Estatístico do Distrito Federal Ano X*, 1946, 163–64.

51 These years were selected based on data availability and on the fact that, after 1925, the amount of fresh meat given to consumption in Rio exceeded the production of the city's slaughterhouses, Santa Cruz and Penha. Hence, outside packinghouses—in the early 1930s, these were probably the Nova Iguaçú and Mendes plants (in the state of Rio de Janeiro) and frigoríficos from São Paulo state—provided the remainder. *Gazeta de Notícias*, February 23, 1930.

52 "Feeding Rio de Janeiro," 979–81.

53 Rio de Janeiro, *Anuário Estatístico do Distrito Federal Ano VI*, 1938 (Rio de Janeiro: Serviço do Gráfico do IBGE, 1939), 70, 219, 427; Brasil, Instituto Brasileiro de Geografia e Estatística, *Repertório Estatístico do Brasil, Quadros Retrospectivos no. 1. Separata do Anuário Estatístico do Brasil – 1939/1940* (Rio de Janeiro: Serviço Gráfico do Departamento de Geografia e Estatística, 1941), 95.

54 "Feeding Rio de Janeiro," 979.

55 Rio de Janeiro, *Anuário Estatístico do Distrito Federal Ano VI*, 1938, 399, 427.

56 *Gazeta de Notícias*, September 26, 1925.

57 "O abastecimento de carne no Rio de Janeiro," *Jornal do Commercio, Retrospecto Commercial do Jornal do Commercio [de 1920]* (Rio de Janeiro: Typ. do "Jornal do Commercio," de Rodrigues & C., 1922), 150–51. Similar arrangements occurred during World War II. For instance, in February 1944, the local press reported that a vessel with 1,700 tons of foodstuff from São Paulo (including meat from the frigorífico Barretos) arrived in Rio. *Jornal do Commercio*, February 23, 24, and 27, 1944.

58 Maria-Aparecida Lopes, "Escasez, epizootia y experimentos sindicales. El abasto de carne en la capital federal mexicana, 1929–1955," in *Integración y desintegración del espacio económico mexicano: mercado interno y abastecimiento de las carnes desde la colonia al siglo XX*, ed. Enriqueta Quiroz (México: Instituto de Investigaciones Dr. José María Luis Mora, Consejo Nacional de Ciencia y Tecnología), 313.

59 Wouter Ronsijn and Niccolò Mignemi, "Introduction: Stocks, Seasons, and Sales," in *Stocks, Seasons and Sales. Food Supply, Storage and Markets in Europe and the New World, C. 1600–2000*, ed. Wouter Ronsijn, Niccolò Mignemi, and Laurent Herment (Turnhout, Belgium: Brepols, 2019), 1–11.

60 Thales A. Zamberlan Pereira, "The North-South Divide: Real Wages and Welfare in Brazil during the Early 20th century," *Revista de Historia Económica – Journal of Iberian and Latin American Economic History* 38, no. 1 (2019): 190–200.

61 Brasil, Ministério do Trabalho, Indústria e Comércio, "Levantamento do custo de vida no Brasil" (Rio de Janeiro: Serviço de Estatística da Previdência e Trabalho, 1946), 90; Pereira, "North-South Divide," 190.

62 Rio de Janeiro, *Anuário Estatístico do Distrito Federal Ano VI*, 1938, 220. These numbers were not abnormal, between 1941 and 1945, annual per capita sugar supply averaged 50 kilos, but they are indeed high. In the early 2000s, Brazilians consumed approximately half of that amount of granulated and refined sugar. Mauricio Jorge Pinto de Souza, Pedro Rodrigues de Oliveira, and Heloisa Lee Burquist, "Lar 'Doce' Lar: uma análise do consumo de açúcar e de produtos relacionados no Brasil," *Revista de Economia e Sociologia Rural* 51, no. 4 (2013): 790, accessed November 29, 2020, www.scielo.br/scielo.php?script=sci_arttext&pid=S0103-20032013000400009&lng=en&nrm=iso. ISSN 0103-2003.

63 The best-known assessment of Brazilians' eating patterns during the 1940s is *Geografia da fome,* published in 1946. Josué de Castro drafted a map of Brazil identifying five food areas according to their natural resources, eating habits, and nutritional deficiencies. Castro placed Rio de Janeiro in an "area of subnutrition," where, in his words, "we verified … the low consumption of milk, vegetables, green vegetables, whole grains, and fruits among the … the proletarian classes." Josué de Castro, *Geografia da fome* (Rio de Janeiro: Edições Antares, 1984), 275–78; "Consultório da alimentação econômica," *SAPS: Boletim Mensal do Serviço de Alimentação da Previdência Social* 1, n. 4 (Rio de Janeiro: Imprensa Nacional, 1945): 30; Rio de Janeiro, *Anuário Estatístico do Distrito Federal Ano X*, 1946, 163, vol. II, Estatística Econômica; Sören Brinkmann, "Leite e modernidade: ideologia e políticas de alimentação na era Vargas," *História, Ciências, Saúde – Manguinhos* 21, no. 1 (2014): 6–8; Rio de Janeiro, *Anuário Estatístico do Distrito Federal Ano VI*, 1938, 219.

64 *Gazeta de Notícias*, September 22, 1918.

65 John J. Crocitti, "Vargas Era Social Policies: An Inquiry into Brazilian Malnutrition During the Estado Novo (1937–1945)," in *Vargas and Brazil: New Perspectives*, ed. Jens R. Hentschke (New York: Palgrave Macmillan, 2006), 149; "Feeding Rio de Janeiro," 983–89; Everardo Backheuser, "Comércio ambulante e ocupacões de rua no Rio de Janeiro," *Revista Brasileira de Geografia* 6, no. 1 (January–March 1944): 6–7.

66 Rio de Janeiro, *Anuário Estatístico do Distrito Federal Ano VI*, 1938, 70, 196–99.

67 John Wells, "Industrial Accumulation and Living Standards in the Long-Run: The São Paulo Industrial Working Class, 1930–75, Part II," *The Journal of Development Studies* 19, no. 3 (1983): 316–17.

68 Crocitti, "Vargas Era Social Policies," in *Vargas,* 152.

69 Pereira, "North-South Divide," 187.

70 Lobo, *História do Rio de Janeiro*, 548; Pereira, "North-South Divide," 191–95.

71 Horace B. Davis and Marian Rubins Davis, "Scale of Living of Working Class in Sao Paulo, Brazil," *Monthly Labor Review* 44, no. 1 (1937): 249.

72 Wells, "Industrial Accumulation," 318–19.

73 Rio de Janeiro, *Anuário Estatístico do Distrito Federal Ano X*, 1946, 163.

Bibliography

Archives Consulted

Arquivo Geral da Cidade do Rio de Janeiro, (cited as AGCRJ)

Government Documents and Publications

Bennett, A. W. "Diplomatic and Consular Reports on Trade and Finance, Brazil, Report for the year 1889–1890 on the Trade of Rio Grande do Sul." United Kingdom. Foreign office, 1890. Annual Series, no. 702. London: Harrison and Sons, 1890.

Brasil. Instituto Brasileiro de Geografia e Estatística, *Repertório Estatístico do Brasil, Quadros Retrospectivos no. 1. Separata do Anuário Estatístico do Brasil - 1939/1940*. Rio de Janeiro: Serviço Gráfico do Departamento de Geografia e Estatística, 1941.

Brasil. Ministério da Agricultura. "Relatorio apresentado ao presidente dos Estados Unidos do Brazil pelo ministro de estado da Agricultura, industria e commercio Rodolpho Nogueira da Rocha Miranda no anno de 1910." Vol. 1. Rio de Janeiro: Oficinas da directoria geral de estatística, 1910.

Brasil. Ministério da Agricultura. "Relatorio apresentado ao presidente dos Estados Unidos do Brasil pelo ministro de estado da agricultura, industria e commercio, Dr. João Gonçalves Pereira Lima. Anno de 1918." Vol. 1. Rio de Janeiro: Typographia da directoria geral de estatistica, 1918.

Brasil. Ministério da Agricultura. "Relatorio apresentado ao presidente dos Estados Unidos do Brasil pelo ministro de estado dos negócios da agricultura, industria e commercio, Dr. Ildefonso Simões Lopes. [Ano de 1920]." Rio de Janeiro: Papelaria e typographia Villas Boas e C., 1921.

Brasil. Ministério da Agricultura. *Relatório dos trabalhos da superintendência do abastecimento durante o anno de 1922*. Rio de Janeiro: Imprensa Nacional, 1923.

Brasil. Ministério do Trabalho, Indústria e Comércio. *Levantamento do custo de vida no Brasil*. Rio de Janeiro: Serviço de Estatística da Previdência e Trabalho, 1946.

Brasil. Senado Federal. Decreto n. 7.778, December 30, 1909. "Dá regulamento ao serviço de registro genealógico de animaes." Accessed November 20, 2020, https://www.camara.leg.br/.

Brasil. Senado Federal. Decreto n. 7.945, April 7, 1910. "Estabelece bases de concurrencia para matadouros modelos e entrepostos frigoríficos destinados á conservação e transporte de productos nacionaes estrangeiros, mediante favores e condições." Accessed November 20, 2020, https://www.camara.leg.br/.

"Decreto no. 2056, de 16 de Dezembro de 1918," Antonio José da Silva Brandão. In *Collecção de Leis Municipaes e Vetos do ano de 1918*, vol. 42, organized by J. B. Horta Barbosa, 95–96. Rio de Janeiro: Typ. do Jornal do Commercio, de Rodriguez & C., 1919.

Momsen, Richard P. "Activities of an Anglo-Brazilian Meat Company." In *Commerce Reports, Daily Consular and Trade Reports*, no. 164. Washington: Government Printing Press (1918): 179.

Rio de Janeiro. *Anuário Estatístico do Distrito Federal Ano VI*, 1938. Rio de Janeiro: Serviço Gráfico do IBGE, 1939.

Rio de Janeiro. *Anuário Estatístico do Distrito Federal Ano IX*, 1941. Rio de Janeiro: Publicação do Departamento de Geografia e Estatística, 1942.

Rio de Janeiro. *Anuário Estatístico do Distrito Federal Ano* X, 1946. Vol. II, Estatística Econômica. Rio de Janeiro: Publicação do Departamento de Geografia e Estatística, 1947.

Rio de Janeiro. *Consolidação das leis e posturas municipaes do Districto Federal.* Segunda parte, legislação districtal. Rio de Janeiro: Oficinas tipográficas de Paula Souza & Comp., 1906.
Roberts, John. "Annual Production of Animals for Food and Per Capita Consumption of Meat in the United States." United States Department of Agriculture, Twenty-Second Annual Report of the Bureau of Animal Industry for the Year 1905. Washington: Government Printing Office, 1907.
São Paulo. "Mensagem apresentada ao congresso legislativo, na 2ª sessão da 14ª legislatura, em 14 de julho de 1929, pelo Doutor Julio Prestes de Albuquerque, presidente do estado de São Paulo." N.p. N.d.

Newspapers and Magazines

A Gazeta (São Paulo)
Correio da Manhã (Rio de Janeiro)
Correio Paulistano
Gazeta de Notícias (Rio de Janeiro)
Jornal do Commercio (Rio de Janeiro)

"A creação do Instituto de Carnes sul rio-grandense." *A Federação. Órgam do Partido Republicano.* October 8, 1935.
"A questão dos matadouros modelos." *O Paiz* (Rio de Janeiro). May 13, 1910.
"Carne podre para a população." *Gazeta de Notícias* (Rio de Janeiro). December 18, 1919.
"Consultório da alimentação econômica." *SAPS: Boletim Mensal do Serviço de Alimentação da Previdência Social* 1, n. 4, Rio de Janeiro: Imprensa Nacional, 1945, 30–31.
"Feeding Rio de Janeiro." *Bulletin of the Pan American Union* 61, no. 1. Washington: Government Printing Office (1927): 978–989.
"Meat Packing in South America." *Refrigerating World. Incorporating Cold Storage & Ice Trade Journal* 54, no. 1 (1919): 23–24, 32.
"O problema da carne verde." *Correio da Manhã* (Rio de Janeiro). September 28, 1918.
"O abastecimento de carne no Rio de Janeiro." Jornal do Commercio, *Retrospecto Commercial do Jornal do Commercio [de 1920].* Rio de Janeiro: Typ. do "Jornal do Commercio," de Rodrigues & C., 1922.

Other Primary Sources

Affonseca Junior, Léo de. *O custo da vida na cidade do Rio de Janeiro.* Rio de Janeiro: Imprensa Nacional, 1920.
Ortigão, A. B. Ramalho. *O anno commercial econômico y financeiro de 1918.* Rio de Janeiro: Typografia Bersnard Frères, 1919.
Simonsen, Roberto C. *The Meat & Cattle Industry of Brazil; Its Importance to Anglo-Brazilian Commerce.* London: Industrial Publicity Service, 1919.

Secondary Sources

Albert, Bill, and Paul Henderson. *South America and the First World War: The Impact of the War on Brazil, Argentina, Peru, and Chile*. Cambridge: Cambridge University Press, 2002.

Backheuser, Everardo. "Comércio ambulante e ocupacões de rua no Rio de Janeiro." *Revista Brasileira de Geografia* 6, no. 1 (January–March 1944): 3–34.

Bell, Stephen. *Campanha Gaúcha: A Brazilian Ranching System, 1850–1920*. Stanford, CA: Stanford University Press, 1998.

Benites, Miguel Gimenes. "Os frigoríficos da grande São Paulo e arredores: estudo geográfico." Master's thesis, Universidade de São Paulo, 1978.

Brinkmann, Sören. "Leite e modernidade: ideologia e políticas de alimentação na era Vargas." *História, Ciências, Saúde - Manguinhos* 21, no. 1 (2014): 1–17.

Castro, Josué de. *Geografia da fome*. Rio de Janeiro: Edições Antares, 1984.

Craig, Lee A., Barry K. Goodwin, and Thomas Grennes. "The Effect of Mechanical Refrigeration on Nutrition in the United States." *Social Science History* 28, no. 2 (2004): 325–336.

Crocitti, John J. "Vargas Era Social Policies: An Inquiry into Brazilian Malnutrition During the Estado Novo (1937–1945)." In *Vargas and Brazil: New Perspectives*, edited by Jens R. Hentschke, 143–171. New York: Palgrave Macmillan, 2006, ProQuest Ebook Central.

Davis, Horace B., and Marian Rubins Davis. "Scale of Living of Working Class in Sao Paulo, Brazil." *Monthly Labor Review* 44, no. 1 (1937): 245–253.

Dean, Warren. *The Industrialization of São Paulo*. Austin: The University of Texas Press, 1969.

Downes, Earl Richard. "The Seeds of Influence: 'Brazil's 'Essentially Agricultural' Old Republic and the United States, 1910–1930." PhD diss., University of Texas at Austin, 1980.

Duffett, Rachel. *The Stomach for Fighting: Food and the Soldiers of the Great War*. Manchester: Manchester University Press, 2015.

Freitas, Benedicto de. *História do matadouro municipal de Santa Cruz*. Rio de Janeiro: Irmãos Pongetti Editores, 1950.

Fritsch, Winston. "Apogeu e crise na primeira república." In *A ordem do progresso: Cem anos de política econômica republicana, 1889–1989*, edited by Marcelo de Paiva Abreu, Dionísio Dias Carneiro Netto, Gustavo Henrique Barroso Franco, and Winston Fritsch, 31–72. Rio de Janeiro: Editora Campus, 1994.

Graham, Richard. *Britain and the Onset of Modernization in Brazil 1850–1914*. Cambridge: Cambridge University Press, 1968.

Guàrdia, Manel, José Luis Oyón, Sergi Garriga, and Nadia Fava. "Meat Consumption and Nutrition Transition in Barcelona, 1709–1935." *Urban History* 45, no. 2 (2018): 193–213.

Haber, Stephen. "Development Strategy or Endogenous Process? The Industrialization of Latin America." Working Paper No. 269, Stanford, CA, 2005, 1–86.

Hanson, Simon G. "The Farquhar Syndicate in South America." *The Hispanic American Historical Review* 17, no. 3 (1937): 314–326.

Jaguaribe, Helio. *Economic and Political Development. A Theoretical Approach and a Brazilian Case Study*. Cambridge: Harvard University Press, 1968.

Laudan, Rachel. "Power Cuisines, Dietary Determinism and Nutritional Crisis: The Origins of the Globalization of Western Diet." *Interactions: Regional Studies, Global Processes, and Historical Analysis,* Conference Proceedings. Library of Congress, Washington, DC, February 28–March 3, 2001. Accessed November 25, 2020, http://webdoc.sub.gwdg.de/ebook/p/2005/history_cooperative/www.historycooperative.org/proceedings/interactions/laudan.html.

Lobo, Eulália Maria Lahmeyer. *História do Rio de Janeiro: do capital comercial ao capital industrial e financeiro.* V. 2 Rio de Janeiro: Instituto Brasileiro de Mercado de Capitais - IBMEC, 1978.

Lopes, Maria-Aparecida. "Escasez, epizootia y experimentos sindicales. El abasto de carne en la capital federal mexicana, 1929–1955." In *Integración y desintegración del espacio económico mexicano: mercado interno y abastecimiento de las carnes desde la colonia al siglo XX*, edited by Enriqueta Quiroz, 295–330. México: Instituto de Investigaciones Dr. José María Luis Mora, Consejo Nacional de Ciencia y Tecnología.

Love, Joseph L. *São Paulo in the Brazilian Federation 1889–1937.* Stanford, CA: Stanford University Press, 1980.

Luna, Francisco Vidal, and Herbert S. Klein. *The Economic and Social History of Brazil Since 1889.* Cambridge: Cambridge University Press, 2014.

Mamigonian, Armen. "Notas sobre os frigoríficos do Brasil Central Pecuário." *Boletim Paulista de Geografia* no. 51 (1976): 7–14.

Neill, Deborah. "Finding the 'Ideal Diet': Nutrition, Culture, and Dietary Practices in France and French Equatorial Africa, c. 1890s to 1920s." *Food and Foodways* 17, no. 1 (2009): 1–28.

Pearce, W. M. *The Matador Land and Cattle Company.* Norman: University of Oklahoma Press, 1964.

Pereira, Thales A. Zamberlan. "The North-South Divide: Real Wages and Welfare in Brazil during the Early 20th century." *Revista de Historia Económica – Journal of Iberian and Latin American Economic History* 38, no. 1 (2019): 185–214.

Perinelli Neto, Humberto. "Nos quintais do Brasil: homens, pecuária, complexo cafeeiro e modernidade – Barretos (1854/1931)." PhD diss., Universidade Estadual Paulista, Franca, 2009.

Ronsijn, Wouter, and Niccolò Mignemi. "Introduction: Stocks, Seasons, and Sales." In *Stocks, Seasons and Sales. Food Supply, Storage and Markets in Europe and the New World, C. 1600–2000*, edited by Wouter Ronsijn, Niccolò Mignemi, and Laurent Herment, 1–11. Turnhout, Belgium: Brepols, 2019.

Saes, Flávio A. M. de. "A controvérsia sobre a industrialização na Primeira República." *Estudos Avançados* 3, no. 4 (1989): 20–39.

Saes, Flávio A. M. de. "Estradas de ferro e diversificação da atividade econômica na expansão cafeeira em São Paulo, 1870–1900." In *História econômica da independência e do império*, edited by Tamás Szmrecsányi and José Roberto do Amaral Lapa, 177–196. São Paulo: Edusp/Imprensa Oficial/Editora Hucitec, 2002.

Sinclair, Upton. *The Jungle.* Minneapolis: Lerner Publishing Group, 1971. ProQuest Ebook Central.

Smil, Vaclav. "Eating Meat: Evolution, Patterns, and Consequences." *Population and Development Review* 28, no. 4 (December 2002): 599–639.

Smith, Peter H. *Politics and Beef in Argentina: Patterns of Conflict and Change.* New York: Columbia University Press, 1969.

Souza, Mauricio Jorge Pinto de, Pedro Rodrigues de Oliveira, and Heloisa Lee Burquist. "Lar 'Doce' Lar: uma análise do consumo de açúcar e de produtos relacionados no Brasil." *Revista de Economia e Sociologia Rural* 51, no. 4 (2013): 785–796. Accessed November 29, 2020, <http://www.scielo.br/scielo.php?script=sci_arttext&pid=S0103-20032013000400009&lng=en&nrm=iso>. ISSN 0103-2003.

Specht, Joshua. *Red Meat Republic: A Hoof-to-Table History of How Beef Changed America*. Princeton: Princeton University Press, 2019.

Suzigan, Wilson, and Tamás Szmrecsányi. "Os investimentos estrangeiros no início da industrialização do Brasil." In *História econômica da primeira república: coletânea de textos apresentados no I Congresso Brasileiro de História Econômica*, setembro de 1993, edited by Sérgio S. Silva and Tamás Szmrecsányi, 261–283. São Paulo: Editora Hucitec/FAPESP/ABPHE, 1996.

Suzigan, Wilson. *Indústria brasileira: origem e desenvolvimento*. São Paulo: Hucitec, 2000.

Turner, Katherine Leonard. *How the Other Half Ate: A History of Working-Class Meals at the Turn of the Century*. Berkeley: University of California Press, 2014.

Waibel, Leo. *Capítulos de geografia tropical e do Brasil*. Rio de Janeiro: Serviço gráfico do Instituto Brasileiro de Geografia e Estatística, 1958.

Wells, John. "Industrial Accumulation and Living Standards in the Long-Run: The São Paulo Industrial Working Class, 1930–75, Part II." *The Journal of Development Studies* 19, no. 3 (1983): 297–328.

Epilogue

The Fragilities of Globalization: Beef and the Environment

In 2019, intense wildfires ravaged forested areas of Brazil. That August, the National Institute for Space Research (*Instituto Nacional de Pesquisas Espaciais*) registered a 70 percent increase in fire activity compared to 2018; most occurred in the Amazon biome. According to the agency, these events resulted from droughts and "the change in land use patterns" in several regions of the country.[1] The latter explanation was a reference to forest clearing for the expansion of agriculture and livestock ventures. The response of the Brazilian government—or lack thereof—drew worldwide criticism. Some news outlets and researchers identified depredatory ranching and non-enforcement of environmental laws as the main culprits.[2] For several decades, experts have warned of the ecological degradation provoked by unfettered agribusiness. The pictures of burned trees immersed in smoke clouds that accompanied the 2019 news seemed to epitomize what is wrong with our ever-growing appetite for beef. Brazil holds roughly 60 percent of the Amazon, the "largest continuous area of forest in the world."[3] The South American rainforest houses numerous Indigenous groups; apart from its biodiversity, it plays a vital role in absorbing carbon dioxide from the atmosphere and generating oxygen, which can mitigate climate change. Developments there are bound to have global repercussions.

Brazil is at the epicenter of global environmental concerns for other reasons as well. The country has one of the largest herds in the world and is a leading beef and soybean exporter (soybean meal is a crucial source of vegetal protein for livestock).[4] These metrics come with significant ecological trade-offs. Ranching requires vast swaths of pastureland (in Brazil, most cattle are raised in natural grasses); demands an enormous amount of water (a major nutrient for cattle); and utilizes massive areas to cultivate cereal for fodder (land that otherwise would be suitable for growing human food). Some studies have concluded that cattle are major emitters of methane produced during digestion, contributing to greenhouse gases. In the area of public health, experts have linked excessive red and processed meat consumption to chronic diseases.[5]

It is almost impossible to disentangle the multiple interests—private and public—that have collaborated in the growth of the livestock industry in Brazil over the past century. External demand, government incentives, and infrastructure developments are just some driving forces in Brazil's admission to the club of meat exporters.[6] Domestic increase in animal protein intake played a part, as middle-class Brazilians—like their peers in the northern hemisphere earlier—craved this dietary feature in part as a means of social leveling. Per capita meat consumption of all types in Brazil quadrupled from 1961 to 2017.[7] A combination of factors—income growth, improvement in cold chain structures, extended cultivation of soybean and maize, and most notably, the rise of the factory-farmed chicken—account for such a dietary shift. Over those years, while the annual per capita supply of beef cattle doubled, that of poultry meat jumped from less than two kilos to almost 50. One can only fathom the day-to-day reality behind these data: if some Brazilians did not feast on expensive beef cuts, they could afford a piece of chicken. On special occasions, they probably visited steakhouses (*churrascarias*). These all-the-meat-you-can-eat restaurants thrived in poor neighborhoods (*periferias*) in the late twentieth century. They embodied economic ascension and extended the dining-out phenomenon—previously available only to the few—to dwellers in periferias. Today, major cities in Brazil and around the world have churrascarias, branded as venues for having an authentic Brazilian dining experience.

The remarkable increase in poultry meat intake in Brazil—which is, in fact, a global development—deserves more attention than is possible in these pages.[8] As for other animal-derived foods, the panorama depicted above contrasts dramatically to a 1963 report on the state of the Brazilian livestock industry, prepared by the Economic Commission for Latin America and the Caribbean (CEPAL) and the Food and Agriculture Organization of the United Nations (FAO). Early in that decade, the study reveals, notwithstanding Brazil's position as a major holder of bovines (with the third largest stock in the world), the proportion of beef cattle to inhabitant was half that observed in Argentina, Uruguay, and New Zealand. Despite some advanced ranching operations, antiquated methods plagued the raising, processing, and distribution of livestock and by-products nationwide. The CEPAL report identifies land concentration, extensive farming, lagging technology, and unfair labor practices as obstacles to the industry's progress in Brazil. Although the report acknowledges that the domestic intake of eggs and milk had improved, meat consumption—again, compared to neighboring countries—was quite low. Moreover, in 1960, most Brazilians still relied on outdated municipal abattoirs to get their meat, and only a few had access to the industrialized product. The report advocates government incentives and drafting a national plan to overhaul ranching, so the beef industry could keep up with population growth.[9]

The CEPAL report paints a dismal picture of Brazil's livestock industry; yet, its publication coincided with an "explosion of ranching activity in upland… regions of eastern Amazonia."[10] Zones of the Amazon, like other biomes in Brazil, have been the "last frontier" for various economic ventures for centuries.[11] The pre-history of the modern Brazilian livestock industry coincided with the nineteenth-century expansion of coffee plantations in the southeast. As sections of the Atlantic forest were cleared to enlarge arable land for agriculture and ranching, population growth followed suit.[12] Indeed, some ranchers and experts argued that such expansion would eventually boost meat consumption by urban dwellers in that region. Others contended that Brazil would be wiser to utilize its vast "unoccupied" lands to escalate exports of animal-derived commodities. By the late nineteenth century, ranchers had displaced the native population and penetrated farther in the central-west region, roughly into the *Cerrado* (savannah) biome, which corresponds to approximately 25 percent of the country's territory, encompasses several states, and houses a multifaceted ecosystem: semiarid savanna, grasslands, and riverine forests. Before reaching the Amazon basin, ranchers performed major experiments to expand livestock operations into tropical and semitropical ecosystems in Brazil's southeast and central regions.[13]

Relative to its South American neighbors, ranching modernization in parts of central-southeast Brazil occurred late and was at odds with European livestock-rearing techniques. For a while, outsiders—experts from São Paulo included—deemed livestock raising in these areas backward and their animals of inferior quality than those in the adjacent countries.[14] Ranching in tropical Brazil serves as a cautionary tale of how nature imposes its limits on economic ventures as well as the difficulties in changing fauna.[15] In a long process of trial and error, and absent consistent government support, ranchers adapted husbandry methods to the ecological imperatives of the Cerrado. That is, the majority practiced extensive farming, relying on traditional practices to tend to their animals, control mortality, and combat epizootics. The few who introduced outside grasses, supplemented fodder with salt, and used barbed wire, did so because it was economically feasible. Speaking of Mato Grosso state in central Brazil, historian Robert W. Wilcox calls these strategies "imposition and negotiation," whereby breeders achieved adequate productivity levels by compromising with natural constraints and economic imperatives. On the other hand, because ranchers settled primarily grassland areas, at least until the early 1900s, certain zones in central-west Brazil escaped significant degradation. Such was the case of "Mato Grosso de Goiás," a tropical forest enclave in today's Goiás state.[16]

The best example of ecological compromise was the introduction of zebu cattle for breeding purposes.[17] Realizing that faunae from the northern hemisphere suffered to acclimatize to the tropical ecosystem—accounts of beef breeds dying of exposure to the elements (heat and plagues) abound, ranchers opted for the zebu, a species developed on the Indian subcontinent. Such a path was divisive, in part because some experts considered that national "races" could only prosper if mixed with European purebred. While this controversy unfolded, zebu specimens continued to arrive, particularly in southeast and central-west Brazil. After World War I, stock raisers from Minas Gerais developed the Indubrasil, a pure zebu breed that reigned in these regions until the 1950s. As soon as Brazil began to publicize its tropical ranching advances to breeders in arid and semiarid Americas, its efforts were engulfed in transnational concerns over animal disease.[18]

The infamous episode of Mexico's purchases of zebu bulls from Brazil in 1946, which coincided with an outbreak of foot-and-mouth disease (FMD), typifies globalization's fragilities and promises. While the animals remained in quarantine for several months before disembarking in Mexico, the epizootic, discovered in the Veracruz port in December 1946, expanded to the rest of the country, reaching 16 states in less than one year.[19] As the ailment threatened to spread to the Mexico–United States border area—where ranching was and still is a bi-national business, the United States carried out a twofold defense scheme. On the one hand, it interrupted live cattle imports from its southern neighbor for several years. On the other, in 1947 and in conjunction with Mexico, it conducted a program that eliminated approximately one million herds infected or suspected of being infected. This measure had major costs for Mexican ranchers (particularly for small proprietors whose wealth depended on their herd numbers), severely curtailing meat for domestic consumption, and had profound, long-term transnational implications.[20]

After this show of force—on occasions, military personnel conducted the slaughter program, local resistance, and some recognition that the initial strategy had resulted in utter failure, the United States' approach shifted. Policymakers seemed to acknowledge that to counter hemispheric threats, it was necessary to recognize other countries' expertise and involve multilateral agencies in the process. Indeed, despite the initial blow to the binational ranching business, Mexico and the United States engaged in an unprecedented diplomatic and scientific collaboration. In addition to forming joint initiatives to develop a vaccine against the disease (and later inoculating millions of animals), the United States government issued contracts to buy canned meat from Mexico. Other agencies granted loans to Mexican ranchers for the acquisition of purebred animals. Most impactful to the binational relationship were the incentives to modernize and increase the capacity of various packinghouses at the United States–Mexico border.[21]

From the Brazilian perspective, the United States manipulated the incident to restrict competition; a common strategy in international livestock exchange was to use a sanitary embargo as a protectionist measure.[22] Nevertheless, the FMD crisis resulted, in 1951, in the creation of the Pan-American Center for Foot-and-Mouth Disease Center, an institute headquartered in Rio de Janeiro linked to the Organization of American States and the Brazilian government. For its part, Brazil gained a foothold in the international veterinary community, entered the global livestock breeders club, and consolidated its brand of tropical ranching.[23] The aforementioned CEPAL/FAO's report singled out central-west Brazil as one of "the most progressive" regions in the country. There, continues the study, in adapting to "tropical hostile environmental conditions" ranchers have "produced a herd that yields meat at high rates and quickly, [these animals] withstand high temperatures, and possess great resistance to plagues and diseases."[24]

On the heels of the CEPAL/FAO publication, a new zebu breed, the Nelore, began to replace the Indubrasil almost everywhere in the country, except in Rio Grande do Sul.[25] The Nelore—whose white hair color contrasts so vividly with gray-burned areas in today's Amazon—resulted from breeding experiments conducted in southeast and central-west Brazil. Its development accompanied the conversion of forested Cerrado areas (mainly in south Mato Grosso) into natural pasturelands. From there, both technologies (animal improvement and tropical husbandry) moved up to the Amazon more systematically. As they did, the region's land cover began to undergo massive changes, including the spread of planted pastures in the 1980s. Government-sponsored infrastructure (highway construction, for instance), tax breaks, and credit incentives accelerated the agriculture and pasture frontier movement from the southeast to the center-west and north Brazil. Such an expansion occurred primarily alongside major rivers and roads and was spurred by cheap land prices, easy access to public land, and domestic and international demand for meat.[26]

Over time, different internal and external stimuli played a part in Brazil's farming advancing. From 1990 to 2011, Brazil increased its exports of beef and soybean by 720 percent and 530 percent, respectively.[27] During that period, studies have identified two seemingly contradictory trends: first, an impressive upsurge in herd numbers, mainly in the northern region;[28] second, between 2005 and 2013, a 70 percent reduction in deforestation in the Amazon. A series of measures that include government oversight, enforcing the Brazilian Forestal Code (which determines limits on forest clearing), establishing Indigenous reserves, extending protected areas, a "market rejection of deforesters," and "cattle ranching intensification" are behind these data.[29] One study "cautiously supports the view that Brazil has the potential for large-scale sustainable development of its agriculture to meet global food security goals."[30] Other works stress that there is no guarantee that this trend will continue. Even if intensification proves profitable, "without complementary policies to curb new deforestation," demand for more land may increase. Still, others warn that progress in the Amazon had overlapped with deforestation in the Cerrado and conversion of pasture into soybean fields.[31]

This mixed picture leads to the following conclusions. The agricultural and ranching sectors are fundamental to the Brazilian economy; they represent approximately 25 percent of its gross domestic product. The livestock industry in central-west and north Brazil comprises big corporations, small-scale proprietors (who rent out pasturelands or raise calves for other ranchers), and cowhands (whose livelihood depend on their labor in midsize and large holdings). Some breeders have humble origins; others, with ranching experience, migrated to the north in the 1970s answering the federal government's call to "develop" the Amazon. They all feel abandoned by the authorities and persecuted by environmentalists.[32] Without the participation of these sectors, alongside Indigenous peoples, in conservation projects maintaining sustainable intensification is almost impossible. If, after the 1950s, government incentives were crucial to the expansion of pasturelands in center-west Brazil and the Amazon, in the 2000s, government surveillance and agricultural and ranching intensification were critical to protecting forested areas.[33] In an article published in the journal *Science*, Raoni Rajão from Universidade Federal de Minas Gerais and colleagues issue calls for other actors with a stake in Brazil's livestock/soybean complex to collaborate in this effort, asking foreign buyers to acquire only agricultural products (soybean, cattle, and meat) from areas designated "free of tropical deforestation."[34]

The 2019 Amazon fires, like the mid-twentieth century FMD episode, reveal the fragilities of globalization, but the latter also offers some lessons. Transnational agreements have a better chance of suppressing deforestation in the Amazon. International condemnations of Brazil's behavior without any reference to the corporations that enable such behavior are bound to have adverse consequences. As this book shows, salted, fresh, or industrial meat that arrived in early-1900s Rio de Janeiro resulted from transnational networks, requiring no small amount of work, technology, and government oversight. Today, meat remains a symbol of progress and economic betterment. To tame our appetite for meat, and indeed to change our relationship with food entirely—a process that seems to be well underway in light of plant-based food innovation, it is necessary to unveil farm-to-table networks and to address food access inequalities. It is also crucial to develop a new global dietary paradigm, one that reconciles food production for human and animal consumption with the environment.

Notes

1 Brasil, *Infoqueima. Boletim Mensal do Programa de Monitoramento e Risco de Queimadas e Incêndios Florestais* 4, no. 8 (August 2019): 5.

2 Raoni Rajão et al., "The Rotten Apples of Brazil's Agribusiness. Brazil's Inability to Tackle Illegal Deforestation Puts the Future of its Agribusiness at Risk," *Science* 17, vol. 369, no. 6501 (July 2020): 247.
3 Christiane C. Leite et al., "Historical Reconstruction of Land Use in the Brazilian Amazon (1940–1995)," *Journal of Land Use Science* 6, no. 1 (2011): 34. See the graphic pictures in Charlie Hamilton James, "As the Amazon Burns, Cattle Ranchers Are Blamed. But It's Complicated," *National Geographic*, August 30, 2019.
4 Mustafa Zia et al., "Brazil Once Again Becomes the World's Largest Beef Exporter," *Amber Waves Magazine, The Economics of Food, Farming, Natural Resources, and Rural America* (July 1, 2019).
5 Julian Baggini, "A Tax on Red Meat? That Won't Save the Planet - or do Much to Improve our Health, *The Guardian*, May 29, 2019. "WHO Report Says Eating Processed Meat is Carcinogenic: Understanding the Findings," *The Nutrition Source*, Harvard T. H. Shan School of Public Health, November 3, 2015, accessed December 21, 2020, www.hsph.harvard.edu/nutrition-source/2015/11/03/report-says-eating-processed-meat-is-carcinogenic-understanding-the-findings/.
6 Jeffrey Hoelle, *Rainforest Cowboy: The Rise of Ranching and Cattle Culture in Western Amazonia*, (Austin: University of Texas Press, 2015), 21–27.
7 Hannah Ritchie, "Carne para alimentação: quais países lideram o ranking," accessed December 21, 2020, www.bbc.com/portuguese/geral-47125834; Hannah Ritchie, "Meat and Dairy Production," (2017) published online at OurWorldInData.org, accessed December 21, 2020, https://ourworldindata.org/meat-production.
8 John Wells, "Industrial Accumulation and Living Standards in the Long-Run: The São Paulo Industrial Working Class, 1930–75, Part II," *The Journal of Development Studies* 19, no. 2 (2007): 316–17; Steve Striffler, *Chicken: The Dangerous Transformation of America's Favorite Food* (New Haven, CT: Yale University Press), 2007.
9 *La ganadería en América Latina. Situación, problemas y perspectivas. Vol. II El Brasil.* Informe preparado con arreglo al programa conjunto de la Comisión Económica para América Latina y la Organización de las Naciones Unidas para la Agricultura y Alimentación (México: Publicación de las Naciones Unidas, 1963), 7–42.
10 Eugenio Yatsuda Arima and Christopher Uhl, "Ranching in the Brazilian Amazon in a National Context: Economics, Policy, and Practice," *Society & Natural Resources* 10, no. 5 (1997): 433.
11 Consider, for instance, the "rubber boom" in the Amazon in the second half of the 1800s, the persistence of logging activities in the Caatinga biome, or the whaling industry on the northeast coast. José Augusto Pádua, "Nature and Territory in the Making of Brazil," in *New Environmental Histories of Latin America and the Caribbean*, ed. Claudia Leal, José Augusto Pádua, and John Soluri, *RCC Perspectives* no. 7 (2013): 36, accessed December 22, 2020, https://doi.org/10.5282/rcc/5921; Warren Dean, *With Broadax and Firebrand: The Destruction of the Brazilian Atlantic Forest* (Berkeley: University of California Press, 1995), 29–40; Bartolomeu Israel de Souza, "Cariri paraibano: do silêncio do lugar à desertificação" (PhD diss., Universidade Federal do Rio Grande do Sul, 2008), chapter 2; Francisco Henrique Duarte Filho and José Otávio Aguiar, "Baleias e ecologistas na Paraíba: uma história do fortalecimento do movimento ambientalista e o debate sobre a crise da economia baleeira (1970–1980)," *Topoi. Revista de História* 15, no. 28 (January–June, 2014): 116–142. For a historiography of Brazil's environmental studies, see José Augusto Pádua

and Alessandra Izabel de Carvalho, "A construção de um país tropical: apresentação da historiografia ambiental sobre o Brasil," *História, Ciências, Saúde – Manguinhos* 27, no. 4 (October–December 2020): 1311–40.

12 Warren Dean, "The Green Wave of Coffee: Beginnings of Tropical Agricultural Research in Brazil (1885-1900), *The Hispanic American Historical Review* 69, no. 1 (February 1989): 92; Dean, *With Broadax*, 178–90; Shawn Van Ausdal and Robert W. Wilcox, "Hoofprints: Ranching and Landscape Transformation," in *New Environmental Histories of Latin America and the Caribbean*, ed. Claudia Leal, José Augusto Pádua, and John Soluri, *RCC Perspectives* no. 7 (2013): 73–79, accessed December 22, 2020, https://doi.org/10.5282/rcc/5921.

13 Robert W. Wilcox, *Cattle in the Backlands: Mato Grosso and the Evolution of Ranching in the Brazilian Tropics* (Austin: University of Texas Press, 2017), 14–16; Sandro Dutra e Silva, *No oeste, a terra e o céu. A expansão da fronteira agrícola no Brasil Central* (Rio de Janeiro: Mauad Editora, Fapeg, 2017), 101–24.

14 A. D. Melvin, "The South American Meat Industry," in *Yearbook of the United States Department of Agriculture* (Washington: Government Printing Office, 1913), 360; Joana Medrado, *Do pastoreio à pecuária.* "A invenção da modernização rural nos sertões do Brasil Central" (PhD diss., Universidade Federal Flumense, 2013), 100.

15 See Tyler Priest, "Extraction Not Creation: The History of Offshore Petroleum in the Gulf of Mexico," *Enterprise & Society* 8, no. 2, Special Issue: Business and Nature (June 2007): 229–30.

16 Robert W. Wilcox, "'The Law of the Least Effort': Cattle Ranching and the Environment in the Savanna of Mato Grosso, Brazil, 1900-1980," *Environmental History* 4, no. 3 (July 1999): 348–59; Dutra e Silva, "No oeste," 101–05.

17 Wilcox, *Cattle in the Backlands*, 204–22.

18 Medrado, *Do pastoreio à pecuária*, 154; Shawn Van Ausdal, "Reimagining the Tropical Beef Frontier and the Nation in Early Twentieth-Century Colombia," ed. Gordon M. Winder and Andreas Dix, *Trading Environments. Frontiers, Commercial Knowledge, and Environmental Transformation, 1750–1990* (New York: Routledge, 2016), 180–83.

19 Newspapers in Mexico, the United States, and Brazil debated the link between the Brazilian specimens and the disease in Mexico, although no connection was proved. *Jornal do Commercio*, July 20, 1946; September 13, 1946, October 11, 1946; *The New York Times*, February 20, 1947; *Gaceta Médica de México*, April 30, 1948.

20 Octavio Herrera Pérez, "La fiebre aftosa en México y la disputa por el control sanitario y el mercado del ganado entre Estados Unidos y América Latina en los años de la posguerra mundial," in *Mercados en común. Estudios sobre conexiones transnacionales, negocios y diplomacia en las Américas (siglos XIX y XX)*, ed. Maria-Aparecida Lopes and María Cecilia Zuleta (México: El Colegio de México, 2016), 244–52; Thomas Rath, "A Tale of Four Laboratories: Animal Disease, Science, and Politics in Cold War Latin America, in *Itineraries of Expertise. Science, Technology, and the Environment in Latin America's Long Cold War*," ed. Andra B. Chastain and Timothy W. Lorek (Pittsburgh, PA: University of Pittsburgh Press, 2020), 162–64.

21 Herrera Pérez, "La fiebre aftosa en México," 252–59.

22 "A importação de gado zebú do Brasil pelo México," *Jornal do Commercio*, October 17, 1946. Arturo A. O'Connell, "La fiebre aftosa, el embargo sanitario norteamericano contra las importaciones de carne y el triángulo Argentina-Gran Bretaña-Estados Unidos en el período entre las dos guerras mundiales," *Desarrollo Económico* 26, no. 101 (April–June 1986): 24–25.

23 Rath, "A Tale of Four Laboratories," 166–68.
24 *La ganadería en América Latina*, 16–17.
25 Wilcox, *Cattle in the Backlands*, 222.
26 Lívia C. P. Dias et al., "Patterns of Land Use, Extensification, and Intensification of Brazilian Agriculture," *Global Change Biology* 22, no. 8 (2016): 2982–95; Maria S. Bowman, et al., "Persistence of Cattle Ranching in the Brazilian Amazon: A Spatial Analysis of the Rationale for Beef Production," *Land Use Policy* 29, no. 3 (July 2012): 559; Leite et al., "Historical Reconstruction," 39–41.
27 David M. Lapola, Luiz A. Martinelli, Carlos A. Peres et al., "Pervasive Transition of the Brazilian Land-Use System," *Nature Climate Change* 4 (2014): 28, accessed December 13, 2020, https://doi.org/10.1038/nclimate2056. Behind these numbers is a great deal of transnational collaboration: phytosanitary accords, technical knowledge exchange, and agreements between institutions of education—to mention a few—that developed over several years. For the case of dairy products in the Common Market of the South (*Mercosul*) context see José Lannes, "La cadena de lácteos en Brasil desde el Mercosur: temas para una historia transnacional," in *Mercados en común. Estudios sobre conexiones transnacionales, negocios y diplomacia en las Américas (siglos XIX y XX)*, ed. Maria-Aparecida Lopes and María Cecilia Zuleta (México: El Colegio de México, 2016), 263–77. On the subject of scientific exchange in the agricultural world, see María Cecilia Zuleta, "Laboratorios de cambio agrario: tecnología y ciencia en el campo," *Historia Mexicana* 70, no. 1 (277) (July–September 2020): 61–97.
28 Merle D. Faminow, "The Brazilian Cattle Sector: Status, Prospects and Controversies," *Canadian Journal of Agricultural Economics/Revue canadienne d'agroeconomie* 45, no. 3 (1997): 182.
29 Daniel Nepstad et al., "Slowing Amazon Deforestation through Public Policy and Interventions in Beef and Soy Supply Chains," *Science* 6 (June 2014), New Series, vol. 344, no. 6188 (6 June 2014): 1118–20; Lapola et al., "Pervasive Transition," 28.
30 Dias et al., "Patterns," 2887.
31 Bowman, et al., "Persistence of Cattle," 560–66; Britaldo Soares-Filho et al., "Cracking Brazil's Forest Code," *Science* 344 (25 April 2014): 364.
32 Pádua, "Nature and Territory," 36–37; Hoelle, *Rainforest Cowboy*, 21–27; 72–90.
33 Lapola et al., "Pervasive Transition," 32.
34 Rajão et al., "The Rotten Apples," 248.

Bibliography

Government Documents and Publications

Brasil. *Infoqueima. Boletim Mensal do Programa de Monitoramento e Risco de Queimadas e Incêndios Florestais* 4, no. 8 (August 2019): 1–15.

Melvin, A. D. "The South American Meat Industry." *Yearbook of the United States Department of Agriculture*. Washington: Government Printing Office, 1913.

Newspapers and Magazines

Gaceta Médica de México
Jornal do Commercio (Rio de Janeiro)
The New York Times

"A importação de gado zebú do Brasil pelo México." *Jornal do Commercio.* October 17, 1946.
Baggini, Julian. "A Tax on Red Meat? That Won't Save the Planet - or do Much to Improve our Health." *The Guardian.* May 29, 2019.
James, Charlie Hamilton. "As the Amazon Burns, Cattle Ranchers Are Blamed. But It's Complicated." *National Geographic.* August 30, 2019.
Zia, Mustafa, James Hansen, Kim Hjort, and Constanza Valdes. "Brazil Once Again Becomes the World's Largest Beef Exporter." *Amber Waves Magazine. The Economics of Food, Farming, Natural Resources, and Rural America* (July 1, 2019).

Other Primary Sources

La ganadería en América Latina. Situación, problemas y perspectivas. Vol. II El Brasil. Informe preparado con arreglo al programa conjunto de la Comisión Económica para América Latina y la Organización de las Naciones Unidas para la Agricultura y Alimentación. México: Publicación de las Naciones Unidas, 1963.
Ritchie, Hannah. "Meat and Dairy Production." *Published online at* OurWorldInData.org. 2017. Accessed December 21, 2020, https://ourworldindata.org/meat-production.
Ritchie, Hannah. "Carne para alimentação: quais países lideram o ranking." Accessed December 21, 2020, www.bbc.com/portuguese/geral-47125834.

Secondary Sources

Arima, Eugenio Yatsuda, and Christopher Uhl. "Ranching in the Brazilian Amazon in a National Context: Economics, Policy, and Practice." *Society & Natural Resources* 10, no. 5 (1997): 433–451.
Bowman, Maria S., Britaldo S. Soares-Filho, Frank D. Merry, Daniel C. Nepstad, Hermann Rodrigues, Oriana T. Almeida. "Persistence of Cattle Ranching in the Brazilian Amazon: A Spatial Analysis of the Rationale for Beef Production." *Land Use Policy* 29, no. 3 (July 2012): 558–568.
Dean, Warren. "The Green Wave of Coffee: Beginnings of Tropical Agricultural Research in Brazil (1885–1900)." *The Hispanic American Historical Review* 69, no. 1 (February 1989): 91–115.
Dean, Warren. *With Broadax and Firebrand: The Destruction of the Brazilian Atlantic Forest.* Berkeley: University of California Press, 1995.
Dias, Lívia C. P., Fernando M. Pimenta, Ana B. Santos, Marcos H. Costa, and Richard J. Ladle. "Patterns of Land Use, Extensification, and Intensification of Brazilian Agriculture." *Global Change Biology* 22, no. 8 (2016): 2887–2903.
Duarte Filho, Francisco Henrique, and José Otávio Aguiar. "Baleias e ecologistas na Paraíba: uma história do fortalecimento do movimento ambientalista e o debate sobre a crise da economia baleeira (1970–1980)." *Topoi. Revista de História* 15, no. 28 (January–June 2014): 116–142.
Dutra e Silva, Sandro. *No oeste, a terra e o céu. A expansão da fronteira agrícola no Brasil Central.* Rio de Janeiro: Mauad Editora, Fapeg, 2017.

Faminow, Merle D. "The Brazilian Cattle Sector: Status, Prospects and Controversies." *Canadian Journal of Agricultural Economics/Revue canadienne d'agroeconomie* 45, no. 3 (1997): 179–199.

Harvard T. H. Shan School of Public Health, "WHO Report Says Eating Processed Meat is Carcinogenic: Understanding the Findings." *The Nutrition Source*, November 3, 2015. Accessed December 21, 2020, www.hsph.harvard.edu/nutritionsource/2015/11/03/report-says-eating-processed-meat-is-carcinogenic-understanding-the-findings/.

Herrera Pérez, Octavio. "La fiebre aftosa en México y la disputa por el control sanitario y el mercado del ganado entre Estados Unidos y América Latina en los años de la posguerra mundial." In *Mercados en común. Estudios sobre conexiones transnacionales, negocios y diplomacia en las Américas (siglos XIX y XX)*, edited by Maria-Aparecida Lopes and María Cecilia Zuleta, 227–259. México: El Colegio de México, 2016.

Hoelle, Jeffrey. *Rainforest Cowboy: The Rise of Ranching and Cattle Culture in Western Amazonia*. Austin: University of Texas Press, 2015).

Lannes, José. "La cadena de lácteos en Brasil desde el Mercosur: temas para una historia transnacional." In *Mercados en común. Estudios sobre conexiones transnacionales, negocios y diplomacia en las Américas (siglos XIX y XX)*, edited by Maria-Aparecida Lopes and María Cecilia Zuleta, 261–299. México: El Colegio de México, 2016.

Lapola, David M., Luiz A. Martinelli, Carlos A. Peres, Jean P. H. B. Ometto, Manuel E. Ferreira, Carlos A. Nobre, Ana Paula D. Aguiar, Mercedes M. C. Bustamante, Manoel F. Cardoso, Marcos H. Costa, Carlos A. Joly, Christiane C. Leite, Paulo Moutinho, Gilvan Sampaio, Bernardo B. N. Strassburg, and Ima C. G. Vieira. "Pervasive Transition of the Brazilian Land-Use System." *Nature Climate Change* 4 (2014): 27–35. Accessed December 13, 2020, https://doi.org/10.1038/nclimate2056.

Leite, Christiane C., Marcos H. Costa, Cleverson A. de Lima, Carlos A. A. S. Ribeiro, and Gilberto C. Sediyama. "Historical Reconstruction of Land Use in the Brazilian Amazon (1940–1995)." *Journal of Land Use Science* 6, no. 1 (2011): 33–52.

Medrado, Joana. *Do pastoreio à pecuária. A invenção da modernização rural nos sertões do Brasil Central*. PhD diss., Universidade Federal Flumense, 2013.

Nepstad, Daniel, David McGrath, Claudia Stickler, Ane Alencar, Andrea Azevedo, Briana Swette, Tathiana Bezerra, Maria DiGiano, João Shimada, Ronaldo Seroa da Motta, Eric Armijo, Leandro Castello, Paulo Brando, Matt C. Hansen, Max McGrath-Horn, Oswaldo Carvalho, and Laura Hess. "Slowing Amazon Deforestation through Public Policy and Interventions in Beef and Soy Supply Chains." *Science* 6, New Series 344, no. 6188 (6 June 2014): 1118–1123.

O'Connell, Arturo A. "La fiebre aftosa, el embargo sanitario norteamericano contra las importaciones de carne y el triángulo Argentina-Gran Bretaña-Estados Unidos en el período entre las dos guerras mundiales." *Desarrollo Económico* 26, no. 1 (April–June 1986): 21–50.

Pádua, José Augusto. "Nature and Territory in the Making of Brazil." In *New Environmental Histories of Latin America and the Caribbean*, edited by Claudia Leal, José Augusto Pádua, and John Soluri, 33–39, *RCC Perspectives* no. 7 (2013). Accessed December 22, 2020, https://doi.org/10.5282/rcc/5921.

Pádua, José Augusto, and Alessandra Izabel de Carvalho. "A construção de um país tropical: apresentação da historiografia ambiental sobre o Brasil." *História, Ciências, Saúde – Manguinhos* 27, no. 4 (October–December 2020): 1311–1340.

Priest, Tyler. "Extraction Not Creation: The History of Offshore Petroleum in the Gulf of Mexico." *Enterprise & Society* 8, no. 2 (2007): 227–267.

Rajão, Raoni, Britaldo Soares-Filho, Felipe Nunes, Jan Börner, Lilian Machado, Débora Assis, Amanda Oliveira, Luis Pinto, Vivian Ribeiro, Lisa Rausch, Holly Gibbs, and Danilo Figueira. "The Rotten Apples of Brazil's Agribusiness. Brazil's Inability to Tackle Illegal Deforestation Puts the Future of its Agribusiness at Risk." *Science* 17, vol. 369, no. 6501 (July 2020): 246–248.

Rath, Thomas. "A Tale of Four Laboratories: Animal Disease, Science, and Politics in Cold War Latin America." In *Itineraries of Expertise. Science, Technology, and the Environment in Latin America's Long Cold War*, edited by Andra B. Chastain and Timothy W. Lorek, 159–177. Pittsburgh, PA: University of Pittsburgh Press, 2020.

Soares-Filho, Britaldo, Raoni Rajão, Marcia Macedo, Arnaldo Carneiro, William Costa, Michael Coe, Hermann Rodrigues, and Ane Alencar. "Cracking Brazil's Forest Code." *Science* 344 (25 April 2014): 363–364.

Souza, Bartolomeu Israel de. "Cariri paraibano: do silêncio do lugar à desertificação." PhD diss., Universidade Federal do Rio Grande do Sul, 2008.

Striffler, Steve. *Chicken: The Dangerous Transformation of America's Favorite Food*. New Haven, CT: Yale University Press, 2007.

Van Ausdal, Shawn, and Robert W. Wilcox. "Hoofprints: Ranching and Landscape Transformation." In *New Environmental Histories of Latin America and the Caribbean*, edited by Claudia Leal, José Augusto Pádua, and John Soluri, 73–79, *RCC Perspectives* no. 7 (2013). Accessed December 22, 2020, https://doi.org/10.5282/rcc/5921.

Van Ausdal, Shawn. "Reimagining the Tropical Beef Frontier and the Nation in Early Twentieth-Century Colombia." In *Trading Environments. Frontiers, Commercial Knowledge, and Environmental Transformation, 1750–1990*, edited by Gordon M. Winder and Andreas Dix, 166–192. New York: Routledge, 2016.

Wells, John. "Industrial Accumulation and Living Standards in the Long-Run: The São Paulo Industrial Working Class, 1930–75, Part II." *The Journal of Development Studies* 19, no. 3 (1983): 297–328.

Wilcox, Robert W. "'The Law of the Least Effort': Cattle Ranching and the Environment in the Savanna of Mato Grosso, Brazil, 1900–1980." *Environmental History* 4, no. 3 (1999): 338–368.

Wilcox Robert W. *Cattle in the Backlands: Mato Grosso and the Evolution of Ranching in the Brazilian Tropics*. Austin: University of Texas Press, 2017.

Zuleta, María Cecilia. "Laboratorios de cambio agrario: tecnología y ciencia en el campo." *Historia Mexicana* 70, no. 1 (277) (July–September 2020): 61–97.

Index

Page numbers in *italics* refer to figures, those in **bold** indicate tables.

For Product Safety Concerns and Information please contact our EU representative GPSR@taylorandfrancis.com
Taylor & Francis Verlag GmbH, Kaufingerstraße 24, 80331 München, Germany

www.ingramcontent.com/pod-product-compliance
Ingram Content Group UK Ltd.
Pitfield, Milton Keynes, MK11 3LW, UK
UKHW022352190926
475702UK00015B/2245
9780367528546